COMPREHENSIVE CLASSROOM MANAGEMENT

SECOND EDITION

Comprehensive Classroom Management

CREATING POSITIVE LEARNING ENVIRONMENTS

Vernon F. Jones
LEWIS AND CLARK COLLEGE

Louise S. Jones
BEAVERTON SCHOOL DISTRICT

Allyn and Bacon, Inc.
BOSTON LONDON SYDNEY TORONTO

Library of Congress Cataloging-in-Publication Data

Jones, Vernon F., 1945–
    Comprehensive classroom management.

    Rev. ed. of: Responsible classroom discipline. c1981.
    Bibliography: pp.
    Includes index.
    1. Classroom management.   2. Interaction analysis in
education.   3. School discipline.   I. Jones, Louise S.,
1949–   . II. Jones, Vernon F., 1945–
Responsible classroom discipline.   III. Title.
LB3013.J66   1986   371.1′024   85–9045
ISBN 0–205–08524–5

Series Editor: Susanne F. Canavan
Production Coordinator: Helyn Pultz
Editorial-Production Services: Bywater Production Services
Cover Coordinator: Linda K. Dickinson

Printed in the United States of America.

10 9 8 7 6 5 4 3 2 1   92 91 90 89 88 87 86 85

To my first mentors, Jere Brophy and Tom Good, whose excellent work continues to inform me; to Dan Duke, a valued friend, colleague, and scholar; and to our children Sarah and Garrett, who bring us so much joy.

Contents

Activities

Preface

Purpose

The numerous reports published between 1982 and 1984 on education in the United States increased public awareness of the importance of quality education. These reports were accompanied or followed by efforts to describe needed changes in the educational system and in teacher training. In March 1984, a ten-member Panel on the Preparation of Beginning Teachers, chaired by Ernest L. Boyer, president of the Carnegie Foundation for the Advancement of Teaching, issued a report listing three major areas of expertise needed by beginning teachers:

1. knowledge of how to manage a classroom,
2. knowledge of subject matter, and
3. understanding of their students' sociological backgrounds.

A publication from the Association for Supervision and Curriculum Development entitled *Effective Schools and Classrooms: A Research-Based Perspective* (Squires, Huitt, & Segars 1983), stated that effective teachers—those whose students demonstrated consistently high levels of achievement—possessed skills in

1. planning, or getting ready for classroom activities;
2. management, which has to do with controlling students' behavior; and
3. instruction, which concerns providing for or guiding students' learning (p. 10).

Walter Doyle (1986), in his comprehensive chapter in *Handbook of Research on Teaching*, explained that the classroom teacher's role involves two major functions—establishing order and facilitating learning. Regardless of changes that may be made in the education system, schooling in the United States will not improve significantly unless teachers develop skill in the widely varied teaching methods generally described as "classroom management."

Fortunately, technology in classroom management has kept pace with the increasing demands placed upon teachers. Research in classroom management has grown explosively in the last fifteen years. Most teachers trained in the 1960s learned only such simple prescriptions as "don't smile until Christmas" or "don't grin until Thanksgiving." By 1985, however, thousands of articles and hundreds of thoughtful research projects focused on student behavior and learning. By this time, the concept of school discipline, which concentrated on dealing with inevitable student misbehavior, was replaced by the concept of "classroom management," which emphasized methods of facilitating positive student behavior and achievement. The purpose of this book is to give the reader a comprehensive, practical description of the current research and extensive methodology of classroom management.

Audience

This book is written for teachers, counselors, administrators, and special educators. Its comprehensive and research-based presentation offers practical ideas for creating positive classroom and school climates, organizing and managing classrooms, improving instruction, dealing with classroom discipline problems, and developing school-wide discipline programs. This enables educators in their various roles to understand the broad issues and skills involved in effective management, instruction, and discipline.

Approach

Materials used to train teachers and administrators have too often focused on isolated aspects of effective instruction and management. To develop a realistic, workable approach to classroom management, educators have had to seek out and integrate information from literally dozens of sources—each of which has claimed to provide "the answer." This book offers a comprehensive, research-based synthesis of current knowledge in effective teaching and in developing effective schools.

"Recent research makes it clear that successful classroom management involves not merely responding effectively when problems occur, but preventing problems from occuring frequently" (Brophy 1983, p. 23). Extensive review of the research and our own experiences in classrooms highlights five major factors or skill areas involved in effective classroom management. Effective classroom management is based upon:

1. developing a solid understanding of students' personal/psychological and learning needs,
2. establishing positive teacher-student and peer relationships that help meet students' basic psychological needs,
3. using organizational and group management methods that maximize on-task student behavior,
4. implementing instructional methods that facilitate optimal learning by responding to the academic needs of individual students and the classroom group, and
5. employing a wide range of counseling and behavioral methods that involve students in examining and correcting their inappropriate behavior.

This emphasis on providing a variety of specific methods to consider does not, however, imply that teachers should implement these by rote. We believe that teachers should (and will) implement recommendations selectively, attending to their own teaching styles, learning goals, students' needs, and other context variables. Because we have always remained heavily involved in schools and teacher training, it seems obvious to us that research "can extend the range of hypotheses (alternative strategies) considered and sensitize the teacher to the possible consequences of his/her actions" (Good & Power, 1976, p. 47). It cannot, however, prescribe a universal set of methods that will be effective in all instances.

The importance of encouraging teachers to consider context variables, including instructional goals and students' age, socioeconomic level, and cognitive skills has been pointed out by a number of writers and researchers (Brophy & Evertson, 1976; Cronbach, 1975; Darling-Hammond, Wise, & Pease, 1983; Doyle, 1979; Peterson, 1979; Soar, 1983; Zumwalt, 1983). As Brophy and Evertson (1976) put it,

> Effective teaching requires the ability to implement a very large number of diagnostic, instructional, managerial, and therapeutic skills, tailoring behavior in specific contexts and situations to the specific needs of the moment. Effective teachers not only must be able to do a large number of things; they also must be able to recognize which of the many things they know how to do applies at a given moment and be able to follow through by performing the behavior effectively. (p. 139)

Any writer (or reader) must be cautious about the manner in which research is used as a framework for making practical decisions, and in determining the methods to be presented in this book and the research offered to support and expand these methods, we have made numerous choices. These choices are based on extensive study of the available research; personal and professional acquaintance with some of the leading researchers and writers in the field; and our own experience as regular classroom teachers, special educators, public school administrator, pre- and in-service teacher trainers, and psychologist and researcher. Our decisions are also based on Elliot Eisner's (1984) ideas about translating educational research into useful prescriptions for practitioners. Responsible use of research, according to Eisner, requires that the educator should, "have examined a body of research studies, extracted generalizations, determined that the theory is supported by the evidence, and then used the theory as a tool for shaping decisions" (p. 448). He also suggests that those involved in educational research (and, we trust, prescription and training) should have "an intimate acquaintance with life in classrooms" (p. 450). The material presented throughout this book meets these criteria.

The methods have been employed by us and by numerous teachers whom we have taught and with whom we have worked over the past fifteen years. During the past four years, the methods have been field-tested by teachers in nearly two hundred classrooms evenly divided among primary, intermediate, middle, and high school settings. These settings include classrooms in inner-city, rural, and suburban schools.

Organization

The book is divided into four parts. Part I provides an overview of classroom management and its relationship to students' personal/psychological and academic needs thus providing a theoretical foundation for understanding and thoughtfully implementing the practical strategies presented in later chapters. Part II focuses on interpersonal relationships in the classroom and on the interaction between school and home as key factors influencing students' behavior and achievement. Part III provides the reader with numerous research-supported, practical strategies for improving classroom organization and instruction. Part IV offers many kinds of specific methods for effectively dealing with discipline problems that occur at both the classroom and the school-wide level, because numerous studies and our combined thirty years of experience indicate that some students will cause disruptions in even the best learning environments.

A major problem in listing a variety of teaching methods, of course, is that the reader can become frustrated or overwhelmed and may fail to attempt any new method. Therefore, throughout the book we have also provided activities that encourage the reader to slow down and take time to implement and practice the methods discussed.

The Second Edition

This second edition includes several new chapters and numerous new methods stemming from the teacher and school effectiveness research completed in the past five years. Specific changes include:

The new introductory chapter that provides a summary of teacher effectiveness and classroom management research and prescription.

The book's increased emphasis on secondary education with many new ideas and case studies.

Added new chapters on school-wide discipline programs and on beginning the school year.

Numerous case studies to demonstrate teachers' use of the methods presented throughout the book.

Many new practical forms.

A new section on instruction highlights the strengths and comparisons of many of the popular instructional methods.

Many ideas for dealing with disruptive students, including a systems approach to working with students prior to referral for special education placement.

New design features making the book easier to read.

New chapter headings and chapter introductions highlight each chapter's major themes. Subsidiary material is printed in smaller type and clearly set off from the text.

Updated chapter bibliographies providing a rich source of reference material for the interested student and professional.

Acknowledgments

We wish to acknowledge the many teachers whose application of the methods presented in this book have validated their effectiveness. Specifically, we would like to thank Dean Long, Marjorie Miller Tonole, and Terri Vann for allowing us to use student behavior change projects they completed in one of our graduate classes. We would also like to thank Cory Dunn for his assistance in developing Figure 12.1. We are grateful to Jere Brophy, Dan Duke, Joyce Putnam, Joseph Witt, and Karen Harvey for giving generously of their time and expertise in providing helpful reviews. Finally, we wish to express our appreciation to David W. Lynch and Wendy Conger for their thoughtful and professional editorial work.

PART I

FOUNDATIONS
OF COMPREHENSIVE
CLASSROOM MANAGEMENT

Theory and practice in classroom management have improved dramatically over the past decade. Unfortunately, practical methods presented to teachers have often been simplistic and piecemeal. Because of public and teacher concern over discipline problems, new ideas have too often been quickly marketed as panaceas. Rather than assisting teachers to understand the issues in effective classroom management and the relationship between various strategies, most published materials have presented unidimensional approaches to small aspects of classroom management. These methods have usually failed to significantly affect students' behavior or have solved only a few of the teacher's problems with discipline. When this occurs, teachers are left with a sense of frustration and impotence. They must either blame themselves or ask if the profession has anything meaningful to offer in the way of ideas on classroom management.

Part I is directed toward alleviating the confusion associated with the topic of classroom management. In this section we examine the major causes of unproductive student behavior and provide a theoretical and philosophical foundation from which to examine approaches to encouraging positive student behavior and achievement and responding to disruptive behavior. In Chapter 1 we place the concept of classroom management in perspective by examining the extent of the problem, considering the reasons for an increase in problems associated with student behavior, defining comprehensive classroom management, describing the history of classroom management, and discussing the relationship between classroom management and the teacher's professional needs. In Chapters 2 and 3 we examine students' personal and academic needs that must be met for them to become productively involved in the learning process. Discussions of classroom management have until recently placed far too much emphasis on controlling unproductive student behavior and too little on creating environments that encourage productive behavior. The concepts presented in Chapters 2 and 3 provide a foundation for refocusing attention on preventive interventions.

After completing Part I you should understand why discipline problems arise and the factors that must be confronted in order to reduce these problems. This perspective provides a basis for employing the preventive and corrective strategies described throughout the book. Perhaps more important, this understanding will enable you to creatively analyze your own classroom or school environment and evaluate how you might implement the ideas presented in this book or create new solutions for dealing with the behavior problems that occur in your school.

CHAPTER 1

Classroom Management in Perspective

Almost all surveys of teacher effectiveness report that classroom management skills are of primary importance in determining teaching success, whether it is measured by student learning or by ratings. Thus, management skills are crucial and fundamental. A teacher who is grossly inadequate in classroom management skills is probably not going to accomplish much.

Jere Brophy and Carolyn Evertson, (1976),
Learning From Teaching

The concept of classroom management is broader than the notion of student discipline. It includes all the things teachers must do to foster student involvement and cooperation in classroom activities and to establish a productive working environment.

Julie Sanford, Edmund Emmer, and Barbara Clements,
"Improving Classroom Management"
Educational Leadership, April, 1983

Student behavior problems have for years been a major concern of teachers, administrators, and parents. National concern about students' achievement has intensified public interest in schools and students' behavior. Although teachers face the task of educating many students whose home and community environments are disruptive, research demonstrates that teachers' skills in managing classrooms are a major factor influencing students' motivation, achievement, and behavior. The concept of discipline, with its emphasis on dealing with inevitable misbehavior among students, has been replaced by a more comprehensive body of knowledge on how to increase students' achievement by preventing management problems.

EXTENT OF THE PROBLEM

The issue of student behavior has been a longstanding concern of laypersons and educators. Since its inception in 1969, the annual Gallup Poll of the Public's Attitudes Toward Public Education has found school discipline to be the public's number one educational concern on fifteen of sixteen occasions. The 1984 poll indicated that 25 percent of those sampled felt that lack of discipline was the biggest problem facing local schools, an increase of 2 percent over the 1983 poll and identical to the 1982 poll. Seven out of ten respondents to both the 1982 and 1984 polls rated discipline problems in their local schools as either "very serious" or "fairly serious." The 1982 poll also reported that 63 percent of those surveyed viewed discipline problems in schools as a "main reason why teachers are leaving their jobs." Similarly, in the 1983 survey, respondents who stated they would not want their children to become teachers rated discipline problems second only to low pay as their main reason.

Teachers echo the public's concern about students' behavior. Sixty percent of teachers agree that public concern over discipline is warranted (Levin, 1980). The National Education Association (NEA) 1983 National Teacher Opinion Poll reported that 45 percent of the teachers responding indicated that student misbehavior interfered with teaching to either a great or moderate degree. Several investigators report that issues of order and control are pervasive troubles for teachers (Pollard, 1980; Woods, 1976; Yinger, 1980), and that these problems are accentuated for beginning teachers (Willower, 1975). Reports also indicate that student behavior problems are contributing to teachers' stress and discontent. Feitler and Tokar (1982) found that 58 percent of their sample of teachers ranked "individual pupils who continually misbehave" as the number one cause of job-related stress. Cichon and Koff (1980), in a study of nearly 5,000 Chicago teachers, reported that managing disruptive students ranked second to being "involuntarily transferred" as the major cause of stress. The 1984 Gallup Poll of Teachers' Attitudes Toward the Public Schools (Gallup, 1984) reported that half the teachers surveyed viewed discipline problems in their local schools as either "very serious" (16 percent) or "fairly serious" (33 percent). Almost without exception, today's teachers view classroom discipline as a key issue that influences the two aspects of their professional lives that are perhaps the most important: (1) the degree to which their students develop personal and cognitive skills, and (2) the degree to which teachers enjoy their jobs.

These findings are no surprise, considering the amount of time teachers are involved in managing students' behavior. Gump (1967) reported that approximately half of teachers' actions involved instruction. The remainder of teachers' behavior involved such management functions as organizing and arranging students for instruction (23 percent), dealing with misbehavior (14 percent), and handling individual problems (12 percent). A study (Wragg, 1984) of 36 British teachers observed during 213 lesson hours in classes of mixed ability found that 54 percent of teachers' behavior involved management functions. Doyle (in press) presents an impressive review of research indicating the interdependence of management and instruction functions. Simply stated, students' learning is directly related to classroom order. The passage of Public Law 94-142 has added to teacher's classroom management burdens. Teachers are increasingly responsible for the instruction and supervision of behavior-disordered and learning disabled students. Research indicates that teachers spend significantly more time instructing and managing these special students and have between 60 percent and 90 percent more interactions with them than students not identified under the law (Thompson, White, & Morgan, 1982).

School administrators share teachers' and parents' concerns, listing discipline as their top concern and stating that more time must be spent resolving the problem (Duke, 1978). The Safe School Study Report to the U.S. Congress, *Violent Schools–Safe Schools* (1978), stressed the problems facing many schools. Based on a mail survey of 4,000 elementary and secondary schools, the authors of the study found that 8 percent of the nation's schools were characterized as having serious behavior problems. A review of data (Moles, 1983) indicates that although disruptive student behavior had not increased during the past five years, neither had there been a substantial reduction in the problem.

While violent student misbehavior was the focus of concern during the 1970s and continues to be an important issue, students' achievement was increasingly the focus during the first half of the 1980s. Studies such as *A Nation at Risk: The Report of the National Commission on Excellence in Education*, and John Goodlad's "A Study of Schooling" (1983) have aroused public worry over the quality of education in the United States. Consequently, classroom management is increasingly seen as vital because of its relationship to students' learning.

Regardless of whether disruptive behavior or low achievement troubles us most, students' attendance and attitudes about school provide additional cause for alarm. The National Center for Education Statistics report, *The Condition of Education* (Plisko, 1983) showed that, nationally, 28 percent of students failed to graduate from high school. But only 61 percent of black and 56 percent of Hispanic nineteen-year-olds had high school diplomas. In inner-city schools the statistics were even worse. "Most inner-city high schools in New Jersey lose more than half of each class prior to graduation" (Hyman & D'Alessandro, 1984, p. 40). Additionally, on any given day, one in twelve students is absent from school, and this figure is nearly one in five students in some large cities. Research (Hollingsworth, Lifler, & Clune, 1984) indicates that nearly one student in ten is suspended from school during any school year. A 1977 study by the Children's Defense Fund revealed that two million students were suspended annually, accounting for eight million lost school days. In a study of 56 schools, Gottfredson (1983) found that 31 percent of black male students had been suspended at least once in the past term.

Fortunately, some reports suggest that students' misbehavior probably peaked during the 1970s, and teachers appear to be less distressed about students' misbehavior. In 1980, 54 percent of the respondents to the NEA's National Teacher Opinion Poll said that student behavior interfered with their teaching to a great (21 percent) or moderate (33 percent) degree. In 1984, 45 percent reported interference, with 15 percent rating the interference as great and 30 percent moderate. The 1984 NEA National Opinion Poll showed teacher concern about disruptive student behavior to be even less than that reported in the 1983 poll. Similarly, the 1984 Gallup Poll of Teachers' Attitudes Toward the Public Schools (Gallup, 1984) indicated that teachers were less concerned about violent or law-violating student behavior and more distressed by problems such as incomplete assignments, cheating, insubordination and truancy. Teachers were less disturbed during the first half of the 1980s for several reasons. In response to teachers' uneasiness about student violence throughout the 1970s, teachers used collective bargaining to seek and obtain agreements on teachers' rights to remove disruptive students from class. (From a contract between West Linn School District No. 3Jt, Clackamas County, Oregon, and the Willamette Falls Bargaining Council [1983–1985]). The example we quote here demonstrates how far some teachers' groups have gone in bargaining for strong teachers' rights in removing students.

Article 5—Student Discipline

1. General

   Definition of duties and responsibilities of all administrators, coordinators, supervisors, and other personnel pertaining to student discipline shall be reduced to writing by the District, and presented to each teacher at the start of each school year. Such definition of the duties and responsibilities of personnel is a retained right of the District.

2. Procedure

   Teachers may temporarily exclude a student from the classroom when the student's behavior is seriously disrupting the instructional program. When a student is so excluded, the following procedure will be utilized:

   a. The student will be sent to the building principal's office. Prior to requesting that the student be placed back in the classroom, the principal will discuss the matter with the teacher involved.

   b. If the teacher does not agree to place the student back in the classroom at the principal's request, the student will not be allowed back in the class pending completion of this procedure.

   c. In the event the teacher and principal disagree, the matter will be referred as soon as possible to the Superintendent. A conference will be arranged with the teacher, principal and Superintendent. The decision of the Superintendent will be final.

d. 1. The parties agree that in such matters a speedy resolution of any disagreement in (b.) above is of paramount importance. The parties agree that a good faith effort will be made to arrange and meet with the Superintendent as provided for in (c.) above; even if it means meeting outside the regular workday.

2. If the Superintendent is not available to meet as per this section, this meeting will be conducted by the Assistant Superintendent. If neither is available, it will be conducted by another certified central office administrator.

In addition to acknowledging teachers' rights to remove disruptive students, many school districts provide teachers with in-service training in classroom management. This training has been further augmented by school districts' efforts to incorporate research on teacher and school effectiveness into their teacher in-service and evaluation programs. Consequently, by the mid-1980s, a large proportion of experienced teachers had received at least some training in methods for preventing and handling disruptive student behavior.

Obviously it is insufficient to merely document the severity of student behavior problems. It is critical that educators understand why these problems arise. The two basic reasons why classroom management continues to be a major problem in our schools are these: First, teachers are asked to instruct a wide range of students, many of whom come to school with varying degrees of emotional distress and inadequate personal skills. Second, teachers have historically been inadequately trained in classroom management and instructional skills.

SOCIAL FACTORS INFLUENCING STUDENTS' BEHAVIOR

Although teachers cannot immediately or directly alter the social factors that create students' problems, understanding them does enable teachers to place students' failure and disruptive behavior in perspective and to create environments that reduce rather than intensify their effect. When discussing the problem of disruptive or disturbed student behavior, teachers often ask why these problems seem to have increased over the past decade. Indeed, as education and psychology have developed an increasingly sophisticated body of knowledge, teachers have entered the classroom better trained than ever before. There is little question that today's teachers better understand such topics as human development and the learning process than did teachers ten years ago. Therefore, although unproductive student behavior is often a response to factors within schools and classrooms, it seems reasonable to assume that today's school environments are, in general, more supportive of students' needs and more conducive to learning than they were ten or twenty years ago. Consequently, though improving teachers' skills remains a major component in combating unproductive student behavior, other variables must be considered in order to develop a comprehensive understanding of the intensified problems of classroom discipline.

When searching for answers to the complex problems faced by schools as social institutions, educators must look at society itself. Perhaps the most dramatic social factor affecting students' behavior is the increased isolation and instability of the nuclear family. As Bronfenbrenner (1974) and numerous other social psychologists have noted, the extensive mobility of the American population has created a situation in which families have become increasingly isolated. As young families have moved away from their extended families, they have frequently found themselves living in rather impersonal suburbs that lack the sense of continuity, support, and security often found in smaller towns where families had lived for many years. The relative isolation experienced by many families has meant that the nuclear family has become the major satisfier of personal and social needs for both parents and children. This situation would undoubtedly place heavy demands upon family units in a relatively stable, unchanging social milieu, but the problem has been intensified by rapid change in American society. Increased emphasis on the individual's right to experience happiness and to place personal fulfillment over obligation has placed even greater demands on the nuclear family. As a result, during the past decades, divorce rates have soared. Consequently, "only 63 percent of all children under 18 in 1978 were living with both natural parents in their first marriage, and nearly one in five was living in a single-parent family, almost double the number 25 years ago" (Conger, 1984, p. 203). Indeed, predictions indicate that nearly 50 percent of children born during the 1970s will experience divorce or death of a parent (Calhoun, Crotberg, & Rackey, 1980; Glick & Norton, 1979). The large number of single-parent families, combined with a rate of inflation that has caused many mothers in two-parent families to seek employment, have created a situation in which well over half of women with school-age children are employed at least half-time.

Even though research (Ahlstrom & Havighurst, 1971) suggests that children may in fact be better off in a single-parent family than in a two-parent family racked by conflict, there is little question that family instability has placed heavy emotional demands upon children (Elkind, 1981). These demands often (though certainly not always) result in emotional turmoil, which frequently affects children's ability to comfortably adjust to the academic and social demands of the school experience.

Stress within the family unit certainly affects students' needs and behaviors, yet this is only one of several social factors that has led to increased discipline problems. Another factor is the move away from the automatic acceptance of adult authority. Today's youngsters are more mature and aware than ever before. For instance, the average age of menarche for American girls is nearly two years earlier today than it was in 1900. Children also appear to possess more sophisticated reasoning skills than we often acknowledge. Research stemming from Piaget's conceptualizations of cognitive functioning suggests that cognitive development can be accelerated by experience and training (Beilin, 1971; Brainerd & Allen, 1971; Kamil, 1972). Children in our society are increasingly provided with educational and media-related experiences that have potential for enhancing their cognitive skills. The extensive availability and excessive use of television has certainly been a factor in enabling younger and younger children to discuss and question issues that were heretofore unquestioningly accepted. One of the authors recently asked her fourth-grade class to write about what they felt to be the major problem facing the world today. Students' answers included energy, pollution, family upheaval, and violence as seen in the increased incidence of rape. Even more interesting than the topics themselves was students' ability to provide surprisingly sophisticated reasons for their statements. As children become able to examine and analyze their environment at increasingly early ages, the concept of child subservience to the unexplained authority of adults will come under increasing strain.

Elkind (1981) suggests that society reinforces this trend by pressuring younger and younger children to achieve academically and socially. As children are pushed to look like adults and to perform athletically, academically, and socially like adults, it is to be expected that adult authority will come into question at an increasingly early age.

Changes in the rate of physical and cognitive development have reduced the age at which youths begin questioning adult authority, and two additional factors have influenced this trend. First, as our society becomes more complex and changes with ever-increasing rapidity, adults' skills and perceptions are realistically less relevant to young people than they were when children grew up to find a society very much like that in which their parents were raised. In a very real sense, adults today are less authorities on the world in which their children will be raised than were adults a century ago. Second, perhaps more poignantly than at any time in our nation's history, young people today are faced with the fact that the adults who parent and teach them are rather ineffective in handling their own world. On the family level, an increasing number of young people vividly view relationships that their parents could not make work. On a societal level, young adults have heard about crises in El Salvador, the Middle East, the environment, potential nuclear war, energy, and inflation. Primary-grade children are not able to comprehend such issues and make the connection between these problems and legitimate adult authority, but they may very well sense and respond to older children's questioning of this authority and even to adults' hesitation about their own legitimacy.

The gradual reduction in adult authority has been reinforced by increasing emphasis on uniform human rights. Minority and women's rights have received more notoriety, yet children have also benefited from this trend. Examples of children's rights include the fight for the rights of the unborn, the rights of delinquent youths as expressed in the In re Gault decision (1967), and the rights of handicapped children as seen in legislation such as P.L. 94-142.

Legislation directly affects classroom discipline. As almost every teacher is aware, classrooms are becoming increasingly heterogeneous. In addition to increased cultural integration, students with a variety of handicapping conditions are experiencing integration into regular classrooms. Although this situation has exciting potential for both students and teachers, it also places increased demands upon teachers' time and energy. These new demands have obvious implications for classroom management, for teachers often find themselves working with students with relatively serious personal or learning problems. Teachers therefore have less time to attend to the emotional and cognitive demands of other students. Consequently, students who may have been only minor discipline problems may act out to receive teacher attention that is being given to other students.

A final social factor influencing students' classroom behavior is the manner in which education is funded in our society. Teacher training programs do not receive money to provide scholarships like those given to athletes or musicians. Teachers' salaries have consistently remained low, and, compared to other areas of employment, teachers' salaries have rated poorly in keeping up with inflation. Therefore, the teaching profession has had difficulty attracting the best candidates and retaining the most capable professionals (Schlechty & Vance, 1981; Robertson, Keith, & Page, 1983; Weaver, 1979). Furthermore, with the current emphasis on reducing taxes, schools are in financial difficulty. One need only read the statement of goals and purposes of any school district to realize that the officially stated goals of public education support the type of teaching associated with positive learning environments and well-managed classrooms. It is an unfortunate reality, however, that these goals are frequently subverted by districts' needs to minimize costs. When a teacher is asked to instruct twenty-five to thirty-five students in perhaps ten subjects, we can expect that the goals of public education will become lost. The material in this book will provide teachers with practical skills that, if thoughtfully applied, will significantly improve their ability to successfully instruct children, but school districts must recognize the reality that teachers often face herculean tasks. If society sincerely believes that schools should perform their role as outlined in the goal statements developed by most school districts, teachers' loads must be reduced and additional support staff must be made available.

This overview of social factors influencing classroom discipline is not intended to suggest that teachers face insurmountable problems, nor to provide an excuse for teachers who experience major problems in classroom discipline. It is important, though, that teachers realize that a variety of social factors have altered many school and classroom situations. If teachers are to work effectively with young people, they must be aware of the factors that are placing somewhat different, and increasing, demands upon them.

SCHOOL FACTORS INFLUENCING STUDENTS' BEHAVIOR

An undetermined yet significant amount of disruptive student behavior is caused by teachers' lack of classroom management skills. Brophy and Rohrhemper (1981) observed and interviewed forty-four teachers from inner-city schools in a large metropolitan school district and fifty-four teachers in a small city. Most of the teachers had ten or more years of experience and half were nominated by their principals as outstanding in working with problem students. The researchers found that few of the teachers had any pre-service or in-service training in classroom management. The study also reported that few of the teachers (including those rated most effective) had a clear, consistent philosophy or understanding of how to manage their classrooms. Instead, they tended to rely on an unsystematic bag-of-tricks approach developed through experience.

The research on teacher effectiveness and school effectiveness discussed in the next section also tells us that teachers' behavior is a key ingredient affecting student's behavior and performance. Schools working with similar student populations differ dramatically in how well students behave and achieve (Edmonds, 1981; Rutter, 1979). Similarly, teachers instructing very similar groups of students show marked differences in their ability to assist students in developing desirable behavior and achievement (Brophy & Evertson, 1976; Evertson & Emmer, 1982; Good & Grouws, 1979; Stallings, 1983).

Students' attitudes toward school are another strong indication that school factors contribute greatly to students' academic and behavior problems. When Jane Norman and Myron Harris (1981) surveyed 160,000 teenagers for their book, *The Private Life of the American Teenager,* they discovered that only 42 percent of the students described school as "necessary," 21 percent found it "interesting" and 27 percent said school was "boring." Additionally, 60 percent of the students said they studied primarily to pass tests rather than to learn. A national poll conducted by the University of Michigan's Institute for Social Research reported that the number of students who thought what they learned in school was "very important" or "quite important" declined from 70 percent to 50 percent in the decade 1970 to 1980. Another study conducted by the National Center for Educational Statistics reported that more than half of the high school seniors sampled found their part-time jobs more enjoyable than school. When John Godland (1983) asked students to identify the best thing about school, 34.9 percent said "friends," 13.4 percent said "sports," 7 percent said "classes," 4.1 percent said "teachers," and 8 percent said "nothing." Given these findings, we should not be surprised that more than 55 percent of teenagers state they cheat in school (Norman & Harris, 1981). The extent of student apathy suggested by these studies was validated when the Carnegie Council on Higher Education surveyed school principals for its 1979 study "Giving Youth a Better Chance." Forty-one percent of the principals surveyed rated student apathy as "very serious" or "serious." In fact, principals rated apathy ahead of absenteeism as a leading school problem.

CLASSROOM MANAGEMENT: AN HISTORICAL PERSPECTIVE

Because approaches to classroom management have developed so dramatically since 1970, teachers have been bombarded with alternative answers to the question, "How do I control my classroom?" Amid the multitude of competing and sometimes conflicting methods presented to teachers, it is helpful for them to develop an understanding of the historical progression of the various methods.

The Counseling Approach

During the 1960s and through much of the 1970s, the emphasis in dealing with student behavior was on discipline. The little training teachers received was focused on what to do after students misbehaved. Because the emphasis in psychology during the late 1960s and early 1970s was on personal growth and awareness, most methods were focused on understanding students' problems and helping them better understand themselves and work cooperatively with adults to develop more productive behaviors. One of the earliest and most widely employed models was William Glasser's Reality Therapy (1965, 1969). Glasser's model derived from the belief that young people need caring professionals willing to assist them in taking responsibility for their behavior and for developing plans aimed at altering unproductive conduct. Rudolf Dreikurs and his associates (1971) developed a somewhat more clinical model based on the belief that acting out children were making poor choices because of inappropriate notions of how to meet their basic need to be accepted. Dreikurs proposed a variety of methods for responding to children's misconduct, depending upon the goal of the behavior. His model provided teachers and parents with strategies for identifying the causes of students' misbehavior, responding to misbehavior with logical consequences, and running family and classroom meetings.

Emphasis on humanistic psychology was most obvious in the models of self-concept theorists. Initially summarized by LaBenne and Green (1969), and Purkey (1970), this work was focused on the relationship between positive student self-concepts, students' learning, and productive behavior. This work was extended to a more practical program for teachers by Tom Gordon (1974) whose *Teacher Effectiveness Training* provided them with techniques for responding to students' misbehavior with open communication and attempts at mutually solving problems.

Behavioristic Methods

As social uneasiness rose about disruptive behavior of youth, the focus of classroom discipline moved in the direction of teacher control. This increased attention to discipline was associated with the development and popularization of behavioristic methodology. Beginning in the mid-1970s, most courses aimed at helping teachers cope with disruptive student behavior were focused almost exclusively on behavior-modification techniques.

Teachers were taught to ignore inappropriate behavior while reinforcing appropriate behavior, write contracts with recalcitrant students, and use time-out procedures. This emphasis on control was most systematically presented to teachers in the form of Lee Canter's (1976) *Assertive Discipline*. Teachers learned to state clear general behavioral expectations, quietly and consistently punish disruptive students, and provide group reinforcement for on-task behavior.

Teacher-Effectiveness Research

While counseling and control-oriented approaches vied for popularity, a new emphasis on classroom management was developing during the 1970s. This new direction emphasized not what teachers did in response to student misconduct, but rather how teachers prevented or contributed to students' misbehavior. This research, later labeled teacher effectiveness, has focused attention on three sets of teacher behaviors that influence students' behavior and learning: (1) teachers' skill in organizing and managing classroom activities, (2) teachers' skills in presenting instructional material, and (3) teacher-student relationships.

Teachers' Organizational and Management Skills
A study that initially displayed the importance of teachers' organizational and management skills was reported in Jacob Kounin's 1970 book, *Discipline and Group Management in Classrooms*. Kounin and his colleagues videotaped thousands of hours in classrooms that ran smoothly with a minimum of disruptive behavior and classrooms in which students were frequently inattentive and disruptive. The videotapes were then systematically analyzed to determine what teachers in these two very different types of classrooms did differently when students misbehaved. The results showed no systematic differences. Effective classroom managers were not notably different from poor classroom managers in their ways of responding to students' misbehavior. Further analysis, however, demonstrated clear and significant differences between how effective and ineffective classroom managers behaved prior to students' misbehavior. Effective classroom managers employed various teaching methods that prevented disruptive student behavior.

The Texas Teacher Effectiveness Study was a second landmark study dealing with organizing and managing behavior. In this study, reported in *Learning from Teaching* by Jere Brophy and Carolyn Evertson (1976), the researchers observed fifty-nine teachers over two years. Teachers were selected to provide two groups whose students differed consistently in performance on standardized achievement tests. Classroom observations focused on teachers' behaviors previously suggested as being related to effective teaching. The results of the study supported Kounin's findings on effective behaviors that prevented disruption and facilitated learning by creating smoothly run classrooms.

The findings of Kounin and Brophy and Evertson were expanded by Emmer, Evertson, and Anderson (1980) in the Classroom Organization and Effective Teaching Project carried out at the Research and Development Center for Teacher Education at the University of Texas at Austin. In the first of a series of studies, these researchers observed twenty-eight third-grade classrooms during the first several weeks of school. The research findings showed that the smooth functioning found in effective teachers' classrooms throughout the school year mostly resulted from effective planning and organization during the first few weeks of school. Effective classroom managers provided students with clear instruction in desirable classroom behavior and carefully monitored students' performance—reteaching behaviors that students had not mastered. Effective teachers also made consequences for misbehavior clear and applied these consistently. This study was followed by research in junior high school classrooms (Evertson & Emmer, 1982a) that verified the importance that early planning and instruction in appropriate behavior have in secondary school settings.

Recent studies building upon those we have cited demonstrate that when teachers are provided information about skills associated with effective teaching and receive feedback on how their behavior in the classroom matches criteria for effective teaching, they can become much more effective teachers (Good & Grouws, 1979; Evertson, Emmer, Sanford, & Clements, 1982; Fitzpatrick, 1982; McDaniel, 1983; Mehlman, 1982; Sanford, Emmer, & Clements, 1983; and Stallings, 1983).

Instructional Skills
A second area of investigation on teachers' behavior that prevents disruptive student behavior and enhances learning examines how material is presented to students. The earliest and most lasting work on this subject has been conducted by Madeline Hunter. Her ITIP (Instructional Theory into Practice) program for nearly two decades has attempted to translate findings in educational psychology into practical strategies that improve instruction. Though her work emphasizes some of the skills pointed out by researchers interested in classroom organization and teacher-student relationships, her major contribution is in helping teachers understand the need to develop clear instructional goals, state these to students, provide effective direct instruction, and monitor students' progress.

This research has been expanded by studies (Berliner, 1979; Fisher & others, 1978, 1980; Good & Grouws, 1979; Stallings, 1983, 1984) that have examined the relationship between various teacher instructional patterns and students' achievement. These studies, often called process-product research because they examine correlations between instructional processes and student outcomes or products, are thoughtfully reviewed by Rosenshine (1983) and Good (1983a). Criticism of this line of research has focused on the fact that no one behavior or group of behaviors of teachers is related to students' achievement with all ages and types of students and for all learning outcomes.

Subsequently, some writers (Darling-Hammond, Wise, & Pease, 1983; Doyle, 1979; Soar, 1983; Zumwalt, 1982) warn against placing too much emphasis on specific teacher skills. These writers suggest that although teachers should be familiar with the results of process-product research, they must selectively employ these findings, taking into account the unique characteristics of the students with whom they work and the educational goals they espouse.

A second field of study examines the relative merits of competitive, co-operative, and individualized instruction. This work, carried out by Roger and David Johnson of the University of Minnesota, demonstrates that cooperative learning activities are associated with many desirable learning outcomes. Students who work cooperatively on learning tasks tend to relate more positively to their peers, view learning as more positive, and learn more information (Johnson & Johnson, 1975, 1983, 1984). Additional work in cooperative team learning was carried out by Slavin (1983), who developed the Teams-Games-Tournaments approach, and by Sharan (1980).

Another area of study is the variability in how students learn best and how teachers can adjust instruction to respond to students' individual learning styles. This work, carried out by Rita Dunn (Dunn, 1983; Dunn & Dunn, 1978), Joseph Renzulli (1983), Anthony Gregore (1982), and others shows that when teachers allow students to study in environments conducive to learning and use approaches to learning that are most productive for each student, the students learn much more effectively and behave appropriately. In their *Models of Teaching*, Bruce Joyce and Marsha Weil describe many types of instructional methods that respond to different learning goals and students' learning styles. Joyce and Weil (1980) write that:

> . . . despite the fearsome troubles besetting education, there presently exists a really delightful and vigorous array of approaches to teaching that can be used to transform the world of schools if only we would employ them.
>
> We believe that strength in education resides in the intelligent use of this powerful variety of approaches—matching them to different goals and adapting them to the students' styles and characteristics. Competence in teaching stems from the capacity to reach out to differing children and to create a rich and multi-dimensional environment for them. [p. xxiii]

Teacher-Student Relationships

The third major research area within the teacher-effectiveness paradigm focuses on the effect teacher-student interactions have on students' achievement and behavior. This field of study can be divided into two basic parts: (1) studies exploring the influence of the frequency and quality of teacher-student interactions on students' achievement, and (2) studies emphasizing the personal, affective dimension of teacher-student relationships and their effect on students' attitudes and, to a lesser degree, achievement.

Robert Rosenthal and Leonore Jacobson's *Pygmalion in the Classroom* (1968) generated tremendous interest in the influence teacher-student relationships have on students' achievement. These authors report that teachers' expectations for students' performance became self-fulfilling prophecies. In other words, students seem to perform as teachers expect them to. The important question became what specifically teachers do to communicate high or low expectations to students. This question was initially studied by Brophy and Good (1969, 1974) at the University of Texas. These researchers, leaders in the field of classroom management for fifteen years, found that teachers' interaction with students was associated with marked differences in students' performance (Brophy & Good, 1974). This research has been replicated and expanded, including examination of attribution theory and factors related to teachers' sense of control (Cooper & Good, 1983).

The second area of study involves the affective quality of teacher-student relationships and its effect on students' attitudes and self-concepts. This research was first widely reported in the late 1960s and early 1970s in books such as LeBenne and Green's *Educational Implications of Self-Concept Theory* (1969) and William Purkey's *Self Concept and School Achievement* (1970). Although interpersonal relationships in the classroom were emphasized less during the mid-1970s, research and practical ideas on this subject received more attention in the early 1980s (Purkey, 1978, 1984).

School-Effectiveness Research

The unique characteristics of unusually effective schools were examined throughout the 1970s, but in the late 1970s and early 1980s a number of well-designed and highly publicized school effectiveness studies were done (Brookover, 1978; Edmonds, 1979; Goodlad, 1984; Lipsitz, 1984; Rutter, 1979; Wayson & Pinnell, 1982). The methodology in these studies included comparing schools that were more or less effective in obtaining high achievement and desirable behavior with similar student populations (Brookover, 1978; Edmonds, 1979; Rutter, 1979), examining characteristics common to exemplary schools (Lipsitz, 1984; Wayson & Pinnell, 1982) and carrying out in-depth analysis of instruction and relationships with a cross-section of schools, then analyzing the resulting data (Goodlad, 1984). School-effectiveness research does show that teachers (and administrators) do make a difference. Factors such as teachers' expectations, the quality of teacher-student relationships, instruction emphasizing careful monitoring of students' progress, opportunities for teacher and student involvement in decision making, administrative leadership, and variety in teaching methods influence students' academic performance and behavior. While it is important to develop thoughtful, effective methods for responding to student misbehavior, the focus of both research and application has clearly moved toward creating learning environments that foster desirable student behavior and the associated increase in learning. Much work needs to be done to synthesize the results of various studies and translate these into specific programs for improving schools (Purkey & Smith, 1983), yet school effectiveness studies provide another strong indication that student achievement and behavior can be dramatically altered by improving schools.

DEFINING COMPREHENSIVE CLASSROOM MANAGEMENT

Many teachers, even though they acknowledge the importance of classroom management, react somewhat negatively to the topic. Perhaps because until recently classroom management was viewed primarily as a collection of methods for handling disruptive student behaviors, such teachers initially feel management is only a necessary evil. The subject is too often linked to authoritarian control and order and, is usually viewed, along with bureaucratic paperwork and inability to control one's curriculum, to the distasteful side of teaching. The contrasting side is the excitement of watching a student learn a new concept or receiving a note of appreciation from a parent or student. Many bright, sensitive teachers leave the profession each year frustrated by their inability to create classroom environments in which the rewarding aspects of teaching significantly outweigh the negative aspects.

The fact that classroom management is so frequently associated with feelings of confusion and concern suggests that the initial step in satisfactorily coping with this issue is understanding the factors and skills involved. Extensive reviews of the research (Brophy, 1983; Doyle, 1984; Good, 1983; Squires, Huitt, & Segars, 1984) and our own experience in classrooms bring out five major factors or skill areas involved in effective management. First, *classroom management should be based on solid understanding of students' personal, psychological, and academic needs.* Our experience in teaching classroom-management courses and consulting with schools suggests that, despite extensive worry about students' achievement and misbehavior, very few teachers understand why problems exist or the relationship between the problem and their own professional behavior. An analysis of data from the 1984 Gallup Poll of Teachers' Attitudes Toward the Public Schools shows that,

> Teachers blame disciplinary problems on outside influences—specifically, the courts, lack of respect for authority, and especially lack of discipline in the home, which is mentioned by virtually all teachers (94%). Only about one-third of the teachers feel that teachers themselves are at fault (Gallup, 1984, p. 99).

Once teachers understand students' needs and how these are related to behavior, the next step in developing a well-managed classroom is to employ teaching methods that enhance learning and positive behavior by ensuring that students' personal needs are met in the classroom. Therefore, a second factor is: *Classroom management depends upon establishing positive teacher-student and peer relationships that help meet students' basic psychological needs.* Creating more desirable student behavior by concentrating on establishing positive, supportive classroom environments is based on a concept presented by numerous psychologists and educators (Covington & Berry, 1976; Glasser, 1969; Maslow, 1968; Purkey & Novak, 1984; Schmuck & Schmuck, 1984; Silberman, 1970): individuals learn more effectively in environments that meet their basic personal and psychological needs.

Most classrooms house twenty-five to thirty-five students. Teachers are responsible for orchestrating the movement, attention, and learning of varied students in a limited space. Therefore, regardless of how well a teacher understands students' needs and creates a positive emotional climate, organizational skills are critical. Consequently, the third factor is: *Comprehensive classroom management involves using organizational and group management methods that maximize on-task student behavior.* Order and control should not of course be viewed as the ultimate goal of effective classroom management, yet they are important means to the end of enhancing students' academic interest and achievement. Teachers' organizational and instructional skills interact to influence students' achievement. Kounin (1970) reported that student task involvement ranged from 98.7 percent for the most successful teacher in his sample to 25 percent for the least effective. Numerous additional studies emphasize the relationship between on-task behavior and achievement (Berliner, 1979; Denham & Lieberman, 1980). Therefore, though teachers must consider providing variety and choice in instructional tasks (Soar, 1983), it is desirable to emphasize strong control in the form of desired student behavior. Doyle (in press) summarizes this relationship between behavior control and instruction:

> The data reviewed in this chapter suggest, however, that the solution to the tension between management and instruction may require a greater emphasis on management. In other words, solving the instructional problems of low ability students cannot be done by de-emphasizing management or by designing more complex instructional arrangements for the classroom. Indeed, such "solutions" are likely to increase the problems they are designed to rectify. A more appropriate answer to the problem would seem to involve improved knowledge and training in management so that teachers can be free to concentrate on instructional solutions to learning problems. . . .

High behavioral standards are critical in creating an effective learning environment, but their importance should not be so interpreted as to diminish the value of instructional excellence. Our observations are supported by numerous studies (Au & Kawakani, 1983; Campbell, 1974; Johnson & Johnson, 1975; Jones, 1980; Silverstein, 1979) indicating that effective instructional methods that actively engage students can increase students' achievement and virtually eliminate misbehavior. Thus, the fourth factor in effective classroom management is: *Comprehensive classroom management involves using instructional methods that facilitate optimal learning by responding to the academic needs of individual students and the classroom group.* This aspect of classroom management is based on the idea that

> . . . low motivation, negative self attitudes, and failure are largely the result of improper learning conditions. According to this learning-theory analysis, we should be able to alter a student's failure rate by changing the conditions of classroom learning and, as a consequence, increase his motivation to succeed. [Covington & Beery, 1976, pp. 12, 13]

Walter Doyle (1983 and in press) reviews extensive research supporting the relationship between effective instruction and classroom management. He writes:

> Obviously the tasks of promoting learning and order are closely intertwined: Some minimal level of orderliness is necessary for instruction to occur and lessons must be sufficiently well constructed to capture and sustain student attention. Indeed, the tasks exist simultaneously so that a teacher often faces competing pressures to maximize learning and sustain order. In many instances, actions toward these ends are complementary. [in press]

Studies have indicated that decisions teachers make in an effort to maintain order significantly affect the type and quality of academic work and therefore the quality of students' achievement (Buike, 1981; Doyle, 1983; Duffy & McIntyre, 1982). Specifically, teachers often select lecture material and seatwork focusing on rote learning because these classroom activities are more easily managed. Goodlad (1983a) highlighted this relationship between order and instruction when he wrote:

> Our data revealed that the teachers we studied were aware of the desirability of having students participate in setting their goals, making choices, solving problems, working cooperatively with peers, and so on. But these views were tempered by conflicting ones having largely to do with maintaining control. Those time-honored practices that appeared to help maintain control won out. [pp. 469, 470]

Because of this emphasis on the preventive, instructional aspects of classroom management, a significant portion of this book will be focused on strategies for creating positive learning environments and employing instructional methods that respond effectively to students' needs. Although it is difficult to calculate how much inappropriate classroom behavior can be reduced by employing such methods, 75 percent may be a conservative estimate. Employing effective organizational and instructional methods and creating a positive classroom environment will reduce minor classroom disruptions, which not only creates a better learning environment, but also assists teachers in identifying students with severe problems and provides more time for working with these students. Finally, unless teachers use effective teaching methods, more direct behavior-change interventions will have limited long-term effectiveness.

The creation of positive, supportive classroom environments characterized by effective teaching skills will go a long way toward reducing behavior problems and increasing students' achievement. Anyone who has taught or worked with behavior-problem children is aware, however, that some children will, at least for a time, behave inappropriately in even the most productive learning environments. Consequently, teachers need a repertoire of problem-solving skills to support their instructional skills. The final factor in management is: *Classroom management involves the ability to employ a wide range of counseling and behavioral methods that involve students in examining and correcting their inappropriate behavior.*

Many teachers will say that they do not have the time to employ in-depth counseling strategies, and we believe this statement is generally accurate and realistic. Teachers cannot be expected to administer sophisticated psychological diagnostic instruments or employ in-depth counseling strategies within the classroom. On the other hand, many relatively simple yet effective approaches are available for helping children examine and change their behaviors. Because, as we have seen, teachers are increasingly faced with the task of teaching children who require special assistance, it has become necessary that teachers acquire problem-solving and behavior-management techniques.

A COMPREHENSIVE APPROACH TO CLASSROOM MANAGEMENT

Most educators are introduced to the topic of classroom management by being exposed to isolated techniques. A major reason for the confusion, frustration, and lack of understanding many teachers experience in attempting to create positive student behavior and high levels of achievement is that no one has honestly described the range of skills needed to effectively manage a classroom. In many pre-service education programs, the topic of classroom management is presented as a brief unit in a methods or educational psychology class. Likewise, in-service presentations aimed at providing teachers with classroom management skills are often scheduled for only a few hours. Subsequently, professors and consultants find themselves teaching a few tricks, or one aspect of classroom management, as if they were presenting the answer to teachers' problems. When these limited techniques fail to help teachers significantly, they must either assume that something is wrong with themselves or their use of the new methods or that no one really knows how teachers can effectively manage classrooms.

Teachers can benefit by becoming competent in employing one or more specific approaches to classroom management. To effectively and responsibly employ a method, however, teachers should understand its relationship to other approaches. Figure 1.1 places many of the major approaches to management in perspective. Under each major approach are listed key writers and researchers who have contributed to that emphasis.

Teachers' approaches to classroom management vary tremendously, but teachers seem to combine the methods outlined in Figure 1.1 in three basic ways. Some simply present instructional material in a manner that is productive for a small segment of students and employ structured, punishment-oriented methods to control students who do not (or cannot) respond positively to the instruction. This approach is not only unproductive and unprofessional but often leaves the teacher feeling unfulfilled and frustrated.

A second group of teachers creatively and conscientiously employ interesting and individualized instructional material while maintaining appropriate

FIGURE 1.1 Continuum of classroom management strategies

Chapters 4, 5, 6 *Interpersonal relationships*	Chapters 7, 8 *Classroom organization and management*	Chapter 9 *Instruction*	Chapter 10 *Problem solving*	Chapter 11 *Behavioristic*	Chapter 12 *School-wide discipline*
Jack Canfield & Harold Wells Thomas Gordon William Purkey Richard & Pat Schmuck	Jere Brophy Ed Emmer Carolyn Evertson Tom Good Madeline Hunter Jacob Kounin Jane Stallings	Walter Doyle Rita Dunn Thomas Good Madeline Hunter David & Roger Johnson Bruce Joyce Robert Slavin Robert Soar Jane Stallings	Rudolf Dreikurs William Glasser Thomas Gordon Frank Maple William Morse Robert Spaulding	Wesley Becker Lee Canter Frank Hewett Daniel O'Leary Hill Walker	Lee Canter Daniel Duke William Glasser William Wayson

behavior by implementing behavioristic methods. This approach is productive and is often a necessary initial combination, especially when working with children who lack positive interpersonal skills and have a history of school failure. It is based, though, on external motivation and, if not integrated with efforts to improve interpersonal skills, may leave students with a major skill deficit as well as a motivational system ensuring that productive behavior will exist only when strong external controls are present.

The third approach to managing a classroom involves implementing interesting, effective instruction and employing an interactive and problem-solving approach to classroom management. This approach has the advantage of creating a positive, supportive environment that simultaneously facilitates learning and personal growth. It would be ideal if this third approach were effective with all children, but children with emotional problems may initially need the additional structure provided by control-oriented discipline methods. Therefore, the skilled teacher is able to employ different methods with individual students.

FIGURE 1.2   Skills the teacher needs to develop responsible classroom management

Correction (Chapters 10–12)		School-wide discipline programs Implementing behavioristic techniques Employing problem-solving approaches
Prevention (Chapters 4–9)	Organization and instruction (Chapters 7–9)	Incorporating teaching methods that motivate students by incorporating multiple learning styles and instructional goals Implementing teaching that maximizes on-task behavior Developing effective classroom rules and procedures
	Interpersonal relationships (Chapters 4–6)	Working with parents Creating positive peer relationships Establishing positive teacher-student relationships
Theoretical Foundation (Chapters 1–3)		Understanding students' personal and academic needs

Even when they understand the relationship among various approaches to classroom management, many teachers become confused and frustrated when faced with the task of translating concepts or methods of classroom management into actual classroom practice. The model presented in Figure 1.2 clarifies the specific teacher skills involved in comprehensive classroom management.

The establishment of comprehensive classroom management depends upon developing and employing the knowledge and skills depicted in Figure 1.2. Furthermore, changes aimed at creating more positive student behavior should proceed in the hierarchic order suggested in the model. Teachers too often begin to intervene at the upper end of the hierarchy before laying a foundation by developing prerequisite knowledge and employing preventive interventions. When they do so, interventions will, at best, cause a limited, short-term improvement in students' behavior.

As indicated by the chapter designations listed in Figure 1.2, this book is designed to offer a comprehensive and hierarchic presentation of classroom management. Our emphasis on (1) understanding students' needs, (2) creating positive classroom environments that foster learning and prevent disruptive behavior, and (3) involving students in learning to responsibly correct their own misbehavior is reinforced by recent work on the importance of positive school climate (Anderson, 1982), effective instruction (Doyle, in press), and students' responsibility (Duke & Jones, in press; Wayson & Lasley, 1984) as key factors related to classroom management. Recent studies conducted by the National Center for the Study of Corporal Punishment and Alternatives in the Schools (Hyman & D'Alessandro, 1984) to examine effective programs for training teachers to discipline students further verify the importance of the skills described in this book. Their analysis of effective programs gives seven general techniques for motivating students and helping them deal with discipline problems:

1. providing feedback to students about their behaviors, feelings, and ideas;
2. using diagnostic strategies to better understand students and student-teacher interactions;
3. modifying the classroom climate;
4. applying techniques of behavior modification;
5. using democratic procedures for solving classroom problems;
6. expressing emotions appropriately; and
7. using therapeutic approaches to behavioral problems (p. 43).

A discussion of classroom management is not complete without recognizing teachers' limitations in dealing with disruptive student behavior. When unproductive student behavior is a response to lack of appropriate instructional materials, negative classroom environment, lack of peer support, or temporary crisis in a child's life, changes in the classroom environment will often immediately and significantly change students' behavior. Unfortunately, in a few children, unproductive behaviors are an indication of serious personality disorders that cannot be immediately altered by changes in environment or limited counseling intervention. When working with these children, we must place our interventions in proper perspective to avoid becoming discouraged. It is important to do everything possible to provide a positive learning environment and to help such children control their behavior. Realize, however, that even psychotherapists are not always able to help children who display severe behavior disorders. Similarly, residential treatment centers are often only modestly successful in working with such children.

Therefore, we must recognize that although most children can be helped by effective management methods, and we should keep high expectations for all children, for some children change will involve long and tedious work. Effective classroom management will not eliminate all problems or guarantee that every child will become a high achiever. By applying a comprehensive approach to management, however, we increase the possibility that each child will have a school experience characterized by optimal academic achievement and personal growth. Equally important, applying these strategies will significantly increase the likelihood that we will be able to meet our own needs to experience a sense of accomplishment and to enjoy the time we spend in the classroom.

CURRENT ISSUES IN CLASSROOM MANAGEMENT

Debate is now considerable over the role teachers should play in creating and maintaining a safe and productive learning environment. In his *Teaching: The Imperiled Profession*, Daniel Duke (1984) states that three roles currently receive support. The first argues for limited teacher involvement in handling students' misconduct. Teachers are viewed as responsible only for teaching, with discipline problems referred to administrators or handled by an increasing array of resource people. A second option involves simplifying the teacher's role in classroom management. Teachers are encouraged to systematize their disciplinary role in order to minimize time spent on behavior problems. Programs such as Lee Canter's *Assertive Discipline* (1976) involve teachers in establishing and consistently enforcing classroom rules. The third option would have teachers become familiar with the ever-broader range of research and related skills in classroom management (Brophy, 1982; Evertson & Emmer, 1982; Jones, 1982, 1983; Jones & Jones, 1981) and incorporate these into a new type of classroom leadership.

The literature on teacher effectiveness and school effectiveness strongly supports acceptance of the third option, yet even within this framework many debate about how teachers should present instruction and manage classrooms. Some researchers on school effectiveness (Edmonds, 1982) have placed almost exclusive emphasis on student on-task behavior and achievement of basic skills. Classroom management and instructional skills that enhance these student behaviors tend to emphasize a high degree of classroom structure and the use of extrinsic rewards to increase student's motivation. Research (Rim & Coller, 1979; Soar, 1983) suggests, however, that an intermediate amount of control is associated with the greatest student gains in achievement. That is, too little or too much control of either students' behavior or students' responsibility for the learning task limits their achievement.

Another reason for avoiding too great an emphasis on controlling students' behavior and enhancing achievement-test scores is that these fail to address important issues about the goals of public education in our society. Research indicates that for simple, low cognitive-level tasks, greater teacher control is desirable. Thus, if the goal is to learn the multiplication tables, greater teacher control of learning activities and students' behavior will result in increased learning. When students are involved in solving complex problems or in creative production, though, less teacher control is associated with better outcomes (Johnson & Johnson, 1975; Soar & Soar, 1972, 1975). Jencke and Peck (1976) reinforced this concept when they wrote:

> If teachers supply immediate reinforcement, they must pay the cost of having students learn to rely on rewards that are external to the problem situation itself. This cost may be worth incurring if the teacher is merely attempting to get children to efficiently commit facts to memory. However, the price may be too high when students are learning new concepts or if they are engaged in problem-solving or pattern-searching. [p. 33]

Corno (1979) reported that although increased classroom structure was associated with student gains in achieving basic learning tasks, it was associated with lower scores in creativity. Similarly, Soar and Soar (1980) found that the degree of students' attention to a task was positively related to low cognitive-level learning but negatively related to high cognitive-level learning. Apparently, creative production requires time to merely "sit and think," as opposed to diligently working as it is normally defined by research in on-task student behavior.

These studies are supported by research (Brophy, 1981; Rowe, 1974; Stallings & Kaskowitz, 1974) suggesting that high levels of teacher praise are associated with increased basic skill achievement but decreased creativity and less student independence, persistence, and self-confidence. When teachers use praise to reinforce on-task behavior and simple, correct answers, students respond by producing more of these responses at the expense of more creative, independent work.

If we wish to enhance students' independence, responsibility, creativity, and motivation, we must employ classroom-management strategies that do more than employ rewards and punishments to increase on-task behavior and high scores on achievement tests. Structure, praise, and reinforcement are important tools that do help many, if not all, students in learning basic skills, yet they are not the best techniques for helping all students to reach all learning goals.

Findings from several major national studies place the issue of teacher control in an interesting perspective. In his book, A Place Called School, John Goodlad (1984) provides strong support for the necessity of viewing student behavior problems as more than a response to poorly controlled classrooms. In summarizing the findings, Goodlad (1983a) states that the students

> . . . scarcely ever speculated on meanings, discussed alternative interpretations or engaged in projects calling for collaborative effort. Most of the time they listened or worked alone. The topics of the curriculum, it appears to me, were something to be acquired, not something to be explored, reckoned with, and converted into personal meaning and development. [p. 468]

In another summary of the study, Goodlad (1983b) stressed the two major problems associated with instructional practices that fail to emphasize varied learning goals and instructional strategies.

> The dominant instructional practices we observed in more than 1,000 classrooms (and which most staff development programs emphasize) appear to provide few opportunities for students to engage in the behaviors implied by the more exalted academic purposes of education, to say nothing of those other goals of citizenship, civility, and creativity to which state documents claim commitment. . . . [p. 553]
>
> Being a spectator not only deprives one of participation, but also leaves one's mind free for unrelated activity. If academic learning does not engage students, something else will. [p. 554]

Additional observational studies have confirmed Goodlad's findings. In *Horace's Compromise*, Ted Sizer (1984) states that, "No more important finding has emerged from the inquiries of our study than that the American high school student, as student, is all too often docile, compliant, and without initiative" (p. 54). This sentiment was reinforced by Ernest Boyer (1983) in his *High School: A Report on Secondary Education in America* and by Joan Lipsitz's (1984) study of effective middle schools, presented in her *Successful Schools for Young Adolescence.*

Walter Doyle's (1983, in press) examination of academic work suggests that teachers often select methods of instruction that, while focusing on rote learning, are easily managed in terms of maintaining control. Also, as discussed in Chapter 4, some teachers handle the problem of classroom control by excluding students of lower ability from active participation in classroom activities or by reinforcing incorrect answers by these students in order to maintain a smooth classroom flow. A comprehensive, realistic examination of students' behavior must consider not only methods of instruction and organization that increase students' attending behavior and basic skill acquisition, but also school climate and instructional factors that provide students with a sense of meaningful involvement in the school and community as well as encouraging thoughtful and creative examination of issues presented in a meaningful, dynamic curriculum.

MEETING TEACHERS' NEEDS

Whether we hope to make significant changes in our approach to managing a classroom or are simply looking for a few techniques for working with a particularly difficult child, the quality of personal and professional support available in the school will significantly affect our ability to reach our goal. Numerous educators and writers have emphasized that teachers are able to work more effectively with children when the teachers themselves are treated as professionals and experience the school environment as safe and supportive (Joyce & Clift, 1984; Robert, 1976; Schmuck & Schmuck, 1974; Wayson & Pinnell, 1982). Research indicates a significant relationship between teachers' positive feelings about themselves, their teaching, and such factors as students' achievement (Aspy & Buhler, 1975), students' statements on teachers' effectiveness (Usher & Hanke, 1971), and how students view themselves in a classroom (Landry, 1974).

Teachers are currently confronted by factors that have made a demanding profession even more complex. Educators are faced with a general lack of public support. Teaching is not viewed as a prestigious occupation, nor do teachers receive professional salaries. Similarly, public financial support for education is often questioned and schools must fight hard to obtain needed funding. At the same time, however, the public is demanding more than ever from schools. Federal legislation mandates that teachers work with groups of students that are increasingly heterogeneous in race, culture, and emotional and academic exceptionalities. This demand has been associated with a simultaneous emphasis on accountability.

Unfortunately, the support needed to cope with these demands is often missing. In addition, many teachers are inadequately prepared to instruct children with learning and emotional problems and the accompanying negative attitudes. It is understandable that teacher turnover is high. Unless schools respond more effectively to teachers' needs, teachers will be unable to meet the increasing demands placed upon them, and we will continue to lose many potentially excellent teachers who leave the profession after one or two frustrating years.

Teachers' professional needs fall into three general categories: (1) personal and professional support from colleagues, (2) material and professional support from administrators and other support personnel, and (3) experience of success and professional fulfillment.

Teaching is a demanding job and teachers need encouragement, suggestions, and expressions of personal interest and support from their colleagues. Support may take the form of sharing materials and supplies, helping colleagues by taking their duty when they are not feeling well, listening with interest, providing ideas for dealing with a difficult parent or student, or reinforcing a colleague's efforts. Discussing this type of support, Schmuck and Schmuck (1974) emphasize the relationship between teachers' needs for personal and professional support and their ability to work effectively with children.

> First, the security, comfort, and stimulation that teachers receive from their colleagues increase the amount of personal esteem they bring to interactions with students and the amount of energy they have for working closely with students. Second, staff interactions offer models to students that represent the actual climate of the school. [p. 124]

Marc Robert (1976) also mentions the importance of meeting teachers' needs for support from their colleagues.

> I believe that no great "humanization" breakthrough between student and teacher will occur unless an organized and concerted effort is made to develop and maintain some realistic human support systems within which staff members can help each other to feel good about their personal and professional effectiveness. [p. 44]

Emphasis has recently been placed on the value of colleagues serving as instructional coaches for teachers seeking to improve their skills (Joyce & Clift, 1984; Joyce & Showers, 1982, 1984). Teachers need time to observe colleagues who are skilled in a teaching method, to attempt new methods while being observed by a colleague, and to discuss the results. The importance of providing this type of collegial support is accentuated by the fact that teacher training programs often fail to adequately prepare teachers in current classroom management or instructional methods. Likewise, neither support provided during the early years of teaching (Arends, 1982) nor standard in-service programs (Gall, Haisley, Baker, & Perez, 1982; Joyce, Bush, & McKibbin, 1981; Mertens & Yarger, 1982) provide teachers with meaningful training.

The second category of teachers' needs is administrative and specialist support. This support includes provision of materials and supplies, involvement in formulating curricular and other building policies, support for advanced training, support for innovative instructional activities, and support in the form of positive feedback as well as specific, nonjudgmental professional criticism. The extensive body of research in school effectiveness and instructional leadership consistently points to the importance of administrators' providing these forms of support for teachers (De Bevoise, 1983). When these aids are not available, teachers will be much less effective in the classroom. Specialists in learning and behavior who assist in developing effective programs for children with special learning needs should also be available.

The final category of teachers' needs is experiencing success and enjoyment in the classroom. These needs can be met by developing and applying teaching methods that facilitate appropriate student behavior and successful student achievement. These methods include:

1.　understanding children,
2.　creating positive teacher-student relationships,
3.　developing skill at creating positive peer relations in the classroom,
4.　obtaining parental support,
5.　encouraging students to behave responsibly,
6.　applying teaching methods that motivate learning and prevent disruptive behavior, and
7.　knowing how to solve behavior problems when they arise.

This book is focused primarily on providing skills to meet needs in the third category. In various sections of the book, though, we provide ideas for more effectively meeting the first two categories as well. For example, the methods for developing positive teacher-student and peer relationships apply equally well to creating more positive and supportive staff relationships. Peer observation and coaching can also be used to develop and improve the various teaching methods described throughout the book.

Developing New Skills

The five steps in developing new and more productive behaviors are:

1. developing awareness and better understanding of the problem,
2. making the decision to change,
3. examining and selecting alternative approaches,
4. implementing new methods, and
5. evaluating the results.

Chapters 2 and 3 provide both a theoretical framework and specific activities aimed at understanding the causes of students' misbehavior and considering specific areas in which the reader may wish to develop new skills in order to reduce discipline problems. Chapters 4 through 9 also include instruments and activities aimed at helping teachers diagnose specific causes of student misbehavior.

Once we understand the causes of misbehavior and can evaluate the extent to which these factors occur in our classrooms, the next step in developing improved management skills is deciding to change. The third step involves selecting alternative methods. Each of Chapters 4 through 12 concludes with an activity aimed at helping you select specific methods discussed in the chapter for implementation in your classroom. Finally, we must implement new teaching methods and carefully analyze the results. Many of the activities in this book offer you ideas for assessing students' responses to the methods described.

RECOMMENDED READING

Alschuler, A. (1980). *School discipline: A socially literate solution.* New York: McGraw-Hill.

Brophy, J., and Evertson, C. (1976). *Learning from teaching: A developmental perspective.* Boston: Allyn and Bacon.

Bronfenbrenner, U. (1970). *Two worlds of childhood: U.S. and U.S.S.R.* New York: Russell Sage Foundation.

Coles, R. (1977). *Eskimos, Chicanos, Indians.* (Volume IV of *Children of Crisis*). Boston: Little, Brown.

Coles, R. (1977). *Privileged ones: The well-off and the rich in America.* (Volume V of *Children of Crisis*). Boston: Little, Brown.

Comer, J. (1980). *School power: Implications of an intervention project.* New York: Free Press.

Duke, D. (1984). *Teaching: The imperiled profession.* Albany: State University of New York Press.

Elkind, D. (1981). *The hurried child: Growing up too fast too soon.* Reading, Mass: Addison-Wesley.

Glasser, W. (1969). *Schools without failure.* New York: Harper and Row.

Good, T. & Brophy, J. (1984). *Looking in classrooms.* New York: Harper and Row.

Goodlad, J. (1984). *A place called school.* New York: McGraw-Hill.

Henry, J. (1963). *Culture against man.* New York: Vintage Books.

Jones, V. (1980). *Adolescents with behavior problems: Strategies for teaching, counseling, and parent involvement.* Boston: Allyn and Bacon.

Kounin, J. (1970). *Discipline and group management in classrooms.* New York: Holt, Rinehart and Winston.

Lipsitz, J. (1984). *Successful schools for young adolescents.* New Brunswick, N.J.: Transaction Books.

Maeroff, G. (1982). *Don't blame the kids: The trouble with America's public schools.* New York: McGraw-Hill.

Purkey, W. (1978). *Inviting school success: A self-concept approach to teaching and learning.* Belmont, Calif.: Wadsworth.

Rutter, M., Maughan, B., Montimore, P., Ouston, J., and Smith, A. (1979). *Fifteen thousand hours.* Cambridge, Mass.: Harvard University Press.

Schmuck, R., & Schmuck, P. (1974). *A humanistic psychology of education: Making the school everybody's house.* Palo Alto, Calif.: National Press Books.

Silberman, C. (1970). *Crisis in the classroom: The remaking of American education.* New York: Random House.

Sizer, T. (1984). *Horace's Compromise: The dilemma of the American high school.* Boston: Houghton Mifflin.

CHAPTER **2**

Understanding Students' Basic Psychological Needs

The needs for safety, belongingness, love relations, and for respect can be satisfied only by other people, i.e., only from outside the person. This means considerable dependence on the environment.

Abraham Maslow, (1968),
Toward a Psychology of Being

When discipline problems occur in school, they can more often be traced to dysfunctions in the interpersonal climate and organizational patterns of the school than to malfunctions in the individual. In short, misbehaving students are often reacting in a predictable and even sensible way to the school as it affects them and as they have learned to perceive it and react to it.

William Wayson and Gayson Pinnell, (1981), D. Duke (Ed.)
Helping Teachers Manage Classrooms

Students behave appropriately and learn more effectively in environments that meet their basic personal and psychological needs. All students learn best in school settings where they are comfortable and feel safe and accepted. In addition, students' needs vary somewhat according to their age, and effective teachers create classroom settings and employ instructional strategies that meet their students' unique needs. Students' academic failure and misbehavior can be understood—and subsequently prevented or corrected—by examining classroom and school environments to determine which student needs are not being met.

Teachers are frequently frustrated by their inability to determine the source of disruptive student behavior that detracts from students' learning. When asked to describe why children misbehave, teachers often include in their responses such factors as poor attitude, poor home environment, lower-than-average IQ, and failure of previous teachers to properly develop self- discipline and social skills. Although several or even all of these factors may well influence students' behavior in some way, a teacher can do little about these factors. This emphasis suggests that teachers can merely coax or bribe these students into behaving more appropriately or remove or punish these children when misbehavior occurs. Teachers may thus absolve themselves of responsibility for students' misbehavior. In this scheme, teachers are merely a reactive force. They must put a finger in the dike when confronted with unpredictable forces over which they have little control.

Another approach to understanding children's unproductive school behavior suggests that most unproductive student behavior is a response to children not having their basic needs met within the environment where the misbehavior occurs (Maslow, 1968). Considerable theoretical work and research supports this contention. Furthermore, our own experiences with children of various ages in widely varied settings consistently confirm this explanation of children's unproductive behavior. This explanation has the advantage of placing the teacher in a creative, exciting position. Rather than simply reacting to uncontrollable forces, the teacher controls a wide variety of factors that influence children's behavior.

This view of teachers as able to positively influence students' behavior is supported by research and theory presented by the behavioristic approach and by social psychology. Behaviorism views individual behavior as determined by the pattern of rewards and punishments to which the person is exposed. Teachers often experience frustration when working with students whose history at home or in school or both has included limited reinforcement for desirable school behaviors and considerable reinforcement for behaviors inappropriate in the school. Teachers can, however, learn to systematically teach and reinforce appropriate behaviors. Teachers can also enlist peers in reinforcing positive behaviors. The work of Bandura (1969) and Bronfenbrenner (1970) highlight the social psychologists' view that students' behavior is heavily influenced by the values and behaviors modeled by individuals who are significant in children's lives. Children learn a great deal by modeling others' behavior. Research suggests that children are more likely to model individuals who (1) are perceived as having a high degree of competence, status, and control over resources, (2) have provided previous support and reinforcement, and (3) play a prominent role in the students' daily life. Because teachers have the potential for possessing these qualities, they can, by thoughtful modeling, significantly affect students' behavior. Similarly, by helping to create classroom norms and procedures that encourage students to behave in a positive, supportive manner, teachers can create settings in which the majority of students serve as effective models for the few students who may initially lack desirable attitudes and behaviors.

Teachers are involved daily in creating the atmosphere in which children spend approximately one-fourth of their waking lives. Although this necessity obviously places considerable responsibility upon the teacher, it simultaneously imparts a positive, creative dimension into teachers' professional lives. Teachers are not faced with the prospect of merely reacting to student behaviors over which they have no control. On the contrary, by creating environments that respond sensitively to students' needs, teachers can ensure that most student behavior will be positive and goal directed.

The reader may wonder whether an emphasis on students' needs means subjugating teachers' needs or expectations. It is important to realize that meeting children's needs does not mean that adults do not provide structure, expect high-quality performance, or hold students accountable for their behavior. Indeed, these factors are part of environments that meet students' needs.

The necessity for presenting a chapter on student's psychological needs and focusing a portion of this book on strategies for creating positive classroom environments is based on the unfortunate but very real fact that classroom environments often fail to meet students' basic needs. Far too many children who enter school excited and eager to learn leave school feeling unliked and unsuccessful. After conducting a survey of more than 600 students in grades three through eleven, Morse writes:

> Eighty-four percent of the third-graders were proud of their school work, while only 53 percent of the eleventh-graders felt the same way. In the low grades, 93 percent felt they were doing the best work they could; only 37 percent of the seniors felt this way. Without regard to their achievement quotients and the fact that the failures tend to drop out, the older pupils who remained in school came to feel they were doing inadequate work. Again, over half the young children said they were doing as well in school as they would like, but only 22 percent of the eleventh-graders felt this way. About 40 percent of the pupils often felt upset in school; and with regard to achievement, 20 percent said their teacher made them feel "not good enough." Over 40 percent reported they often became discouraged in school and this discouragement too increased with age. [Morse, 1964, p. 198]

Similar results are reported by Cormany (1975), based upon a study in which the Pennsylvania Department of Education surveyed students' feelings about school. Cormany reports that although 64.4 percent of the kindergarten children expressed positive feelings about school, only 12.8 percent of sixth graders reported such feelings. A variety of other studies support the findings that, as children become older and progress through the grades, they often develop poorer self-esteem and less positive attitudes toward school (Landry & Edeburn, 1974; Stanwyck & Felker, 1974; Yamamoto, Thomas, & Karnes, 1969). A recent survey of more than 8,000 students in grades five through nine reports a similar change in students' attitudes and behavior (Currence, 1984). Results showed that 61 percent of fifth graders said they "try their best at school," compared with only 30 percent of the ninth graders. Similarly, while 60 percent of fifth, sixth, and seventh graders said they never cheated, only 33 percent of ninth graders said this.

It can be argued that children simply become more critical as they grow older, but there is more than enough evidence in other works (Glasser, 1969; Goodlad, 1984; Holt, 1969; Purkey, 1984; Rutter, 1979; Silberman, 1970) and in our own experience in schools to suggest that at least a significant amount of this negativism and the associated acting-out or withdrawal behavior is a response to school settings that fail to meet students' needs. Teachers certainly do not mean to create such environments and are often not even aware that they are doing so. Most teachers sincerely wish to provide an optimal learning environment for their students. Unfortunately, many teachers are hampered by a combination of limited skills resulting from ineffective teacher training programs and the multiple demands placed upon them. This book cannot alter the latter situation, but it does provide teachers with skills that enable them to more effectively cope with these demands.

In this chapter the basic psychological needs that must be met for students to behave in a positive, productive manner are described. No attempt has been made to present an in-depth description of any one theorist's work or to describe child and adolescent development. Rather, the chapter highlights those needs which, when met within the school setting, enhance positive teacher and student behavior and thereby facilitate learning. This and the following chapter provide the foundation for subsequent chapters. The effectiveness of any teaching strategy or behavior-change approach will be influenced by the degree to which it responds to students' needs. Similarly, when a teacher's behavior elicits an unproductive student response, it is likely that the teacher has in some way infringed upon or blocked an important student need.

THEORETICAL PERSPECTIVES

Various writers have attempted to categorize and describe children's basic psychological needs. Rudolph Dreikurs (1971), basing his work on the concepts developed by the Viennese psychiatrist Alfred Adler, centered his ideas for working with children on the belief that children's basic need is to be socially accepted.

> We see the child as a social being who wants to find his place at home, in school, and in the world. If he misbehaves, he has developed erroneous ideas about how to belong. . . . All behavior is goal-directed; it indicates the ways and means that each child has discovered as his expression to gain status and significance. . . .
>
>   The child can function fully only if he feels accepted by the group as a worthwhile member. . . . The restriction of social interest is usually due to inferiority feelings, to the doubts of a child to find a place through useful means. [Dreikurs et al., 1971, p. xi]

In Dreikurs' model, children who misbehave are simply trying to be accepted. Unfortunately, their behavior is based upon the faulty logic that the misbehavior will provide for them the social acceptance they desire.

In his well-known conceptualization of the eight stages of man, Erikson (1963) postulates that elementary-age children are in the stage that he labels Industry vs. Inferiority. During this stage, children must move away from playing make-believe and develop an ability to produce things. Children must learn to do something well and to develop a sense of their own competence. Erikson describes the essence of this stage when he writes:

> . . . and while all children need their hours and days of make-believe in games, they all, sooner or later, become dissatisfied and disgruntled without a sense of being able to make things and make them well and even perfectly: it is this that I have called the sense of industry. . . . For nothing less is at stake than the development and maintenance in children of a positive identification of those who know things and know how to do things. [Erikson, 1968, pp. 123, 125]

In Erikson's writing we can see the dual emphasis upon viewing oneself as competent and having this competence verified and expanded through meaningful contact with others.

Another useful concept on students' needs is offered by Coopersmith (1967). In his research on the factors associated with self-esteem, Coopersmith found that in order to possess high self-esteem, individuals need to experience a sense of significance, competence, and power. Significance can best be defined as the sense of being valued that an individual attains from involvement in a positive two-way relationship in which both parties sincerely care about each other. Competence is developed by being able to effectively perform a socially valued task as well as or better than others at one's age level. For example, winning a free-throw shooting competition involving her peers would provide a third-grader with a sense of competence. Being able to tie her shoe or add one-digit figures would provide her with a much smaller sense of competence. Finally, power refers to an ability to control one's environment. Therefore, youngsters whose parents employ a democratic parenting style that involves them in decision-making will experience a sense of power. Similarly, students who are allowed to choose a topic of special interest for their social studies project or who are asked to provide input into how the classroom is arranged will experience a sense of power.

In addition to understanding theories that deal with children's needs, upper-grade elementary or middle school teachers must be aware of the unique needs of adolescents. The physical onset of adolescence is occurring at an earlier age (Elkind, 1979). In addition, children are becoming cognitively more sophisticated at an earlier age due to the availability of television and adults' tendency to encourage sophisticated behavior in children (Elkind, 1981). Consequently, fifth- and especially sixth-grade teachers find themselves dealing with students who are experiencing the early stages of adolescence.

Erikson describes the next developmental stage—that experienced by young adolescents—as the search for a sense of identity. During the initial phase of this stage (ages eleven to thirteen) there is a dramatic increase in self-consciousness and a lowered self-esteem. Young adolescents feel "on-stage," as if everyone is observing them. Elkind (1967) labels this the "imaginary audience." Young adolescents also view themselves and their personal problems as unique and cannot understand that others are experiencing similar feelings, a concept Elkind labels the "personal fable."

Young adolescents are also beginning to challenge previously accepted beliefs and values. With the gradual increase in their ability to consider abstract ideas and better understand the concepts of past and future, adolescents began to view their world more subjectively and critically (Kohlberg, 1976; Piaget, 1970). Therefore, adolescents have a basic need to critically examine ideas, rules, and decisions. They are likely to question why they must study a topic, complete an assignment, or follow a rule that does not apply to the adults who share their environment. This often frustrating behavior increases as students move through mid-adolescence (ages fourteen to sixteen) and become somewhat less absorbed in egocentric, self-oriented matters and more interested in their relationship to others and in better understanding and controlling their environment. Students during grades eight through ten are often testing their new personal, physical, and cognitive skills by challenging rules or adult behavior they view as illogical or indefensible. During these early and mid-adolescent years, students need fair, clearly articulated structure and adults who are personally strong and flexible enough to become involved in openly discussing questions adolescents have about subject matter, teaching techniques, and school rules and procedures (Jones, 1980).

Work by Joan Lipsitz (1984) and her colleagues at the Center for Early Adolescence at the University of North Carolina at Chapel Hill further emphasizes the importance of developing school environments that meet young adolescents' developmental needs. These needs include:

1. the need for diversity,
2. the need for opportunities for self-exploration and self-definition,
3. the need for meaningful participation in school and community,
4. the need for positive social interaction with peers and adults,
5. the need for physical activity,
6. the need for competence and achievement,
7. the need for structure and clear limits. (Dorman, 1981, p. 1)

Joan Lipsitz's thoughtful book, *Successful Schools for Young Adolescents* (1984), examines four schools that have successfully met these needs. Schools interested in assessing their effectiveness in responding to these needs as well as creating more productive learning environments for young adolescents can refer to Lipsitz's book and can also employ Dorman's *Middle Grades Assessment Program* (1981).

In *The Hurried Child*, Elkind (1981) adds an interesting dimension to the topic of children's psychological needs. He states that relationships among all individuals, but especially between children and adults, involve basic patterns of dealing with each other. He describes these patterns as implicit contracts, and notes that they are constantly changing. He further comments that children's needs are met when contracts change in response to changing personal and cognitive skills demonstrated by children, but that contracts must not change primarily in response to adults' needs.

Elkind describes three basic contracts between parents and children: (1) responsibility-freedom, (2) achievement-support, and (3) loyalty-commitment. The freedom-responsibility contract refers to adults' "sensitively monitor[ing] the child's level of intellectual, social, and emotional development in order to provide the appropriate freedoms and opportunities for the exercise of responsibility" (p. 124). The achievement-support contract refers to adults' expecting age-appropriate achievements and providing the necessary personal and material support to assist children in reaching expected goals. The loyalty-commitment contract emphasizes adults' expectations that children will respond with loyalty and acceptance of adults because of the time, effort, and energy adults give. Although Elkind focuses on the parent-child relationship, these contractual areas apply to all adult-child relationships.

Elkind's key concept related to contracts is that they are frequently violated by adults and that this violation causes stress for youngsters. Violation of the freedom-responsibility contract occurs when adults fail to reward responsibility with freedom. For example, when students act responsibly in making a reasonable request from a teacher or administrator and are met with disrespect, this contract has been violated. Likewise, students who have demonstrated skill in directing portions of their own learning but are not allowed to do so experience frustration and stress through violation of the responsibility-freedom contract. The achievement-support contract is violated when adults do not provide adequate support for students' achievement. The low-achieving student who receives few opportunities to respond in class, little assistance in answering questions, and less reinforcement for appropriate answers is not receiving support commensurate with desired and potential achievement. Difficulties in the loyalty-commitment contract occur when children, especially adolescents, fail to provide adults with indications of loyalty commensurate with the efforts or commitment that adults see themselves as having made. When adults respond with removal of commitment rather than by understanding and discussing the problem, contract violation occurs. This condition is more likely to happen with low-achieving students who may not immediately repay teachers for what appear to be considerable amounts of time and effort.

Maslow's Hierarchy of Needs

Although each of the theoretical conceptualizations described in the previous section provides a valuable increment of insight into childrens' needs, Maslow's concept of the basic human needs incorporates the key components of many theories in a form that allows teachers to systematically assess and respond to students' needs. Maslow suggests that there is a hierarchy of basic human needs and that lower-level needs generally take precedence over higher-order needs. His hierarchy of needs has been broken down in a variety of ways, but it includes these components:

Self-actualization
Self-respect
Belongingness and affection
Safety and security
Physiological needs

Maslow's theoretical position is that people are basically good and that they have an innate need to be competent and accepted. Unproductive behavior is therefore not viewed as an indication of a "bad" child but rather as a reaction to the frustration associated with being in a situation in which one's basic needs are not being met. Maslow further suggests that these basic needs cannot be met without assistance from others. Finally, he postulates that only when the basic needs are met can the individual become motivated by self-actualization or the need to take risks, learn, and attain one's fullest potential.

The major goal of our educational system is to assist children in developing demonstrable academic and social skills and the related ability to solve meaningful problems. Within the school environment, then, children are expected to demonstrate new understandings and new ways of perceiving and manipulating their environment. Therefore, in a very real sense, the school's primary goal requires students to be involved in the process of self-actualization. Maslow's theory suggests, however, that children will not be able to accomplish this task unless the environment first provides adequately for lower-level needs. The message is clear. If we expect students to perform appropriate academic tasks, we must first create environments that meet children's basic needs. Conversely, if we fail to meet these needs, we can expect that children will become frustrated and anxious and will behave in an unproductive manner.

Physiological Needs

It is easy for teachers to pass over the importance of meeting students' physiological needs. Because schools provide shelter, heat, and food that is certainly adequate and is more substantial than many children receive at home, it is perhaps natural to assume that students' physiological needs are being met. Nevertheless, schools may fail to respond sensitively in many subtle ways to students' physiological needs and thereby unwittingly cause varying degrees of unproductive students' behavior.

In her extensive work on students' learning styles, Rita Dunn (1978, 1983) has discovered twenty-six variables that influence students' learning (Figure 3.2). Examining the elements she describes, we find that these ten deal directly with physiological factors: (1) sound, (2) light, (3) temperature, (4) design, (5) auditory learning preference, (6) kinesthetic learning preference, (7) ·visual learning preference, (8) intake, (9) time, and (10) mobility. Students vary significantly in the amount of sound and light that is optimal for their learning. One of the authors recalls spending much effort attempting to block out noise generated by a sister who studied best with a radio and phonograph playing simultaneously at high volume. As many schools have realized, students respond more productively when they have had an adequate breakfast. We recall working with a fifth-grade boy whose only nutrition between the evening meal and his school lunch was a bottle of cola. A change in the student's eating habits brought about a dramatic improvement in his behavior. Likewise, some students (and many adults) are unable to function effectively if they must work for several hours with nothing to eat or drink. Teachers should consider that students who eat breakfast at seven or eight o'clock must often wait at least four hours between meals. Teachers also need to be sensitive to any visual or auditory deficits experienced by a student and alter classroom structures to respond to these factors. Teachers should also attempt to develop classroom procedures that include a simple, unembarrassing method for students to quietly leave the room to use the lavatory.

Although these factors are obvious examples of physiological needs, a variety of more subtle factors appear that adults frequently fail to recognize. For example, studies involving both primates (Harlow, 1958; Mason, 1965) and infants (Casler, 1965; Dennis, 1960; White & Held, 1967) indicate that touch is an important physiological and psychological need. Direct classroom research in this area is lacking, but we suggest that touch is a very real need for children and that there is a relationship between meeting this need and productive student behavior.

Another physiological factor is the degree to which the classroom environment provides a comfortable, stimulating atmosphere for students. Simple adjustment in standard furniture is common, yet it is less common for teachers to respond to the fact that some students need quite different seating, such as a chair, table, or the floor. Similarly, teachers who frequently move around the room may forget that their students are expected to remain relatively immobile for much of the school day. Though some students may adapt to this requirement of schooling, others learn less effectively or misbehave, partly because they cannot cope with behavioral expectations that violate their basic need to move. Teachers of preadolescents and young adolescents must be particularly sensitive to students' needs for mobility and social interaction. Research (Goodlad, 1984) indicates that students are seldom actively involved in the learning process. This expectation of passive, immobile behavior is a major cause of acting-out behavior in many middle schools and junior high schools.

Readers can undoubtedly envision a room in their home that has been decorated to provide a relaxing, comfortable place to study, sew, or enjoy family activities. As adults, we go to considerable lengths to create environments that we find pleasant. Although children have much less control over the physical aspects of their environment, they too feel more comfortable and can be more productive in environments that provide comfort and stimulation. Classrooms should be colorful and should include a variety of visually interesting materials such as posters and mobiles, as well as a comfortable corner in which students can relax and read or discuss problems, or to which they can move when they need a respite from the tasks associated with a busy school day. Some teachers enjoy collecting and displaying such materials, but it is important to encourage students to incorporate materials that they bring from home. Students' input can also involve having them decorate the walls or having their artwork displayed on classroom walls and in hallways.

Although teachers normally associate comfort and physiological needs with the physical aspects of the classroom, the pacing of learning activities is also a significant factor. All teachers experience days when the pace is so demanding that at the end of the day they retreat to a long jog, a hot bath, or two aspirins. We often forget, though, that students are also faced with numerous academic and social tasks each day. In fact, the strain associated with the pace of classroom activities may be more pronounced for children, for they are generally not controlling the pace. It is therefore important that teachers provide time other than the traditional lunch and recess breaks (which sometimes prove to be more tension-producing than academic activities) for children to relax and synthesize their learning. This time may be particularly important for slower learners, because within the normal academic program of the school day, these children may never complete all their assignments and thereby experience the satisfaction of having time to relax and reflect upon what they have learned.

During a recent seminar, one of the authors asked a group of beginning teachers to state the one factor they believed to be most responsible for disruptive student behavior. Working separately, nine of the ten students listed the pace of the classroom day—too many activities with too little time to relax—as the most significant cause.

Although the classroom is certainly the hub of a student's school day, it is important to examine other aspects of school environments for situations in which physiological needs may not be met. Perhaps the best example of such settings is the school cafeteria. Most elementary and many secondary school cafeterias consist of long tables with attached benches. Although this arrangement is economical, relatively indestructible, and easy to move, it also tends to create a noisy, crowded, uncomfortable, impersonal atmosphere. A variety of small tables would provide a calmer, more relaxing lunch break for students. To verify the difference between these two environments, we encourage the reader to spend, if possible, several lunch periods in each setting. Each time the authors spend time in a traditional lunchroom environment, we come away with a fresh appreciation for why teachers often find that students return from their lunch break in anything but a relaxed state.

Safety and Security Needs

Certainly the most basic aspect of safety and security is that students feel safe from physical harm when going to and from school and when they are in the school or on the playground. It is terribly important that schools respond to this need by providing adequate supervision by caring adults and by developing procedures for working with children to effectively confront situations in which this need is not being met. In addition to ensuring that students are safe from physical abuse by peers, schools must also ensure that students are safe from physical abuse by adults. Several days before writing this portion of the book, one of the authors witnessed a teacher towering over a second-grade student and screaming angrily. The child had lowered himself to the floor and cowered in a near fetal position. The teacher concluded her tirade by screaming at the child that if he repeated his misbehavior she would paddle him soundly. This incident took place in an upper middle-class school and was a response to the student violating a minor school rule. One cannot help but wonder how many times a scene like this occurs every day. If teachers wish to create schools in which children experience a sense of physical and psychological safety, they must ensure that their behavior and that of their colleagues does not violate this important human need.

Though it is paramount that teachers create school environments in which students feel safe from physical harm, it is also important to attend to students' needs to feel safe from unnecessary and unproductive psychological pressures. Unfortunately, it is often difficult for adults to directly and immediately pinpoint factors that may be causing subtle pressure for students. An excellent example occurred several years ago in a school district in Oregon. Much to their credit, district administrators became worried about what they perceived as a negative attitude among a significant number of their young school children. The district subsequently sought the services of an outside agency to examine the situation. The consultants decided initially to examine the ratio of positive to negative statements made by teachers. They began their intervention by simply asking children in second-grade classrooms to answer yes or no to the question, "Do you like school?" As indicated in the fourth column of Figure 2.1, at the beginning of the school year, most students in all classes responded yes to this question. The consultants discovered, however, that, for students who experienced classrooms characterized by a low rate of positive teacher verbalizations, these positive feelings about school changed dramatically within the first fifteen weeks of school.

More specifically, in the eight classes in which teachers provided less than 65 percent positive statements, the percentage of students responding that they liked school dropped an alarming 48 percent during the fifteen weeks. In the seven classrooms in which 70 percent or more of the teachers' statements were positive, though, students' responses to the question of whether or not they liked school remained, on the average, exactly the same after fifteen weeks of school. These data suggest that children are much less comfortable in classroom environments characterized by a low rate of positive teacher statements, probably because students frequently feel attacked and punished under such conditions, which significantly reduces their psychological safety. In his sensitive and creative book, *Inviting School Success*, Purkey (1984) reinforces this concept by poignantly emphasizing that the quality of the learning environment is significantly influenced by the degree

FIGURE 2.1   Influence of positive and negative teacher statements on students' feelings about school

| Teacher | Pre 2 weeks after start of school (September 20-27) | | | Post January 22-24 | | |
	Pos.	Neg.	Students responding yes to: "Do you like school?"	Pos.	Neg.	Students responding yes to: "Do you like school?
1	.72	28	90%	.76	24	90%
2	.34	66	90%	.33	67	20%
3	.66	34	80%	.70	30	70%
4	.69	31	90%	.65	35	80%
5	.54	46	100%	.61	39	20%
6	.80	20	100%	.87	13	100%
7	.22	78	90%	.19	81	20%
8	.64	36	70%	.64	36	40%
9	.79	21	100%	.77	23	100%
10	.92	08	80%	.89	11	90%
11	.52	48	100%	.63	37	60%
12	.73	27	90%	.65	35	90%
13	.45	55	90%	.61	39	80%
14	.67	33	80%	.73	27	80%
15	.58	42	90%	.60	40	70%
16	.51	49	60%	.58	42	10%
17	.76	24	70%	.77	23	70%

[a]Personal correspondence with Bud Fredericks, Teaching Research, Monmouth, Oregon.

to which teachers' supportive, inviting statements outweigh their critical, uninviting statements.

Psychological safety can also be enhanced by applying instructional methods ensuring that students are given work they feel able to master and by ensuring that students understand and take part in the evaluation process. Students will not experience a sense of safety and security when they are involved in classrooms where they have little understanding of, or control over, their environment and yet where their ability to function must be judged daily.

Need for Belonging and Affection
Experiencing a sense of belonging and affection is an extremely important psychological need. In addition to being important in itself, this sense is a key

ingredient in feelings of both safety and respect for others. We have all, at one time or another, been in a situation in which we felt we did not belong and that others in the environment did not feel affection for us. Put the book aside for a moment and try to visualize one such situation. See if you can focus on how you felt about being in that situation. How did you feel about remaining in or returning to that situation? Would you want to work in that environment? If you were required to work in such an environment, how do you think it would influence your performance and behavior?

Teachers must realize that children experience these same feelings when they are involved in settings in which they do not feel they belong. Indeed, because their sense of self is less well defined and consequently more dependent upon outside influences, it is likely that children experience lack of belonging with more intensity than do most adults. Children who feel that they do not belong are likely to withdraw or to seek attention through unproductive behaviors. It is no surprise that research (Schmuck, 1963; 1966; and Tagiuri, Bruner, & Blake, 1958) suggests that individuals' behavior in a group setting is significantly influenced by the degree to which the person views other group members as liking them.

> Although educators generally have not considered student friendships relevant to individual students' cognitive and affective development, our research evidence . . . and experience indicate that they are related. In fact, the friendships classmates have for one another, along with their willingness to help and support one another, represent important ingredients for the enhancement of individual academic achievement. Moreover, learning groups in which friendship and influence are dispersed among many peers have more supportive work norms and are more cohesive than groups in which the friendship and influence processes are hierarchical. Strong relationships with others are not only valuable in themselves; they also can enhance cognitive development in the classroom. [Schmuck & Schmuck, 1974, p. 101]

The peer group is very important to students and the extent to which a student experiences acceptance or rejection from the group can dramatically influence their behavior.

> Positive interpersonal relations among students is necessary both for effective problem solving in groups and for general classroom enjoyment of instructional activity. The psychological security and safety necessary for open exploration of instructional tasks is based upon feelings of being accepted, liked, and supported by fellow students. Class cohesion is based upon positive interpersonal relationship among students. [Johnson & Johnson, 1975a, p. 188]

While writing this chapter, one of the authors conducted a workshop with the leadership team of a high school that was experiencing attendance problems with minority students bussed to the school. After discussing a wide range of teacher-student relationship and instructional factors, the staff agreed that a significant cause of the problem was that students in the school—and especially those bussed to school—did not know the other students in their classes. The staff agreed that attendance could not be significantly improved unless nonattending students felt more comfortable and wanted in their classes.

Although the sense of belonging resulting from peers' statements can be extremely important, it is equally, if not more, important that students feel accepted and respected by their teachers.

Because children are highly dependent upon adults for satisfaction of many of their basic needs, the respect they receive from adults affects them in a major way. Patterson (1973) states this reality powerfully: "The concepts which the teacher has of the children become the concepts which the children come to have of themselves" (p. 125).

The therapeutic value inherent in providing individuals with a sense of being cared for and respected is sensitively presented by Carl Rogers and his colleagues (Carkhuff, 1969; Rogers, 1958; Truax & Carkhuff, 1967). In describing the essential ingredients of a relationship that facilitates positive personal growth and learning, Rogers states:

> There is another attitude which stands out in those who are successful in facilitating learning . . . I think of it as prizing the learner, prizing his feelings, his opinions, his person. It is a caring for the learner, but a non-possessive caring. It is an acceptance of this other individual as a separate person, having worth in his own right. [Rogers, 1969, p. 109]

Need for Self-Esteem

Self-esteem has been defined in various ways, but it can, perhaps, best be described as a general positive or negative view one holds of oneself. Therefore, whether or not a child has positive self-esteem will be heavily influenced by the extent to which the previously discussed needs have been met. All individuals have a strong need to experience a sense of significance, competence, and power, and thereby to have basically positive self-esteem. Unfortunately, young people often find that they are unable to acquire these ingredients through socially acceptable channels. This situation occurs when parents fail to provide love and support and when schools do not foster positive personal relationships, fail to develop instructional patterns that enable each child to experience success, and consistently place all power in the hands of adults. In such situations, youngsters attempt to acquire significance, competence, and power by methods which adults find less desirable and which are almost always ultimately less beneficial to the youngster.

An excellent example of the powerful influence self-esteem can have on an individual's behavior is reported by Combs, Avila, and Purkey (1971) in *Helping Relationships*. These authors describe an incident in which what a young man believed about himself significantly influenced his school performance.

> What a boy believes about himself is really important. We had a student at Greeley who scored in the 98 percentile on the entrance test, and he thought that he had a 98 IQ. And because he thought he was an average kid, he knew college would be hard for him. He almost failed in his first term. He went home and told

his parents, "I don't believe I'm college caliber," and the parents took him back to school and talked with the college counselor. When he found out that 98 percentile score meant that he had a 140 IQ, he was able to do "A" work before the year was over. [p. 43]

Many research findings support the fact that, at all grade levels, students with high self-concepts achieve more effectively than do those with poor self-concepts. Studies in elementary schools (Campbell, 1967; Farls, 1967; Williams & Cole, 1968), junior high schools (Brookover, Paterson, & Thomas, 1965), high schools (Farquhar, 1968; Gowan, 1960), and college (Brunkan & Sheni, 1966; Irwin, 1967) all indicate varying degrees of positive correlation between positive self-concept and successful school achievement. If we wish to assist all students in becoming effective learners, we must create classroom settings that facilitate the development of positive self-esteem. This task involves creating warm, safe environments, in which students feel they belong and are an accepted part of the group. It also involves employing instructional strategies that assist students in clearly understanding the learning goals, becoming actively involved in the learning process, and experiencing success.

Need for Self-Actualization
In Maslow's conceptualization, self-actualization refers to each person's intrinsic need to reach his or her potential and to express himself or herself completely and creatively.

> So far as motivational status is concerned, healthy people have sufficiently gratified their basic needs for safety, belongingness, love, respect and self-esteem so that they are motivated primarily by trends to self actualization (defined as ongoing actualization of potentials, capacities, and talents). . . . [Maslow, 1968, p. 25]

The existence of this need is seen in children's curiosity, in their need to understand their environment, and in their need to express themselves creatively, whether by building a treehouse or painting a picture. Therefore, though it is important for schools to meet students' basic needs, it is also important to provide settings that encourage this higher-level self-need. This can be accomplished by varied strategies, including allowing students to choose special learning projects, encouraging individual goal setting and self-evaluation, stimulating class discussions, and encouraging students to constructively challenge both academic and procedural issues.

A number of writers have emphasized that we live in a rapidly changing society in which the knowledge and skills that adults possess will often be dated by the time children reach adulthood. It appears therefore that the most effective and useful skills teachers can help children acquire are skills in creatively analyzing situations and making effective decisions. These skills are closely related to the need to experience self-actualization. Educators should attempt to develop schools that meet students' basic needs, simultaneously providing them with opportunities to experience learning activities associated with self-actualization.

NEEDS OF INNER-CITY STUDENTS

Teachers tend to underestimate the anxiety and concern inner-city students experience in school (Hawkes & Furst, 1973). Inner-city students are too often viewed as unmotivated and unconcerned about their schoolwork. However, studies (Hawkes & Koff, 1970; Hawkes & Furst, 1971) comparing the anxiety level of inner-city and suburban students indicate that inner-city elementary and middle school students experience greater worry about schoolwork, self-adequacy, and life in general. Teachers' misperceptions of inner-city students' needs often lead to inappropriate emphasis on authoritarian control methods with these students.

> The teacher, thinking that his students are unmotivated, worry-free, and uncon-
> cerned about their school work, fails to address these emotionally focused areas
> of student concern. Because the students' anxiety fails to be addressed in the
> classroom, they become unruly and disruptive in response to their anxiety. The
> teacher, faced with losing control of the classroom, may become dogmatic and
> inflexible in response to this increasing experience of stress. A real cause of dis-
> cipline problems (high student anxiety and worry regarding school perfor-
> mance) is left unaddressed. [Mendler & Curwin, 1983, p. 200]

Research findings indicate that low-socioeconomic-status (SES) and minority students differ from their higher SES counterparts in that they need greater psychological support and praise (Brophy & Evertson, 1974; Soar & Soar, 1975; Solomon & Kendall, 1976), clearer classroom structure (Brophy & Evertson, 1974; Moskowitz & Hayman, 1976; Soar, 1983; Sanford & Evertson, 1981), and more active involvement in the learning process (Aronson, 1978; Kagan, 1980). These findings as well as comments by skilled inner-city teachers who reviewed and field tested the methods presented throughout this book suggest that although all students benefit from teachers' implementing these methods, they are critical when teaching inner-city students.

NEEDS OF EXCEPTIONAL STUDENTS

The emphasis on placing students in the least restrictive educational environment and the lack of funds available to provide special education services to students ensure that regular classroom teachers will continue to be responsible for a large portion of exceptional children's education. The use of effective classroom management methods influences all students, but has a particularly strong impact on exceptional students. Emotionally disturbed students are more responsive to negative teacher or peer responses and require classroom environments in which relationships are characterized by safety and support (Epanchin & Paul, 1982; Jones, 1980; Wood, 1975). These students also benefit from structured environments in which academic and behavioral expectations and consequences are clearly taught, monitored and implemented (Haring & Phillips, 1972; Kerr & Nelson, 1983; Walker, 1979). Learning disabled students also benefit from supportive, well structured environments. In addition, these students have special needs for instructional methods and materials that meet their unique learning needs (Dunn, 1983; Gold & Siegel, 1983; Smith, 1983; Weber, 1982). Although often ignored, gifted students also have unique learning needs that are best served by teachers employing the classroom management methods described throughout this book (Jones, 1983a). Because many gifted students possess a questioning attitude, skepticism, and sense of their own power (Seagoe, 1974) and because they have intensified needs to learn problem solving skills, participate in decision making and set and evaluate goals (Culross, 1982), they are especially resentful of and harmed by classroom management methods that emphasize rigid teacher control.

In working with exceptional students, you will be called upon to employ a wider range of teaching skills than with students who display more normative behavior. In fact, the teaching methods presented throughout this book are those that are employed by effective special education teachers. Interestingly, these methods not only enable teachers to effectively manage and instruct a wide range of exceptional students, they also improve the behavior and achievement of the more typical students.

METHODS FOR DISCOVERING STUDENTS' PERSONAL NEEDS

We have three basic methods for determining students' needs. First, teachers can examine what theories and associated research results say about those needs. This approach has the advantage of providing teachers with information based on a large sample of students in varied settings. Perhaps even more important, this method is relatively free from the teachers' own biases and needs. For example, the teacher who does not feel comfortable allowing students to take an active part in the learning process may, in fact, interpret student behavior as indicating that students do not want or cannot handle even a limited amount of this responsibility. Theoretical statements that have stood the test of time and data collected using sound research designs are not influenced by such individual biases and may therefore provide us with a clearer picture.

The second approach to determining students' needs within the school setting is to ask students what they need in order to feel more comfortable and better able to learn. An individual is the world's best expert on himself and herself. Students basically know better than anyone what factors make them comfortable, productive, and happy. It is a fact of life that students have had fewer experiences than adults, and consequently are less knowledgeable about the relationship between behavior and its consequences. Nevertheless, students are often much more sensitive and aware than teachers acknowledge. A fourth-grade child has been involved in observing and influencing human behavior for ten years. Similarly, this child has spent ten years attempting to manipulate the environment in order to meet needs. Consequently, even elementary school children have considerable expertise in understanding the variables that influence their behavior. They know which environmental factors create comfort, safety, and belongingness and which factors elicit discomfort, rejection, and the accompanying withdrawal or aggression. Given that a teacher's goal is to create environments that facilitate students' learning, it seems only reasonable that teachers should systematically involve students in providing information about the learning environment.

The third method for obtaining information about students' needs is systematic observation. By carefully monitoring how children behave in various situations, teachers can learn a great deal about unmet student needs. One of the authors recently taught a child who often appeared very sluggish, unmotivated, and slow in both speech and comprehension. At times, however, the student was quite animated and aware. Before making a referral, and following an uninformative parent conference, the author began collecting data on the relationship between the student's behavior and food consumption. The student consistently seemed more animated after lunch. Data also revealed a consistent pattern between the mornings when the student seemed sluggish and those when he reported having no breakfast or merely a cookie or a similarly poor breakfast. When the mother was shown these data, she reported that the child had hypoglycemia. This realization led to a discussion that culminated in the mother's agreeing to provide the necessary morning diet, and this change was followed by significant improvement in the child's behavior.

A young teacher provided another example of the benefits associated with carefully observing student's behavior as a means of assessing students' needs. When describing a student's behavior, the teacher noted that the student did not get along well with his peers and that this unmet need was very likely to be the cause of his problem. A more thorough examination of the boy's behavior, however, indicated that he had few negative peer contacts in situations such as recess or at lunch when fights might be expected. Instead, nearly all his negative peer contacts occurred when the class was involved in seatwork. Therefore, though it was quite possible that a need for belongingness influenced the boy's behavior, a more appropriate initial intervention involved responding to his academic needs by providing him with seatwork that he could complete successfully.

ACTIVITIES FOR EXAMINING STUDENTS' PERSONAL NEEDS

In this section we present several activities that can be used to examine students' personal/psychological needs within the classroom. The first two activities are based upon the theoretical work described earlier in the chapter and therefore stem from the first method of determining students' needs. The third activity directly involves students in providing teachers with information about students' needs in a classroom setting. Because Chapter 11 includes a section on collection of data, activities for incorporating this third approach to assessing students' needs are included there.

ACTIVITY 2.1   Responding to students' basic needs—Examining the classroom setting

Because this activity will require some time and thought, select a time when you can work relatively uninterrupted for perhaps an hour. Begin by writing the words *Physiological Needs* at the top of a sheet of paper. Now list two ways in which you ensure that these needs are being met in your classroom. Be specific when listing the factors. For example: The teacher provides five minutes of calm music and silent reading following lunch. Next, list two situations in the classroom that might hinder meeting students' physiological needs. Continue this activity by following the steps above for each of the remaining four needs presented by Maslow. If you are not currently teaching full time, complete this activity by selecting a classroom you have observed recently. Finally, after reading Chapters 4 through 9, return to this activity and describe two specific changes that could be made in the classroom in order to more effectively meet each of the five student needs.

ACTIVITY 2.2   Responding to students' basic needs—Examining an individual case

Select a student who is having particular difficulty in behaving appropriately in class. List at least one specific example to indicate how each of Maslow's needs is not being met in the classroom or school environment.

It is possible that you may not be able to list an example under one particular need but may be able to list three or four examples under another. The important point is that this activity will assist you in thoughtfully considering the student's actions in light of his or her needs. After completing Chapters 4 through 9, return to this activity and list at least one method that can be employed to ensure that each of these situations

ACTIVITY 2.3   Discovering students' own thoughts about their needs

This activity provides students with an opportunity to describe the extent to which their needs are being met in the classroom. The questionnaire presented in Figure 2.2 has been employed in a variety of classrooms. We encourage you to use this form or to alter it in any manner that will provide a more accurate tool for determining student's needs.

continued

FIGURE 2.2   Student need assessment questionnaire

Check the appropriate box.

Your thoughts about our class	Always	Most of the time	Some-times	Seldom	Never
Physiological needs					
1. Do you eat a good breakfast each morning?					
2. Does your teacher touch you enough?					
3. Can you see the blackboard and screen from where you are sitting?					
4. Do I talk loud and clear enough for you to hear?					
5. Do you have time to relax during the day?					
6. Do you have enough time to complete your assignments?					
7. Do we go slow enough in class?					
8. Do you need a study period at the end of the day?					
9. Is the room a quiet place to work?					
Safety and Security					
10. Are your grades fair?					
11. Does each day in this class seem organized?					
12. Do you follow the school and classroom rules?					
13. Is the discipline used in this classroom fair?					

Check the appropriate box.

Your thoughts about our class	Always	Most of the time	Some-times	Seldom	Never
14. Can you say what you'd like to in this class?					
15. Do you feel free enough to ask me questions?					
16. Can you trust your teacher?					
17. Can you get help when you need it?					
18. Are you calm when you take your report card home?					
Love and Belonging					
19. Is the room a happy place to be?					
20. Do you think that the students in this class like you?					
21. Am I friendly and do I smile at you?					
22. Do I take time with you each day?					
23. Does your teacher show that she or he likes you?					
24. Do you feel that I listen to you when you have a problem?					
25. Do I praise you when you deserve it?					
26. Do other students respect your property?					
27. Do people praise you when you do well?					

continued

Check the appropriate box.

Your thoughts about our class	Always	Most of the time	Some-times	Seldom	Never
28. Do I listen to your suggestions?					
Self–Esteem					
29. Do you feel involved in this class?					
30. Do you feel proud when you share a project with the class?					
31. Do you take part in class discussions?					
32. What subject area do you feel most successful at? _____					
33. What subject area could you improve in? _____					
Self-actualization					
34. Are you able to study things that interest you?					
35. Can you use what you learn in school?					
36. Do you have a chance to be creative in your schoolwork?					
37. Do you like to continue your studies at home on your own?					
38. Are you excited about what you are learning at school?					

Once you have prepared an instrument for obtaining information from students, set aside a suitable amount of time for introducing and administering the questionnaire. Be sure to adequately prepare the students by briefly discussing your reasons for seeking their ideas and sincerely expressing your desire that they take the activity seriously and feel free to provide honest responses.

The reader who has requested written feedback from students is aware of how easy it is to simply scan the material for any positive or negative comments, feel good about having asked for feedback, and file the material away. There are two problems with this approach to responding to student feedback. First, by merely scanning the feedback you may either fail to notice subtle but consistent feedback or overreact to several negative statements that are not representative of the feelings expressed by the majority of students. If you receive a piece of negative feedback from only one or two students, you may want to discuss the findings with the students (if students have signed their names) or consider why a few students responded as they did (it may simply be that the student(s) had a bad experience immediately preceding the administration of the questionnaire). It is unlikely, however, that you would want to make a major change in the classroom, or even raise the issue with the entire class. On the other hand, if three-fourths of the class respond that they would like a change, it is important that the issue be thoughtfully examined and discussed with the class. Unless student feedback is clearly summarized and tabulated, it is easy to confuse major issues that need attention with comments from a few students that are taken too personally and blown out of proportion.

A second danger associated with merely scanning student feedback is that unless the results are shared with students and obvious responses are made to their suggestions, students begin to feel that the activity is not meaningful and that their input is not valued. Consequently, it is advisable to create a method for displaying the results so that they can be shared with students. The easiest approach is often to simply tally the results. Figure 2.3 provides the tallied results obtained by employing the first nine questions on the student feedback form presented in Figure 2.2.

A simple tally enables you to see where changes may be needed, as well as areas that students view as strengths. An interesting extension to simply tallying data is to determine a numerical average score for each item. When using a five-choice rating scale, as in Figure 2.3, a score of five can be assigned for each student who marked the most positive response, a score of four can be given for the second response, and so on. The scores can be added and divided by the number of students completing the form in order to achieve a class score for each item. Therefore, the results shown in Figure 2.3 indicate that the class score for item 1 in Figure 2.2 would be 3.6. Obtaining a class score for each item allows you to compare students' attitudes and feelings at different times throughout the school year. For example, if you responded to a low score on item 1 by teaching a unit on nutrition or sending a letter home to all parents about students' breakfasts, you could check the results of the intervention by administering the questionnaire again after sever-

FIGURE 2.3   Results of Administering a student needs questionnaire

Check the appropriate box.

Your thoughts about our class	Always	Most of the time	Some-times	Seldom	Never
1. Do you eat a good breakfast each morning?	////	̶H̶H̶ ̶H̶H̶	̶H̶H̶ /	////	
2. Does your teacher touch you enough?	̶H̶H̶ ̶H̶H̶	̶H̶H̶	̶H̶H̶/	//	//
3. Can you see the blackboard and screen from where you are sitting?	̶H̶H̶ ̶H̶H̶ ////	̶H̶H̶ /	//	//	
4. Do I talk loud and clear enough for you to hear?	̶H̶H̶ ̶H̶H̶ ̶H̶H̶ ///	̶H̶H̶ //	//		
5. Do you have time to relax during the day?	///	̶H̶H̶ ////	̶H̶H̶ ///	//	////
6. Do you have enough time to complete your assignments?	̶H̶H̶ //	̶H̶H̶ ̶H̶H̶ /	///	//	
7. Do we go slow enough in class?	̶H̶H̶	̶H̶H̶ ̶H̶H̶ //	̶H̶H̶	//	
8. Do you need a study period at the end of the day?	///	̶H̶H̶ //	̶H̶H̶ //	̶H̶H̶ //	/
9. Is the room a quiet place to work?	//	̶H̶H̶ ////	̶H̶H̶ ////	//	///

al weeks and comparing the class scores on item 1 to see whether or not a change had taken place.

ACTIVITY 2.4   Interpreting and responding to student feedback

After developing and administering a student feedback form and summarizing the results, you should interpret the results and decide what changes, if any, need to be made. The following tasks and questions will help to facilitate this process.

List the three statements students marked most frequently in the two most positive categories. For every three of these statements, write one factor in the classroom that contributes to this positive student reaction.

List the three statements students marked most often in the lowest categories. For each of these statements, write one factor in the classroom that contributes to this negative student reaction. After completing Chapters 4 through 9, return to the activity and, following each classroom factor, list one change (including teacher's behavior) that could be made in the classroom to reduce or eliminate this factor.

Complete this activity by listing three things you learned about your students' needs based upon the results of the questionnaire.

Recommended Reading

Allers, R. (1982). *Divorce, children, and the school.* Princeton, N.J.: Princeton Book Company.

Coopersmith, S. (1967). *The antecedents of self-esteem.* San Francisco: W. H. Freeman.

Dreikurs, R., Grunwald, B., & Pepper, F. (1971). *Maintaining sanity in the classroom: Illustrated teaching techniques.* New York: Harper and Row.

Elkind, D. (1981). *The Hurried child.* Reading, Mass.: Addison-Wesley.

Erikson, E. (1963). *Childhood and society,* 2nd ed. New York: Norton.

Erikson, E. (1968). *Identity, youth and crisis.* New York: Norton.

Glasser, W. (1969). *Schools without failure.* New York: Harper and Row.

Holt, J. (1979). *The underachieving school.* New York: Pitman.

James, M., & Jongeward, D. (1971). *Born to win: Transactional analysis with Gestalt experiments.* Reading, Mass.: Addison-Wesley.

Jones, V. (1980). *Adolescents with behavior problems: Strategies for teaching, counseling, and parent involvement.* Boston: Allyn and Bacon.

Kohl, H. (1971). *Half the house.* New York: Bantam Books.

Maslow, A. (1968). *Toward a psychology of being.* New York: Van Nostrand.

Purkey, W., & Novak, J. (1984). *Inviting school success: A self-concept approach to teaching and learning.* Belmont, Calif.: Wadsworth.

Spaulding, R., & Spaulding, C. (1982). *Research-based classroom management.* San Jose, Calif.: Maple Press.

Wood, M. (1975). *Developmental therapy.* Baltimore: University Park Press.

CHAPTER **3**

Understanding Students'
Academic Needs and Interests

Being a spectator not only deprives one of participation but also leaves one's mind free for unrelated activity. If academic learning does not engage students, something else will.

John Goodlad, (1983),
Phi Delta Kappan, "A Study of Schooling"

Thus low motivation, negative self-attitudes, and failure are largely the result of improper learning conditions. According to this learning-theory analysis, we should be able to alter a student's failure rate by changing the conditions of classroom learning and, as a consequence, increase his motivation to succeed. Actually there is considerable experimental evidence on this point.

Martin Covington and Richard Beery, (1976),
Self-Worth and School Learning

Recent studies have demonstrated that students learn best and behave more appropriately in classroom settings that meet their learning needs. Students' misbehavior and failure can often be traced to failure to create an educational environment conducive to learning. Educators have also begun to appreciate that students vary in the type of classroom struc-ture and instruction that best facilitate their learning. Understanding the instructional needs of an individual child or group of children provides teachers with information essential for creating a positive learning environment.

Although meeting personal needs is the foundation for creating environments that support growth and learning, closely related and equally important needs exist within environments that are specifically designed to assist children in acquiring academic knowledge. Therefore, the use of teaching methods that fulfill students' academic needs should be paralleled by efforts to meet their basic personal needs.

The importance of understanding students' academic needs has been shown by numerous studies, described in Chapter 1, indicating that students spend most of their time involved in passive learning activities aimed at developing factual knowledge. "The emphasis on management of group contingencies and on answering often appear to focus the attention of teachers and students on getting work done rather than the quality of work" (Doyle, 1983, p. 186). As we have mentioned, teachers often select instructional methods that enhance order at the expense of engaging students in meaningful learning activities. An understanding of students' academic needs that must be met in order to enhance their motivation and academic achievement provides the groundwork for teachers to begin implementing more diverse, creative teaching methods. The academic needs listed in this chapter are based on the authors' own categorization of research on student learning. This list has been validated by lists generated by more than 200 teachers. We encourage you to continually review the literature and consider this list in light of your own experience.

STUDENTS' ACADEMIC NEEDS

Students' academic needs include the need to:

1. understand the teacher's goals,
2. be actively involved in the learning process,
3. relate subject matter to their own lives,
4. follow their own interests,
5. experience success,
6. receive realistic and immediate feedback,
7. experience an appropriate amount of structure,
8. have time to integrate learning,
9. have positive contact with peers, and
10. receive instruction matched to their skill level and learning style.

Research and our own experiences indicate that when teaching methods respond effectively to these needs, students' learning is significantly increased, and misbehavior is dramatically decreased.

Understand the Teacher's Goals

People are more likely to become involved in activities that have a clear goal. You can undoubtedly recall sitting through a meeting that seemed to have no direction or purpose. Compare the feelings generated by this type of situation to those from a meeting in which goals were clearly stated and the activities moved smoothly toward reaching the stated goals. Similarly, children will derive more satisfaction and enjoyment from an activity that has a definite aim. Compare a child who merely bounces a basketball against a wall to the youngster who is shooting baskets. The child will remain involved in the latter activity much longer because it includes a designated goal.

Studies indicate that students often complete work merely to earn grades, with little interest in or awareness of content goals (Anderson, 1981; Blumenfield, Pintrich, Meece, & Wessels, 1982; Stake & Easley, 1978). Walter Doyle (1983) writes that:

> . . . the quality of the time students spend engaged in academic work depends on the tasks they are expected to accomplish and the extent to which students understand what they are doing. It is essential, therefore, that direct instruction include explicit attention to meaning and not simply focus on engagement as an end in itself. . . . [p. 189]

One of us recently had an opportunity to observe how important clear goal setting is when working with a student-teacher. During the initial observation, students seemed confused and inattentive as the student-teacher wandered through a lesson that appeared rather directionless. Based on this observation, the student-teacher was encouraged to write a clear goal statement on the board before beginning each lesson and to discuss his goals with the students. Later observations, as well as the teacher's reports, indicated that this approach markedly influenced students' attentiveness and on-task behavior. In his *Motivation and Teaching*, Wlodkowski (1978) discusses the role of goal setting in improving motivation.

> With the goal-setting model, the student knows that she/he is in command and can calculate what to do to avoid wasting time or experiencing self-defeat. Thus, before even beginning the learning task, the student knows that her/his effort will be worthwhile and has an actual sense that there is a good probability for success. [p. 54]

To no one's surprise, research indicates that students ranging from middle-class college students (Bryan & Locke, 1967) to lower-class elementary school children (Kennedy, 1968) achieve better when they are presented with specific learning goals.

Be Actively Involved in the Learning Process

Probably you have been involved in a variety of learning experiences characterized by almost total lack of learner participation. Over the years we have noticed that teachers' behavior at faculty meetings often resembles students' behavior that teachers find annoying. We should consider our own response to lack of involvement before punishing the same behavior in students.

Put the book aside for a moment and try to recall the feelings you experienced the last time you were involved in a learning situation in which you were simply a passive recipient of information. As you recall this situation, it is quite likely that you remember experiencing boredom, frustration, annoyance, or anger. Furthermore, it is probable that you did not learn as much from this experience as you would have if you had been involved in the learning process. As George Leonard wrote in his *Education and Ecstasy* (1968), "No environment can strongly affect a person unless it is stronlgy interactive" (p. 39). Summarizing his extensive, systematic study of education in a sample of thirty-eight schools, Goodlad (1983a) writes:

> Teachers appear to teach within a very limited repertoire of pedagogical alternatives, emphasizing their own talk and the monitoring of seatwork. The customary pedagogy places the teacher very much in control. Few activities call for or even permit active student planning, follow-through and evaluation. [p. 467]

Regardless of whether one views learning as based on reinforcement of appropriate responses, modeling, or reconstruction of cognitive concepts, learning will take place only when the learner is actively involved in attempting new skills. Piaget (1977) emphasizes that, especially for young children, learning must involve doing. Children tend to learn what they do rather than what they see or hear.

> Good pedagogy must involve presenting the child with situations in which he himself experiments, in the broadest sense of that term—trying things out to see what happens, manipulating things, manipulating symbols, posing questions and seeking his own answers, reconciling what he finds one time and what he finds at another, comparing his findings with those of other children. [Duckworth, 1964, p. 2]

Studies completed at the Center for Early Adolescence suggest that this age group, along with primary-age children, requires particular emphasis on active participation in the learning process. The *Middle Grades Assessment Program* (Dorman, 1981), designed to help schools for young adolescents assess the effectiveness of their instruction, asks schools to assess the extent to which:

18. Teacher encourages students to ask questions of each other as well as of the teacher.
19. Teacher builds on students' comments and ideas.
30. Students are actively engaged in activities, manipulating materials and objects. They are not just listening.
42. In many classrooms, small groups of students are working independently on projects or assignments.
46. Students and teachers relate what they are learning in class to field trips or visits into the community that they are planning or have completed. [pp. 44–46]

A large number of researchers and writers support the concepts outlined in Dorman's assessment instrument (Johnson & Johnson, 1975, 1983, 1984; Jones, 1980; Lipsitz, 1984; Slavin, 1983).

Robert White's (1959) theory of competence motivation and DeCharms's (1968, 1976) work relating this theory to the educational setting further emphasize the importance of actively involving students in the learning process. These writers report that individuals seek to control their own behavior and to resist consistent external control over their behavior. DeCharms's major thesis is that students who are involved in directing their own learning will produce better work and will enjoy their work more than will students who are merely responding obediently in order to receive reinforcement. DeCharms (1976) writes that schools should provide children with small but real choices and that this effort should be associated with adults' expectations that students will act responsibly.

Rotter's (1954, 1966) theory and research, related to locus of control, reinforces the concept that students should be meaningfully involved in the learning process. Students who possess an internal locus of control believe that their own efforts determine their success or failure, and external locus of control students believe that outside forces have a major influence on outcomes. Research (Bar-Tal & Bar Zohar, 1977; Coleman, 1966; Stipek & Weisz, 1981) indicates that students who possess an internal locus of control are more likely to achieve academic success. Furthermore, studies (Bar-Tal & Bar-Tal, 1975; Chandler, 1975; Chapin & Dych, 1976; Fowler & Peterson, 1981) indicate that children can develop an internal locus of control by being involved in learning environments in which they are provided with responsibility and choice.

Finally, even if theorists did not suggest that students need to be actively involved in the learning process, anyone who has been around elementary-age children must be impressed with their intense curiosity and their almost limitless energy in exploring their world. It should not surprise parents or teachers of these children that an effective learning environment must actively involve these youngsters in exploring and ordering their environment.

Relate Subject Matter to Their Own Lives

Undoubtedly you have attended meetings at which the topic was of little interest because it dealt with material that seemed to have no direct influence upon immediate concerns. For a moment, put the book aside and try to envision the last time you attended such a meeting. What were you feeling? What did you do? What did you want to do? If you are like most people, you experienced boredom, resentment, and frustration. It is also likely that you were somewhat inattentive and perhaps even talked to someone or graded papers during the meeting. Finally, it would not be unusual if you strongly desired to leave the meeting.

Unfortunately, students all too often do not view their schoolwork as pertaining to their needs or interests, and consequently experience feelings similar to those just described. This situation may be intensified for students who find that they have difficulty understanding the material. Consider how you would feel if you were required to take a course in advanced biochemistry or quantum theory. It is very likely that your frustration over the irrelevance of the subject would be compounded by your inadequacies in understanding the material. Many children experience similar frustration and impotence as they struggle to learn material that seems neither related to their lives nor within their ability to master. Examining the reasons for school failure, William Glasser (1969) describes this factor poignantly.

> ... with increasing frequency from grade one through the end of graduate school, much of what is required is either totally or partially irrelevant to the world around them as they see it. Thus both excess memorization and increasing irrelevance cause them to withdraw into failure or strike out ... [p. 30]

McClelland's theory and subsequent research on achievement motivation (McClelland, Atkinson, Clark, & Lowell, 1953; McClelland & Alschuler, 1971) suggests that individuals will be more highly motivated to achieve if they can be shown how their efforts relate to their everyday lives. Ausubel's (1968) concept of the value of meaningful learning supports the importance of relating subject matter to pertinent issues in students' lives. When the material being learned cannot be related to existing cognitive structures, retention is limited (Dooling & Mullet, 1973). The concepts highlighted by the techniques of values clarification (Harmin, Kirschenbaum, & Simon, 1973); Simon, Howe, & Kirschenbaum, 1972) provide further insight into, as well as specific approaches to, the importance of relating subject matter to students' lives. Stinchcombe (1964) concisely states the results associated with learning that fails to relate to students' lives.

> When a student realizes that he does not achieve status increment from improved current performance, current performance loses meaning. The student becomes hedonistic because he does not visualize achievement of long-run goals through current self-restraint. He reacts negatively to a conformity that offers nothing concrete. He claims autonomy from adults because their authority does not promise him a satisfactory future. [Stinchcombe 1964, pp. 5, 6]

If we want students to remember information, we must relate the information to some meaningful event or idea in their lives. It is much more difficult to initially learn and to retain nonsense syllables than it is to learn meaningful information. Material is forgotten not because the brain fails to retain the information, but because the information is not retrievable due to interference from other associations that are more accurate, important, or relevant.

That students' motivation, learning, and retention are enhanced by relating material to events within their lives is certainly a major reason for ensuring that subject matter meets this criterion. It is equally important to realize, however, that, if children are to develop the skills that will enable them to sensitively operate a democratic social system, they need more than knowledge of facts. They need to know how to make decisions about current issues and how to weigh values against facts. This wisdom is not learned through an education based primarily upon memorization and an emphasis on improving scores on standardized tests. Rather, it is learned by applying knowledge to meaningful issues in children's lives. John Dewey stated this concept clearly when he wrote:

> ... What avail is it to win prescribed amounts of information about geography and history, to win ability to read and write, if in the process the individual loses his own soul: loses his appreciation of things worth while, of the values to which they are relative; if he loses desire to apply what he has learned and, above all, loses the ability to extract meaning from his future experiences as they occur? [Dewey, 1963, p. 50]

Follow Their Own Interests

Students need opportunities to delve into topics they find exciting and interesting. Anyone who has worked with students has seen and been impressed by the energy and enthusiasm they display when searching for information associated with a topic they find interesting. Similarly, we have, on numerous occasions, been amazed by the extent and sophistication of students' knowledge of these self-chosen topics. Although it may not be in students' best interest to allow them to learn only about topics of their own choosing, it is equally if not more destructive to fail to reinforce and support their self-initiated inquiries.

It is interesting that, after reading the autobiographies and biographies of 400 of the most famous people of the twentieth century, Goertzel and Goertzel (1962) commented that nearly 60 percent of these people experienced major school problems, and many intensely disliked school. It is quite probable that many of the school problems experienced by these noted individuals were related to the fact that schools often demand conformity and reinforce learning unrelated to students' special interests. Torrance (1960), a leading researcher in creativity in the schools, stated that schools tend to suppress creativity in order to increase conformity.

One probable factor leading to students' decreased satisfaction with school as they progress through the grades (Flanders, Morrison, & Brode, 1968) is that students learn that they must study what they are told rather than what interests them. In an interesting study, Asher and Markell (1974) found that, though fifth-grade girls were much better readers than boys when reading low-interest materials, boys read as well as girls when both were given high-interest material. Mahoney (1974) found that students enjoy school more and achieve better when they are allowed to make choices during their school day. Additional research clearly indicates that providing children with a sense of personal control increases school achievement (DeCharms, 1972; Lepper & Greene, 1975; Maehr, 1974). Furthermore, students are more willing to follow classroom rules when they are involved in making the rules (Tjosvold, 1977; Tjosvold & Santamaria, 1977). If we wish to increase students' motivation, enhance creativity, and reduce unproductive student behavior, we must create learning environments that provide time for students to follow their own interests.

Experience Success

None of us enjoys being in a setting in which we consistently fail. Most adults can recall situations in which they responded to failure by dropping an activity and attempting something at which they were more adept. To a large degree, this behavior was influenced by the need to view oneself as competent. Success experiences are instrumental in developing feelings of self-worth and confidence in attempting new activities.

> It is through achievement that academic self-confidence grows, and increased confidence in turn promotes achievement through inspiring further learning. In short, confidence and competence must increase together for either to prosper. When they do not grow apace, students are likely to suffer. [Covington & Beery, 1976, p. 5]

Recent teacher-effectiveness research suggests that students' learning is increased when they experience high rates of success in completing tasks. When the teacher is available to monitor and assist students, success rates of 70 to 80 percent are desirable (Brophy & Evertson, 1976). When students are expected to work on their own, success rates of 95 to 100 percent are desirable (Fisher et al., 1980). Studies suggest that when students are given inappropriate tasks, the tasks are much more likely to be too difficult than too easy (Fisher et al., 1980; Gambrell, Wilson, & Gantt, 1981; Jorgenson, 1977).

Following successful experiences, individuals tend to raise their expectations and set higher goals, whereas failure is met with lowered aspirations (Diggory, 1966). Success or failure also influences individuals' self-evaluations (Wylie, 1961). Studies also indicate that praising students' work produces greater performance gains than does criticism (Costello, 1964; Page, 1958) and that the positive effects in self-rating and performance tend to spread to areas related to those in which praise was provided for success experiences (Maehr, 1976).

A strong relationship also connects success and both long-term school performance and positive mental health. Carrino (1966) reported that 90 percent of high school dropouts in his study scored below grade level in reading and spelling in the second grade. Only 10 percent of the students who graduated fell into this category, however. Studies on adolescent suicide (Jacobs, 1971), schizophrenia (Holmes & Barthell, 1968; Watt, Stolorowrd-Lubensky, & McClelland, 1970), and other serious mental disorders (Holzman & Grinker, 1977) indicate that continued failure in the school and home can have devastating effects on young people.

If we fail to provide students with activities in which they can succeed, we should expect that they will withdraw or act out. Because children have a basic need to experience a sense of competence, they will reject settings and activities that attest to their failure, and will, instead, become involved in activities at which they can be successful. These alternative behaviors often include actions adults label unproductive. The actions, however, are often merely attempts to display competence and receive acknowledgment in the only way a child has found successful.

Receive Realistic and Immediate Feedback

Closely associated with the need for success experiences is the need to receive immediate and specific feedback. Because students care about being successful, it is important that they receive feedback clearly designating the extent to which they have succeeded at a task. Several studies (Burrows, 1973; Collins, 1971) show that students' achievement is enhanced by providing them with information about their current level of performance (based on results of diagnostic tests), followed by specific learning tasks aimed at mastering the material. Page (1958) found that supportive comments, accompanied by statements about specific strengths and weaknesses in students' work, were more effective in improving students' performance than either grades or brief positive comments. In fact, students who care most about failing are most in need of immediate feedback, for, without it, they tend to judge their performance as unacceptable (Meunier & Rule, 1967).

Not all feedback is effective in improving students' performance. Studies show that hostile or extensive criticism creates negative attitudes and lowers achievement, creativity, and classroom control (Brophy & Evertson, 1976; Dunkin & Biddle, 1974; Flanders, 1972; Rosenshine, 1976). Praise is often overused and is not a powerful reinforcer for many children (Brophy, 1981; Ware, 1978). Praise can be an effective form of feedback when it provides students with specific information about the quality of their work and the effort made to complete the work. Praise is, however, often misused. Teachers frequently praise incorrect answers (Anderson, Evertson, & Brophy, 1979; Mehan, 1974), and this false praise is more often given to lower-achieving students (Brookover et al., 1978; Kleinfeld, 1975; Weinstein, 1976). "To the extent that praise is important, the key to its effectiveness lies in its quality rather than its frequency. Effective teachers know both when and how to praise" (Good & Brophy, 1984, p. 193).

An Appropriate Amount of Structure

Students need guidance from adults. Schools are designed to place young people in settings where concerned, educated adults can structure an environment so that students develop the skills they will need to function effectively in society. This statement may appear to present the obvious, but a decade of criticism of the schools has not only productively challenged, but also destructively confused, the concept of legitimate adult authority. The positive aspect of this challenge to structure and authority is that it has served to make educators aware of the danger associated with arbitrary, repressive authority that ignores students' rights and thereby reduces ther self-concepts and creativity. The unfortunate aspect of this criticism is that freedom has too often been stated as a solution rather than a concept that highlights a problem. Freedom, however, does not in itself constitute an educational program that is an answer to discipline problems. The question of how best to provide children with necessary and appropriate structure while maintaining their dignity and teaching them responsibility remains. When viewed in this manner, the issue becomes how to more actively and meaningfully involve children in the learning process and how to assist teachers in developing personal and instructional skills that will allow them to effectively control a classroom without being negative and repressive in their interactions with students.

Research in parenting provides some useful hints on the type of structure that is most beneficial for children. Parenting styles are frequently divided into three major categories: authoritarian, authoritative, and laissez-faire (Baumrind, 1968; Elder, 1963). In authoritarian parenting parents maintain complete control over all decisions, and seldom involve children in meaningful dialogue about choices. Laissez-faire refers to permissive parenting, in which the parent is frequently absent and provides few limits or guidelines for the child. Authoritative parenting involves parents' maintaining ultimate responsibility for the child's behavior while involving the child in discussions that may lead to compromise but, at the very least, providing the child with both a sense of involvement and a clear understanding of the reasons for the decision. A wide variety of research and theory stresses the benefits derived from employing an authoritative parenting style (Elder, 1963; Enright, Lapsley, Drivas, & Fehr, 1980; Kandel & Lesser, 1972; Mead, 1970). The findings strongly support the value of developing an approach to working with children that blends structure and support with flexibility, open dialogue, explanations, and conflict resolution. Children need to work in environments which are clearly organized and in which rules and expectations are understood. It is equally important, though, that children be involved in creating the rules, discussing the expectations, and evaluating the results.

Research in classroom management also supports the importance of structure. In his often-cited study on classroom discipline, Kounin (1970) cites a variety of teacher behaviors that enhance classroom order and control. He writes that students misbehave less frequently when teachers communicate their awareness of classroom happenings and are able to respond to several issues simultaneously. Similarly, teachers who make smooth transitions between activities and who keep their students alert by involving all students in learning activities have fewer classroom problems than teachers who lack these skills. These findings suggest that students want and respond more effectively to adults who are better able to monitor and react to situations and who create a well-organized atmosphere in which students are actively involved. As discussed in detail in Chapter 7, recent research shows that teachers who early in the school year help children learn and master classroom rules and procedures have fewer behavior problems and are more effective in bringing about increased achievement.

Finally, we must be aware that children vary considerably in the amount of structure they find most beneficial (Jones, 1983a). Grimes and Allinsmith (1961) compared the reading achievement of children with high, medium, and low amounts of anxiety and found that high-anxiety children did better in more-structured school settings, and low-anxiety children tended to function better in less-structured classrooms. Soar (1983) reports evidence that lower-achieving students and students from lower socioeconomic environments generally learn more effectively in highly structured environments. Similarly, young children learn best in classroom settings characterized by relatively high rates of teacher-directed learning, consistent structure, and high rates of correct responses (Anderson et al., 1979; Good & Grouws, 1979; Rosenshine, 1978).

Although all students benefit from working in well-organized environments where expectations and goals are clearly understood, some students function more effectively when given more choices and somewhat less structure. Soar (1983) reports that older, higher-achieving and higher-SES students tend to learn more effectively in classroom settings that provide opportunities for active student involvement. There is also convincing evidence (Jones, 1983a; Soar, 1983) that highly structured classroom environments facilitate rote learning but hinder divergent, creative thinking. It is the job of a skilled teacher to discover these individual differences and provide opportunities for different children to work in different ways in the classroom.

Time to Integrate Learning

The school provides a busy and varied environment. During the day students may learn a new concept in math, master several new spelling words, discuss a new concept in social studies, sing a new song, complete a science experiment, and be involved in numerous social interactions in the classroom, in the lunchroom, and on the playground. This diversity and fast pace will often be stimulating and interesting, but it also presents a very real problem to many if not all students. Students need time to integrate the new ideas that they encounter.

In his work on how learning occurs, Jean Piaget (1952, 1970) points to the fact that the learner must take new information and either assimilate the material into existing cognitive structures or create new structures by accommodation. Piaget writes that, because the learner is actively involved in this restructuring, learning requires considerable time and energy.

Students need time during the school day to slow down and integrate what they have learned. All too often students are rushed from one activity to another, with no time allotted for summarizing the learning that has taken place in each activity. When this hurry occurs, students begin to feel confused and often experience a sense of failure, for they frequently have not understood what it was they were supposed to have learned from the preceding activity. As teachers, we are often lulled into believing that everyone has understood because several of our students who learn quickly provide us with an indication that the material has been learned and understood. Students learn at varying rates, however, and in different ways, and it is important to slow down and provide all students with an opportunity to organize the new ideas that have been presented. Effective teachers develop specific instructional activities designed to help students summarize new learning and relate this new knowledge to previous and future learning and the students' own lives.

Have Positive Contact with Peers

The need to interact with peers is an academic need as well as an important personal and psychological need. Piaget (1952) writes that social interactions are important in influencing learning. Numerous studies have supported this contention. Studies comparing the amount of learning that takes place when students work together, as opposed to working individually, indicate that initial learning, retention, and transfer of concepts tends to be higher when cooperative learning is employed (Davis, Laughlin, & Komorita, 1976; Johnson & Johnson, 1975, 1984). Students also seem to enjoy working together, and this approach to learning promotes positive attitudes toward instructional activities and subject areas (Dunn & Goldman, 1966; Wheeler & Ryan, 1973). In discussing the positive effects of cooperative learning, David Johnson, one of the leading researchers in the field, writes:

> The more cooperative students' attitudes and experiences, the more they see themselves as being intrinsically motivated, persevering in pursuit of clearly defined learning goals, believing it is their own efforts that determine school success, wanting to be good students and get good grades, and believing that ideas, feelings, and learning new ideas are important and positive. [Johnson, 1979, p. 151]

As discussed in Chapter 2 and expanded in Chapter 5, creating positive peer relationships also appears to meet a basic personal need that serves as a prerequisite to productive involvement in the learning process (Lewis & St. John, 1974; Schmuck & Schmuck, 1983). This evidence makes it somewhat surprising to find that peer work groups are rare in American schools (Clements, 1983; Goodlad, 1984; Stodolsky, 1983). Anyone who has worked with students knows that they find their peers to be perhaps the most consistently interesting aspect of the school environment. Educators can choose either to attempt to squelch the energy inherent in this interest or to channel this energy toward their learning goals.

Have Instruction Matched to Level of Cognitive Development and Learning Style

Even though we recognize that the personal and academic needs described throughout this chapter apply to all children, we must also be aware that children differ considerably in their levels of cognitive development and learning styles. Teachers who employ the same instructional methods with every student or who employ a limited range of instructional activities will create a situation in which some students become frustrated, experience failure, and respond by misbehaving.

Cognitive Development
Piaget's theories on the sequential stages of cognitive development suggest that teachers should consider the complexity of the subject matter as compared with students' current level of cognitive development. Therefore, when considering the concepts to be presented and the degree of abstractness with which these can be discussed, we should constantly monitor the degree to which students are able to understand and generalize—rather than merely mimic—the material being taught.

Figure 3.1 indicates the variability in cognitive development among students at each age from five to eighteen. The data indicate that fewer than one-quarter of thirteen-year-olds have reached even the onset of formal operational thought—the ability to consider abstract concepts apart from concrete exam-

FIGURE 3.1   Distribution of percentages of children at Piagetian stages

Age (years)	Preoper-ational (%)	Concrete onset (%)	Concrete mature (%)	Formal onset (%)	Formal mature (%)
5	85	15			
6	60	35	5		
7	35	55	10		
8	25	55	20		
9	15	55	30		
10	12	52	35	1	
11	6	49	40	5	
12	5	32	51	12	
13	2	34	44	14	6
14	1	32	43	15	9
15	1	14	53	19	13
16	1	15	54	17	13
17	3	19	47	19	12
18	1	15	50	15	19

From Herman T. Epstein, Cognitive growth and development. *Colorado Journal of Educational Research*, 1979, *19*, 35. Reprinted by permission.

ples. Consider the typical junior high school English, social studies, or math class that presents a wide range of abstract material without using concrete learning activities or relating material to students' own experience. When presented with material related to historical events or literary and mathematical abstractions, few seventh or eighth graders can truly understand the material. Though some higher-achieving students can provide correct answers to abstract questions, many even of these do not understand what they have learned. Toepfer (1979) offers evidence that many students with tested high IQs who have achieved well during the elementary school years experience school failure during early adolescence because the material is simply too abstract for them to comprehend. Unfortunately, his data suggest that many of these potentially fine students began to develop a sense of school failure and inadequacy during the sensitive early adolescent years and become behavior problems and dropouts. Dembo (1977) describes the key relationship between instruction and cognitive development:

> A teacher who uses the best textbooks available and develops the most interesting and stimulating lesson plans can still fail to reach a majority of students in his class who do not have the necessary structures (operations) to enable them to "understand" the presented material. This means that the classroom teacher must be able to (1) assess a child's level of cognitive development, and (2) determine the type of abilities the child needs to understand the subject matter. [p. 273]

Learning Style

In addition to attending to students' current level of cognitive development, teachers who wish to increase students' motivation and success need to respond effectively to the individual student's learning style. Students differ in their approaches to learning. Every student has a cognitive or learning style that represents the general approach he or she takes to learning and organizing material (Sigel & Coop, 1974). Riessmann (1964) writes that teachers too often examine students' failure by considering personal and social problems and do not focus on the child's learning style and determine the best approach to providing instruction.

Research (deHirsch, Jansky, & Langford, 1966; Smith, 1964; Wheeler, 1980) suggests that students' learning can be enhanced by providing them with material that enables them to use the sensory modality with which they are most comfortable. Students also differ in their pace of learning (Kagan, Moss, & Siegel, 1963; Shumsky, 1968). In addition, Bernard (1973) comments that, though teachers have generally been aware of students' individual needs in amount of time needed to complete various tasks, they have generally ignored other aspects of students' learning styles. For example, several authors (Ramirez & Castaneda, 1974; Witkin & Moore, 1974) suggest that students differ according to whether they depend upon personalized, social factors in learning (field-dependent students) or more impersonal, abstract factors (field-independent students). Ramirez and Castaneda (1974) suggest that field-independent students are less concerned about relationships within the classroom and prefer abstract material. They enjoy independent work and competition. Conversely, field-dependent students seek teacher and peer approval and want learning material to be concrete and related to their own interests. Students also differ on such factors as their ability to attend to relevant cues and ignore inappropriate stimuli (Hagen & Hale, 1972), to accept new ideas and surroundings (Messick, 1970; Sperry, 1972), and the ability to reflect upon questions before responding (Kagan, 1966; Messick, 1970). Artley (1981) reviewed many of the major techniques used in reading instruction during the past eighty years. He reports that all programs help the reading problems some students have, while at the same time creating (or at least failing to respond to) the difficulties experienced by other students.

Rita Dunn for a decade has been a leader in the field of understanding individual learning-style preferences. Extensive research conducted by Dunn and her colleagues provides support for the studies cited in the paragraph above. Dunn's research demonstrates that a variety of elements differentially affect individuals' learning. Figure 3.2 is a chart designed by Kenneth and Rita Dunn to demonstrate these variables or elements. Dunn (1983) reports various studies demonstrating that allowing students to work in classroom settings in which environmental, physical, and sociological factors were similar to those preferred by the student dramatically enhances student learning.

Anthony Gregorc, another leader in the field of learning styles, states that people learn in combinations of dualities: (1) concrete-sequential, (2) concrete-random, (3) abstract-sequential, or (4) abstract-random. Figure 3.3 outlines the learning characteristics of individuals who have these four styles. As discussed in Chapter 9, these learning styles have implications for the types and variety of instructional methods we must employ in order to adequately respond to our students' diverse learning needs.

Other theorists, including David Kolb (1978), Joseph Renzulli (1978, 1983), and Bernice McCarthy (1980, 1983) have, like Gregorc, divided individual learning styles into categories and found that when instructional methods match students' preferences for learning style, student achievement is significantly enhanced. Bernice McCarthy has developed the 4-mat system, a cycle of learning that identifies four distinct styles of learning, as well as four distinct instructional roles for the teacher. The goal of this program is to work in every learner's preferred style while simultaneously increasing students' abilities in diverse ways of learning.

McCarthy divides learners and teachers into four quadrants. The four learning styles include:

1.   innovative learners,
2.   analytic learners,
3.   common-sense learners, and
4.   dynamic learners.

Innovative learners seek meaning and want reasons for learning new material. They need to be personally involved in the learning process. These learners are innovative and imaginative people. They enjoy working with people. Ana-

FIGURE 3.2 Diagnosing learning styles

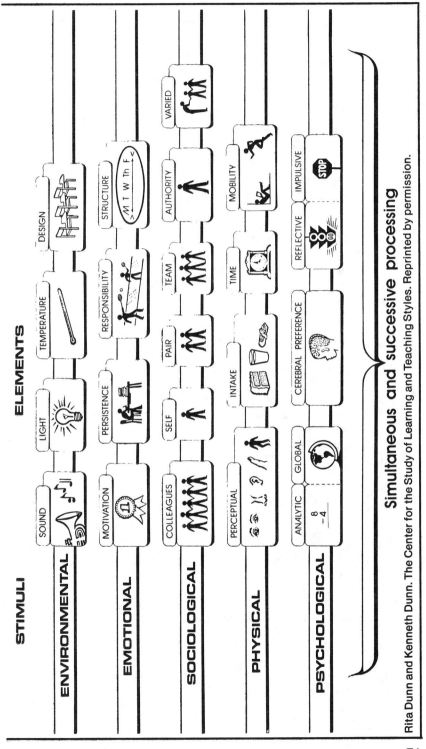

Simultaneous and successive processing

Rita Dunn and Kenneth Dunn. The Center for the Study of Learning and Teaching Styles. Reprinted by permission.

71

FIGURE 3.3   Gregorc's four types of learning

CS: Concrete sequential
1. uses his or her senses
2. direct experience
3. sees only right and wrong
4. loves knowledge
5. accepts authority
6. loves step-by-step directions
7. likes detail
8. sees individual parts
9. low toleration for distraction

AS: Abstract sequential
1. pictures words in mind
2. sees only one answer
3. figures out "why"—analyzes
4. needs written proof
5. sees logical parts
6. likes general guidelines but must have purpose
7. highly verbal
8. low tolerance for distraction

AR: Abstract random
1. uses "sixth sense"—feelings
2. notices body language
3. sees "maybes"—gray areas rather than right and wrong
4. people oriented
5. reluctant to evaluate
6. needs approval
7. looks at whole
8. likes freedom
9. likes having lots going on

CR: Concrete random
1. uses insight
2. gets gist of ideas—makes mental leaps
3. likes to answer but can see many answers
4. likes knowledge if it involves (many) people
5. creative
6. accepts authority if he or she considers it legitimate
7. likes to solve problems
8. accepts positive and negative comments
9. sees whole with parts
10. follows guidelines within limits
11. likes lots going on that involves him or her

lytic learners want to know the facts. They perceive information abstractly and process it reflectively. The analytic learner can effectively create concepts and build models. Schools today are designed for this type of learner. Common-sense learners need to know how things work. They enjoy solving problems and seek "hands-on" experiences. Practical application of ideas is important to them. Dynamic learners learn most effectively by the self-discovery method. These learners take risks, are flexible, and relish change. Dynamic learners seek action and tend to follow through with plans.

McCarthy states that the role of the teacher has to change with each type of learner. With innovative learners the style of teaching is matched when the teacher is a motivator and uses the discussion approach with much teacher-student interaction. With analytic learners, the teacher provides information by direct instruction. The type of teaching style that best meets the needs of the common-sense learner is the "coaching method," in which the teacher models, involves the student, and provides immediate feedback. A teacher who serves as a resource and evaluator best serves the needs of the dynamic learner. The teacher tends to be more involved and active while working with learners who are innovative and analytic, but the common-sense and dynamic learner is more involved in the learning process, with the teacher serving as facilitator and evaluator.

Having divided learning into four styles or quadrants, within each quadrant McCarthy believes that an effective teacher plans activities to cover both left- and right-hemisphere dominant students so that growth in each area may occur. In Chapter 9 we present ideas for developing lesson plans following McCarthy's model.

It is interesting but no surprise that students can provide us with useful information about how they learn best. As part of a required audit, the Little Rock School District asked a random sample of 566 students in grades 7 to 12 to state what classroom factors helped them to learn. The results (Mosley & Smith, 1982) showed the top five factors to be:

1. clear, complete explanations and concrete examples;
2. positive, relaxed learning environments in which students could talk to and learn from other students;
3. individualized instruction, in which teachers know that students are different, occasionally divide students into groups, check on students' progress, and assign varied tasks;
4. adequate academic learning time in class; and
5. motivation and interest by using a variety of instructional methods and teacher's enthusiasm.

It is informative that these factors listed by students incorporate most of the academic needs presented in this chapter.

Students can also provide information about their own learning styles. Much of the research on students' learning styles involves questionnaires asking students to report how they learn best. In the bibliography at the end of this chapter, we list several assessment tools that are available to teachers and have been used and researched extensively in classroom settings. The key to selecting a method of assessing student learning styles is that the assessment needs to be prescriptive; that is, it needs to help the teacher select materials and instructional methods that better fit the learning needs of individual students or the class. Assessing learning styles also provides us with an additional avenue for working cooperatively with our students to facilitate learning. Assessment of learning styles involves students in understanding how they learn and can serve as a powerful motivating and clarifying device for both teachers and students.

Because one of the goals of schooling is to increase students' skills in obtaining knowledge, we want to help children expand their cognitive style, rather than merely accommodate their current style. Therefore, though we would ideally, especially when teaching such basic skills as reading and mathematics, individualize material to respond to each student's preferred style, we should also incorporate various methods of instruction and help children learn how to assimilate material presented in various manners. As discussed in Chapter 9, materials are increasingly available for helping us develop lessons that incorporate varied student learning styles, simultaneously directing learning at a range of cognitive outcomes.

The concept of brain hemisphericity is closely linked to the work on students' learning styles. During the past few years considerable research has been done supporting the notion that those who tend to be left-brain dominant learn in different ways and have different environmental and organizational needs in the classroom than right-brain dominant people (Dunn et al., 1982). Right-brain dominant people in general are bothered by noise when working, prefer dim lighting, are less persistent and motivated when doing detailed, logical, sequential kinds of tasks, prefer a tactile mode of learning, and like to learn while working with peers. Left-brain dominant students tend to learn best when it is quiet, and they like bright light, prefer to work by themselves, and learn visually, auditorily, or both. These students enjoy analyzing situations, like tasks to be logical and sequential, and pay attention to detail.

Most of the curriculum in the public school deals with facts and knowledge: logical, sequential, linear concepts; systems, rules, and symbols. ". . . In elementary and many secondary classes, students spend two-thirds of their time doing seatwork with printed worksheets" (Doyle, 1983, p. 180). Durkin (1981) analyzed five basal reading programs and reported that they emphasized practice and assessment and included little instruction in comprehension. Findings from national studies by Boyer (1983), Goodlad (1984), Lipsitz (1984), and Sizer (1984) all reinforce the fact that most instruction is teacher-dominated and fact-oriented. This type of instruction favors left-brain dominant students. Many students are right-brain dominant, however, and learn best when they are actively involved in the realm of creativity, imagination, intuitiveness, spatial concepts, and inventiveness. Therefore, as discussed in Chapter Nine, when designing curriculum and instruction, it is important to create a balance of activities that focus on the learning-style preferences of right- and left-brain dominant students.

ACTIVITIES FOR EXAMINING STUDENTS' ACADEMIC NEEDS

As discussed in Chapter 2, we can discover students' needs by analyzing the classroom environment in light of theories and research, by asking students to provide specific feedback, or both. In this section we provide three activities you can use to consider how effectively you are meeting students' academic needs. The first two activities are based on the theories and research described in this chapter; the third activity involves students' feedback.

ACTIVITY 3.1   Evaluating a classroom environment in light of students' academic needs

For each of the ten student academic needs, list two ways in which you currently meet the need within the classroom. Be specific. For example: I employ interest centers to respond to students' needs to follow their own interests. If you are not currently teaching, select a classroom that you have observed recently.

After completing Chapters 4 through 9, return to this activity and list two specific ways in which you could alter your teaching methods in order to more effectively meet these needs.

ACTIVITY 3.2   Responding to students' academic needs—Examining an individual case

Select a student who is having particular difficulty behaving appropriately in class. List at least two academic needs that are not being met for this student. After completing Chapters 4 through 9, return to this activity and list at least one specific approach that can be employed to ensure that each of the needs you have listed can be more effectively met for this student.

ACTIVITY 3.3   Employing students' input to determine extent to which their academic needs are being met in a classroom

Students can provide us with helpful information on how well the classroom environment is meeting their academic needs. The questionnaire in Figure 3.4 is an example of an instrument that can be administered to discover how students feel about their classroom.

continued

FIGURE 3.4 Student academic needs questionnaire

Please check the appropriate box	Always true 100%	Most of the time 75%	Half of the time 50%	Occasionally 25%	Never true 0%
Understand the teacher's goal					
1. Do you understand the goals for each lesson?					
2. Do you know the purpose of or reason why assignments are given?					
3. Do I explain néw material well enough to you?					
4. Are the directions in class clear?					
Actively involved in the learning process					
5. Do you frequently raise your hand to answer a question?					
6. Do you get a chance to share your ideas in class?					
7. Have you suggested changes for our classroom?					
8. Is there a good balance for you in the amount of time spent in small- and large-group activities?					

continued

Relate subject matter to their own lives

9. Do you see the skills taught in this class as being useful in some other area of your life?

10. Are you asked to collect information or materials from outside of school to use in school assignments?

Follow own interests

11. Are you able to study subjects or ideas that interest you?

12. Do you get to make choices about the topics you study?

Experience success

13. Do you feel good about how much you are learning?

14. Do you experience success in your academic work?

15. Do you accomplish academic goals that you set?

Receive realistic and immediate feedback

16. Are my comments on your work helpful?

17. Do tests give you information about what you have learned?

18. Do tests and assignments help you see what skills you still need to practice?

FIGURE 3.4 continued.

Please check the appropriate box	Always true 100%	Most of the time 75%	Half of the time 50%	Occasionally 25%	Never true 0%
Experience an appropriate amount of structure					
19. Does this class seem organized?					
20. Do you know when work is due?					
21. Are deadlines reasonable?					
22. Are you aware of your progress in this class?					
23. Do you understand the class rules and procedures?					
Time to integrate learning					
24. Do I allow enough time for questions?					
25. Is there enough review time before a test?					
26. Is there enough practice on each skill before going on to a new one?					

Have postive contact with peers

27. Are other students accepting of your ideas?

28. Do people listen carefully to whomever is speaking?

29. Do students in this class help each other?

Receive instruction matched to skill level and learning style

30. Are most of the assignments in class challenging to you?

31. Do you feel that you have a variety of choices for exhibiting your knowledge?

32. Does the way I teach help you learn the material?

continued

Activity 3.3 continued.

To complete this activity, administer the questionnaire provided or modify it to fit the skill level of the children completing the form. Tally the results as suggested in Figure 2.3. When the results have been tallied, analyze the data by completing these items:

1. List all the statements that more than five students responded to with the responses "Always true" or "Most of the Time."
2. List all the statements to which a majority of students responded with the responses "Occasionally" or "Never True."
3. Write three responses to the statement: "I learned that. . . ."
4. Based on this new information, write three statements about changes you would like to make in your classroom.

RECOMMENDED READING

Ault, R. (1977). *Children's cognitive development*. New York: Oxford University Press.

Bybee, R., and Sund, R. (1982). *Piaget for educators*. Columbus, Ohio: Charles E. Merrill.

DeCharms, R. (1976). *Enhancing motivation*. New York: Irvington.

Dewey, J. (1963). *Experience and education*. New York: Macmillan.

Dunn, R., and Dunn, K. (1978). *Teaching students through their individual learning styles: A practical approach*. Reston, Va.: Reston.

Edwards, B. (1979). *Drawing on the right side of the brain*. Boston: Houghton Mifflin.

Fox, R., Luszki, M., and Schmuck, R. (1966). *Diagnosing classroom learning environments*. Chicago: Science Research Associates.

Hart, L. (1983). *Human brain and human learning*. New York: Longman.

Holt, J. (1967). *How children learn*. New York: Dell.

Johnson, D., and Johnson, R. (1975). *Learning together and alone: Cooperation, competition and individualization*. Englewood Cliffs, N.J.: Prentice-Hall.

McCarthy B. (1980). *The 4-MAT system: Teaching to learning styles with right/left mode techniques*. Oak Brook, Ill.: Excel.

Rogers, C. (1969). *Freedom to learn*. Columbus, Ohio: Charles Merrill.

Rotalo, S. (1982). *Right-brain lesson plans for a left-brain world—A book of lesson plans for English and speech*. Springfield, Ill.: Charles C. Thomas, Publisher.

Silberman, C. (1970). *Crisis in the classroom: The remaking of American education*. New York: Random House.

Slavin, R. (1983). *Cooperative learning*. New York: Longman.

Toepfer, C. (1983). Brain growth periodization data: Some suggestions for rethinking middle school education. *High School Journal*. 63, 222–227.

MOTIVATING LEARNING AND MINIMIZING DISRUPTIVE BEHAVIOR BY CREATING POSITIVE INTERPERSONAL RELATIONSHIPS IN THE CLASSROOM

It has been said that an ounce of prevention is worth a pound of cure, and the statement is the key to effective classroom management. A large percentage of classroom problems can be prevented by creating positive, safe classroom environments. Books on classroom management all too often are focused on techniques for modifying individual students' behavior through a system of rewards and punishments, while failing to acknowledge the vital role the social atmosphere plays in influencing students' behavior. Unfortunately, this major oversight frequently creates situations in which students are manipulated into behaving appropriately in environments that do not meet their basic psychological or academic needs. This approach is not only thoughtless and unfair to students, but also creates a situation in which the new behavior is maintained only as long as desired rewards are present. Therefore, we can understand why programs based solely on behavioristic interventions have had limited success in generalizing behavior change to new environments.

In Part II we focus on specific methods for preventing unproductive student behavior by creating positive interpersonal relationships in the classroom and throughout the school. These methods are important because they help to create environments in which students feel happy and excited about learning. This atmosphere, in turn, tends to elicit more positive student behavior and to facilitate learning. Because the school's primary goal is to transmit knowledge, it seems logical to assume that schools should create learning environments that allow all students to view the acquisition of knowledge as an exciting, enjoyable activity. Unless we create such environments, we will continue to find that many students see learning as a solemn and difficult task to be engaged in only when appropriate rewards or punishments exist and to be terminated as soon as possible. In a democratic society characterized by amazingly rapid change, this attitude creates not only poor mental health but also citizens who cannot adequately govern themselves.

Educators should be aware of the dangers inherent in the completely un-substantiated belief that time spent in creating classrooms in which students feel involved, safe, and happy could somehow be better spent in additional instructional time. As we saw in Part I, students' academic performance is enhanced when we take time to respond to their personal and psychological needs. Research (Purkey & Novak, 1984; Johnson & Johnson, 1984; Soar, 1983; Walberg & Waxman, 1983) indicates that positive affect is associated with im-proved student attitudes and higher-level thinking skills. Another important reason for blending academic and personal-social skill building is that if schools' goals include preparing young people to be involved citizens, activi-ties aimed at developing a sound base of knowledge must be balanced with skills in interpersonal relations and problem solving.

In Chapter 4 we examine two pivotal aspects of teacher–student rela-tionships: (1) the personal, affective quality of these relationships, and (2) ways in which we communicate expectations to students. Chapter 5 is focused on the quality of peer relationships within classrooms. The chapter provides numerous activities for enhancing positive, cooperative peer relationships. Parents can do much to encourage positive student attitudes toward school, and in Chapter 6 we examine methods you can employ to create positive, sup-portive relationships with parents.

CHAPTER 4

Establishing Positive Teacher–Student Relationships

It seems to the writer that the most important single factor in establish-ing sound mental health is the relationship that is built up between the teacher and his or her pupils.

Virginia Axline, (1947),
Play Therapy

Teachers retain their effectiveness as professional persons only so long as they remain warmly human, sensitive to the personal needs of chil-dren, and skillful in establishing effective relationships with them.

Robert Bush, (1954),
The Teacher–Pupil Relationship

The quality of teacher–student relationships dramatically affects whether students' personal needs are met in the classroom. Students spend nearly a quarter of their waking lives between ages six and seven-teen with teachers. Because teachers are responsible for evaluating students' work and controlling the quality of life in the classroom, they are powerful adult figures in students' lives. Effective teachers under-stand the influence they have on students and use this influence posi-tively. An increasing body of research and theory provides teachers with helpful guidelines for using their influence to enhance students' feelings of worth, their motivation, and their achievement.

The teacher–student relationship is very important for students. Young people spend between six and seven hours a day (between 40 and 50 percent of their waking hours) for almost half of the days each year in schools. By the time a youngster reaches sixth grade he or she has spent more than 7,000 hours with teachers. The significance of the teacher–student relationship is also influenced by the simple fact that adults are very important to children. Children depend on adults to provide them with the essentials of food, shelter, and protection. Adults also provide children with satisfaction of such important psychological needs as love, structure, and modeling of important social behaviors. Furthermore, adults possess an immense amount of information that young people find exciting and desirable. Adults hold the answers to many of the "why" questions students ask. Young people also depend upon adults for satisfaction of a variety of less essential, but nevertheless important needs such as entertainment, transportation, and spending money. In a very real sense, adults control the rewards and punishments that control young people's lives. Because they control the satisfaction of essential physical and psychological needs, adults clearly possess the power to hurt or to sensitively guide students. The extent of teachers' influence over students is intensified by their view of our possessing considerable knowledge and responsibility for evaluating their knowledge, social skills, and attitudes.

A significant body of research indicates that academic achievement and students' behavior are influenced by the quality of the teacher–student relationship. Students prefer teachers who are warm and friendly (Rosenshine, 1970; Norman & Harris, 1981). More important, positive teacher–student relationships, in which teachers employ the skills described in this chapter, are associated with more positive student responses to school (Aspy & Roebuck, 1977; Conger, 1977; Norman & Harris, 1981) and increased academic achievement (Aspy, 1969, 1972; Aspy & Roebuck, 1977; Berensen, 1971; Brookover, et al., 1978; Brophy & Evertson, 1976; Davidson & Lang, 1960; Hefele, 1971; Kleinfield, 1975; Rosenshine & Furst, 1973; Soar, 1977; Stallings, 1975; Stoffer, 1970). Davidson and Lang (1960) reported that students who felt liked by their teachers had higher academic achievement and more productive classroom behavior than students who felt their teachers held them in lower regard. Similarly, Morrison and McIntyre (1969) reported that 73 percent of the low-achieving students in their study perceived their teachers as thinking poorly of them, but only 10 percent of high achievers held such beliefs. When examining students' adjustment, Truax and Tatum (1966) found that children adjusted more positively to school, teachers, and peers when teachers displayed empathy and positive regard for children.

An excellent example of the importance of combining acceptance with respect for students was reported by Kleinfeld (1972) in a powerful analysis of teachers' interactions with Eskimo and Indian students who had recently moved to urban settings. Kleinfeld found that teachers who were effective with these children were able to combine showing a personal interest in the students with demands for solid academic achievement. Summarizing her findings, she states:

... The essence of the instructional style which elicits a high level of intellectual performance from village Indian and Eskimo students is to create an extremely warm personal relationship and to actively demand a level of academic work which the student does not suspect he can attain. Village students thus interpret the teacher's demandingness not as bossiness or hostility, but rather as another expression of his personal concern, and meeting the teacher's academic standards becomes their reciprocal obligation in an intensely personal relationship. [Kleinfeld, 1972, p. 34]

Support for the importance of improving teacher–student relationships can also be found in numerous studies indicating that teachers demonstrate a low rate of positive statements when working with children (Brophy, 1981; Greenwood & Hops, 1976; Luce & Hoge, 1978; Thomas, Presland, Grant & Glynn, 1978; White, 1975).

In general, praise for appropriate and desired behavior is a rare event, particularly between adult and child. Studies of natural rates of teacher praise and approval to individual children have shown them to be extremely low in an absolute sense and also in relation to other categories of teacher behavior. [Walker, 1979, p. 95]

In her *Successful Schools for Young Adolescents*, Joan Lipsitz (1984) remarked that successful schools for this age group provide a warm, personal environment. Describing these schools, Lipsitz writes:

Gradually, students gain increasing amounts of independence. They remain, however, in a highly personalized environment. The nature of the schools' organizational structure establishes continuity in adult–child relationships and opportunities for the lives of students and adults to cross in mutually meaningful ways. In each school, students express their appreciation for being cared about and known. They are actively aware of being liked, which is notable only because, in most schools, young adolescents are generally disliked. [p. 181]

Taken together, this research points to a real need for teachers to learn and conscientiously apply skills in relating more positively to their students.

Fortunately, research (Aspy & Roebuck, 1977) demonstrates that teachers' behavior in the area of interpersonal relationships can be significantly changed by in-service training. Furthermore, these changes can positively affect students' attendance, achievement, and self-concept.

In examining children's behavior from a behavioristic perspective, we can say that teachers control the consequences (rewards and punishments) that influence children's behavior during a significant number of hours each day. Because we selectively reinforce desired behaviors, we have a major influence on students' behavior. The quality of the teacher–student relationship significantly influences the value children place on reinforcers controlled by the teacher. Behavioristic concepts stress the importance of social reinforcement (praise) and specify that when tangible or token reinforcers are needed to influence students' behavior, we must pair these with social reinforcement so that the child gradually begins to respond to our praise. How well students will respond to either concrete reinforcers dispensed by the teacher or to teachers' praise, however, is very much based on the quality of the teacher–student relationship.

Modeling theory provides another approach to the significance of a teacher's role and the importance of the teacher–student relationship. Children learn a great deal by watching adults. Much of children's behavior is developed by emulating the behaviors of adults who play significant roles in their lives.

> One of the most salient developments in American social psychology during the past decade has been what for many laymen appears as a demonstration of the obvious; namely, children learn by watching others. Or, to put the issue in more provocative form: the behavior of others is contagious. [Bronfenbrenner, 1970, p. 124]

Bronfenbrenner also reported that young people are more likely to model behavior that is exhibited by several adults. Furthermore, youngsters tend to model behaviors if they think adults benefit from the performance of these behaviors. The latter factors directly demonstrate the importance of creating schools in which a large percentage of adults demonstrate the skills and attitudes described in this chapter, and in which teachers are reinforced by their peers and administrators for exhibiting these skills.

PLACING TEACHER–STUDENT RELATIONSHIPS IN PERSPECTIVE

Before presenting specific approaches for improving teacher–student relationships, we must place this issue in a proper perspective. The quality of teacher–student relationships has great influence upon the amount of productive or disruptive behavior students display in a school setting. By improving the quality of our interactions with students, we can significantly increase the amount of productive student behavior. Creating positive teacher–student relationships, however, will obviously not solve all classroom problems. We must be careful not to confuse the importance of establishing positive teacher–student relationships with the belief that all classroom problems can be solved by love and understanding. Regardless of how concerned, positive, and fair a teacher is, students frequently misbehave in classes that are poorly organized and in which students are not provided with appropriate and interesting instructional tasks.

Furthermore, as anyone who has taught for very long realizes, students need and want positive teacher behavior to be associated with firmness, realistic limits, and competent teaching. The ability to blend warmth and caring with realistic limits is frequently a difficult task for young teachers. Unfortunately, this confusion is occasionally intensified by advice suggesting that beginning teachers should be less warm toward and more distant from their students. The main issue is not whether teachers should be less warm or friendly, but that they must simultaneously assert both their right to be treated with respect and their responsibility for ensuring that students treat each other with kindness. Warmth and concern can exist side by side with firmness. Indeed, effective teaching involves blending these vital ingredients.

EVALUATING THE QUALITY OF TEACHER–STUDENT RELATIONSHIPS

Before implementing any of the varied behaviors that you can employ to create more positive teacher–student relationships, you should evaluate the current quality of your own interactions with students. Just as effective teaching involves both a diagnostic and a prescriptive component, any decision to alter our behavior will be aided by first assessing the students' reaction to the current behavior. This approach enables us to focus changes in areas where students' feedback suggests that changes may be needed in order to improve teacher–student relationships. Figures 4.1 and 4.2 present forms that many teachers have found useful in assessing the quality of their relationships with their students.

FIGURE 4.1   Questionnaire

Check the appropriate box	Home run	3rd base	2nd base	1st base	Strike-out!
1. Am I courteous toward you?					
2. Do I treat the students fairly?					
3. Am I honest?					
4. Do I touch you?					
5. Do you seem excited about my teaching?					
6. Do I talk over problems with you?					
7. Are you praised for your work?					
8. Am I patient and understanding?					
9. Do I keep my temper?					

continued

FIGURE 4.1   Questionnaire

Check the appropriate box	Home run	3rd base	2nd base	1st base	Strike-out!
10. Do I listen to you when you want to talk?					
11. Am I polite?					
12. Do you think that I like you?					
13. Am I too strict with the class?					
14. Do I seem happy?					
15. Am I willing to admit I am wrong?					
16. Can you trust me?					
17. Do I embarrass you?					
18. Do I listen to your suggestions?					
19. Do I expect too much from you?					
20. Do I smile at you?					
21. Am I friendly?					
22. Am I a good sport?					
23. Do I have sense of humor?					
24. Do I show appreciation for special things you do?					
25. Do I encourage you?					
26. Can you ask me questions?					
27. Do I have any nervous habits?					
28. Do I help you when you need it?					

Check the appropriate box	Home run	3rd base	2nd base	1st base	Strike-out!
29. Do I give you helpful feedback?					
30. Do I look at you when I talk to you?					
31. Do I share my feelings?					
32. Do I think you can do your work?					

Thank you for completing this questionnaire. Your responses help me evaluate my teaching.

COMMENTS

thank you!

FIGURE 4.2   Teacher–student relationship evaluation form

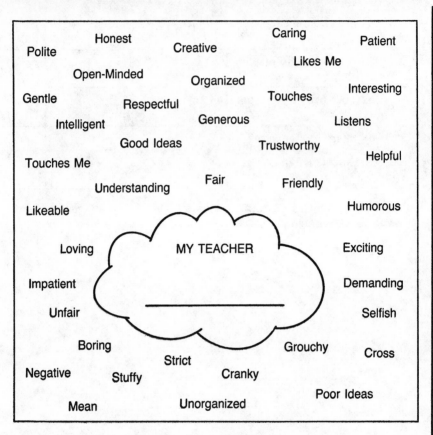

Circle the words that describe your teacher.

Circle in red if the words describe your teacher most of the time.
Circle in blue if the words describe your teacher sometimes.
Circle in green if the words seldom describe your teacher.
Cirlce in orange if the words never describe your teacher.

Although information collected by individual teachers provides more specific information, when students work with several teachers each day it is useful to periodically assess students' general attitude toward adults in the school. Many student attitude surveys include items that provide a school staff with such information. While working on this book, one of us conducted a school assessment for a middle school that was experiencing significant problems with students' achievement, students' behavior, and community support. As part of the assessment, students were asked to complete the DEMOS

FIGURE 4.3   Students' perceptions of teachers: Percentage of students responding "nearly always" or "most of the time"

Question	6th grade	7th grade	8th grade
Teachers understand the problems of students	37	33	20
Teachers care about students	76	43	41
The Principal and Vice-Principal help the students	43	32	21
Teachers pick on some students	25	40	51
Teachers give most of their help and attention to the good students	31	36	51
A student can get help from a teacher	50	43	25

D scale (a dropout-prediction scale developed by George Demos). Figure 4.3 shows the results of the items directly related to the quality of teacher–student relationships.

The data presented in Figure 4.3 show a dramatic pattern of students who have spent more time in the school perceiving teachers as less understanding, caring, helpful, and fair professionals. Though slight decreases in students' attitudes might be expected as youngsters move into early and mid-adolescence, our work in middle schools suggests that significant changes are unusual. When such changes do occur, they are inevitably associated with lower achievement and greater student misbehavior.

The results of this survey led the staff to include in their school-improvement plans considerable effort to incorporate many of the skills discussed in this chapter. Tentative results indicate that these changes have significantly influenced students' attitudes, achievement, and behavior.

ACTIVITY 4.1   Evaluating the teacher–student relationship

Have every student in your class(es) complete the form in Figure 4.1 or a similar form you devise.

Tabulate the results so that you have a summary of all students' responses. Keep in mind that one or two low statements may indicate that a change is needed with only several students. Five or more low statements suggest, though, that a major change may help to improve your relationships with students.

continued

After tabulating the results, complete these statements:

I learned that . . .
I was surprised that . .
I was pleased that . . .
I was disappointed that . . .
I would like to change the fact that . . .

EMPLOYING EFFECTIVE COMMUNICATION SKILLS

The importance of employing effective communication skills cannot be over-emphasized. The use of effective communication skills is the foundation for good classroom management. Unless we employ effective communication skills, all other attempts at creating a well-managed, positive learning environment will be severely limited and usually short-lived. Caring interpersonal interactions are essential in meeting such important individual needs as safety and security, belongingness, and self-esteem.

In addition to creating relationships that meet essential student needs, using effective communication skills benefits us by allowing us to more effectively meet our own personal needs and simultaneously achieve our professional goals. Using the skills presented in this section enables us to:

1. be warm and friendly and enjoy relationships with students,
2. clearly express our own needs and wants within the classroom,
3. better understand and accept students and experience more positive feelings toward them, and
4. create situations in which students feel understood and cared for and therefore respond more positively to us and to their peers.

Communication skills can be divided into the two categories of sending skills and receiving skills. Sending skills are those commonly employed when speaking to someone. Receiving skills are techniques that can be used to become a more effective listener.

Before examining the communication skills presented in this section, realize that the effective use of these skills is based on specific beliefs about children and the goals and roles adults choose to follow when working with children. The use of communication skills is based on these premises:

1. We wish to share with students responsibility for resolving problems.
2. We believe that students are, for the most part, responsible individuals when the atmosphere is conducive to their being so.
3. We accept that there can be more than one perspective to a problem and consider perspectives other than our own to be valid.
4. We do not perceive our objective in a teacher–student confrontation as being "to win."

Implementing the skills outlined in this chapter will help you meet your needs and reach important educational goals. The effective use of these skills, however, depends on your acceptance of these four premises.

Before presenting specific communication skills that assist us in developing open, effective relationships with students, it is useful to consider the various types of teacher–student relationships we may choose. In an earlier work (Jones, 1980) one of us wrote that teachers can select from among three general types of teacher–student relationships. Although teacher–student relationships vary on numerous dimensions, a primary factor involves the level of openness we choose. We can choose a teacher–student relationship characterized by:

1. almost complete openness, in which we share a wide range of personal concerns and values with students,
2. openness related to our reactions to and feelings about the school environment, with limited sharing of aspects reflecting our out-of-school life, and
3. an almost exclusive focus on a role-bound relationship; that is, we share no personal feelings or reactions, but merely perform our instructional duties.

The choice we make on how to relate to students will depend on our own personalities, the school setting, the students' age, and perhaps community factors. For example, many teachers working in secondary alternative schools choose very open, self-disclosing relationships with students. Conversely, primary-grade teachers, while being very warm and supportive with their children, may choose to employ a very limited amount of open communication. In general, students prefer and learn best when working with warm, concerned teachers whom students perceive as willing to go out of their way to assist them in the learning process (Conger & Petersen, 1984; Purkey & Novak, 1984; Rutter, 1979). Our own experiences support the value of teachers' employing open communication at least at the second level described above.

If we wish to monitor the classroom environment and adjust it according to students' needs, we must be willing to encourage and even systematically seek students' feedback. We must be willing to become involved in openly discussing our own and the students' reactions to how the classroom is operating. A central theme of this book is that effective classroom managers are aware of classroom processes and are willing and able to engage students in assessing and adjusting classroom procedures and instructional methods. This act involves not only our own awareness and self-analysis, but also involving students in open dialogue and problem solving.

An interesting example of the decision we must make about openness to student feedback occurred while this book was being written. A student–teacher being supervised by one of us was challenged by a student in his sophomore biology class. Frustrated by his inability to understand a lecture, the student stood up at the back of the class and stated loudly, "This class stinks!"

Rather than sending the student to the office, the teacher responded by stating that, though he wished the student would share his frustration in a more polite manner, he was glad that he was able to state his anger rather than simply not come to class. The teacher proceeded to inform the student that he would like to discuss the student's concern, but that first he needed to determine whether it was shared by a majority of the class or only a few students. The teacher's inquiry indicated that only three students shared this concern. Therefore, the teacher indicated that it made better sense for him and the three students to work together to consider how to make the class better for them. The student responded positively, and several discussions led to a positive resolution.

An interesting sidelight to this story involved the supervising teacher's reaction. The teacher, a veteran of teaching in low-income-area schools, firmly informed the student–teacher that if he wished to maintain students' respect and order in the classroom, the only acceptable response to this type of disruption was to immediately and firmly send the student to the office and to inform the class that any additional outbursts would be similarly handled.

A third option was offered by a friend of ours who is a highly skilled physical education teacher. This teacher indicated that she agreed that the student should be immediately dismissed from the class. She said, however, that this action should be taken firmly yet politely, and that the student should know that he would, at a later time, be provided an opportunity to discuss his concerns and behavior.

The different reactions chosen by these three teachers exemplifies the decision we must make on the level of openness to students' input we select. Throughout this book, we provide strategies you can employ should you choose to accept open dialogue and an interactive process in the classroom. Similarly, many of the ideas presented can be employed by teachers who select a somewhat less open and role-bound style. Regardless of which approach you select, the key is to be aware of the choice that has been made and to thoughtfully select and implement classroom–management methods that enable you to effectively and consistently implement these methods.

You can use the communication skills described in the following sections regardless of your decision on the degree of teacher control. If you choose a more open, interactive classroom–management style, however, you will find these skills particularly important in effectively developing your classroom–management skills.

Sending Skills

The sending skills that are most essential in working with children include:

Deal in the Present
Information is more useful when it is shared at the earliest appropriate opportunity. Young people are very "now" oriented. It is unfair and ineffective to

bring up issues after several days have elapsed. Therefore, though it may be necessary to wait until you can speak with the student alone or until the student has better control of his or her emotions, it is best to discuss important matters as soon after they occur as possible.

Talk Directly to Students Rather Than About Them

Adults have a tendency to talk to parents or colleagues about students rather than talking directly to the student. The assumption seems to be that students could not understand or would be overpowered by the information. Our experiences strongly contradict these beliefs. Indeed, it appears that students suffer more from worrying about what has been said about them than they ever do from receiving skillfully presented direct feedback. By talking directly to students, we show respect for them while ensuring that they receive accurate (rather than second-hand) information about adults' feelings.

Speak Courteously

Nothing does more to create positive interactions than employing simple courtesy statements such as "thank you," "please," and "excuse me." Because teachers serve as important models for students, their interactions with them should include more (certainly not less) frequent use of courtesies than do their interactions with other adults.

Make Eye Contact and Be Aware of Nonverbal Messages

An old saying states that children often respond more to what adults do than to what they say. Because young people are so dependent upon adults, they become adept at reading adults' nonverbal messages. It is therefore very important that we attempt to make our nonverbal messages congruent with our verbal messages. If you are talking to a student but looking over their shoulder, the student will find it difficult to believe that you feel positive about her or him and are sincerely concerned. Similarly, when we shout that we are not angry with a class, the students will be more likely to listen to the tone of voice than to the words.

Take Responsibility for Statements by Using the Personal Pronoun "I"

In their *Discovering Your Teaching Self,* Curwin and Fuhrman (1975) provide a succinct and sensitive statement about this skill:

> Meaningful communication between people (the communication between adults and children is of special interest to us) often breaks down because one party (or both) continually tells the other what's wrong with him rather than identifying how he himself is feeling in the situation. When I tell someone what's wrong with him, I virtually take away from him all responsibility for himself. Since I know what is wrong, I also know how to "correct" it. Thus I leave him powerless and probably defensive. [p. 196]

If we say to a student, "You are being disruptive," or "You're late again!" the student is likely to feel attacked and defensive. If, however, we say, "It distracts me and I feel uncomfortable when you talk while I am talking (or when you come in late)," the student has been provided with some useful information about his or her effect on other people. Similarly, using the pronoun "we" is unfairly ganging up against a student. When confronted with statements beginning with "we feel" or "the entire class believes," the student is likely to feel attacked and defeated. Though they are flexible, children are also very sensitive and need to be confronted by one person at a time. Furthermore, because each of us is an expert on only our own feelings, it appears reasonable that each of us should share our own feelings and dispense with the pronoun "we."

In his *Teacher Effectiveness Training* (TET), Thomas Gordon (1974) writes that when expressing a concern about students' behavior that affects the teacher, the teacher should employ an "I" message consisting of three components: (1) the personal pronoun "I," (2) the feeling the teacher is experiencing, and (3) the effect the student's behavior is having on the teacher. For example, a typical teachers' response to a student's interruption might be, "If you can't stop interrupting me, you can leave the room." If we employed an "I" message in this situation, we might say "When you interrupt me I become frustrated because I get distracted and have difficulty helping the other students."

Because "I" messages express personal feelings and often deal with student behaviors that require change, it is best to send them privately. We should do so especially when we are dealing with adolescents. Adolescents, being particularly sensitive to peer pressure, will often respond to even the most thoughtful public criticism defensively. Because most adolescents value being treated as adults, though, they will usually respond positively to private expressions of our concern.

Another, less open, way to send an "I" message involves politely yet firmly expressing a demand utilizing the first person singular. Therefore, if a student began talking to another student during a teacher's presentation, the teacher might say in a nonthreatening manner, "I expect students to listen quietly while someone in this class speaks." Although this type of "I" message will more likely elicit a defensive response from older students, it is a clear, straightforward way to present your expectations.

Give Specific Descriptive, Nonevaluative Feedback

Feedback is most useful when it clearly describes what a child has done and does not evaluate or judge the behavior. If a student is constantly talking out, it would be effective to respond by stating, "When you talk to other students while I am talking I find it hard to lead the discussion." Compare this response to a general, evaluative statement such as, "You are so rude in class, it is hard to believe." The first statement provides the student with specific information; the latter is too general and borders on name calling.

When discussing teachers' feedback, teachers inevitably ask: How much praise should I give? and How is praise most effectively presented? The answer to the first question is probably somewhat more but not too much.

Based on results of a three year study involving data collection in more than 100 fourth-, sixth-, and eighth-grade classrooms, Sadker and Sadker (1985) express concern about the quantity and quality of teachers' feedback to students. These researchers found that teachers demonstrated low rates of praise or criticism and high rates of acceptance. "Acceptance included teacher comments that implied that student performance was correct and appropriate. . . (Examples include: "O.K.," "uh-huh," "I see," or simply teacher silence)" (Sadker & Sadker, 1985, p. 360). The Sadkers' main interpretation of their findings was that teacher feedback was too bland. They found that "In two-thirds of the classrooms observed, teachers never clearly indicated that a student answer was incorrect" (p. 360). Similarly, only 11 percent of teacher feedback involved praise, and in more than one-fourth of the classrooms, teachers never praised students' answers. These findings regarding the general lack of critical or specific feedback are reinforced by data reported by Goodlad (1984) indicating that 20 percent of both elementary and secondary students stated that they were neither informed nor corrected following a mistake. The Sadker's also expressed concern about the finding that in nearly half the classrooms observed a few students received three times their share of teacher–student interactions and that 25 percent of students in all classes observed were not involved in any classroom interaction. On a more positive note, the researchers report that nearly one-third of all teacher feedback involved remediative comments including, ". . . probing questions and teacher comments that encouraged or cued a more acceptable or more accurate student response" (p. 360).

We should distribute praise more evenly so that not only high-achieving students or students with the social skills to elicit praise from us receive praise. In fact, research (Brophy & Evertson, 1976; Good, Ebmeier, & Beckerman, 1978; Soar, 1975; Stallings, 1975) suggests that praise is more effective with lower-SES students and low-achieving students—the very students who research suggests receive the least praise. Praise is also a more effective reinforcer for primary students.

When considering how to praise, O'Leary and O'Leary (1977) state that to serve as an effective reinforcer, praise must have three qualities:

(1) *Contingency:* Praise must immediately follow desired behaviors rather than being applied simply as a general motivator. Anderson et al. (1979) found that teachers failed to use praise contingently because the rate of praise following reading turns that contained mistakes was similar to the rate following correct responses.

(2) *Specificity:* Praise should describe the specific behavior being reinforced. Again, Anderson et al. (1979) suggest that teachers needed improvement in this area. Their data showed that teachers were specific in only 5 percent of their praise for academic work and 40 percent of their praise for behavior.

(3) *Credibility:* Praise should be appropriate for the situation and the individual. Older, high-achieving students are aware that praise is used primarily

for motivation and encouragement and may find praise unnecessary and even insulting.

Specific information on how to employ praise more effectively can be found in Jere Brophy's (1981) work on praise. Figure 4.4 presents Brophy's summary of how to effectively praise students.

FIGURE 4.4   Guidelines for effective praise

Effective praise	Ineffective praise
1. is delivered contingently	1. is delivered randomly or unsystematically
2. specifies the particulars of the accomplishment	2. is restricted to global positive reactions
3. shows spontaneity, variety, and other signs of credibility: suggests clear attention to the student's accomplishment	3. shows a bland uniformity that suggests a conditioned response made with minimal attention
4. rewards attainment of specified performance criteria (which can include effort criteria)	4. rewards mere participation without consideration of performance processes or outcomes
5. provides information to students about their competence or the value of their accomplishment	5. provides no information at all or gives students information about their status
6. orients students toward better appreciation of their own task-related behavior and thinking about problem solving	6. orients students toward comparing themselves with others and thinking about competing
7. uses student's own prior accomplishments as the context for describing present accomplishments	7. uses the accomplishments of peers as the context for describing students' present accomplishments
8. is given in recognition of noteworthy effort or success at difficult (for this student) tasks	8. is given without regard to the effort expended or the meaning of the accomplishment (for this student)
9. attritubes success to effort and ability, implying that similar successes can be expected in the future	9. attributes success to ability alone or to external factors such as luck or (easy) task difficulty
10. fosters endogenous attributions (students believe they expend effort on task because they enjoy it and/or want to develop task-relevant skills)	10. fosters exogenous attributions (students believe they expend effort on the task for external reasons—to please the teacher, win a competition or reward, etc.)

Effective praise	Ineffective praise
11. focuses students' attention on their own task-relevant behavior	11. focuses students' attention on the teacher as an external authority figure who is manipulating them
12. fosters appreciation of, and desirable attributions about, task-relevant behavior after the process is completed	12. intrudes into the ongoing process, distracting attention from task-relevant behavior

From Jere E. Brophy, "Teacher Praise: A Functional Analysis." *Review of Educational Research* (Spring 1981): 5, 32. Washington, DC: American Educational Research Association, 1981. Reprinted by permission.

The research on praise is supported by work in what has been called attribution theory (Anderson & Prawat, 1983; Weiner, 1979). According to Weiner (1979), students attribute their success or failure to: ability, effort, luck, or difficulty of task. If students attribute their success or failure to effort, they are able to view their performance as influenced by factors within their control (an internal locus of control) and are therefore able to expect success in similar situations if they make the effort (Andrews & Debus, 1978; Harter & Connell, 1981). When failure is attributed, however, to ability, luck, or difficulty of task, students feel less control over results and begin to believe that making a concerted effort in the future will have little effect on the outcome. Praise that helps students focus on factors within their control that influenced performance allows students to develop on internal locus of control.

Make Statements Rather Than Asking Questions

When children misbehave, they are frequently bombarded with questions. This approach leaves the child feeling intimidated and defensive. Questions such as "Are you feeling all right?" "Would you like to leave the room for a few minutes?" or "Can I help?" can be extremely productive. Teachers should, however, be aware of opportunities for replacing questions with statements. Consider the different feelings a child might have upon coming late to class and hearing "Where have you been?" compared to "I was concerned when you were late because we have to leave on our field trip in five minutes." It is important to keep in mind that questions are often important tools for helping children understand and change their behavior. Asking students what they were doing or how their behavior helped them is an important component in solving problems. Questions often misdirect students from taking responsibility for their own behavior, however, while creating defensiveness. Therefore, when dealing with students' behaviors, use questions sparingly and in the context of a problem-solving approach.

Maintain a High Ratio of Positive to Negative Statements

Children are sensitive to praise and criticism given by adults. Unfortunately, many teachers find that disruptive behavior is more noticeable, and therefore respond to it more frequently than to on-task behavior. As indicated in Figure 2.1, frequent negative remarks by the teacher are usually accompanied by students' dislike for school. Though we often fall into the trap of believing that critical remarks will improve students' behavior, research suggests that quite the opposite is true.

> In one study we took a good class and made it into a bad one for a few weeks by having the teacher no longer praise the children. When the teacher no longer praised the children, off-task behavior increased from 8.7 percent to 25.5 percent. The teacher criticized off-task behavior and did not praise on-task behavior. When the teacher was asked to increase her criticism from 5 times in 20 minutes to 16 times in 20 minutes, the children showed even more off-task behavior. Off-task behavior increased to an average of 31.2 percent, and on some days was over 50 percent. Attention to the off-task behavior increased its occurrence when no praise was given for working. Introduction of praise back into the classroom restored good working behavior. [Becker, Engelmann, & Thomas, 1975, p. 69]

Most children need and want attention from their teacher. If they find that it is easier to obtain this attention by negative actions they will understandably increase the frequency of such behavior. Unfortunately, this interchange not only negatively affects the student's self-concept but also creates a ripple effect that often produces a generally negative classroom atmosphere. In a very real sense teachers in such cases are actually responsible for increasing unproductive student behavior.

In a more positive vein, attending to on-task behavior and increasing the ratio of positive to negative statements can increase on-task behavior and quite rapidly create a more positive classroom environment. In his *Inviting School Success,* William Purkey (1978) discusses the benefits of teachers' sending inviting rather than disinviting statements to students. In defining these terms Purkey writes:

> As used here, an invitation is a summary description of message—verbal and nonverbal, formal and informal—continuously transmitted to students with the intention of informing them that they are responsible, able, and valuable. Conversely, a disinvitation is intended to tell them that they are irresponsible, incapable, and worthless. [p. 3]

Purkey explains the importance of inviting statements when he writes:

> Rather than viewing students as physical objects to be moved about like puppets on strings, the teacher's primary role is to see students in essentially positive ways and to invite them to behave accordingly. Students, like all of us, greatly benefit from others who see and communicate to them the positive traits and potentials that they may not see in themselves. . . . Judging by what we now know about school life, an invitational approach to education very likely increases the probability of student success and happiness in the classroom. [pp. vi, vii]

An example of a disinviting statement was recently provided by a high school vice principal. He stated that the day before finals week began, he observed a student requesting assistance from a teacher. The teacher's response: "Don't worry, you haven't got a chance of passing the test anyway" was devastatingly disinviting. Conversely, a teacher reported hearing a colleague respond to a similar request, "I'm glad you came in Jeremiah, I believe that if you study this you can earn the grade you want." This inviting comment evoked a wide smile from the student and could be expected to contribute to an increased effort. If we wish to create positive environments in which students feel safe, respected, significant, and competent, it is imperative that we make far more inviting than disinviting statements.

Activities for Improving Sending Skills

It is easy to react positively to ideas and yet never take the time or risk to incorporate these into our repertoire. The activities presented below are intended to help you practice the sending skills discussed in this section. Even teachers who frequently employ these skills will find that the structured practice will improve their awareness of and fluency in implementing these skills.

ACTIVITY 4.2   Talking directly to children rather than about them

1. During a two-day period, list every statement (positive or negative) you make to an adult about a child.
2. In front of each statement, write either "yes" or "no" to indicate whether or not the content of the statement was shared with the child.
3. For each statement with a no placed in front of it, write out a statement that you could have made to the child.

ACTIVITY 4.3   Monitoring courteous remarks

1. Make a tally of the courteous remarks you make to students during a one-day period. You may want to carry a counter or a small note pad.
2. If you used fewer than 25 such statements (recall that research indicates that elementary teachers have approximately 1,000 interactions with children each day), try to double the number the next day.
3. Briefly write (or discuss with a colleague) how it felt to increase the number of courteous statements. Did your students respond any differently the second day?

ACTIVITY 4.4   Sending "I" messages

1. To test your knowledge of "I" messages, change each of these five
    statements into an "I" message:
    a.   Late again! What's the matter with you?
    b.   I don't want to hear another word out of anyone.
    c.   No book again? How do you expect to learn anything?
    d.   How can you be so inconsiderate as to stand there drinking
          water for so long when you know other children want a drink?
    e.   If you get in trouble on the playground one more time you can
          miss the rest of your recesses this month!
    If you have difficulty with this task, consult a colleague or refer to
    Thomas Gordon's *TET: Teacher Effectiveness Training.*
2. Tape-record your classroom for at least one hour. While listening to
    the tape, list all the "I" messages you sent and all the "you" or "we"
    messages you sent. Next, change all the "you" or "we" statements
    to "I" messages. Finally, repeat the activity and try to increase the
    ratio of "I" to "you" or "we" statements.

ACTIVITY 4.5   Giving useful oral feedback

Change each of these general statements into a statement that provides
the student with specific, nonevaluative feedback.

1. That's a nice picture, Susan.
2. Jimmy, your behavior on the playground was terrible.
3. Class, you were very rude during the assembly.
4. Erin, your penmanship has improved a lot since the last writing as-
    signment.
5. Bill, if you keep disrupting the class I will send you to the principal's
    office.

Write a specific example of effective and ineffective praise for each of the
twelve aspects of praise listed in Figure 4.4.
    From the list of twelve aspects of effective praise, select three you
believe would be most helpful in improving the quality of your praise. If
you are currently working with students, employ each of these at least
once a day over a five-day period.

ACTIVITY 4.6   Improving your positive–negative ratio

1. Have a student or colleague tally the positive and negative state-
    ments you make during a minimum of two hours of instructional
    time. Try to include several types of lessons and do not code more

than thirty minutes at a time. Especially when using students to tally remarks, it is helpful to define positive and negative statements and provide the coder with a list of commonly used positive and negative remarks. Neutral remarks such as statements related to instruction or comments such as "Okay," "Alright," or "Yes" should not be coded.

2. If your ratio of positive to negative statements was less than three to one, repeat the activity and try to focus on responding positively to productive student behavior. Following a period in which your ratio was very high, ask the students to evaluate the lesson.

3. Write ten inviting statements that you could employ in your teaching. During the next two teaching days, make at least ten inviting statements each day.

Inviting statements: Examples

a. I really enjoyed your presentation. Would you be willing to share it with the other fifth-grade class?
b. I'm really glad you're back and feeling better.
c. I'm very glad you are in my class this year.
d. Those are two good causes; can you think of any more?
e. Would you like some help with that work?

Inviting Statements: Your list

a.   f.
b.   g.
c.   h.
d.   i.
e.   j.

Receiving Skills

Listening skills are extremely important because when used effectively they create relationships that allow students to feel significant, accepted, respected, and able to take responsibility for their own behavior. By effectively employing listening skills, adults assist youngsters in clarifying their feelings and resolving their own conflicts. Unfortunately, adults all too often provide quick answers for children rather than carefully listening in order to assist the youngster in clarifying the problem and then aiding them in developing a solution. Stop for a moment and reflect upon the last several situations when a student came to you with a problem or expressed a strong emotion. What did you do? If you are like most adults, at least half of the time you provided a quick answer to the problem or attempted to stop the expression of emotion by providing assurances or by suggesting that the student should not be expressing the emotion. Both of these responses are commonly employed because they require a minimum of time and effort and prevent adults from having to deal with a youngster's emotions. When adults consistently provide answers, however, they subtly inform students that they do not care enough to really listen to them and do not trust their ability to resolve their own conflicts.

Before examining the major listening skills, we must clarify an important point. There are numerous instances (perhaps even a significant majority) during a school day when a student is merely requesting information. If a student requests permission to leave the room or asks for clarification of directions, it is appropriate to simply provide them with information. However, when students share personal problems, express confusion with their work, or display emotions, it is often most effective to initially employ one or more of the listening skills discussed in this section.

The primary goal of using listening skills is to help students express their real concern, need, or want. Students often initially make general, angry statements that disguise their real concerns. A student who says, "I hate this class" might be feeling frustration at his or her inability to understand the material or concern over lack of acceptance by peers. By employing the methods described in the following pages, you can assist the student in clarifying the underlying problem. Once the problem has been exposed, you must switch from merely listening to an active role in helping the student examine and solve the problem.

Empathic, Nonevaluative Listening

This skill involves providing the speaker with a sense that she or he has been clearly heard and that the feelings being expressed are acceptable. Several major benefits can be derived from employing these skills. First, students learn that their feelings are acceptable, which reduces the tension and anxiety associated with having to hide one's true feelings. This act in turn makes students feel more accepted. Second, when thoughts and feelings can be expressed openly and are received nonjudgmentally, students are much less likely to express feelings through unproductive behaviors. Acting-out in the classroom, vandalism, and truancy are often indirect methods of dealing with feelings that could not be expressed openly and directly. Third, when adults listen nonevaluatively they provide young people with an opportunity to examine and clarify feelings that are often confusing and frightening. This exchange frequently enables youngsters to better understand a situation and to consider approaches to effectively coping with the situation.

There are two basic approaches to nonevaluative listening. First, the listener can simply acknowledge the speaker's statement by looking at them and making oral responses such as "M-hm," "Yes," "Uh-uh," "I see," and "I understand." This form of listening encourages the speaker to continue talking by indicating that the listener is attentive and involved. Quite obviously, this type of response is least effective when employed in isolation, for most children wish to hear more than a simple acknowledgment.

The second method for employing empathic, nonevaluative listening is commonly called paraphrasing, active listening, or reflecting. In their *Learning Together and Alone*, Johnson and Johnson (1975a) present seven guidelines for employing this skill.

General Guidelines for Paraphrasing

1. Restate the sender's expressed ideas and feelings in your own words rather than mimicking or parroting her exact words.
2. Preface paraphrased remarks with, "You think . . . ," "Your position is . . . ," "It seems to you that . . . ," "You feel that . . . ," and so on.
3. Avoid any indication of approval or disapproval.
4. Make your nonverbal messages congruent with your verbal paraphrasing; look attentive, interested, and open to the sender's ideas and feelings, and show that you are concentrating upon what the sender is trying to communicate.
5. State as accurately as possible what you heard the sender say and describe the feelings and attitudes involved.
6. Do not add or subtract from the sender's message.
7. Put yourself in the sender's shoes and try to understand what it is he is feeling and what his message means. [p. 102]

An example will help to clarify the manner in which this skill can be used. Several years ago, a friend of ours reported having this interchange with her nine-year-old daughter. The daughter approached the mother one morning and informed her that she hated the babysitter who had been with her the previous night. Several factors might then have prevented the mother from effectively listening to her child. First, she could have responded to the word "hate" by informing her daughter that she should not hate anyone. Second, because the family lived in an area where it was difficult to find a babysitter, the mother could understandably have attempted to convince her daughter that the babysitter was really a nice person. Instead, perhaps because she was an excellent elementary school counselor, the mother effectively paraphrased her daughter's statement. Her initial response to her daughter was, "You really don't like the babysitter, do you?" The daughter responded by agreeing and mentioning that the babysitter burned the dinner. Because the babysitter never washed the dishes and the mother had never seen a burned pan, she again had an excellent opportunity to deny and correct the daughter's perception of the situation. Instead, however, she said, "You really don't like the way she does things, do you?" The daughter again agreed and said that the babysitter also made the children go to bed early. Because the children were allowed to stay up half an hour later when a babysitter was present, the mother had yet another opportunity to confront her daughter with the inaccuracy of her statements. Instead, the mother again paraphrased the daughter's statement by saying, "You really don't like having the babysitter here, do you?" At this point, the daughter responded, "No, and you're gone too much, Mom." By listening nonjudgmentally, the mother had allowed both herself and her daughter to discover an important issue.

Paraphrasing has the advantage of making the speaker feel listened to while allowing the listener to be somewhat more involved than is possible when employing only acknowledging responses. Furthermore, by providing a summary of the speaker's statement, the listener may help the child to clarify his or her thoughts or feelings. If the paraphrased statement is not congruent with what the speaker wanted to say, the speaker has an opportunity to correct the listener's paraphrase and thereby clarify the initial statement.

One word of caution about the use of paraphrasing: Students may say that they do not like having someone repeat what they have just said. This response is more common in the upper elementary and secondary grades than among young children. If students frequently indicate that they view your statements as parroting their own, you will need to either reduce the amount of paraphrasing used or attempt to employ responses that vary slightly from the student's original statement. One method of providing a more creative and useful paraphrase is to respond to the feeling as well as the content of the student's statement. Consider the case where a student says to a teacher, "You're picking on me!" If the teacher responds by saying, "I'm not being fair with you?" the student may feel good because he or she was listened to and not punished, yet may also perceive the response as overly reflective. By incorporating a response to the student's feeling, such as, "You're feeling bad because you don't think I'm being fair," the teacher adds another dimension to the response. Another approach to diversifying paraphrasing responses is to vary the response from the student's initial response. This step may include simply creatively paraphrasing the response or adding an interpretation such as, "You're angry because I just asked you to turn around but I didn't say anything to Bob?" Activity 4.7 provides several methods for helping you improve and diversify skills in empathic, nonevaluative listening.

ACTIVITY 4.7   Practicing listening skills

1. To examine and improve your skills in employing paraphrasing, imagine that each of the following statements has just been said to you. Write two responses to each of the ten statements. In the first response, simply paraphrase the statement without mimicking the student's words. In the second response, add a feeling component.
    a. Someone stole my lunch ticket!
    b. This work is too hard.
    c. Can we have ten extra minutes of recess?
    d. Bill has had the book for two days.
    e. I hate you!
    f. I didn't get into trouble in music class today.
    g. Nobody in the class likes me.
    h. Do I have to take my report card home?
    i. I never get to take the roll.
    j. Mary is always picking on me.
2. During one school day, list five statements children make to you and five questions they ask you that could best be responded to by empathic, nonevaluative listening. When the list is complete, write a response to each of the ten student statements.

THE TEACHER AS MODEL

Social learning theorists have shown that individuals learn many things primarily by observing and modeling the behavior of others. Research (Bandura, 1969, 1977) indicates that individuals are more likely to model the behavior of people whom they view as possessing competence and control over resources, and who are a major source of control, support, and reinforcement. Because teachers possess these characteristics, they are in an excellent position to serve as models for their students. Studies (Schachter, 1964) also suggest that people are more likely to model the behavior of others in unfamiliar situations in which rules and expected behaviors have not been established. Because the beginning of the school year is the time when many students experience the classroom as most uncomfortable and unclear, it is important that early in the school year we model behaviors we wish them to emulate. On several occasions when we have presented information about current educational research to professionals in fields other than education, someone in the audience has commented that the research on the importance of the first few days of school coincides with their own experiences. These professionals relate that in their own public school experiences they invariably knew after only a few school days if the teacher was someone who would run a well-organized class and whom they could respect. One participant recently recalled that teachers usually got back what they gave out. If they were well organized and treated students warmly and politely, students responded in kind.

We must realize that our influence as models continues throughout the school year. In many schools, student turnover is high and the many students who transfer into the school have their initial and most influential contacts with the teacher at times other than the first days of school. Teachers frequently comment that transfer students often gravitate to a less-than-ideal group of students. If we wish to have new students accept our values, we must make a special effort to provide them with an adult model who demonstrates competence and warm care for the new student. A few minutes of extra time spent going over classroom procedures and meeting privately with the students to discuss their work and offer any needed assistance can dramatically increase the likelihood that they will model us rather than the behavior of any potentially negative group of peers.

Students model what adults do, not what they say should be done (Bryan & Walbek, 1970). Therefore, we should consistently monitor our behavior to determine whether we are treating students respectfully, modeling attentive listening, avoiding favoritism, and modeling organized, committed behavior as a teacher and learner. An excellent example of effective modeling occurred several years ago while we visited the classroom of an extremely effective teacher. The eighth-grade students in his class were actively involved in a science project and the room buzzed with noise and interest. A boy called across the room to his friend, John, and requested that John throw him the scissors. John immediately obliged and the airborne scissors narrowly missed hitting another student. Rather than shouting at John, the teacher walked over to him and put his hand on John's shoulder. He proceeded to share with John the fact that the near miss had frightened him because he cared about and felt responsible for the students in his class. He then asked John if in the future he would carry the scissors across the room.

After class the teacher explained why his intervention had been so calm and personal. He stated that young adolescents are involved in so many changes that their egos are very fragile and they personalize almost everything. He went on to say that his goal was to provide the student with information in a manner that would enhance the likelihood that the student would listen. Had he yelled at the student or made an example of him in front of the class, the student probably would have responded by focusing on the teacher's "mean" behavior rather than examining his own behavior. The teacher stated that by admitting to his own feeling and sharing it with the student, he had provided the student with valuable information without making him defensive. This incident is an excellent example of a skilled teacher's ability to spontaneously synthesize a working knowledge of adolescent development with practical communication skills. The result of this synthesis was that the teacher was able to respond in a way that facilitated the student's personal growth while modeling emotional control and sensitivity to the student's feelings.

Beginning teachers frequently grapple with the extent to which they should "join in" with students, share students' interests, use student slang, and so on. Our experience suggests that students respond best to adults who are comfortable with themselves, their values, and their personal preferences and who, when appropriate, can share these nonjudgmentally with students. Consequently, if a teacher enjoys the same music as many students do, discussing it with students offers a format for relaxed, personal interaction. Likewise, when our preferences or values differ, encouraging a two-way exchange of ideas can prove stimulating and educational to both the students and ourselves. We should, however, avoid becoming overly involved in students' interests or activities outside of school, particularly those of us who are secondary teachers. Adolescents are working at developing their own identity and generally view adulthood as a positive stage in which individuals have reached desired personal and social adjustment. Consequently, adolescents are confused by adults who show intense interest in students' social activities and interests. It confuses them to see adults who appear to want to be similar to young people or a part of their peer group. If adults do not have something more interesting or valuable to offer, a major goal of adolescence—moving toward partnership in the adult community—is devalued. Students need to know that we have interesting lives apart from them and that we find life stimulating and challenging in some ways that are different from theirs. At the same time, they need us to be interested enough in them and open enough with our own values to share our ideas with them and engage them in discussions of personal as well as academic matters.

COMMUNICATING POSITIVE EXPECTATIONS

The communication skills we use or fail to use dramatically influence the teacher–student relationship. But we also greatly influence the quality of these relationships through the expectations we communicate to students. School effectiveness research (Brookover et al., 1979; Edmonds, 1979; Rutter et al., 1979) has consistently pointed to teachers' high expectations of students' performance as a key factor associated with students' achievement. In a variety of subtle and not-so-subtle ways, we communicate to some students that they are bright, capable, and responsible while other students receive the message that they are dull, incapable, and irresponsible. It is obvious that our behaviors that create positive expectations almost always enhance the teacher–student relationship, and those which indicate negative expectations not only create poor relationships but also create poor self-concepts and reduce learning.

An example of a teacher expressing differential expectations to different students occurred a number of years ago when one of us was collecting data in a rural elementary school. The teacher had arranged her class by seating her students as pictured in Figure 4.5. When presenting information to the

FIGURE 4.5

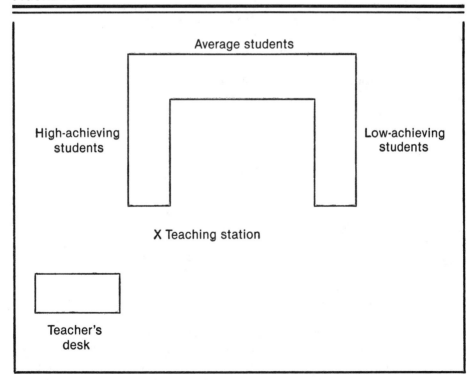

group she almost always stood in front of her high-achieving students. One day while she was making a presentation to the class, the low-achieving students became somewhat noisy. The teacher responded by glaring at the low achievers and stating firmly, "Be quiet over there; we're trying to learn something over here."

Our expectations of students are influenced by a variety of factors other than actual performance or behavior. Frericks (1974) found that teachers viewing a group of students labeled low in ability described the students' behavior more negatively than did teachers who viewed the same students but were told they were observing "regular students in a normal classroom." Spencer Hall (1981) reported that some students nominated for a citizen-of-the-year reward had misbehavior rates as high as that of any student in the class. Teachers are obviously influenced by the way in which students present themselves or are labeled, as well as by students' behavior.

Results from classroom interaction studies indicate that teachers generally respond more favorably to students they perceive as high achievers. High-achieving students receive more response opportunities (Brophy & Good, 1971), are given more time to answer questions (Rowe, 1974; Bozsik, 1982), receive more positive nonverbal feedback such as smiles, nods, and winks (Chaikin, Sigler, & Derlega, 1974), and are less likely to be ignored (Willis, 1970). Cooper and Good (1983) provide this list of common ways in which teachers respond differently to high- and low-achieving students.

1. Seating low-expectation students far from the teacher and/or seating them in a group.
2. Paying less attention to lows in academic situations (smiling less often and maintaining less eye contact).
3. Calling on lows less often to answer classroom questions or to make public demonstrations.
4. Waiting less time for lows to answer questions.
5. Not staying with lows in failure situations (i.e., providing fewer clues, asking fewer follow-up questions).
6. Criticizing lows more frequently than highs for incorrect public responses.
7. Praising lows less frequently than highs after successful public responses.
8. Praising lows more frequently than highs for marginal or inadequate public responses.
9. Providing lows with less accurate and less detailed feedback than highs.
10. Failing to provide lows with feedback about their responses as often as highs.
11. Demanding less work and effort from lows than from highs.
12. Interrupting performance of lows more frequently than highs. [p. 10]

This list is reinforced and expanded in Jere Brophy's (1983) review of the self-fulfilling prophecy and teachers' expectations research. These findings suggest that teachers expect more from students they view as more capable and that these students have more positive interactions with their teachers. As you would expect, the fact that teachers have more frequent and positive interactions with some students affects who learns most effectively in the classroom. In reviewing the research on expectation effects, Brophy (1983) cites studies suggesting that "teacher expectations do have self-fulfilling-prophecy effects on student-achievement levels, but that these effects make only a 5 to 10 percent difference, on the average" (p. 635). Brophy goes on to state:

> These conclusions clearly imply that even ideal teacher education related to the topic of teacher expectations will not work miracles in our schools, but they do not imply that the topic is unimportant. Even a 5% difference in educational out-comes is an important difference, the more so as it is compounded across school years. Furthermore, the presentation so far has been confined to consideration of the average effect across all teachers of expectations concerning student achievement. The story becomes much more complicated, and the implications for teacher education much more obvious, when we turn attention to other kinds of expectations and to differences among teachers in predisposition to expectation effects. [p. 635]

As demonstrated by Kleinfeld's (1975) research with Eskimo and Indian children, students' performance is enhanced by combining a warm, personal teacher-student relationship with high, yet realistic expectations for achievement. In addition to consistently employing the communication skills previously described, we must avoid the trap of communicating low expectations to students. We must attempt to involve lower-achieving students in class discussions, help them respond when they have difficulty, and provide individual assistance and follow-up (including correspondence with parents) when they fail to complete assigned work.

Confronted with this suggestion, many teachers respond that lower-achieving students would be uncomfortable if asked to answer questions or if confronted with silence when they failed to answer a question. This interpretation may be accurate, but there are numerous relatively simple solutions to these problems. For example, we can meet individually with students who seldom volunteer answers and who fail to respond when called upon. During such a conference we may agree with the student on the types of questions the student wishes to answer, or we may agree to call on the student immediately after he or she raises his or her hand. We can also talk to our classes about waiting for students' answers. Students can be informed that we will attempt to assist all students who have difficulty with an answer and request that other students not raise their hands or call out the answer until the teacher asks for assistance. Individual conferences and classroom procedures such as these help us make the classroom a safe and inviting environment for all students. Furthermore, they clarify and equalize expectations so that all students feel that we believe they are valuable and capable class members.

We must realize that the concept of holding high expectations for all students does not mean that we should provide identical treatment for all students. To a considerable extent, the differential treatment students receive from teachers is a logical and often thoughtful response to individual student needs. Nevertheless, teachers should become aware of the potential for allowing successful students to dominate classroom interactions. Brophy (1983) sheds light on this important issue:

> Clearly, if teachers merely react consistently to the student behavior that confronts them, group statistics will reveal that the high expectation students receive more response opportunities (because they volunteer and call out more often), have more academic and fewer procedural or behavioral interactions with the teacher (because they are oriented more toward academic learning, can work more independently without supervision, and seldom become disruptive), receive more praise (because they succeed academically more often), and receive less criticism (because they show less classroom disruption and academic failure). [p. 637]

It is often desirable that we initiate a higher percentage of our academic contacts with low-achieving students during individual or small-group instruction. Similarly, especially when introducing new material to younger children, we should try to maximize the percentage of correct responses so that students do not become confused by competing, inaccurate information. The critical issue is that we must become aware of ways in which we respond differently to various types of students and thoughtfully and systematically implement differential interaction patterns that support individual student and group learning.

Activities for Monitoring Teachers' Expectations

The activities that follow are examples of methods we can employ in order to systematically examine our interactions with low- and high-achieving students. You can use these data as a reference for considering whether your differential interactions are supporting optimal learning for all students or are inadvertently disadvantageous to low-achieving students.

Additional information and activities dealing with communication of teachers' expectations may be found in a packaged in-service program entitled "Teacher Expectations and Student Achievement" (TESA) Kerman (1979).

Before beginning the activities listed below you should know that research indicates that when teachers are made aware of how they differentially treat students and are involved in monitoring their teacher-student interactions, inequitable interactions can be eliminated (Good & Brophy, 1974; Sadker & Sadker, 1985).

ACTIVITY 4.8   Monitoring students' response opportunities

List the four highest- and four lowest-achieving students in your class. Place these students' names in the form provided in Figure 4.6. Have a colleague tally your interactions with these students during at least two half-hour periods when the class is involved in group instruction.

FIGURE 4.6 Monitoring teacher–student dyadic interactions

| Student's name | Student volunteers answer | Teacher asks student a question | Student response | | | Teacher assists student | Teacher praises student | Teacher criticizes student | Teacher calls on another student |
			correct	partially correct	incorrect				

continued

FIGURE 4.7   Monitoring teacher–student interactions

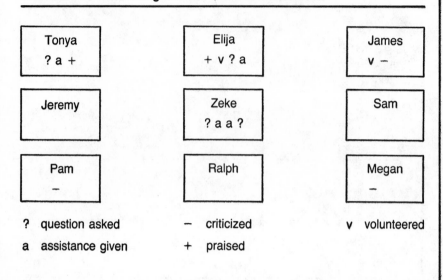

Tonya ? a +	Elija + v ? a	James v –
Jeremy	Zeke ? a a ?	Sam
Pam –	Ralph	Megan –

?	question asked	–	criticized	v	volunteered
a	assistance given	+	praised		

      This activity can also be completed by presenting the observer with a seating chart and a label for each type of teacher–student interaction on which you wish to obtain data. An observer might be asked to observe several students and tally the number of times they were asked a question, given assistance in answering a question, criticized, praised, or volunteered an answer. Figure 4.7 is a sample of the data you might collect using this procedure.

After examining the results, respond to these statements:

      Two things I learned about my interactions with these students were . . .

      Two things I will try to do differently the next time I teach a large group lesson are . . .

ACTIVITY 4.9   Mapping a teacher's classroom movement

Draw a map of your classroom, including location of the furniture. Ask a colleague to come into your classroom during a period of at least half an hour when the class will be involved in seatwork and you will be free to assist students. Have the observer mark your movement with a solid line during the entire observation. The observer should place a number by each place where you stop. To record the amount of time spent at each spot, have the observer place a tally mark next to the number for every fifteen seconds that you remain in that spot.

After examining the walking map, answer these questions:

1. Where did you spend the most time? least time?
2. Were any students ignored? Were there specific reasons for not interacting with these students?
3. Did the classroom arrangement influence your movement? How?
4. What changes, if any, would you make in your walking pattern during this type of instruction?
5. What changes, if any, would you make in your classroom arrangement?

Teachers who frequently employ lecture or large-group discussions almost inevitably look at one area of the class much more than others. Almost all teachers have some blind spot. While teaching, one of us almost always sits with his left leg on his right knee. Because this position twists his body to the right, students on the left side of the class are often ignored. The author periodically asks his students to tally the number of contacts he has with students from each side of the class in order to make him more aware of (and accountable for) his behavior.

ACTIVITY 4.10   Balancing positive statements

For three days, make one inviting statement to each child in your class. In order to ensure that each child receives such a statement, make a class list and place a check by each child's name when he or she has been given an inviting statement. After completing the activity, answer these questions:

1. Were there some students whom you had to consciously remind yourself to provide with an inviting statement? If so, did these students have anything in common?
2. Did students respond any differently during the three days? If so, how?
3. Did any students make a positive comment to you about your behavior during these three days?

A good supplement to this activity is to again list your four highest- and lowest-achieving students. Ask a colleague, an aide, or even the principal to tally the number of positive and negative statements you make to each of these students during two half-hour instructional periods.

Student's name	Positive comments	Negative comments
High achievers 1. 2.		

continued

Student's name	Positive comments	Negative comments
3.		
4.		
Low achievers		
1.		
2.		
3.		
4.		

After completing this activity, answer these questions:

1.   What do the data indicate about how you respond to high- as opposed to low-achieving students?
2.   Did you find yourself behaving differently because you were being observed? If so, what did you do differently?
3.   Did any of the eight students appear to respond differently than usual while you were observed? If so, how did their behavior change?

ESTABLISHING RAPPORT WITH STUDENTS

As we discussed earlier, positive student self-concepts are developed and students' achievement is enhanced by combining high expectations with a warm, personal teacher–student relationship. Establishing positive teacher–student relationships is facilitated by employing the communication skills presented earlier in this chapter. Although these skills provide the essentials for developing positive relationships, we can express our interest in and caring for students by creating opportunities for personal discussions with students and by demonstrating our interest in activities that are important to them.

In addition to their value in increasing positive student attitudes, these invitational interactions provide the basis for creating teacher–student relationships that facilitate the use of corrective interventions described in Chapters Ten and Eleven. An excellent example of this concept was provided by a student-teacher with whom one of us was working during the final editing of this book. The student-teacher was working with one of the most disruptive third-graders we have encountered. Each day the boy was involved in numerous instances of aggressive behavior toward peers as well as a high rate of insubordination to adults. Because the assertive discipline program employed by the school had only increased the student's acting-out behavior, and because the boy's parents would not allow the school to provide special education services, the principal was considering expelling the student.

The student-teacher decided to work with the student as part of her assignment in a classroom management course. In so doing, she was asked to attempt many of the methods described throughout this book. In doing so, the student-teacher was encouraged to consistently (and persistently) work on establishing rapport with the student. The student's initial responses were extremely negative. He frequently and vividly informed the student-teacher that he hated teachers (a value reinforced by his parents), and that he wanted nothing to do with her. But the teacher persisted. She discovered that the boy's mother raised show dogs, and she watched a cable television show from New York in which the mother's dog took second place in a national competition. The student-teacher discussed this event with the student and attempted to discover other aspects of the boy's life. One day when a professional athlete with the same name as the boy's was traded, the teacher laminated the article in plastic and placed it on the bulletin board with a large red arrow pointing to it. The class was understandably curious, and the boy received considerable attention. Gradually, he increased his willingness to work cooperatively with the teacher. Although he would not become involved in problem solving, he did agree to a contract that was associated with considerable changes in behavior. Although the dramatic improvement in the student's behavior required behavioristic methods, these were not effective until the student was willing to work with the teacher. The improved relationship made possible other interventions that led to important changes.

The following twelve ideas are examples of methods the authors and their colleagues have found effective in improving rapport with students. In addition to improving teacher–student relationships, these activities are interesting and enjoyable.

Eating Lunch with Students
Most teacher–student contact occurs in the presence of twenty-five to thirty other children. Unless they take the initiative by staying after school, students may never have individual private time with their teacher. One way to provide this personal time is to have lunch in the classroom with individual students. This time can be arranged by simply providing a sign-up sheet so that students who are interested can reserve a time to eat lunch alone with you. You and the student can use the lunch period to share personal interests. You should be willing to listen to the student's concerns about personal or school problems, but the time together should not be used as a conference in which you discuss the student's school work or behavior.

Arranging Interviews
Anyone who has taught young children for several years has experienced an instance in which a student appeared surprised to see the teacher in a non-school setting such as the grocery store. Children often view the teacher solely as a teacher and are quite unaware of our interests and life outside the school setting. One approach for making you seem more real is to allow the children to interview you. You can expand this activity by having your spouse or older children visit the classroom and be interviewed by the class.

Attending Students' Performances

Many students are involved in performance activities that are unrelated to the school. Students play a variety of sports and are involved in musical and dance performances. You can express your sincere interest in your students by occasionally attending these performances. Keep a record of these visits so that they can be evenly distributed among the students. Though it is a good idea to ask students whether they would like you to attend, they are almost always excited by and appreciative of your visit.

Inviting Students to Visit on Halloween

Because Halloween is a time set aside for visiting homes, it provides an excellent opportunity for students to visit your home. Also, because parents frequently set aside Halloween to be with their family, it often proves to be a convenient time for them to transport their child to your home for a short visit. The visit allows the youngster to see another aspect of your life and therefore to view you less as a role and more as a person. In addition, inviting someone into your home is a demonstration that you care about that person.

Sending Letters and Notes to Students

Beginning the school year with a personal letter from you is an effective technique for establishing rapport with students. A positive individualized letter placed on each student's desk informs each student that you are happy to have him or her in class, eager to get to know him or her, and excited about the upcoming school year. Notes given to students throughout the school year can enhance the personal relationship between you and the student. Appropriate times for expressing thoughts or providing information by notes or letters include when a student has been successful at a new or difficult task, when a student's behavior has improved, when a personal matter seems to be worrying a student, and on a student's birthday. Students also appreciate receiving a note or a get-well card along with their homework when they are sick and must miss school for several days.

Employing a Suggestion Box

Students often perceive their teacher as relatively uninterested in their ideas about the classroom. Although we may view this situation as undesirable, it is to some degree an understandable response to the reality that we have primary responsibility for creating an appropriate classroom environment. One method we can employ to indicate our interest in students' ideas is to display a suggestion box and encourage students to write ideas for making the class a better place in which to learn. This approach can be expanded to include holding class meetings in which students discuss their ideas and concerns about the classroom. When classroom meetings are used, having students place agenda items on the board can replace the suggestion box. Either way, our willingness to request, accept, and respond to students' suggestions can be an effective method for improving teacher–student rapport.

Joining in Playground Games

Students enjoy having teachers participate in their playground activities. There are few better ways for us to show our humanness and demonstrate that we enjoy our students than to occasionally share in their recess activities. Not only can this activity enhance teacher–student relationships, but it can also provide us with an excellent form of relaxation. The physical activity and the opportunity to interact with children in a relaxed and nonacademic setting can provide us with a refreshing break in the school day.

One way to formalize this type of teacher–student interaction is to develop several opportunities for friendly athletic competition between students and teachers. We have both worked in schools in which faculty-student competition was organized in such sports as flag football, soccer, volleyball, basketball, and softball. Faculty–sixth-grade games provide a forum for friendly athletic competition in elementary schools, and middle schools can involve a variety of grade levels in this type of activity. These events are an excellent oportunity for students and teachers to have fun together and to see each other in roles other than that of teacher and student. Just as it is important for families to play together and share enjoyable, active experiences, schools that incorporate such activities are likely to find that students and teachers enjoy each other more and confront each other more productively and less frequently.

Sharing an Ice Cream Treat

As warm weather arrives, ice cream cones become a favorite treat for students. Taking time to have an ice cream cone after school with each child provides an excellent opportunity for teacher and student to relax and enjoy each other in a slightly different role. This informal activity affords an opportunity for each to learn a little more about the other. Furthermore, the simple act of taking time with a child and purchasing an ice cream cone indicates to the child that we care.

Making Birthday Cards

A birthday is a very special day for children. A thoughtful way to respond to children's excitement is to make a birthday card when each student has a birthday. The card can include a birthday greeting as well as a positive statement about some aspect of the student's work or behavior.

Placing Stickers and Statements on Students' Work

We can express our respect or appreciation for students' work or behavior by using special stickers such as holiday stickers, smell stickers, and stickers of phrases such as "terrific," "fantastic," or "hard worker." Friendly statements written on students' work and bright stickers can communicate our excitement about teaching and create a more positive teacher–student relationship.

Discussing Report Cards, Projects, or Students' Behavior

Although the activities described above all focus on personal, relaxing activities, positive teacher–student rapport can also be enhanced by taking time to individually discuss students' work or behavior. By taking time to discuss each student's report card, we not only reduce the anxiety often associated with evaluation, but also indicate a sincere interest in and respect for the student. Similarly, creating opportunities to discuss students' positive or negative behavior communicates similar concern. Specific methods for holding conferences with students are discussed in later chapters.

Joining in School and Community Events

Schools often organize special events such as hat days, carnivals, and bike rodeos. Similarly, communities have picnics, carnivals, and other social events. We can demonstrate our interest in students and our own enjoyment of a good time by becoming involved in these activities. Schools can also organize special events or displays that provide an opportunity for students to view teachers in a personal light and increase positive teacher–student interaction. We have both worked in buildings where a childhood picture of each staff member was placed in a display case and students attempted to match the teachers with the childhood pictures. Similarly, we have taught in schools where a bulletin board was arranged so that teachers and students could publicly write positive statements to other students or teachers. Our involvement in activities such as these helps to create a positive school atmosphere and thereby significantly reduce unproductive student behavior.

ASSESSING THE EFFECT OF ATTEMPTS TO IMPROVE TEACHER-STUDENT RELATIONSHIPS

Although it is easy to read about new ideas but not take time to implement them, we may also become excited about new ideas and fail to assess whether implementing the ideas did in fact have the desired results. The final activity in this chapter reminds you to attend to both of these potential pitfalls.

ACTIVITY 4.11   Assessing the effect of attempts to improve teacher–student relationships

Complete each of the activities presented in this chapter. In addition, implement at least three of the activities for improving teacher–student rapport.

When these activities have been completed, repeat Activity 5.1 and compare the results. From these results, complete these statements.

My students now see me as more . . .
My students now see me as less . . .
My feelings toward my students have changed in that I now . . .
I particularly like the fact that . . .
I will certainly continue . . .

RECOMMENDED READING

Alberti, R., and Emmons, M. (1974). *Your perfect right.* (2nd ed.). San Luis Obispo, Calif.: Impact.

Brophy, J., and Good, T. (1974). *Teacher–student relationships: Causes and consequences.* New York: Holt, Rinehart and Winston.

Combs, A. (1982). *A personal approach to teaching beliefs that make a difference.* Boston: Allyn and Bacon.

Gazda, G. (1973). *Human relations development: A manual for educators.* Boston: Allyn and Bacon.

Ginott, H. (1972). *Teacher and child.* New York: Macmillan.

Gordon, T. *T.E.T.: Teaching effectiveness training.* (1974). New York: Peter H. Wyden.

Hurt, H., Scott, M., and McCroskey, J. (1978). *Communication in the classroom.* Reading, Mass.: Addison-Wesley.

Jones, V. (1980). *Adolescents with behavior problems: Strategies for teaching, counseling and parent involvement.* Boston: Allyn and Bacon.

Jourard, S. (1971). *The transparent self.* New York: D. Van Nostrand.

Kraft, A. (1975). *The living classroom: Putting humanistic education into practice.* New York: Harper and Row.

Lang, A. and Jacobowski, P. (1976). *Responsible assertive behavior: Cognitive/behavioral procedures for trainers.* Champaign, Ill.: Research Press.

Liberman, R., King, L., DeRisi, W., and McCann, M. (1975). *Personal effectiveness: Guiding people to assert themselves and improve their social skills.* Champaign, Ill.: Research Press.

Purkey, W. (1978). *Inviting school success: A self-concept approach to teaching and learning.* Belmont, Calif.: Wadsworth.

Rogers, C. (1961). *On becoming a person.* Boston: Houghton Mifflin.

Schmuck, R. and Schmuck, P. (1983). *Group process in the classroom.* Dubuque, Iowa: William C. Brown.

Seiler, W., Schuelke, D., and Lieb-Brilhart, B. (1984). *Communication for the contemporary classroom.* New York: Holt, Rinehart and Winston.

CHAPTER 5

Establishing Positive
Peer Relationships

*Classrooms that have a climate of competitiveness, hostility and alien-
ation cause anxiety and discomfort and do not facilitate the intellectual
development of many students. Classrooms in which students and
teachers support one another facilitate the development of self-esteem
and the satisfaction of fundamental motives. They also provide the
opportunity for students to use their intellectual capacities to their
fullest.*
Richard Schmuck and Patricia Schmuck, (1983),
Group Processes in the Classroom

*Positive interpersonal relations among students are necessary both
for problem solving in groups and for general classroom enjoyment of
instructional activity. The psychological security and safety necessary
for open exploration of instructional tasks is based upon feelings of
being accepted, liked, and supported by fellow students. Class cohesion
is based upon positive interpersonal relationships among students.*
David Johnson and Roger Johnson, (1975),
*Learning Together and Alone:
Cooperation, Competition, and Individualization*

Peers have an important role in determining the quality of the learning
environment. With today's increased emphasis on students' achievement, teachers are often hesitant to allocate time for creating positive
peer relationships in the classroom. In addition, teacher education

programs seldom provide teachers with specific skills for developing positive, supportive group norms. A considerable body of research indicates, however, that time spent creating a positive peer group can eliminate much misbehavior and provide a classroom climate that enhances students' achievement.

Peer relationships influence students' achievement in several ways. First, peer attitudes toward achievement affect students' academic aspirations and school behavior (Coleman, 1966; Lewis & St. John, 1974; Rutter, 1979; Sharan & Sharan, 1976). Second, the quality of peer relationships and personal support in classrooms affects the degree to which students' personal needs are met and, subsequently, their ability to be productively involved in the learning process (Lewis & St. John, 1974; Schmuck, 1963, 1966). Finally, peer relationships can directly affect achievement through cooperative learning activities (Johnson & Johnson, 1975, 1983; Johnson, Marayama, Johnson, Nelson, & Skon, 1981; Sharan & Hertz-Lazarowitz, 1981; Slavin, 1983).

Anyone who has worked with groups of students has witnessed the role peers play in influencing students' behavior. When discussing the differences between confronting an adolescent in front of the group and having a private talk with the student, teachers frequently remark that it seems as if they are dealing with two completely different students. We should not be surprised that students' feelings and behaviors are significantly influenced by their classmates. During the school year, students spend more than 800 hours with their classmates. And, because most elementary school classrooms are composed of children who live close together, friendships and conflicts that develop in the classroom often have a very real influence on youngsters' lives outside the school. Peer pressure is somewhat less complex and extensive for early primary-grade children whose egocentricity reduces the influence of their peers. Nevertheless, at all grade levels the values, norms, and behaviors of the group significantly affect individual students' feelings of safety, belongingness, respect for others, and self-esteem.

In their *Group Processes in the Classroom*, Richard and Patricia Schmuck (1983) write of the classroom group's importance:

> The classroom clearly offers a setting in which high levels of feeling exist daily and wherein covert psychological dynamics often come into play. As students interact, and students and teachers relate, they communicate—however indirectly—their feelings about one another. Such gestures of affect influence how students view themselves, their abilities, their likability, and their general worth. Morever, feelings, evaluations, or defenses about oneself make up students' self-esteem and have impact on the degree to which they use their intelligence and the manner in which they form their current educational aspirations. [p. 24]

UNDERSTANDING THE CLASSROOM GROUP

The classroom by nature elicits numerous interactions and feelings. By placing twenty-five to thirty-five individuals in a thirty-by-thirty-foot room, schools create a highly interactive environment. Peer interaction is a natural and desirable aspect of almost all learning environments. Group instruction is employed both because it is frequently more expedient and because a good education involves learning how to function as a group member. The group's influence is intensified by the competition found in most classrooms. Students compete for the highest test scores, strive to move into a higher reading group, or run for class office. Even when we employ individualized programs that deemphasize competition, students have numerous opportunities to compare their work to that of their classmates. It is understandable and perhaps unavoidable that classrooms are characterized by a fairly high level of interaction and the accompanying spontaneous interchange of feelings.

Although teachers often express concern and frustration over the negative aspects of peer pressure, the peer group can be a positive and supportive factor in the classroom. When students feel liked by their peers and when interactions are characterized by thoughtfulness and helpfulness, students experience a sense of safety and security, belongingness and affection, significance, respect of others, and power. Students are then able to concentrate more fully on learning and are willing to take greater risks in attempting to master new skills. Consequently, it is extremely important that we implement strategies that encourage development of positive, supportive peer interactions in the classroom.

It is beyond the scope of this book to thoroughly examine group dynamics, but we must realize that groups, like individuals, have needs that must be met before the group can function effectively. If the classroom group is to function in a supportive, goal-directed manner, we must initially set aside time for activities that enable students to know each other, develop a feeling of being included, and create diverse friendship patterns. Only after these feelings have been developed can a group of students proceed to optimally respond to the learning goals of the classroom.

A large body of both theory and research supports these observations. Several major theories of group development support the concept that interpersonal issues must be clarified before groups can begin to function effectively in meeting their task goals. Tuckman (1965) and Schmuck and Schmuck (1983) observe that the functions groups serve can be divided into interpersonal and task functions. This two-stage theory of group development and functioning is supported by work with classroom groups (Runkel et al., 1971). Schutz's theory (1966) states that during the early stages of a group's development, members care primarily about being included in the group. Discussing this aspect of group dynamics in their *Group Processes in the Classroom*, Schmuck and Schmuck (1975) write:

> Issues of interpersonal inclusion characterize the beginning of a group's life. In the classroom, the students and teacher confront one another's presence and raise questions such as: How will I fit in here? Who will accept me? Who will reject me? What do I have to do to be accepted? Academic work cannot easily be accomplished until these questions of inclusion are answered satisfactorily. [p. 171]

Gibb's (1964) theory of group dynamics also supports the importance of initially dealing with interpersonal issues. Gibb states that groups begin to function effectively only after members feel accepted and develop a sense of interpersonal trust. He says that, following resolution of this primary issue, groups move on to the issues of making decisions and group norms and goals.

Much research also suggests that group norms greatly influence individual students' behavior. The Coleman Report (1966) is perhaps the best-known study of the effect of peer norms. This study, commissioned by the U.S. Office of Education and directed by James Coleman, was an attempt to determine the factors that influenced school achievement among high school students. Coleman's data suggest that factors such as funds available for equipment and salaries, the racial makeup of the school, and the teachers' educational level make little difference in determining students' achievement. Instead, the major factors are the socioeconomic composition and achievement orientation of fellow students. When students attend schools in which academic achievement is valued, their interest in academic endeavors and their academic achievement increase. Similarly, attendance at schools where academic performance is not valued tends to decrease students' academic interest and achievement. Coleman's study has been criticized on several grounds, yet it appears that peers' attitudes do account for a significant amount of variance in students' achievement. In a closely related study, Lewis and St. John (1974) attempted to determine the variables that influenced achievement of black students in classrooms where the majority of students were white. Their research showed that higher achievement among black students was related to norms that stressed both achievement and acceptance of black students within the classroom. The results indicated that the presence of high-achieving white students was not sufficient to significantly enhance academic achievement among the black students. It appeared that this factor had to be combined with white students' accepting their black peers as friends.

Other studies (Alexander & Campbell, 1964; Berenda, 1950; Hargreaves, 1967; McDill et al., 1969; Wilson, 1959; Wax, 1971) reaffirm that students are heavily influenced by the attitudes and information of their peers. Berenda's (1950) study examined the extent to which seven- to thirteen-year-old children would respond to group pressure by contradicting material they could clearly see was correct. The experiment involved placing each child in a room with the eight highest-achieving students in the child's class. The eight peers were instructed to give incorrect responses to comparisons of the lengths of two lines. The results showed that 57 percent of the seven- to ten-year-olds and 46 percent of the thirteen-year-olds agreed with obviously wrong answers provided by their peers. This powerful influence of peer conformity is partially explained by the fact that:

> Individuals rely on group norms to guide them, especially when they are unsure about social reality. . . . For students especially there is a pull toward the peer group to make the complex world of the school more understandable. . . .
>   Students feel insecure when their personal response is in opposition to a group norm. [Schmuck & Schmuck, 1975, p. 121]

Group values and norms so deeply influence the individual student's behavior that we can expect that the student's self-esteem will be significantly affected by the group, and that the student's self-image will mirror the group's attitudes about the student (Mannheim, 1957). Similarly, research (McGinley & McGinley, 1970; Reese, 1961; Stevens, 1971) suggests a correlation among the student's popularity, self-esteem, and achievement. Although the influence of these factors undoubtedly is complex, most teachers would agree that students who are well liked by the group generally feel better about themselves and tend to function more productively in the classroom. The influence of positive group feelings upon learning is directly supported by studies from various grade levels indicating that students' achievement is higher in classrooms characterized by diverse, positive peer relationships (Muldoon, 1955; Schmuck, 1966; Walberg & Anderson, 1968).

The relationship among positive group norms, diverse liking patterns, and productive student behavior and achievement is a major incentive for teachers to develop skills in creating positive peer relationships in the classroom, but we have a second important reason for acquiring these skills. Today's students live in a world which is increasingly urban and in which people are more and more interdependent. The time when the average person lived in relative isolation and was basically self-sufficient is long past. Individuals depend upon others for needed goods and services as well as for meeting emotional needs. Likewise, individuals are rediscovering the importance of coming together in order to combat social problems ranging from burglary to an energy crisis. This increased interdependence can also be seen in the move away from the Renaissance scholar toward increased specialization. In producing anything from automobiles to ideas, individuals focus on an ever more specialized aspect of their work and must cooperate with others in order to create increasingly sophisticated products.

If schools are to adequately prepare students for a society characterized by interdependence and cooperative effort, they must provide students with frequent and meaningful experiences in functioning cooperatively in groups. Rather than continually stressing competition and individual learning, teachers must employ cooperative group work in the classroom. More than three decades ago, John Dewey emphasized that life in a classroom should mirror the processes students will face in society. He wrote too that the goal of schooling was to provide students with skills that would enable them to create a better living situation.

Activities for Examining Peer Relationships in the Classroom

We have three basic methods of determining the degree to which children in the class are accepted by and feel involved in the classroom group. One method is the sociometric test for determining which students are most frequently chosen by other students as desired work or play partners. To collect these data, students can be asked to list (younger children may tell you their choices) the two students in the classroom with whom they would like to eat lunch, work on a school project, or do some other activity. The data can then be tabulated and displayed in chart form, as shown in Figure 5.1.

The data in Figure 5.1 were obtained in a fourth-grade classroom. The chart indicates that six students were not chosen by any of their classmates and two students were chosen seven times. We can obtain additional information by also asking students to list the three classmates toward whom they feel least friendly. We would then have a total number of times each student was chosen positively and negatively. In *Group Processes in the Classroom*, Schmuck and Schmuck (1983) provide more methods for collecting this type of sociometric data.

A sociogram can also be developed by actually observing a class for a time and recording every instance in which a child has a positive or negative interaction with another child. This method has the advantage of providing an indication of the actual interaction patterns in a classroom.

The third method for determining students' feelings about their position in the classroom group as well as their general feelings about the group is to develop a questionnaire that allows them to report their feelings about the group. The advantage of this approach is that it can provide us with more detailed information than is available through a sociometric test or observation. The main problem with this approach is that students must experience fairly high trust before they will accurately report the information. Even during the initial stages of group development, however, this approach will often reveal useful information. Figure 5.2 is an example of a questionnaire that can be used at several grade levels.

A questionnaire can also be used for gathering information about group norms. "Norms are group agreements, usually implicit, which help to guide the psychological and behavioral processes of the group members" (Schmuck & Schmuck, 1983, p. 203). Because norms have a major influence on students' attitudes, beliefs, and behaviors, it is useful for us to be aware of group norms and to discuss these with students. One method for obtaining information about group norms is to devise parallel questionnaires asking students to report their views about how the class thinks and how they think. We then have information not only on the accepted group norms, but also on the degree to which individual students' values support the group norm. Not uncommonly, we find that though most students perceive the group as supporting one set of values, the actual collective values of individual members are quite different. For example, class members may believe that their peers do not value asking

FIGURE 5.1 Sociogram data display based on the question: "Whom would you most enjoy sitting by at lunch?"

Chooser	Chosen																								
	1	2	3	4	5	6	7	8	9	10	11	12	13	14	15	16	17	18	19	20	21	22	23	24	25
1															1	1									1
2																								1	1
3																									
4							1												1		1				1
5																									
6										1		1										1		1	
7		1																							
8										1	1	1				1						1			1
9																									
10		1																							1
11																									
12		1											1			1								1	

128

	1	2	3	4	5	6	7	8	9	10	11	12	13	14	15	16	17	18	19	20	21	22	23	24	25
13	1	1													1			1				1			1
14															1										
15													1	1											
16				1	1												1							1	1
17				1	1		1									1									
18					1	1																			
19									1																
20										1															
21											1														
22														1	1										
23	1	1																						1	1
24														1											
25		1																						1	
Total times chosen	7	4	0	3	4	2	2	0	1	4	1	0	1	2	2	7	1	1	1	0	0	2	0	3	2

FIGURE 5.2   Group assessment questionnaire

Please answer these questions as carefully as you can.

1. Do you like being in this class? ___ ___
                                        Yes No
    Why? _____

2. Would you say that you are a leader or a follower in this class?
    (Circle your answer in red)   Leader   Follower

3. Would you rather be the opposite of the answer that you gave in
    question 2?
    (Circle your answer in green)   Yes   No   Maybe

4. Do you listen to people in our class?
    (Circle your answer in yellow)   Usually   Sometimes   Seldom

5. Do other children listen to you when you are talking? ___ ___
                                                            Yes No

6. Are you comfortable helping people in this class?

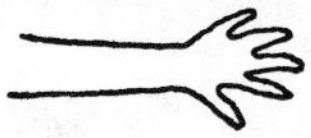

                                        ___   ___   _____
                                        Yes   No   Sometimes

7. Are you comfortable asking for help from class members?

                                        ___   ___   _____
                                        Yes   No   Sometimes

8. Name three things that you contribute to our group.
    a.
    b.   Help ?!!
    c.

9. Name two things you would like to contribute to our group.
    a.
    b.

10. How do you feel about the students in your class?

                        _____   I like all the students

    (check in blue)   _____   I like most of the students

                        _____   I like only a few students

11. Do the students like you?

_____ Most of the students like me.

(check in orange)   _____ Some of the students like me.

_____ I don't think the students like me very much.

12. Do you have friends to sit with at lunch? ____ ____

Yes   No

13. When you are at recess, do members of this class let you play with them?

____ ____ _____

Yes   No   Sometimes

14. If you could change one thing about the people in this class, what would you change? _____

_____

_____

Thank you for filling out this questionnaire for me.

the teacher for help or doing well in class, when in fact most students do indeed value these behaviors. Figure 5.3 is a form that can be administered on two occasions using the two sets of directions and criteria to determine group norms.

After administering this form using both directions, we can tally the results and share them with the class. This sharing can lead to useful discussion of group norms and reasons for discrepancies between individual values and perceived group values. We can use this opportunity to share our values on each item. Finally, the class can become involved in discussing ways in which the more supportive individual values can become incorporated into the classroom.

Once we have discovered the dynamics in the classroom, the next step is to implement activities that create more positive peer relationships and group norms. There are several methods for developing positive peer relationships in the classroom. We can begin the school year by helping students to become better acquainted with their peers. This endeavor can be accompanied by activities that create a class spirit and positive group identity. Throughout the year we can support these activities by involving students in others aimed at building friendships. We can also enhance positive peer relationships by implementing instructional strategies, such as peer tutoring and group projects which reinforce the value of supportive, cooperative learning. Finally we can employ problem-solving approaches focused on helping peers resolve their own conflicts.

FIGURE 5.3 Determining individual and classroom norms

Introduction:	First administration:	Each classroom has different sets of beliefs about good and bad behavior. Put an X in the boxes below to indicate how you think other students in this class feel.
	Second administration:	Indicate how *you* feel about each of the statements by placing an X in the box that describes your feelings.
Heading:	First:	How many students in this class believe
	Second:	My feelings are

	First	*Almost everyone*	*About half*	*Only a few*
	Second	*Almost always*	*About half the time*	*I disagree*
1. It is good to raise your hand and let the teacher know that you do not understand what is being presented.				
2. It is good to do your best work.				
3. It is good to answer questions and share what you know.				
4. It is good to praise and encourage other students.				
5. It is good to follow class rules and procedures.				
6. It is good to help others with their work (except on tests).				
7. It is good to cooperate with and help a substitute teacher.				
8. It is good to politely let another student know when his or her disruptive behavior bothers you.				

ACQUAINTANCE ACTIVITIES

You can undoubtedly recall experiencing discomfort when walking into a party or other group setting knowing very few individuals. Compare the feelings experienced in such instances with those elicited when you walk into a room filled with acquaintances and friends. People usually feel more relaxed and comfortable in discussions or other activities with people they know. Students experience similar feelings. The new student who is confronted by thirty unfamiliar faces is likely to respond either by withdrawing until the environment becomes more familiar or by acting-out as a means of controlling the environment by eliciting an expected response.

Several years ago, one of us was contacted by a teacher who was experiencing much frustration because the students in his sophomore English class were not becoming involved in group discussions. Furthermore, the teacher said that absenteeism in class was relatively high and students were not handing in the number of assignments he had expected. The teacher, a hardworking, dynamic young man, indicated that the material being read and discussed seemed to be of high interest and that he had made a special effort to consistently relate aspects of the literature to students' lives. Finally, students were seated in a circle and open discussion was encouraged.

While discussing this situation, I asked the teacher whether students in the class knew each other. The teacher seemed surprised by the question and indicated that because the students came from only two feeder schools and had been in his class for nearly six months, he assumed they were well acquainted. The students' behavior suggested, however, that they felt some discomfort, and the teacher agreed to assess how well they knew one another. He was surprised to discover that only a quarter of the students in his class knew the first names of more than half of their peers. He discussed this figure with the class and explained his decision to allocate time to helping students become better acquainted. Following a series of activities aimed at helping them do so, he again collected data on attendance, percentage of assignments handed in, and students' participation in class discussions. All three variables showed changes that were statistically significant at the .01 level. These results were so striking that the teacher's English department decided to incorporate a peer-acquaintance unit into the first nine weeks of the school year.

The peer-acquaintance activities described below include several that were used by the teacher described in the previous paragraph. These activities are designed to help students get better acquainted with one another so that they will feel safe and secure and will therefore become more actively engaged in the learning process. As students become better acquainted, the likelihood that they will interact with and be influenced by a wider range of students increases and cliquish behavior decreases.

The Name Chain

A name chain is the most effective method for helping students to learn each other's names. These steps will help make this activity run smoothly.

1. Ask the students to sit in a circle so that each can comfortably see all the students in the group.
2. Clearly explain the reasons for being involved in the activity. You might say that one benefit of knowing everyone's name is that it increases their knowledge of the environment and thereby makes them more comfortable and more likely to become actively involved. Similarly, you may indicate that knowing other students' names will enable students to greet each other in a friendlier, more relaxed manner, which will have a tendency to make both the classroom and the school a more positive place.
3. Ask the students if they have any questions about why they are being asked to do the activity.
4. Explain to the students that each person will be asked to say their first name and tell the group one thing about themselves. They may choose to tell the group something they like to do, something interesting that happened to them recently, how they are feeling, and so on. Inform the class that they will be asked to repeat each student's name and the statement they have made. They will begin with the person who spoke first and stop when they have given their name and have said something about themselves. The first student may say, "I'm Bob, and I went to the beach this weekend." The next would say, "That's Bob (or you're Bob), and he (or you) went to the beach last weekend. I'm Sandy, and I enjoy backpacking." Because we are faced with the difficult task of learning a large number of names and because having an adult remember their names seems particularly important to adolescents, it is best to have you be the last person to speak. You will therefore be able to list each student's name and what they have shared with the class.
5. Have everyone take a paper and pencil and change seats. Ask the students to start with a designated individual and go clockwise around the circle, writing down each person's name. It is not necessary to have them list what each student shared.
6. Ask for a volunteer who will begin with the person designated as the starting place and slowly give the name of each person in the circle. This recital serves as an opportunity for students to check the accuracy of their list and to learn the names of any students they might have missed.

It is important to provide follow-up for this activity. For example, for several days following the activity you may want to attempt to go around the class listing each student's name or ask for a volunteer to do so. We must continue to be aware of whether or not students are remembering names and continue to emphasize the value of knowing names. If you ask students to work in groups, you may suggest that they make sure they know each member's name before beginning the group activity. Teachers all too often involve students in activities and then fail to follow up with behavior that reinforces the learning derived from and the values implied by the activity.

What's in a Name

This activity is excellent as a first-acquaintance activity or as an activity following a name chain. Students are placed in groups of five or six. Briefly lead a discussion on the value of names. You might include comments about how names may reflect a cultural heritage, refer to a loved relative, or be chosen because a parent liked the name. The discussion can also focus on how names may evoke positive or negative feelings, depending on how each of us likes our name or what people do with the name. Then, tell the class that the activity involves sharing some things about the students' names as a way of becoming better acquainted. Ask students to tell these facts about their name:

1. State their full name.
2. How did they get their name? For example, were they named for someone? Does the name represent a family heritage or nationality?
3. Do they have any nicknames? Who calls them by this name? Do they like the nickname(s)?
4. Do people change their name in any way? For example, is it often shortened and so on? How do they feel about this?
5. Do they like their name? If not, what would they prefer?
6. What name do they want used in the class?

After all groups have finished, one student in each group can volunteer to introduce each member of the small group to the entire class. They do so by giving the name each student wants to be called in the class.

Know Your Classmates

Each student will need a ditto sheet entitled "Know Your Classmates" and a pencil or pen. Ask students to find a person in the class who fits each description listed on the sheet and to obtain the person's signature on the line in front of the description. To encourage students to interact with numerous peers, inform them that they cannot have the same person sign their sheet more than

FIGURE 5.4   Know your classmates

Name _____

Collect the signatures of the appropriate persons:
_____ 1. A person whose birthday is in the same month as yours.
_____ 2. A person who has red hair.
_____ 3. A person whom you don't know very well.
_____ 4. A person who has an interesting hobby. What is it? __
_____
_____ 5. A person with freckles.
_____ 6. A person whose favorite color is yellow.
_____ 7. A person who loves to read.

continued

_____ 8. A person who takes gymnastic lessons.
_____ 9. A person who is left-handed.
_____ 10. A person with naturally curly hair.
_____ 11. A person who has a dog. The dog's name is _____ .
_____ 12. A person who belongs to a Scouting troop.
_____ 13. A person shorter than you.
_____ 14. A person taller than you.
_____ 15. A person with the same color shirt or dress as you are wearing.
_____ 16. A person who plays an instrument. What instrument?
_____
_____ 17. A person who traveled out of the state this summer. Where? _____
_____
_____ 18. A person who wants to play professional sports when he or she grows up. Which one? _____
_____ 19. A person with more than four children in the family. How many? _____
_____ 20. A person who plays soccer.
_____ 21. A person with braces on his or her teeth.
_____ 22. A person who rides horseback.

twice. Figure 5.4 is an example of this activity. The descriptions can be adapted to fit the specific interests of children at different ages and in different settings.

Interviews

Interviews are an excellent means for students to become better acquainted with each other. This activity will often foster new friendships and feelings of self-importance. Lack of information about others is often a major barrier to establishing new friendships. When children do not know their peers, they tend to make assumptions and develop unrealistic fears or unfounded biases. As students interview each other, they learn new and exciting information about their peers. This knowledge, in turn, promotes diversified friendship patterns in the classroom.

We can employ interviews in the classroom in many ways. One method involves introducing the interviewing process by having students list ten questions that would help them know a classmate better. This list provides some examples of questions that might be asked by nine-year-olds:

1. What is your favorite color?
2. What is your favorite sport to play? to watch?
3. What are you proudest of?
4. Do you have any pets? If so, what are their names?
5. What is your favorite professional team in football? basketball? baseball?
6. What kinds of foods do you like to eat?
7. If you could go anyplace on a vacation, where would you go? Why?
8. Do you take any lessons?

9. Do you have any hobbies?
10. Do you like your first name? If not, what would you change it to?

We write these on the chalkboard and tell the students to each choose a person whom they do not know very well and, using the ten questions as a guide, learn as much as they can about their partner. After ten minutes ask each pair to separate but stay within viewing distance and draw their partner. These portraits are later shared and displayed. The next step consists of the pairs drawing a map of how to walk to each other's homes (only students old enough to understand the streets in their neighborhood). The final step is for each student to share the information about their partner with the rest of the class. Because you are a group member, you should participate in this activity.

Another approach to interviewing also begins by developing a list of questions students might ask each other. These are written on the board and referred to as students interview each other in pairs. After these questions have been asked, each pair of students joins with another pair. The four children share the new information they have learned about their partners. After a few minutes ask the class to reconvene and each person to share five things about his or her partner with the class.

A third interviewing technique has a student sit in a place of honor at the front of the classroom. The student is asked questions by the other class members. Students enjoy being in the limelight and often state that this is their favorite approach to interviewing.

A final interviewing approach has several students serve as reporters. They interview their peers and obtain such information as: where students were born, the number of members in their family, a student's favorite television show, food, color, or animal, a special hobby or pet, any unusual places they have traveled to, and students' future goals. The information is tabulated and can either be duplicated and given to each student or you can make a large chart in the hall for other classes to read.

The results of these interviewing activities can often be seen in new friendships and more open communication in the classroom. This atmosphere in turn makes the classroom a safe and more relaxed learning environment for students.

Guess Who

An acquaintance activity used by a number of secondary teachers gives students an opportunity to discover how well they know their peers. The steps for setting up this activity are:

1. Briefly describe the activity to the students and elicit their willingness to take part in the activity.
2. Ask students to write brief (two- or three-line) statements about themselves, which can include facts about their personal history, family, hobbies, and so forth.
3. Collect all the autobiographical statements.

4.   Ask each student to take out paper and pencil. Read each description and ask the students (you, too, should be involved) to write the name of the student who they believe wrote the description.

5.   After all the descriptions have been read, reread them and ask the authors to identify themselves. Ask the students to indicate on the list whether they made the correct choice. Upon completing the task, you can ask students to indicate the number of their peers whom they correctly identified. These results can be used to initiate a discussion about the degree to which class members have become acquainted.

6.   An interesting alternative to this activity is to have students write brief statements that include one false statement about themselves. Then give the class the student's name and personal description and ask them to decide which statement is false. This activity can be performed by the entire group or can be developed as a contest between two groups.

7.   A second variation of this activity is to have each student write a poem or riddle about himself or herself. These poems are put into a box. Each student draws a poem from the box and reads it aloud to the class. From the information on the poem the class tries to identify the author of the poem. As a follow-up, each student could draw a self-portrait that could be placed on a bulletin board with his or her poem below it.

Dyads

This acquaintance activity simply involves providing students with an opportunity to spend several minutes getting to know someone with whom they are not well acquainted. This activity is most beneficial when it gives students a chance to interact both with peers whom they would like to get to know better and peers whom they might intially not choose to meet. These are the specific methods for involving students in this activity.

1.   Explain the reasons for employing the activity. Inform the participants that it simply provides them with an opportunity to sit down and talk to several peers whom they do not know well. Be sure to give the students a chance to question and discuss the activity.

2.   Ask the students to stand in a circle so that they can see all members of the group. Then ask them to look around the group and see whether there are people whom they would like to get to know better. This may be a person whom they have not met but would like to meet or a person whom they know a little and would like to get to know better. At this stage in the activity it is helpful to point out that picking someone does not mean you want to date them or become their best friend. It simply means they are a person whom you do not know well.

3.   Suggest that each person determine several people whom they would like to meet, because the person they choose may be chosen by someone else. Here it is helpful to state that a situation sometimes arises in which the last few people remaining already know each other. This situation can be handled in two ways. First, these individuals can simply form dyads and get to know each other better. Second, these adolescents can

each join a dyad that includes two people whom they do not know well. Because the activity is much less effective if groups are larger than three, limit their size.

4.   Before having students make their selection, inform them that their task is simply to spend four or five minutes getting to know the person they choose or who chooses them. It is useful to tell the students that they can learn something about themselves by paying attention to the way in which they choose or are chosen. For example, if they turn their back slightly, look at their feet, and think, "I'm not very interesting, no one will choose me," they may be creating a situation in which they are less likely to be chosen. Also inform the class that because this is not an easy task they may have a tendency to take the easy way out by choosing their best friend. Point out that even though it may be easier, they may be cheating both themselves and other students out of some interesting learning.

5.   Inform the students that they can now choose someone and that they will be called back together in about five minutes.

6.   About one minute before the time is up, inform the students that they have about one minute to complete their conversation.

7.   When the students are once again in the large group, ask them how the activity went and how they felt. Allow several minutes for this discussion and then, unless they found the activity very difficult and do not want to try it again, ask them to once again look around the group and choose a person whom they would like to get to know better. Depending on the time available, the leader's goals, and the students' interest, this activity can be repeated any number of times. If the students indicate that the activity was difficult and they do not want to continue, follow up by asking what they found difficult. Their difficulty may stem from such factors as well-formed cliques that need to be dealt with in order to create an open, safe environment.

8.   One interesting alteration that teachers and group leaders find beneficial is to have the students select someone whom they might normally not get to know. Indicate that this does not mean that they do not like the person, but simply that that person might be a little more difficult for them to approach. It is helpful to provide the students with examples and for teachers to share their own concerns about meeting certain types of people. The leader might say that when he or she was in high school, he was not athletic, and therefore, he found it difficult to approach "jocks." He might also say that people tend to have difficulty approaching someone they have never met or who has interests different from their own. Though this version of the activity is more difficult, it does have payoffs in reducing tensions and expanding the pattern of students' interactions.

Having students know and feel supported by their peers is valuable at all grade levels, but it may be particularly critical as young people move through early adolescence. Students in grades six through eight are experiencing rapid cognitive and physical changes. This is a time of heightened self-consciousness and decreased self-esteem. Consequently, students learn much more effectively in environments where teacher-student and peer relationships are characterized by warmth, support, and stability. Schools for young adolescents should not only employ a wide range of acquaintance activities, but should also be organized so that students spend a sizable portion of the school day with students and teachers whom they know. Describing successful schools for young adolescents, Joan Lipsitz (1984) writes:

> The groups of students are small enough that, as the teachers and paraprofessionals in the schools say, they know the students' moods and do not make the interpersonal mistakes that would be unavoidable in large, more impersonal settings. The students are secure in being known, and staff members are relaxed because of their deep familiarity with the students and their confidence in dealing with them. . . . The schools have adopted policies that strengthen and stabilize peer groupings by extending the time students remain together, both during the day and also over a period of several years. . . . Antisocial behavior that results from the randomness and brevity of student groupings in most secondary schools is substantially reduced in these schools. [p. 182]

If you are interested in incorporating additional acquaintance activities into your lesson plans, you can find numerous resources. Among those we have found most useful are: Bailey and Kackley, *Positive Alternatives to Student Suspensions* (1981); David Johnson's *Reaching Out* (1982); Jack Canfield and Harold Wells's *One Hundred Ways to Enhance Self-Concept in the Classroom* (1976); Nickerson et al., *Miraculous Me* (1980); and Michele and Craig Borda's *Self-Esteem: A Classroom Affair* (1978).

ACTIVITIES FOR ESTABLISHING A COHESIVE GROUP

Group cohesiveness refers to the extent to which a group experiences a sense of identity, oneness, and esprit de corps. Cohesive groups are characterized by warm, friendly interactions among all members rather than by positive interchanges limited to small cliques within the group. Cohesive groups provide settings in which students feel safe, experience a sense of belonging, and view themselves as being liked and respected by others. Research (Lewis & St. John, 1974; Schmuck, 1966) indicates that students who are accepted by their classmates have more positive attitudes toward school and are more likely to achieve closer to their potential than are students who feel rejected and isolated. These findings are supported by research (Combs & Taylor, 1952), which indicates that students perform less effectively when they feel threatened by the environment.

> Cohesiveness is correlated with the productivity of a group, provided the norms are supportive of production. Cohesive groups are more goal-directed than noncohesive groups, and as long as the goals of the individuals are in line with pro-

ductivity, cohesiveness is a facilitating factor. Classroom groups which have strong goals have satisfied students. Moreover, students who know what is expected of them and who are involved and close to their peers in pursuing educational goals are more satisfied than students in classrooms that are disorganized and fragmented. [Schmuck & Schmuck, 1976, p. 31]

Group cohesiveness and a positive group identity do not develop simply because students spend time together. Rather, positive feelings about being a group member are developed by making the group seem attractive, distinguishing it from other groups, involving the group in cooperative enterprises, and helping students to view themselves as an important component in the group. The activities described in this section are designed to accomplish these goals. These activities are most effective when used in association with acquaintance activities and activities for creating diverse liking patterns.

Activities aimed at creating a cohesive classroom group will be most effective when introduced at the beginning of the school year. One important reason for developing group cohesion early in the school year is that cohesive groups are desirable only if the group's norms support your learning goals. If you can begin the year by establishing a positive group feeling while creating norms that support academic achievement and productive behavior, the school year will be pleasant and productive.

Activities for Elementary School Classrooms

Ways of Having a Happy Classroom
Focusing on the positive qualities of a classroom sets a tone for the entire year. In the fall we can ask students to list things they can do to make the classroom a happy place to be. Students can be encouraged to describe ways of positively interacting with each other, ideas for having fun in the classroom, and so on. The students' ideas can be written on a large sheet of paper and posted in the classroom. Every month students can be asked whether they are acting in accordance with the ideas expressed on the chart and they can evaluate each item to see if it is still applicable. New ideas may be added at any time.

Group Contributions
To establish a cohesive classroom it is important that students focus on their contributions to the group. We can enhance this theme by creating a bulletin board. Give each child paper, pencil, and crayons and ask them to draw a picture of himself or herself. After these have been completed, ask students to think about what contribution they can make to the group. After you have led a short discussion to clarify the concept and provide students with ideas, give them a strip of paper and tell them to write down their contribution. Collect the pictures and contributions and mount them on a bulletin board for all to see. This is an excellent way of reinforcing the fact that everyone can contribute to the classroom and that the classroom will be a better place if all contribute some of their special talents.

Class Charter

The development of a class charter strengthens the feeling of group cohesiveness and helps students learn how a government works and how to govern themselves.

Three steps are involved in developing a charter. First, the class selects a committee of students to write the charter. The committee writes a preamble or statement of purpose, a section on class officials and their responsibilites, a section on qualifications for the candidates, a section on election procedures, and a section stating the laws or responsibilities of the classroom. The second step is a class discussion and debate on the charter. The final step is a vote and ratification by a two-thirds majority of the class.

To implement the class government, students hold elections based on national election procedures. Candidates petition for office, make campaign posters, and give speeches. A primary and a general election are held. Any student may hold an office but may not run for reelection until each child has had an opportunity to hold that office. Elections are held every three weeks.

Students become responsible for the classroom operation as various officers assume responsibilities such as supervising the class when you are not in the room; facilitating class meetings; taking lunch count; sorting, straightening, and passing out books and papers; controlling audiovisual equipment; cleaning sink and shelves; or being certain that everyone is present during a fire drill. To involve students in becoming more responsible for classroom functioning without employing a formal class charter, we can simply create as many classroom jobs as there are students. Jobs can be assigned by having students' names drawn out of a hat, returning the name to the hat if students have previously had the job. Students enjoy being involved in developing and performing class jobs, which enables them to view themselves as integrally involved in running the class.

Classroom Arrangements

Developing a comfortable classroom environment can enhance students' motivation and provide opportunities for increasing their sense of competence and power. It is desirable to involve students in decisions about the classroom arrangement whenever possible. Give them a basic floor plan of the room including all "built-ins." Then ask them to sketch in the desks and any other movable furniture. The arrangements can be displayed and the students and you can choose the floor plan with which all would be most comfortable. By giving students responsibility for a room arrangement, we indicate our respect for their judgment and they gain a sense of significance, competence, and power.

Students can also be active in decorating the room. They can be encouraged to bring posters from home, take part in designing bulletin-board displays, and determine the types of plants they would like in the room. Increased student involvement in organizing and decorating the room is almost always associated with an intensified group feeling, higher motivation, and reduced vandalism.

Class Spirit

At the beginning of the school year most students are excited and motivated. Teachers can take advantage of this excitement by establishing a "class spirit" that creates a bond among the students. Many activities throughout the year can revolve around this "class spirit."

To create a class spirit, teacher and students discuss the kinds of group identity they would like to develop and formulate a list. The list might include: a class animal, name, flower, insect, song, flag, color, cheer, game, cartoon character, sport, bird, and poem. Suggestions are welcomed and eventually students vote to determine their choices in each category. When the "class spirit" is completed it is displayed proudly in a prominent place in the room.

It is very important to reinforce this activity by using parts of the class spirit whenever possible throughout the year. For example, when sending a newsletter to parents we might draw several of the class symbols on the letter and mimeograph the newsletter onto paper that is the class color. Similarly, stating the class cheer prior to special sporting events or singing the class song at the close of each week continues to enhance class spirit.

Class History

An effective activity that helps to mold students into a cohesive group is development of a class history or class yearbook. When approached with this idea in the fall, students are always overwhelmingly in favor of making a class history.

Four to six students are chosen either by the teacher or by their peers to write the history and all students are encouraged to contribute ideas. Every month the history writers meet and decide what events, assemblies, new lessons, etc. they wish to incorporate into their class history. The historians then divide the writing assignments. At the end of the year students have a collection of the year's events. In addition to these events the class history can include poems written by students, a student directory of addresses and phone numbers, an autograph page, a page about students' thoughts on the year, and a letter written to the students by the teacher. The class history helps create a sense of group purposefulness and commitment and is a memorable treasure for each student.

Photo Album

Whenever a special event occurs, capture the moment in a picture. Students can become actively involved by learning to use a camera. Pictures taken by students can be accompanied by written statements and put on the bulletin board until replaced by a picture and description of a new event. The old material can then be placed in the class photo album and some of the written material can be incorporated into the class history.

The photo album can be shown to parents during scheduled conferences or when a parent drops by the school. Parents enjoy seeing pictures of their children involved in special school activities. This sharing enhances parent interest in their child's school experience and increases parental support for the teacher and the school. When a particularly good picture of a child is obtained, the teacher can make a copy and send it to the parents along with a short note. Parents appreciate this thoughtful gesture and their increased interest in their child's classroom experience helps their child to develop a sense of pride and commitment.

When there are a few moments left in a day, it is enjoyable to recall several of the special events by looking at the pictures in the class photo album. This is an effective means of reinforcing a sense of identity and creating positive feelings about the class.

Opening and Closing Questions

Students arrive at school with many different feelings and needs. Some students may arrive in an irritable mood resulting from an argument with a younger brother or lack of a proper breakfast. Another student's favorite goldfish may have died, while yet another child may be extremely happy because it is his or her birthday. It is often hard for students to make the transition from home to school. Therefore it is important that students be given a few minutes at the beginning of each day to share any events that are significant to them.

Students are asked to meet in a circle. The teacher then asks whether any person needs or wants to share anything. A student who has just broken his or her foot may need someone to carry his or her lunch tray while another student whose dog just died may need some care and understanding. Teachers also have days when they are tired or not feeling well and therefore would like the students to be particularly quiet and helpful during the day. When students are treated kindly and their needs are accepted and respected, they will respond to your needs and desires.

For students who are less comfortable sharing their needs in a group, an optional activity is to have them write down their needs and place them in a box or bag. You can check several times during the day to see whether any child has put a need in the box.

The end of the school day can be an important time to establish closure on any issues that occurred during the day. Questions such as, "What did you learn today?" "How do you feel about the day?" or "What did you like and dislike about today?" often evoke serious discussion. It is advisable to allow at least twenty minutes for this session. Taking time at the end of each day encourages students to examine what they have accomplished and also helps to ensure that the day will end on a positive note.

Special Days

Creating special days allows students to have some influence over their environment while enhancing a sense of group identity. Special days might include a day on which everyone wears the same color, a day for wearing favorite buttons, a day when students wear their baseball, soccer, ice skating, or Scout uniforms, a day for dressing as students did during the 'fifties, and a day when everyone wears their favorite hat. You can add to the special day by relating various subjects to the day's theme. Math problems to solve batting averages could be included on uniform day, music of famous singers during the rock 'n roll era might be discussed and listened to during music class on 'fifties day, or students might read stories involving hats on hat day.

My School Bulletin Board

Creating a cohesive group is very important, but it is often useful to expand this concept beyond the classroom. One way to do so is to have students make a hall display or bulletin board with the theme: "What I Like about My School." Use pictures, essays, or a collage. This activity enhances school spirit and focuses on the positive aspects of a school. This concept can be extended to include a large hall mural with the same theme to which each class contributes their ideas as to why they like their school.

Baby Pictures Bulletin Board

An activity that enhances group or school cohesiveness is the display of teachers' or students' baby pictures. A contest can be held to determine which students can correctly identify the teachers' or students' baby pictures. Students enjoy this activity and it often leads to increased dialogue between students and teachers and among students.

A somewhat similar activity is to display samples of students' or teachers' hobbies in the main showcase. Students and teachers can try to match the hobby with the person involved. This activity can be used to generate positive feelings and a sense of esprit de corps either within the classroom or throughout the school.

Activities for Secondary Classrooms

Because secondary school students spend considerably less time in one classroom group, most secondary teachers will choose to incorporate only one or two of the types of activities described in the previous section. A teacher of Junior Writing and American Literature recently shared with us one of her techniques for incorporating group cohesiveness activities. During the first week of school she has the class brainstorm ways in which individuals contribute to the class as a whole. These are listed on the blackboard and may include such statements as:

breaking the ice
listening carefully and quietly
making perceptive observations
contributing their own experiences
bringing the group back to the topic being discussed
asking someone to clarify a point
summarizing
asking questions

This material is used to stimulate a discussion about how there are many ways of contributing to a class and that students will differ in their contributions. About a week later, pass out slips of paper with the name of a student on each slip. Each student in the class receives one slip and is asked to write one positive comment about a contribution the student listed on the slip has made to the class. The slips are handed in and students volunteer to read several of them.

Two additional and complementary methods can be employed with secondary classes to enhance group cohesiveness. We can involve students in cooperative-learning activities. Cooperative learning is described by David and Roger Johnson (1975, 1984) in *Learning Together and Alone* and *Circles of Learning*. Cooperative learning involves students working together to attain a goal. This activity may include group projects in which all students obtain the same grade for work completed, cooperative studying for an exam, cooperatively obtaining material to be used individually or generating creative ideas.

Because they have limited time with their students, most secondary teachers emphasize cooperative learning or other academic learning activities as the basis for creating positive peer relationships that enhance students' motivation and achievement. It is important to keep in mind, though, that these activities will be more successful when students have first been taught basic group skills. Students enjoy activities aimed at teaching these skills, and you will find numerous materials available for developing these skills.

We have found several activities and processes particularly valuable in helping secondary students develop skills in functioning as supportive, effective group members. The process includes involving students in an activity that requires cooperation to reach a goal, followed by systematically discussing the behaviors that facilitated the group activity. The game "five square" (Figure 5.5) is perhaps the best activity for stimulating this student learning. As described in Figure 5.5, students are placed in groups of five, and each group is given the task of passing puzzle pieces until each group member has an equal-sized square in front of him or her. Tell students that groups who complete their task can quietly observe groups still at work. Finally, if one or more groups has difficulty completing the task, members of these groups can raise a hand, signaling that they would like to be replaced by a student from a group that has completed the task. This student then joins the group still working and continues to follow the rules. The addition of a new member who has seen the correct pattern will usually facilitate quick task completion.

When all groups have completed the task, you can involve students in discussing the groups' functioning. On a chalkboard or butcher paper, make columns labeled "Behaviors that facilitated task completion" and "Behaviors that hindered the group." Then ask students, without mentioning names, to describe behaviors that helped their group complete their task. Next, students can list behaviors that blocked their group. Then lead a discussion on group behavior. Interestingly, this activity may also highlight additional factors related to establishing effective learning environments. For example, when using the activity recently, a student in one of our classes indicated that he had experienced considerable anxiety when other students began watching

FIGURE 5.5   The five-squares game

Preparation of Puzzle

A puzzle set consists of five envelopes containing pieces of stiff paper cut into patterns that will form six-inch squares, as shown in the diagram. Cut the squares into parts and lightly pencil the letters a through j as shown below. Then mark the envelopes A through E and distribute the pieces thus:

Envelope   A – j, h, e
B – a, a, a, c
C – a, j
D – d, f
E – g, b, f, c

Erase from the pieces the lower-case letters and write instead the envelope letters A through E, so that the pieces can easily be returned for reuse.

Several combinations of the pieces will form one or two squares, but only one combination will form five squares.

Instructions for Students

Each person should have an envelope containing pieces for forming squares. At the signal, the task of the group is to form five squares of equal size. The task is not complete until everyone has before him or her a perfect square and all the squares are of the same size. These are the rules: (1) No member may speak, (2) No member may signal in any way that he or she wants a card, (3) Members may give cards to others.

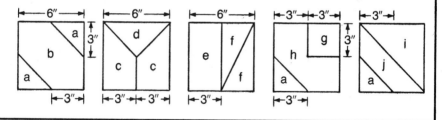

his group. This comment led to a productive discussion on the advantages and disadvantages of anxiety in learning and a further discussion on how anxiety could be limited in the class.

A second activity we have found useful in secondary classrooms is called "real estate." This activity (Figure 5.6) involves students in cooperative decision making and is arranged so that each student has information essential to the group. Therefore, a premium is placed on involving all group members in making the decision. After the students have completed the activity, it

FIGURE 5.6 Real estate

Preparation

Preparation involves cutting 144 two-by-two-inch squares for each group of eight players. These squares serve as the sections students will be asked to select. The squares are numbered and stars are drawn or attached to the backs of these squares: 1, 2, 3, 4, 7, 8, 13, 14, 15, 19, 20, 25, 26, 37, 38, 49, 55, 56, 59, 60, 67, 68, 72, 79, 80, 98, 99, 100, 111, 112, 117, 118, 121, 122, 125, 126, 127, 128, 129, 130, 133, 134, 137, 138, 139, 140, 141, 142. Before beginning the game, the squares are laid out in twelve *rows* of twelve. Preparation also includes making a set of eight maps (see Appendix) for each group of eight players.

Directions

Imagine your team to be a real estate firm commissioned to purchase lands appropriate for grape culture for United Wineries, Inc. Ideally, such land should have adequate rainfall, fertile soil, gentle slope, and adequate subsoil drainage.

Inadequate rainfall can be compensated for by irrigation wells. Infertile soil can be corrected by fertilizers and soil-building practices. Hilly land can be terraced. Inadequate drainage can be corrected by laying drainage pipes. Such corrections are expensive, however, and United Wineries has told your firm that they will not purchase land that requires more than one such corrective program. They will be willing to stand the expense for correcting one deficiency but not two or more.

For each section of land you find that meets United Wineries' standards you will receive $2,000 in commissions. (Such land will be represented on the gameboard by a star beneath the tab.)

Sections of land that require more than one corrective program are represented by a white blank under the tab.

It will cost your firm $1,000 to investigate a section; that is, to remove a tab in order to determine whether the land actually does meet the standards of United Wineries.

Teams of soil analysts and agricultural experts have been gathering information about the large geographical area represented by the cards in front of you. Their findings are not complete, but the maps they have prepared give your real estate firm some information about the area.

Each of your members will be allowed to study and memorize one of eight maps that gives information about rainfall, soil fertility, subsoil drainage, or slope for a portion of the 144 sections available to your company. Notice that there are two maps for each agricultural condition surveyed. These maps are not identical because the surveying was done by a team and was not completed.

You must decide as a team which sections you wish to investigate. Remember, each investigation costs you $1,000. Each suitable section of land you find will pay you $2,000 in commissions from United Wineries. QUESTIONS?

You now have several minutes to study and memorize your maps. Then you must turn them in and work from your memory.

is important to assist them in examining their group behavior to distinguish between productive and unproductive behavior. First, have the most successful group describe the procedure they followed in making choices. Then ask them to list specific behaviors that facilitated their effective decision making. Finally, ask the group to describe any behavior that they believed interfered with making their decision. This series of questions can then be asked of the group that was least successful at making good choices. When this information has been recorded, the remaining groups can add to the lists.

Group skill-building activities have the advantage of serving several functions. While teaching students the behaviors associated with effective group work, they help students become better acquainted and can increase the feeling of group cohesiveness. Additional group skill-building activities can be found in the books listed in the Recommended Readings.

We can also enhance group cohesiveness by involving students in shared decision making about classroom organizational factors or problems. As discussed in Chapter 7, students can cooperatively develop classroom rules and procedures. Also work with students to resolve problems that arise. We recently spoke with a friend who reported working with his junior English class to resolve the problem of student papers being late. The teacher reported that more than half his class worked part time and several teachers were requiring that major projects be due on the same day. The teacher and his students collected data on due dates for each student's assignments and developed a series of due dates that was approved by all students in the class.

ACTIVITIES FOR ENHANCING DIVERSE LIKING PATTERNS

You have undoubtedly been involved in groups in which everyone was comfortable with and enjoyed every group member. Whether it was an extended family, school staff, church group, or group of close personal friends, you probably looked forward to being with this group and found that the group supported personal and intellectual growth. Compare this experience with working in a group characterized by cliquishness and numerous isolated individuals. Anyone who has been unfortunate enough to work in such a group knows that it is far less supportive of creativity, risktaking, and productivity.

Students are similar to adults in that they are happier and more productive in environments that provide warmth and friendship. You may recall the Lewis and St. John (1974) study discussed earlier in this chapter. The study indicates that the presence of high-achieving students was not in itself enough to increase achievement among lower-achieving students. In addition to being exposed to norms that supported academic achievement, the lower-achieving students needed to be accepted as friends by their classmates. When students feel liked by their peers they experience a sense of significance, belonging, safety, and respect for others. Unless these basic personal needs are met, students will have less energy to expend in learning.

The activities described in this section increase the likelihood that all children in the classroom will be liked and accepted by their peers. Though it is important to employ several of these activities early in the school year, we should reinforce positive peer interactions by using activities such as these at least two or three times a month throughout the school year.

As with the activities connected with group cohesiveness, elementary and middle school teachers will be most likely to use the specific activities described in this section. Because teachers in grades K–8 work with groups of students longer, it is appropriate that they spend more time involving students in activities encouraging positive peer relationships and improved self-esteem. Secondary teachers will find that by incorporating the methods described in the previous section, student friendships will become more widespread and cliquishness will be reduced. This result is more likely to occur if elementary and middle school teachers have employed activities such as those found on the following pages.

Friendship Bulletin Board

"The only way to have a friend is to be one," can be the theme of a bulletin board in the hall. This bulletin board can take many forms. One method is to have students draw pictures of friends doing things together and to share with the class what they are doing. A second approach is to make a collage of friends and write words around the collage about the qualities a friend has. Another method is either to have students draw self-portraits or to pair students and have each person draw or make a silhouette of his or her partner.

Students can then put feelings that describe themselves or their partner into words in the heart of the silhouette. Thoughts and ideas the students have can be put in the brain. By the hands and feet of the silhouette, students can draw in things that they can do well. These can be mounted and each person can write a paragraph about why the partner is a friend.

This activity introduces the concept that children in the class can be friends. It also encourages children to begin to consider positive characteristics of their classmates. These concepts provide a basis for establishing a safe, positive environment characterized by diverse liking patterns.

Good Deeds Tree

To build upon the theme of helping others, a large paper tree or branch is placed on the bulletin board. Students are asked to pay special attention to the nice things people say and do. Whenever they see something nice being done, students write down what happened on a leaf made of green paper and pin it to the tree. The result is a tree full of leaves and a room filled with happy children.

Variations of this activity can be created by using pumpkins in a pumpkin patch at Halloween or shamrocks in a field near St. Patrick's Day. When working with children who cannot write their responses, we can set aside several times a day to ask children to list nice things they have seen or heard. We can write these on the appropriate paper and allow the children to pin them on the bulletin board.

Wanted Posters

Another activity that helps to create an environment of warmth and friendship is construction of wanted posters. Students are given a piece of parchment paper. They burn the edge of the paper to make it look like a poster from the old West and print the word "WANTED" on the paper. Next the student mounts a picture of himself or herself in the center and writes the phrase, "For a friend because . . . " underneath the picture. Around their picture each student writes words describing the qualities that make them a good friend. A piece of tagboard or brown construction paper can be used as a backing or support. A discussion about friendship and an opportunity to share the posters should follow this activity.

Warm Fuzzies

People enjoy receiving compliments. Everyone likes to receive positive attention and recognition in the form of a warm smile, physical touch, or kind word. Unfortunately, children often receive more criticism and frowns than compliments and smiles. In response to this situation Claude Steiner (1977) wrote a children's book entitled *A Warm Fuzzy Tale*. This delightful story can be read to students of all ages. After reading the story you can lead a discussion that assists students in clearly understanding the concepts of "warm fuzzies" and "cold pricklies" and how they make people feel. Following this discussion, students will often initiate the idea of giving warm fuzzies to each other.

One approach to helping children learn to be more positive with their classmates is to actually make warm fuzzies. Warm fuzzies can be made by wrapping yarn around one's fingers several times. The wrapped yarn is then tied in the middle and the ends are cut off. The ends are then fluffed up and a warm fuzzy has been created. After students have made a warm fuzzy they are asked to think of a reason why they deserve a warm fuzzy. Students are encouraged to share their reasons. Each student then keeps his or her first fuzzy. The class should continue making fuzzies until each child has between five and ten fuzzies. To conclude this activity students can be asked to give a fuzzy to a friend. When giving a fuzzy students are asked to tell the reason why it is being given. While the teacher may choose to set time aside daily to hand out fuzzies, students should also be encouraged to give a fuzzy whenever they wish.

Another way to give warm fuzzies is to have a Fuzzy Box where students place positive notes about their peers (students often choose to attach a warm fuzzy to their note). These can be read aloud during the last few minutes of the day. Students enjoy receiving compliments in front of their peers.

Friendship Kites

This activity is an opportunity for students to share some positive thoughts about other students. Spring is usually kite season, and so students make personal paper kites. To implement this activity, students will need four sheets of construction paper: one twelve-by-eighteen-inch white sheet for the kite and three nine-by-twelve-inch sheets of any other color. The three colored sheets can be used to make paper flowers or other designs. Students will also need crepe paper streamers cut and twisted and stapled to the kite. To complete the project they will need string, glue, scissors, a ruler, a pencil, and felt pens or crayons.

Once the kites have been constructed they are passed around the room and each student writes a positive statement about the designer on each kite. The kites can then be displayed for several days. In addition to reinforcing a diverse liking pattern, this activity helps to increase students' feelings of worth and self-esteem.

Valentine Booklets

Another activity that encourages sharing positive feelings is creating Valentine booklets. Give each child a Valentine's Day booklet cut in the shape of a heart. The front and rear covers are red hearts and the inside pages are white hearts. There should be as many white heart pages as there are members in the class (including the teacher). A booklet is created by punching each heart and attaching the pages with string.

Students sit in a circle with their Valentine booklets on their laps. Simply ask the children to "pass to the right." Students then write a nice phrase about the person whose booklet they receive. When you or the timekeeper see that each child has finished writing, speak the phrase, "pass to the right" again. This activity continues until each individual has his or her own booklet. It takes about one hour to complete, but the results are well worth the time spent. Students enjoy this activity and are often seen reading through their booklets when they need a lift.

This activity can be employed in association with a variety of special days. Shamrock books can be used on St. Patrick's Day and the words: "I am lucky to know Scott because . . . " written on the outside. Similarly, booklets can be developed around the theme of being thankful at Thanksgiving and special qualities each student possesses that will help him or her to succeed can be used as a theme on a holiday celebrating the birthday of a famous person.

Secret-Pal Books

Positive communication is vital in a classroom. The secret-pal book activity is a strategy for increasing positive communication. Every Monday each child draws the name of another student. During the week, the students observe the nice things that they see their secret pal doing and write these in their secret-pal book. These books can be made of colored construction paper cover and plain newsprint pages. Students can be encouraged to decorate the books by drawing pictures, writing positive adjectives that describe their secret pal, or writing a word that begins with each letter of the child's name; e.g., Brian— B = brave, R = responsible, I = interesting, A = athletic, N = neat. On Friday, students reveal their secret pals and present them with their books. Students enjoy this activity very much and always look forward to finding out who will be their new secret pal.

A daily variation in the week-long secret-pal books involves having children write their own names on a "secret-pal smiley face." These are placed in a basket and each child draws one, making sure that it is not their own name.

Throughout the day, each child watches his or her "secret pal" and writes down two or three friendly or helpful things he or she observes the secret pals doing. At the end of the day the secret pals are revealed and the "smiley faces" may be taken home.

Discovering Me

This activity gives students an opportunity to interact positively with each other and enhances their self-esteem. Each student draws a class member's name from a hat. Beneath the drawn name the student writes a positive adjective to describe the class member. When everyone has finished writing an adjective the papers are pinned to students' backs. Each student may ask another student three questions that can be answered only with yes or no. Each child continues asking questions until he or she has guessed the adjective pinned to his or her back, at which time they sit down. Students enjoy this type of peer involvement.

All About Me

This activity helps students identify what their feelings are and what they value. Students are given a large manila file folder and nine manila card pockets like that inside the back cover of a library book. Students then open the folder and on the left side write the words, "What I." Under these words students glue five card pockets. On each pocket front they write one of these words: love, feel, like, dislike, and the phrase want to know. Then ask them to title the right-hand side of the folder "What I Value in. . . . " The four pockets glued under this heading are labeled friendship, school, world, and my relationship with my parents. These categories may vary depending on the age of students. Then encourage them to personalize the outside of their folders by writing their name on it and drawing a picture or coloring a design.

After the folders are decorated, students are given several strips of paper and asked to write down items and thoughts that fit into each of the nine categories. A third-grade girl might write that she loves her cat, her parents, and her baby brother. She might report that she values kindness, sharing, trust, and friends who like to play games with her. When doing an activity of this kind, it is important to incorporate a discussion of the students' responses. Students should, however, be given the option not to share what they have written.

I Booklet

Each child cuts eight capital I letters out of colored construction paper. The student uses the first I to decorate a cover using his or her name in colored cut-out pieces of construction paper. On the first page of the book the child focuses on his or her name by writing it in as many unusual ways as possible. On the second page of the I booklet the student illustrates such favorite things as food, toys, colors, friends, television shows, and so on. On the third page the students draw pictures of things they like to experience with each of their five senses. On page 4, ask students to think about the seasons and what they enjoy doing on the weekends during the various seasons. They can either cut out pictures or draw favorite activities for each season. The next page is devoted to pictures of family, their house, a special friend, pets, and something special their family enjoys doing, such as camping. On the sixth page of the book the I is divided into black and white, representing night and day. Students draw several things they do during the day and several things they do in the evening. Page seven focuses on facts about the student such as age, height, address, brothers and sisters, or pets. On the last page students write a poem about themselves, list positive words that describe them, or write a story about themselves. When all the I pages are completed they can be assembled to form an "I" booklet. These should be shared with other classmates. Unlimited topics can be chosen to form an "I" booklet, and topics should be adjusted according to the grade level. For primary students we could have a laminated person in blue jeans but without hair or eye color. Each week a student's name is drawn and the child colors in his eyes and hair on the laminated figure. The chosen child adds patches to the blue jeans with titles such as height, weight, favorite color, favorite food, phone number, address, or friends, and fills in the patch with the designated information.

Positive Bombardment

Positive self-concepts are sustained and strengthened in an atmosphere of trust and security. When this type of environment has been established, a positive bombardment can be effectively employed. This activity can be implemented in a variety of ways. One technique is to have a child seated on a stool in a circle. The students take turns sharing reasons they like or respect the person being bombarded.

Once students have become familiar with this activity and have learned how to give specific positive feedback, the positive bombardments can take place in small groups. Students can now assume greater responsibility for the activity and more children can become involved in a shorter time.

Another alternative is to choose a theme such as "I felt really happy when you . . . " or "You really are a friend because . . . " and have students complete this phrase as they talk to the person being bombarded. Positive bombardments can also be employed as an ending to class discussions or class meetings. For example, children can be asked to make one nice statement to the person seated on either side of them.

Class Awards

Providing students with daily awards is one way to develop positive self-concepts and a feeling of pride. Furthermore, when children receive praise for acceptable behavior, they are more likely to continue to act positively. Students enjoy receiving an award in front of their peers and parents appreciate the special recognition.

At the close of each day eight different awards are presented to students (Figure 5.7). At first we administer the awards and record which students received each award. It is important that all students receive an award within the first week of this activity. As the year progresses, students can become

FIGURE 5.7   Classroom awards

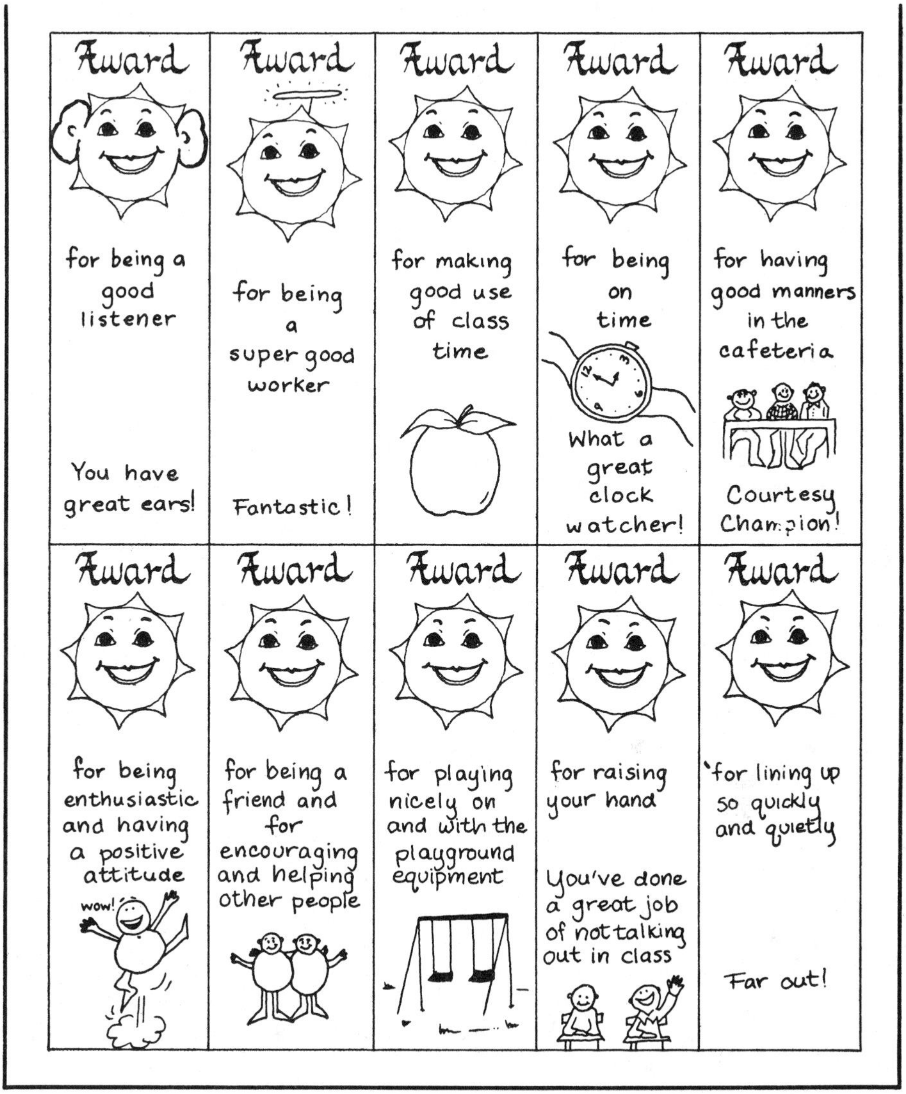

Award	Award	Award	Award	Award
for being a good listener / You have great ears!	for being a super good worker / Fantastic!	for making good use of class time	for being on time / What a great clock watcher!	for having good manners in the cafeteria / Courtesy Champion!
for being enthusiastic and having a positive attitude / wow!	for being a friend and for encouraging and helping other people	for playing nicely on and with the playground equipment	for raising your hand / You've done a great job of not talking out in class	for lining up so quickly and quietly / Far out!

responsible for determining who will earn the awards. We do so by having students nominate classmates and state why they should earn an award. The class president or appointed official can then determine which students will receive the awards and record their names as having received them. If we have not yet developed an atmosphere in which a student can make this type of decision without repercussions from peers, we can initially select the child from the list created by the students.

One special award that helps students focus on the nice things that are done for others is the "Good Citizen Award." Students are asked to pay attention to the sensitive and thoughtful responses their peers make to each other. At the end of the day students share their observations and the class decides who should receive the honor of "Good Citizen" for the day. The chosen citizen receives a special certificate and the child's name is added to the "Good Citizens' " list. This is a simple way to build strong positive feelings within a classroom.

Student Directory

Almost all students have special interests and abilities about which they feel confident. When students feel comfortable in the classroom, they will often be excited about sharing their expertise with their peers. The creation of a student directory is an activity designed to help students identify their strengths and encourage them to use each other as resources.

Students are asked to identify the activities or skills they believe they perform effectively enough to teach another child. These topics should not be limited to school subjects. They may include skills such as basketball dribbling, downhill skiing, working with dogs, model rocketry, borrowing in subtraction, organizing desks, writing a report, or calligraphy. These lists are collected, tabulated, and placed in alphabetical order with the name(s) of the student(s) listed after each skill (Figure 5.8). The student directory is typed and mimeographed and each student receives a copy. A directory is also placed in the front of the room for use by the students. The directory can be a valuable tool for a child who needs assistance with a topic. Students will often use this directory as a way to improve their skills by asking an expert to help them.

The "I Can" Can

This activity provides students with a visible means of becoming aware of their successes and achievements. We give each child a soup or coffee can and ask them to decorate the cans in some way that represents themselves, such as favorite color, activities, or hobbies. Next, students write the words I CAN on their can. Each time a student masters a new skill, he or she writes the mastered skill on a piece of paper, rolls it up like a scroll, ties it with ribbon, and places it in the can. Periodically the students should take their cans home and share their successes with their parents.

Social-Skill Training Programs

Another increasingly popular approach to creating positive peer relationships and integrating isolated or aggressive children into their peer group involves implementing social skills and problem-solving training activities with the entire class (Akita & Mooney, 1982; Cartledge & Milburn, 1978; Jackson, Jackson, & Monroe, 1983; LeCroy, 1983; Waksman & Mesmere, 1981; Walker et al., 1983). In its simplest form, social-skill training can be accomplished by instructing students in many of the skills described in Chapters 4, 5, and 10 of this book. For example, we could instruct children in sending "I messages"

FIGURE 5.8   Student directory

Organizing desks
Lisa

Otters
Janelle

Painting
Tanya
Kori

Photography
Kori

Piano
Marla
Gwyn
David

Pickleball
Scott H.

Racquetball
Gwyn
Brian

Radio-controlled cars
Scott H.

Reading
John
Larry
Beth
Kori
Claire
Cindy
Jennifer
David

Rearranging furniture
Kori

Recorder
John
David
Gwyn
Ted

Reports
David

Roller skating
Marla
Ted
Cindy
Brian
Jennifer
Kim
Scott A.

Science
Beth

Skateboarding
Scott H.
Brian

Soccer
Claire
Scott A.
Mark
Ted
Robbie
Scott H.
Jennifer
Brian
David

Softball
Kim

Spelling
Gwyn
Ted
Tanya
Cindy
Lisa
Jennifer
Kori
David
Tara
Scott A.

Subtraction
Claire
Gina
David
Kim
Scott A.
Brian

Swimming
John
David
Maria
Tanya
Cindy
Jennifer
Kim

Telling time
Kori

Tennis
Ted

Tetherball
Gwyn

Track events
Brian

*Veterinary
information*
Claire

Violin
John
Kori
Janelle

and "warm fuzzies." Students could practice these skills as a group and be encouraged to use them frequently in their daily classroom interactions. Similarly, we can teach students active listening (Chapter 4) and problem-solving skills (Chapter 10).

Social-skill training can also be implemented with one of several curricular programs now available. Recently we heard about an inner-city middle school that was confronted with the need to reduce suspensions of minority students. Investigating the cause of suspensions, the administration discovered that most were in response to students' fights. Further investigation suggested that most fights began with students becoming involved in verbal "put-downs." The staff decided to approach this problem by teaching all students in the school some basic communication and problem-solving skills. Each home room was scheduled for one full day of training in a program developed by the school district. Teachers joined their students and also received special training so that they could encourage students to use the new skills. Follow-up after six months and one year showed a nearly 50 percent reduction in suspensions for fighting.

Rose (1983) states several advantages to employing social-skill training in the classroom or other school-group setting. First, youngsters generally find a group setting more attractive than individual work. Second, a group makes better use of the teacher's or counselor's time. Third, the group provides diverse models and an opportunity for students to receive feedback from peers. Fourth, the group provides an opportunity for students to teach each other, thus facilitating development of their own social competence.

We have worked with numerous schools whose faculties have chosen to implement social-skill training in their curriculum. Most frequently these have been middle schools and junior high schools whose faculties were interested in reducing the anxiety and conflicts that occur when students from several small neighborhood schools are combined into a larger school. Figure 5.9 lists a number of commercially available social-skills curricula and the grade level or special population for which they were developed.

FIGURE 5.9   Social-skill training materials

Title	Author(s)	Publisher	Date
AWARE: Activities for Social Development	P. Elardo, & M. Cooper	Addison-Wesley	1977
Skillstreaming the Adolescent: A Structured Learning Approach to Teaching Prosocial Skills	A. Goldstein, R. Sprafkin, M. Gershaw, & P. Klein	Research Press	1980

Title	Author(s)	Publisher	Date
ASSET: A Social Skills Program for Adolescents	J. Hazel, J. Schumaker, J. Sherman, & J. Sheldon-Wildgen	Research Press	1981
Getting Along with Others: Teaching Social Effectiveness	N. Jackson, D. Jackson, & C. Monroe	Research Press	1983
Skillstreaming the Elementary School Child	E. McGinnis & A. Goldstein	Research Press	1984
Social Skills Training: A Manual for Teaching Assertive Behaviors to Children and Adolescents	S. Waksman & C. Messmer	Enrichment Press (1920 NW Johnson #10 Portland, OR 97209)	1979
The Walker Social Skills Curriculum: The Accepts Program	H. Walker and others	Pro-Ed (5341 Industrial Oaks Boulevard Austin, TX 78735)	1983
The Rochester Social Problem Solving Program	R. Weissberg, E. Gesten N. Lebenstein, & K. Schmid	Center for Community Study (575 Mt. Hope Avenue Rochester, NY 14620)	1980
Teaching Behavioral Self-Control to Students	E. Workman	Pro-Ed	1982

ASSESSING THE EFFECT OF IMPLEMENTING ACTIVITIES FOR IMPROVING PEER RELATIONSHIPS IN THE CLASSROOM

Whenever a teacher implements a new academic or behavior-change program, it is important to periodically assess its effectiveness. Educators too often employ new ideas simply because they appear interesting or educational and fail to determine whether the new program meets its stated goals. The following activity will assist you in assessing the outcomes of implementing the procedures described throughout this chapter.

ACTIVITY 5.1   Assessing the effect of implementing new peer-relationship activities

Select and implement at least three activities from each of the three approaches to improving peer relationships. These activities can be selected from those described in this chapter or from the resources listed at the end of the chapter. Secondary teachers will want to select several acquaintance activities as well as involving students in several cooperative activities.

After implementing these activities, repeat activities 5.1 and 5.2. Compare the results obtained earlier with the new data. Summarize this comparison by completing these statements:

The number of students who were not selected by any of their peers changed from _____ to _____.
I was surprised to find that . . .
I was happy that . . .
More students stated that they. . .
Fewer students stated that they. . .
My thoughts about improving peer relationships in the classroom are that . . .

SCHOOL CLIMATE

Improving the classroom climate by systematically monitoring and improving the quality of teacher-student and peer relationships will do much to create positive student behavior and increased achievement. Students' and teachers' attitudes and behavior are also affected, however, by the quality of life in the school at large. An increasing body of research points to the importance of school climate (Anderson, 1982).

The importance of classroom and school climate was emphasized by John Goodlad in his *Study of Schooling*. Goodlad and his colleagues studied thirty-eight schools in seven regions across the country. The study involved interviews with all thirty-eight principals, 1,350 teachers, 8,624 parents and 17,163 students, as well as intensive observations in 1,016 classrooms (Goodlad, 1984). Analyzing the results of this study, Goodlad reports that schools differed very little in the type of instruction found within classes. Goodlad reports, though, that differences did appear between schools. Summarizing these findings, Goodlad (1983b) wrote:

I have used the adjectives, "healthy," "satisfying," and "renewing" to describe schools in our sample that pay more than average attention to the quality of interactions among those inhabiting the school and to the physical and social context in which those interactions occur. . . . Schools differed in their ability to create an academic ambience, but the differences appear to be more related to school and classroom climate factors than to methods of teaching per se. [p. 555]

Based on their survey of numerous effective schools, Wayson and Pinnell (1982) drew a similar conclusion. They stated that:

> When discipline problems occur in school, they can more often be traced to dysfunctions in the interpersonal climate and organizational patterns of the school than to malfunctions in the individual. In short, misbehaving students are often reacting in a predictable and even sensible way to the school as it affects them and as they have learned to perceive it and react to it. We are not blaming the teacher, the principal, or the custodian for student misbehavior. But we would have them see that the system or roles and relationships in which they engage are often to blame for misbehavior. In most cases, better behavior may be taught more easily by altering patterns of rules and relationships in the school organization than by viewing and treating the student as a pathological problem. [p. 117]

More specifically, Wayson and Pinnell (1982) cite a variety of studies to support their contention that "eight features of schools have a strong relationship to the quality of discipline" [p. 118].

1. Patterns of communication, problem solving, and decision making.
2. Patterns of authority and status.
3. Procedures for developing and implementing rules.
4. Student belongingness.
5. Relationships with parents and community forces.
6. Processes for dealing with personal problems.
7. Curriculum and instructional practices.
8. The physical environment. [p. 118]

In their study of twelve London high schools, reported in *Fifteen Thousand Hours,* Rutter and his colleagues (1979) reported that a variety of schoolwide factors differentiated schools with positive student behavior and high achievement from schools facing serious problems in these areas. Factors within the school's control that significantly influenced students' behavior and performance included the degree to which teachers emphasized academic achievement; teachers' organizational, instructional, and classroom-management skills; high teacher expectations about students' performance; teachers' willingness to see students about problems at any time; an emphasis on rewards rather than punishments; teachers' involvement in decision making and the associated consistency in teachers' expectations and behavior; and students' involvement in positions of responsibility within the school. Rutter and his associates concluded that:

> ... the pattern of findings suggested that not only were pupils influenced by the way they were dealt with as individuals, but also there was a group influence resulting from the ethos of the school as a social institution. [p. 205]

The factors described by Pinnell and Wayson, and Rutter and his colleagues, have also been reported in two books whose authors conducted ecological analyses of effective secondary schools. Joan Lipsitz's (1984) analysis of four high-quality middle schools reported in *Successful Schools for Young Adolescents* and Sarah Lawrence Lightfoot's (1983) study of six high schools,

The Good High School, offer thoughtful portraits of secondary schools that are serving youths well.

Educators interested in assessing their school's climate can turn to an ever-larger number of instruments and procedures (Bebermeyer, 1982; Dorman, 1981; Howard, 1981; Kelley, 1980, 1981; Lindelow & Mazzarella, 1981; Squires, 1983; Wood & Johnson, 1982). We have employed Dorman's (1981) *Middle School Assessment Program* with several schools and found it to be extremely helpful in assisting middle-school staff in determining directions for improving the quality of their school's climate.

The important point is that teachers should work together to consider not only how their classroom management and instruction influence students' behavior and achievement, but also how the school environment can be altered to encourage positive student attitudes. This can prove to be an exciting, cooperative project that effectively and creatively utilizes teachers' creativity and concern for students. We have taught in and worked with schools in which a committee consisting of students and teachers was established to generate ideas for improving school climate. Figure 5.10 offers some examples of positive school-climate activities instigated by these committees.

FIGURE 5.10   Activities for creating a positive school climate

1. Take pictures of students (including those with a history of school problems) involved in positive behavior. Enlarge these and post them in the hallway.
2. Hold assemblies at least each quarter to reinforce positive student accomplishments. Emphasize improvement as well as standard excellent achievement.
3. Involve students in beautifying the school. Plant flowers around the outside of the school.
4. Provide a space in the hallway where teachers can post positive comments about students and students can write positive statements about their teachers.
5. Create an award (a stuffed turtle or giraffe works nicely) to be presented each week to the staff member who "stuck their neck out" to help students. The award can initially be given by the school climate committee with subsequent selection made by the previous recipient.
6. Involve students and staff in a fund-raising activity such as a jog-a-thon, with proceeds going to a local charity or other worthy cause.
7. Rather than have an attendance officer call absent students, have an adult with whom the student relates well call.
8. Involve the entire school in a day-long evaluation of the school, with ideas generated to resolve problems and make the school even better.
9. Set aside some time each day or week when everyone in the school stops what they are doing and reads quietly.

10. At the end of each day, have everyone in the school write on a three-by-five-inch card one positive experience they had that day.
11. Release teachers to spend a day experiencing the same schedule as a student who is having an unsuccessful school experience. Have the teachers report to the faculty what they saw, how they felt, and any suggestions they have for making the school a better place for their student to learn in.
12. Encourage the school staff to write notes to their colleagues whenever they observe a colleague involved in an especially helpful or thoughtful interaction with a student or staff member.

RECOMMENDED READING

Beane, J., & Lipka, R. (1984). *Self-concept, self-esteem and the curriculum.* Boston: Allyn and Bacon.

Berger, T. (1971). *I have feelings.* New York: Behavioral Publications.

Berger, T. (1971). *Reach, touch and teach.* New York: McGraw-Hill.

Borba, M., & Borba, C. (1982). *Self-esteem: A classroom affair. Volume 2.* Minneapolis, Minn.: Winston Press.

Borba, M., & Borba, C. (1978). *Self-esteem: A classroom affair. 101 ways to help children like themselves.* Minneapolis, Minn.: Winston Press.

Brown, G. (1971). *Human teaching for human learning: An introduction to confluent education.* New York: Viking Press.

Burns, M. (1976). *The book of think.* Boston: Little, Brown.

Canfield, J., & Wells, H. (1976). *100 ways to enhance self-concept in the classroom.* Englewood Cliffs, N.J.: Prentice-Hall.

Castillo, G. (1974). *Left-handed teaching: Lessons in affective education.* New York: Praeger.

Chase, L. (1975). *The other side of the report card.* Pacific Palisades, Calif.: Goodyear.

Covington, M., & Berry, R. (1976). *Self-worth and school learning.* New York: Holt, Rinehart and Winston.

Daniel, B., & Daniel, C. (1978). *Warm smiles, happy faces.* Carthage, Ill.: Good Apple.

Dinkmeyer, D. (1973). *Developing an understanding of self and others (DUSO).* Circle Pines, Minn.: American Guidance Service.

Eberle, B., & Hall, R. (1975). *Affective education guidebook: Classroom activities in the realm of feelings.* Buffalo, N.Y.: DOK.

Farnette, C., Forte, I., & Loss, B. (1977). *I've got me and I'm glad: A self-awareness activity book.* Nashville, Tenn.: Incentive.

Freed, A. (1973). *T.A. for tots.* Sacramento, Calif.: Jalmar.

Goldstein, A. (1980). *Skillstreaming the adolescent: A structured learning approach to teaching presocial skills.* Champaign, Ill.: Research.

Jensen, J., & Cooley, S. (1982). *The elementary guidance connection.* Springfield, Ill.: Charles C. Thomas.

Johnson, D. (1982). *Reaching out: Interpersonal effectiveness and self-actualization.* Englewood Cliffs, N.J.: Prentice-Hall.

Johnson, D., & Johnson, F. (1975). *Joining together: Group theory and group skills.* Englewood Cliffs, N.J.: Prentice-Hall.

LaBenne, W., & Greene, B. (1969). *Educational implications of self-concept theory.* Pacific Palisades, Calif.: Goodyear.

Lalli, J. (1984). *Feelings alphabet: An album of emotions from A to Z.* Rolling Hills Estates, Calif.: B. L. Winch.

McElmurry, M. (1983). *Belonging.* Carthage, Ill.: Good Apple.

McElmurry, M. (1981). *Caring.* Carthage, Ill.: Good Apple.

McElmurry, M. (1981). *Feelings.* Carthage, Ill.: Good Apple.

Nickerson, C., Lollis, C., & Porter, E. (1980). *Miraculous me.* Seattle, Wash.: Comprehensive Health Education Foundation.

Pincus, D. (1983). *Sharing.* Carthage, Ill.: Good Apple.

Plum, L. (1980). *Flights of fantasy.* Carthage, Ill.: Good Apple.

Polland, B. (1975). *Feelings, inside you and outloud too.* Millbrae, Calif.: Celestial Arts.

Purkey, W., & Novak, J. (1984). *Inviting school success: A self-concept approach to teaching and learning.* (2nd. ed.). Belmont, Calif.: Wadsworth.

Purkey, W. (1970). *Self-concept and school achievement.* Englewood Cliffs, N.J.: Prentice-Hall.

Rainbow activities: Fifty multi-cultural human relations experiences. (1977). South El Monte, Calif.: Creative Teaching Press.

Richards, J., & Standley, M. (1982). *Dealing with feelings.* Santa Barbara, Calif.: Learning Works.

Schwartz, L. (1976). *The month to month me.* Santa Barbara, Calif.: Learning Works.

Simon, S. B., Howe, L. W., & Kirschenbaum, H. (1972). *Values clarification: A handbook of practical strategies.* New York: Hart.

Stanford, G., & Roark, A. (1974). *Human interaction in education.* Boston: Allyn and Bacon.

Stanish, B. (1982). *Connecting rainbows.* Carthage, Ill.: Good Apple.

Stanish, B. (1977). *Sunflowering, thinking, feeling, doing activities for creative expression.* Carthage, Ill.: Good Apple.

Stevens, J. P. (1973). *Awareness:* New York: Bantam Books.

Stevens, J. P. (1971). *Awareness: Exploring, experimenting, experiencing.* Moab, Utah: Real People Press.

Thayer, L. (Ed.). (1976). *Affective education: Strategies for experiential learning.* La Jolla, Calif.: University Associates.

Vacha, E. (1979). *Improving the classroom social climate.* New York: Holt, Rinehart and Winston.

Waksman, S., & Messmer, C. (1979). *Social skills training: A manual for teaching assertive behaviors to children and adolescents.* Portland, Ore.: Enrichment Press.

CHAPTER 6

Working with Parents

What are optimal conditions for a parent-teacher conference? A quiet corner, protection from interruptions and a teacher who listens. The words exchanged during the conference may be forgotten, but the mood of the meeting will linger on. It will decide the subsequent attitudes and actions of the parents.

Haim Ginott, (1972)
Teacher and Child

Parents are the most important and influential adults in students' lives. Even at the secondary school level, parents' attitudes toward school dramatically affect students' feelings and behavior. With few exceptions, parents want to know about their children's progress and sincerely desire to have their youngsters be successful in school. Parents are delighted to hear that their youngsters are performing well and appreciate and expect to be informed immediately when problems arise. Effective teachers accept the important role parents play in students' lives and implement methods for communicating positively with parents.

Although a teacher's primary role is to work with students, for several reasons, teachers must also work with parents. First, children's attitudes about school are influenced by their parents (Coleman, 1966; Simpson, 1962). When parents feel good about their child's teacher and school, the youngster is more likely to receive encouragement and reinforcement for desirable school behavior. Second, because parents are, most often, legally responsible for their children, they should be kept informed about their children's behavior and academic performance. Third, parents can be valuable resources for teachers. They can volunteer time to tutor students, assist teachers by typing or mimeographing materials, or share their expertise on special topics with students. Finally, in a very limited number of instances the rewards and punishments available in school are simply not powerful enough to elicit desirable behavior from a youngster. When this occurs, school personnel need to involve parents in developing a behavior-change program for the student.

Even though teachers can derive numerous benefits from interacting with parents, many indicate that parent contacts are a difficult and relatively undesirable aspect of teaching. Teachers' discomfort in working with parents is based on several factors. First, parent contacts are often time consuming and energy draining. When teachers have worked with students for seven hours and had approximately one thousand interchanges (Jackson, 1968), it is understandably difficult to enthusiastically approach additional school-related interactions. Similarly, by the end of the day teachers are usually tired and face several hours of grading and planning. Time spent contacting parents simply means that a larger amount of this work must be completed at home in the evening. Teachers also find parent contacts difficult because local funding of education makes parents aware that they pay for their children's education and they therefore believe they should be able to monitor teachers' performance. This situation is intensified because the teaching profession has never been viewed with the awe or respect bestowed upon professions such as medicine or the law. Perhaps because every parent has been a student, they believe themselves knowledgeable about what their youngster needs in order to function effectively in school. These factors cause many teachers to be somewhat intimidated by parents and therefore to minimize their parent contacts.

These factors increase the likelihood that contacts with parents will be seen as a necessary task rather than an enjoyable sidelight. Teachers can, however, develop attitudes and skills that will make parent contacts much more enjoyable and productive. In this chapter we will provide methods for making positive contacts with parents throughout the school year, implementing effective parent conferences, and handling parent confrontations. In Chapter 11 we present methods for involving parents in assisting us in dealing with students' consistent or extremely disruptive behavior.

As with most classroom-management methods, each of us must decide how much time and effort we wish to invest in working with parents. Elementary school teachers are expected to maintain frequent contact with parents, and children at this age generally respond well to parents' encouragement. At the middle school and junior high school level, most teachers will, because they work with between 80 and 150 students, choose to implement only a few of the ideas presented in this chapter. At this age, and increasingly during the high school years, students desire to solve their own problems and may resent parental involvement. Nevertheless, most students enjoy having parents informed of their activities and successes, and parents of students at every grade level should be informed when students are experiencing serious or persistent problems.

KEEPING PARENTS INFORMED

Importance of Early Contacts

Obtaining parental support is facilitated by familiarizing parents with our instructional goals and classroom methods as soon as possible. Parents are no different from children or teachers. They are more likely to feel positive about and support issues they clearly understand and have had an opportunity to discuss. Parents who perceive themselves as being treated warmly and respectfully by us and who are familiar with our instructional goals and classroom-management procedures are much more likely to encourage student achievement and support us if problems arise.

By introducing parents to the curriculum and major classroom procedures early in the year, we are also able to work with the parents before any worries about their child's achievement or behavior make contacts less positive. A major reason for teachers' concerns about parental contacts is that, except for parent-teacher conferences, most teacher-parent contacts focus on negative student behavior. When our initial interaction with the parents is positive, we are more likely to feel comfortable contacting the parents as soon as their involvement appears necessary. Relationships based on infrequent interactions are seldom as warm and comfortable as those in which contacts are more frequent. Therefore, if we wish to feel comfortable in our contacts with parents, we must instigate relatively frequent, positive contacts with them. Contacts with parents are an excellent example of the idea that an ounce of prevention is worth a pound of cure. In this section we offer several suggestions for instigating such contacts.

Methods for Obtaining Parental Support

There are many approaches to developing parental support for student achievement and positive classroom behaviors. The ideas presented here are among those which we and teachers with whom we have worked have found particularly useful. We encourage you to creatively modify these methods in order to develop an approach best suited to your unique situation.

An Introductory Letter

Perhaps the easiest approach for making the initial contact is to send a letter to each student's parent(s). Because the letter will include information that you will want to present personally to students, it is best to send the letter so that it arrives one or two days after school begins. In the letter you can introduce yourself, state your interest in developing positive teacher-parent contacts, and invite the parents to attend a back-to-school night or similar event in which you and they have an opportunity to meet and discuss the school year. Figure 6.1 is an example of an introductory letter.

The Initial Meeting

It is very important that we attempt to meet parents as soon as possible. The most expedient approach to meeting between 30 and 150 parents seems to be to provide an evening when parents are invited to visit their child's class-

FIGURE 6.1   Introductory letter to parents

Date

Dear Parents,

With school under way, I'd like to take a moment of your time to welcome you to the fourth grade and to introduce myself. My name is Mrs. Louise Jones and I have taught in the Beaverton School District for fifteen years in both open and self-contained classrooms. I completed my undergraduate work at Oregon State University and received my Masters Degree from Lewis and Clark College.

I am very interested in making this a successful and happy school year for you and your child. To ensure this success, we must keep the lines of communication open. I respect the fact that you know your child very well, and so when either you or your child feel worried, please contact me. Likewise, if there is an activity or project that you enjoy, please let me know. I am available at school until 4:00 P.M. each day. I will be contacting you throughout the year about projects, upcoming events, the nice things I see your child doing, and problems, if any arise.

In a few weeks our school will have its annual Back-to-School Night. At that time I will discuss in detail the academic program, my discipline procedures, grading, and my goals and expectations for the year. There will also be a display of books and materials that your child will be using during the year. I encourage you to attend this special evening, because it will give you an opportunity to understand the fourth-grade program and to become better acquainted with the room and materials that your child will be using throughout the coming year.

Sincerely,
Mrs. Louise Jones

room(s) and discuss our approach to instruction and classroom management. It is helpful if the school supports this concept by arranging a formal back-to-school night. If this opportunity is not available, though, it is well worth our effort to arrange such an event for ourselves and any colleagues who may be interested. Our experience also suggests that it is sometimes necessary to arrange an alternative meeting time for parents who are unable to attend an evening session. Information about the times that are most convenient for parents can be obtained by requesting this information in the initial letter sent to parents.

Prior to the initial meeting with parents it is important for elementary teachers to make a telephone contact in which we report something positive about the child and obtain the parents' commitment to attend the parent orientation meeting. This telephone contact also breaks the ice and sets the stage for future telephone conversations.

First impressions are extremely important—especially when a relationship involves sporadic and somewhat role-bound interactions—and it is imperative that we do everything possible to create a positive initial meeting. In addition to the obvious factors of being well-groomed and personable, the teacher should be well organized and the classroom should look interesting and include a personal touch. Parents are very impressed by competence. We can start the meeting on a positive note by placing an outline of the evening's topics on the board. Figure 6.2 provides an example of an outline for a parent orientation meeting. This outline can be accompanied by a folder for each parent, including:

1. a description of the curriculum for the grade level,
2. an introductory letter about yourself that includes professional background and a philosophy of education,
3. a class schedule,
4. a handout describing the emotional and social characteristics of a child at the grade level,
5. a list of special projects that may require some parental assistance,
6. a statement of your classroom-management procedures,
7. book ideas for book reports, and
8. a parent resource form eliciting information about what parents can offer to the class.

By providing parents with written information, we indicate that the information is important. A folder also creates ready-made notes and thus increases the likelihood that parents will learn and recall the information presented.

Another popular idea is to display the textbooks the students will be using throughout the year. This exhibit is most effective if we place a card beside each book indicating the subject, an overview of the topics covered in the book, and why the book is being used.

We can also facilitate a positive meeting by providing a personal touch. There are obviously as many ways to do so as there are creative teachers. One

FIGURE 6.2   Outline for parent orientation meeting

I.   Introducing the Teacher
    A.   College training and degrees earned.
    B.   Professional experience:
        1.   length of teaching experience,
        2.   type of classroom—open vs. self-contained.

II.   Social and Personal Expectations for Students During the Year
    A.   Students will develop responsibility:
        1.   for themselves,
        2.   for their property,
        3.   for their assignments.
    B.   Students will learn to respect their peers' successes and weaknesses.
    C.   Students will develop a feeling of pride for their accomplishments.
    D.   Emphasis will be placed on maintaining and improving self-concept:
        1.   focus on the positive at school,
        2.   encourage parents to reinforce positive behavior at home.
    E.   Students will learn to work harmoniously in groups: emphasis on sharing.
    F.   Emphasis will be placed on teaching students the skills to communicate openly with each other and adults.

III.   Academic Curriculum and Goals
    A.   Students will increase their learning by one grade level in all subject areas by the end of the school year.
    B.   A short discussion on the major topics covered in each academic subject:
        1.   Reading
        2.   Math
        3.   Language Arts
        4.   Handwriting
        5.   Spelling
        6.   Social Studies
        7.   Science
        8.   Physical Education
        9.   Music
        10.   Library

IV.   Emphasis Will Be Placed on Organizational Skills
    A.   Notebooks will be organized by subjects and returned papers will be filed under the proper heading.
    B.   Spiral notebooks will contain students' creative-writing work.
    C.   Desks will remain neat and orderly

V. Grading System
    A. Students' grades are determined by the marks: 0 – outstanding; S – satisfactory; N – needs improvement.
    B. Report cards are given four times a year.
    C. Conferences are held in the fall and spring quarters.

VI. Students Will Have Homework under these Conditions:
    A. To reinforce a weak skill area,
    B. To reinforce a new concept: short practice on the multiplication factor or weekly spelling word list.
    C. When students have failed to use their academic time wisely in school.
    D. Students are encouraged to read for a few minutes each night.

VII. Students Will Be Assigned Three Major Projects During the Year
    A. Parents will be informed by letter.
    B. The date on which the project is due will be set realistically so that it will not interfere with family obligations.
    C. Students are encouraged to start the projects when they are assigned.

VIII. Discipline Procedure
    A. Parents will be contacted when necessary.
    B. Parents are given a copy of the Class Rules.

IX. Teachers' Comments on the Student's Study Habits So Far This Year

X. Miscellaneous Comments
    A. Mark all clothing with the student's full name.
    B. Keep emergency card current.
    C. Please send a note when your child has been ill, is riding a different bus home, or is leaving during the day.

activity that is fun is to have each child make a silhouette of her or his head or a life-size outline of her or his body. The silhouette can be placed on the desk and the outline seated in the child's chair. The parent(s) can then be asked to find their child's seat. Children can also write a note to their parent(s) to indicate several things they would like their parent(s) to see in the classroom.

During the parent orientation we can discuss our approach to classroom management. Parents can be provided with copies of the classroom rules and we can discuss how both minor problems and consistent behavior problems will be handled. For example, we can outline the use of class meetings, describe the problem-solving approach that will be used, and discuss behavior contracts. We should also make a clear statement on when parents will be contacted about students' behavior.

Similarly, we should clearly outline the instructional methods that will be employed to assist the students. We can discuss the class schedule and indicate the types of instruction that will be used in teaching each topic. We might inform the parents that during reading their children will be grouped by ability and will receive numerous homework assignments. We can discuss the types of homework that the students will be assigned and describe how parents can best respond to the homework. You may want to state that should students ever be confused and overly concerned about a particular homework assignment, the student or parent is welcome to call you at home for assistance. Our experience indicates that though parents appreciate and are impressed by this offer, teachers receive very few evening phone calls about assignments.

When discussing academic work, we will want to describe the various special services, such as reading or gifted programs, which are available for providing students with individualized instruction outside the classroom. Similarly, we should discuss how individual differences are attended to in the classroom. Along these lines, it is helpful to outline the grading system that will be employed and to discuss issues such as whether grades will reflect improvement or performance measured against some external standard. We will also want to describe any special instructional methods such as peer tutoring, individual goal setting, or group projects. Finally, parents can be informed that they will receive letters from us announcing any special projects or assignments that may require that they provide their child with some assistance. By clarifying the academic program and informing parents when and how they will be involved in assisting their children, we can begin to create an accepting supportive parent response.

We should also inform parents that they can expect to receive telephone calls and notes when their child has had a particularly good day or done something new or especially interesting. Similarly, the parents should be informed that they will also be notified when problems arise so that they are aware of what is happening. We can indicate that although we accept the responsibility for providing an exciting educational experience and helping the students to learn social skills and responsibility, the most effective approach to motivating student learning and dealing with any problems that arise is for the home and school to work together effectively.

Follow-Up
We must not wait too long before reinforcing the ideas presented in the orientation meeting. We can do so by arranging to involve parents in an instructional activity within a week or two following the meeting. The involvement may include an assignment in which parents are asked to assist their children in obtaining information. We might ask the students to develop a family tree or to interview their parents for a career day. Another follow-up activity involves sending positive notes to parents about improvements or achievements their children have made in the specific areas discussed during the orientation meeting.

An additional aspect of follow-up is contacting parents who did not attend an orientation session. One approach is to send the parents their folder along with a letter stating that they were missed and inviting them to schedule a time to visit the classroom and discuss the material in the folder. It is helpful to call parents who do not respond and ask them whether they had any questions about the material they received. Although such contacts do require additional time, they are well worth the effort, for they create a foundation for increased parental support.

Continuing Teacher-Parent Communication

One method of communicating with parents is to send informational letters about coming areas of study, field trips, long-term projects their child will be asked to complete, or newsletters about class happenings. Parents appreciate receiving information regularly, and a bimonthly or monthly letter seems most appropriate.

Another approach is to have students make personalized stationery during the first weeks of school. They can design their own patterns and decorate their stationery using felt pens, charcoal, paint, or any other art medium. We can use this stationery to send positive notes home about the student. It is best if elementary teachers send a positive note home at least twice a term. Most teachers find it helpful to record when notes were sent as well as the content of the notes. In this way we can send notes to all students and focus on different positive events each time a note is sent for each child.

Phone calls are yet another method for contacting parents. Teachers who call each child's parent(s) at least once before scheduling the initial conference and at least once a term thereafter find that parent-teacher contacts are more relaxed and enjoyable. Teachers often shy away from parents who have a reputation for being difficult to deal with. These, however, are the parents whom we should make the most effort to know. Parents appreciate knowing that their child's teacher cares enough to make a phone call, and the most critical parent will frequently become a supporter of the teacher who takes time to call. When making phone calls, always begin and end the conversation with a positive statement about the child. We should also ask the parent how the child is reacting to school and whether the parent has any information that might assist us in making the school experience more productive for the child. Like children, parents respond more positively when given a sense of competence and power.

We should also contact parents when a child begins to consistently act out in class, falls behind in his or her school work and may need special assistance, or needs to complete some work at home. As in any relationship, it is much better to deal with problems when they first arise than to wait until a crisis has occurred. Parents are justified in their annoyance when they attend a conference and discover that their child has been behind for six or eight weeks. Though it is true that some parents either do not care or cannot provide assistance in working with their child, it is important that we hold positive expectations. It is surprising how often parents with a reputation for lack of concern or for ineptness in helping their child can respond productively when contacted early and treated thoughtfully. There is an important distinction between teachers' constantly calling parents for support and calling parents to provide them with information. Parents have a right to expect teachers to handle minor problems and seek professional assistance in coping with major problems. Parents should be informed, however, when minor problems such as incomplete assignments or failure to bring supplies become frequent occurrences. Similarly, parents should be informed when major behavior or academic problems arise.

A final method for keeping parents informed is to ask them to serve as volunteers in the classroom. Parents are more likely to support us if they understand and feel a part of what goes on at school. Many parents of behavior-problem students had negative experiences when they were in school. Consequently, they respond negatively to and are often intimidated by teachers. Involving these parents in a positive manner in the classroom can do a great deal to alleviate these negative feelings. Parent volunteers who are treated with respect by teachers almost always become strong supporters of the teacher. As anyone who has worked with parent volunteers knows, we will initially need to spend time discussing the volunteer's role and assisting volunteers in understanding and responding consistently with our instructional and discipline style. We will also need to recognize situations in which a parent's style of interacting with children may contradict our methods. In such cases, we may wish to channel the volunteer's efforts into support activities that involve minimal contact with students.

Assessing Parent Contacts

Awareness is almost always the first step in changing one's behavior. Before deciding whether or not to take the time and risks involved in trying new behaviors, most people choose to carefully examine their present behavior. Activity 6.1 provides you with an opportunity to examine your current parent contacts. It also offers several ideas for systematically improving these contacts.

ACTIVITY 6.1   Assessing and improving parent contacts

Assessing your parent contacts
To assess the current level of your contact with parents, answer these questions:

1. How many informational letters have you sent out to every parent so far this year? _____
2. What percentage of your students' parents have received a positive phone call about their child's work or behavior? _____
3. What percentage of your students' parents have received a positive note about their child's work or behavior? _____

4. How many students in your class are experiencing what you would define as significant academic or behavior problems? _____

5. How many parents of these students have you talked to about the problem and your approach to dealing with it? _____

6. How many parents have served as volunteers in your classroom this year? _____

7. How many hours a week is a parent present in your class-room? _____

Improving your parent contacts

1. Send an informational letter to your students' parents. After two weeks evaluate this effort by answering these questions.
    a. How many parents made a positive comment about the letter? _____
    b. How many students said something positive about the letter? _____
    c. List two advantages to sending the letter:
        (1) _____
        (2) _____
    d. List any disadvantages associated with sending the letter.

2. Over a two-week period, send a positive note home with each child in your class. After two weeks evaluate this effort by answering these questions:
    a. How many parents made a positive comment about the note? _____
    b. How many students said something positive about the note? _____
    c. List two advantages to sending the note:
        (1) _____
        (2) _____
    d. List any disadvantages associated with sending the note.

PARENT CONFERENCES

For most teachers, parent conferences are a required form of parent contact. Parent conferences can play a vital role in eliciting parents' support for us and assistance in helping us work with students who are experiencing difficulties. Unfortunately, a poorly organized or otherwise negative conference can create or intensify parental dissatisfaction. This dissatisfaction will frequently be reflected in students' behavior. Furthermore, coping with parental criticism diverts valuable teacher time and energy. Therefore, parent conferences have a very real influence on classroom discipline.

By thoughtfully preparing for a conference and implementing a well-organized conference, we can reduce our own anxiety about conferring with parents while increasing the likelihood that parents will leave the conference feeling positive about and supportive of us. In this section we offer suggestions for improving skills in conferring with parents.

Preparing for a Conference

Because teacher, parent, and student all care about the outcome of a teacher–parent conference, we must consider how to best prepare each of these individuals for the conference. A conference will be more comfortable and productive when each person involved (the student is integrally involved even if he or she is not present) is prepared for the conference.

Preparing Students

The first step in preparing students is to discuss the goals of conferences and allow children to ask questions and express their concerns. Students need to know why their parents are being given a report and what will happen at the conference. The next step is to provide students with an opportunity to evaluate their own work. Because the primary goal of periodic teacher–parent conferences is to clarify and communicate students' accomplishments, it is logical that students should be involved in this process. Providing students with an opportunity to evaluate their own work also reduces their anxiety about the type of information their parents will be receiving. Self-evaluation provides children with a sense of significance, competence, and power.

There are several approaches to involving students in self-evaluation. The most specific and valuable method is to allow students to fill out a report card on themselves. The easiest and most effective method of developing a self-evaluation report card is to simply ask students to rate themselves on the same items on which the district or school requires us to rate students. Figure 6.3 is an example of such a form. Once the student has completed a self-evaluation form (younger children or students who have difficulty with reading will require assistance in completing a form), we can schedule time to discuss the results individually with each student. We should inform the students that this conference will allow the teacher and student to discuss any discrepancies between the teacher's and student's evaluation. It is extremely important to discuss these differences. Student resentment and hostility is often the outcome of a conference in which parents are given negative information about a student before this information has been systematically discussed with the student. The implications for classroom management are obvious and dramatic. Students will treat their teacher and peers with greater kindness and respect when they feel they have been treated fairly.

Another method that can be incorporated with a self-evaluation report card is to have students examine their behavior and academic achievements

FIGURE 6.3   Self-evaluation report card

Name _____

Reading

1. Approximately how many pages of outside reading have you done this term? _____
2. Have you done as good a job on outside reading as you could have? _____
3. Have you kept up your daily assignments in your workbook and reading text? _____
4. What grade do you deserve in reading?
    grade: _____   effort: _____

Math

1. Have you worked hard to get all your assignments done on time? _____
2. Are there any of the mutiplication tables that you are not sure of? _____ If so, which ones? _____
3. Are there any areas of math that you are not clear about or need more help in? _____
4. What grade do you deserve this term in math?
    grade: _____   effort: _____

Spelling

1. Have you studied your list words each week? _____
2. Have you been completing your workbook assignments each week on time? _____
3. Do you think you remember the words that you learn to spell each week? _____
4. How well do you spell your words in your creative writing and on daily assignments?
    superior   very good   fair   poor   (Circle one)
5. What grade should you receive for spelling this term?
    grade: _____   effort: _____

Cursive Writing

1. What grade do you feel you have earned this term in cursive writing?
    grade: _____   effort: _____
2. What do you need to work on? _____

Science, Social Studies, and Art

What grade would you give yourself in each of these areas for this term? Please give a reason for each grade.
Science: grade: _____   effort: _____
Reason _____

continued

Social Studies: grade: _____   effort: _____
Reason _____
Art: grade: _____   effort: _____
Reason _____
What areas are you doing well in at school? _____
What do you need to work on? _____

In what ways do you feel you have grown personally this year?
_____

Please evaluate your study habits and personal growth, using these ratings.

+ = outstanding growth
= = okay or satisfactory growth
√ = need to improve in this area

Put the appropriate mark on each line below.

Study Habits

_____ Following directions
_____ Completing assignments on time
_____ Working well in (your) a group
_____ Working well alone
_____ Listening well to whomever is speaking
_____ Showing neatness in your work and desk
_____ Assuming responsibility for your work

Personal Growth Areas

_____ Considering other people's feelings
_____ Following school rules in a positive way
_____ Taking care of your personal belongings
_____ Controlling your own behavior
_____ Being able to accept responsibility for your own actions
_____ Being able to get along well with others.

Is there anything that you would like to share with me about yourself or your work? _____

Is there anything you would like me to write on your report card or share with your parents? _____
Do you have any comments about my teaching this term? _____
_____
_____

Other comments that might be helpful for me to know? _____
_____
_____

Thank you for your help!

compared with their stated goals. If students have been involved in writing goals for the grading period, they can be asked to write a short statement about the degree to which they met these goals. This procedure not only places their learning and subsequent grade in perspective but also reinforces the concept of students' responsibility for their own learning.

Preparing Parents

There are two basic methods for preparing parents for a teacher–parent conference. First, as discussed earlier, we should already have had several positive contacts with the parents. These contacts ideally include a back-to-school night, a phone call, and several notes sent home on their child's progress. Second, about one week before the conference we should send the parent(s) a note reminding them of the conference and providing them with an agenda for the conference. Figure 6.4 provides an example of such a note and outline.

FIGURE 6.4   Agenda for a parent conference

Dear Mr. and Mrs. Smith:

I am looking forward to our conference on Wednesday, November 6 at 3:30 P.M. In order to help us use the time most effectively I will try to follow the agenda listed below. I hope that this list will cover all areas you would like to discuss. If you have any special questions, it might be helpful to jot them down prior to the conference.

Conference Agenda
1. Share positive personal qualities about the student.
2. Read student's self-evaluation.
3. Discuss the report card and examine samples of the student's work.
4. Discuss the student's behavior and peer relationships.
5. Time for any final parent questions or concerns.
6. Summarize the conference by discussing the student's strengths, weaknesses, and areas that need improvement.

Sincerely,

Mrs. Johnson
3rd Grade Teacher

Teacher Preparation

We are responsible for providing the parent(s) with clearly presented information in the context of a positive, comfortable interaction. The three basic steps in accomplishing this goal are these: First, as discussed in the preceding paragraphs, we should adequately prepare the student and parent(s) for the conference. Second, we should acquire and clearly organize important information about the student. Third, we should create a comfortable, relaxed environment.

Parents are impressed with data. Data indicate that we have invested time and energy in preparing for a conference. Data also testify directly to our professional competence. By focusing on specific data, we quickly move ourselves out of the parents' conception of teachers as professional babysitters and into the category of skilled professional educator. Data also have the obvious advantage of objectifying a discussion. The presence of data greatly diminishes the likelihood that a conference will turn into a debate over whether a student's grade is fair or whether a student's behavior really warrants concern.

Data also provide protection for the educator. Data provide a record of the student's academic progress and behavior as well as our attempts to make thoughtful interventions aimed at improving skills and behaviors. The availability of data prevents us from being accused of exaggerating a problem, picking on a student, or not having attempted to solve the problem ourselves. Regardless of how competent we may be, lack of specific information significantly undermines our position when working with parents. Consequently, well-organized data are a necessary component of any parent conference and are especially important when a conference focuses on dealing with inappropriate student behavior or poor student achievement.

The four major types of data that are useful in a parent conference are:

1. data on the students' and parents' feelings about the class;
2. data on students' behavior and the results of attempts to improve the behavior;
3. data on the student's academic work; and
4. data on conferences with colleagues and specialists aimed at developing a solution to any matter that is a problem.

It is helpful to acquire information about how the parents view the school year as progressing for their child. By requesting this information, we acknowledge the importance of the parents' concerns and ideas. Information about the parents' perceptions of their child's reactions to school and the parents' own wishes can also enable us to be better prepared for the conference. Figures 6.5 and 6.6 provide an example of a cover letter and parent questionnaire used by intermediate grade teachers.

Data on a student's behavior will be necessary only when conferring with parents whose child is having serious behavior problems. In such cases we should present the parents with specific data on the child's behavior and our approaches to helping the child in improving the behavior.

FIGURE 6.5   Cover letter to pre-conference parent questionnaire

Dear Parents,

I am attempting to make parent conferences more productive for myself, your child, and you.

In order to do so, I would like to have as much information as possible for the conference. You can help me by responding to the questions on the attached sheet. If there are any questions that you do not care to answer, please feel free to leave them blank. I would very much appreciate your returning this questionnaire to me at least one day before the conference. If that is not possible, please bring it to the conference with you.

I appreciate the time you are taking to help make this a rewarding conference for all of us.

I look forward to seeing you next week.

Miss Wilson

FIGURE 6.6   Pre-conference parent questionnaire

Please complete this questionnaire and return it as soon as possible. Thank you.   Name: _____

1. My child's general attitude toward school this year is _____
    _____

2. My child expresses most interest in school in _____
    _____

3. My child's greatest concern in school seems to be_____
    _____

4. Some things my child does very well are (these do not have to pertain to school)
    a. _____   d. _____
    b. _____   e. _____
    c. _____   f. _____

5. An area I would like to see my child work especially hard in is _____
    _____

6. Please list some positive qualities that your child has so that we can discuss good qualities at school (such as: trustworthy, patient, understanding, punctual) _____

7. Something I have wondered about this year is_____
    _____

8. Some things my child would like to do but has never done are _____
    _____

continued

9.   Some things that seem difficult for my child are (not necessarily school work: example, doing small tasks with fingers) _____
_____

10. Something my child would like to do in school is _____
_____

11. Several subjects that my child seems to enjoy are (include interests and hobbies) _____
_____

12. I would appreciate any suggestions or comments you have that would help me work more effectively with your child. _____
_____
_____
_____

Thank you for taking time to complete this questionnaire.

Because the school's primary function is to provide students with basic academic skills, the teacher—parent conference should heavily emphasize informing parents about their child's academic progress. We should prepare for each conference by readying a folder that includes samples of the student's work in each major subject. The folder should include specific examples that will help the parent to understand any areas in which the student is having particular difficulties.

If the data on the student's academic progress indicate that the student is not functioning well, we should be prepared to provide the parent(s) with examples of ways in which the student's academic program has been adjusted in order to meet the student's special needs. If we have worked with specialists in developing an individualized program, it is helpful to provide information about these conferences. We can do so by employing a standard form to record the results of such conferences. Figure 6.7 is an example of a form you can use for this purpose. There are several advantages to presenting this type of data. Data on professional consultation evince our concern and resourcefulness. Furthermore, they indicate to the parents that their child's problem is not simply a personality conflict with a teacher or the result of an incompetent teacher's having difficulty teaching their slightly energetic student. Another advantage to having consulted with specialists is that this procedure should present the parents with clearer and more thorough data. Especially in the area of academic difficulties, classroom teachers often have limited skills in diagnosing the specific factors that may be causing a student's problems. By consulting specialists, we can not only provide the parents with more detailed information, but can simultaneously acquire information that can assist in developing a more appropriate academic program for the student.

It is helpful to provide parents with a conference summary. This review can focus the conference and can also refresh our minds, for we often hold

FIGURE 6.7   Teacher–specialist conference form[a]

Consultant's name _____ Date _____

Consultant's position or role _____

Reasons for holding the conference:

Goals for the conference:

Information obtained:

Decision(s) reached:

Additional comments:

[a]From Vernon F. Jones, *Adolescents with Behavior Problems: Strategies for Teaching, Counseling, and Parent Involvement.* © 1980. Reprinted by permission of Allyn and Bacon, Inc.

several consecutive conferences. The parent should be given the summary sheet at the end of the conference. Figure 6.8 is an example of a conference summary form.

Once we have prepared students and parents and have collected and developed the important data, the final preparation involves creating a comfortable conference setting. If possible, the conference should be held at a round table so that neither party is in a dominant position. The atmosphere can be made more relaxed by placing some flowers on the table and having cookies and coffee available. The agenda should be placed on the board or on a large sheet of butcher paper as a reminder for both parties. Parents also appreciate knowing what topics and skills have been covered during the term. A piece of paper listing these skills can be placed next to the agenda for reference during the conference. Pencil and paper should be provided so that the parent(s) can take notes during the conference.

FIGURE 6.8   Conference summary form

Student's name: _____

Academic Achievement

Reading

Doing well in: _____
Needs to work on: _____

Math

Average of math scores: _____   _____
                                    tests   daily work
   Strong areas: _____
   Needs to improve on: _____

Other subjects: _____
_____

Behavior and Personal Characteristics

Postive personal qualities that I see in your child: _____
_____

Improvement needed in: _____
_____

Comments about how your child is relating to his or her classmates: _____
_____
_____

Final Comments

You could help at home by: _____
_____
_____

Any additional comments: _____
_____
_____

Providing an Effective Conference

If we have prepared effectively, the actual conference will usually be quite easy and comfortable. After greeting the parent(s) warmly and chatting for a moment about any positive topic, we should begin the conference by sharing several positive personal qualities the child displays at school. We can encourage the parent(s) to discuss any aspects of the student's behavior they have enjoyed or been particularly pleased with recently. The next step is to ask the parent(s) to read the student's self-evaluation report card and any other material the student has written about his or her progress during the term. Students are often so critical of their own work that this is an interesting and sensitive preparation for any critical comments we may need to make. Once they have read their child's own critical evaluation, parents are less likely to question our statements about areas in which their child needs improvement.

Many parents are very concerned about their child's report card, so that the next step is to discuss the actual report card and examine specific examples of the student's work. When doing so, we should initially focus on positive aspects of the student's work. Parents respond well to the "sandwich theory of feedback," in which critical comments are sandwiched between positive comments about their child. Another strategy is to introduce an area that needs improvement with the statement, "I would like to encourage your child to. . . ." By focusing on the positive, we can minimize parental defensiveness and criticism.

Once academic matters have been discussed, we can focus on the student's behavior and peer relationships. It is important to discuss positive aspects of the student's behavior as well as aspects that require improvement. Also, if the student has experienced serious behavior problems, we must provide the parent(s) with specific data on the student's behavior and efforts to assist the student in changing behavior. During this portion of the conference it may be appropriate to invite the principal or any other specialists to join in the discussion. The last section in this chapter provides specific strategies for conferring with parents of seriously acting-out children.

After we have discussed the student's academic progress and behavior, the parent(s) should be encouraged to ask questions and make comments. If the parents do not have any questions, we can assist them in focusing on their thoughts and concerns by referring to any pertinent items on the Pre-conference parent questionnaire (Figure 6.6).

We can conclude the conference by summarizing the student's academic and behavior strengths and weaknesses. Goals for improvement can be written down (Figure 6.9) and we can discuss any ways in which the parents can assist the child at home. These should be listed on the Conference summary form (Figure 6.8). We should discuss any follow-up contacts that appear desirable based on the information discussed during the conference and we should express sincere appreciation for the parents' efforts and input.

The final step in implementing an effective conference is to ask parents to evaluate the conference (Figure 6.10). This provides us with valuable information about aspects of the conference that parents find most and least beneficial. Perhaps equally important, by requesting an evaluation we conclude the conference with an activity that acknowledges the parents' value and provides them with a sense of competence and power.

FIGURE 6.9

PLAN FOR IMPROVEMENT

STUDENT'S NAME: _____

TEACHER'S NAME: _____

PARENT'S NAME: _____

DATE: _____

AREA TO BE IMPROVED: _____
_____

THE TEACHER WILL: _____
_____

THE STUDENT WILL: _____
_____

THE PARENT WILL: _____
_____

LONG-RANGE GOAL: _____
_____

FIGURE 6.10   Conference evaluation form

Would you please take a moment to evaluate our conference? This review helps me as I plan our next one.

excellent	10	_____
	9	_____
	8	_____
	7	_____ Please check the
		appropriate line.
	6	_____
average	5	_____
	4	_____
	3	_____
	2	_____
poor	1	_____

Was there a subject which you especially appreciated my sharing or which was very helpful to you?
Was there an area we neglected to discuss that you feel I should have brought up?
Do you have any other comments to share?

Implementing and Assessing New Methods

Having examined a variety of methods for preparing and implementing parent conferences, the next step is to select specific methods you believe would make your next set of conferences more productive and enjoyable. If you are somewhat tentative about a new method, you might wish to employ it with several parents with whom you are most comfortable.

ACTIVITY 6.2   Implementing and assessing new methods

Select one method for improving student, parent, and teacher preparation. Write these on a sheet of paper and make a specific statement about how you will implement each method. Next, select one method from the section on implementing an effective conference.

During your next series of parent conferences, implement each of the methods you have selected. After the conferences are completed, evaluate the new methods by completing these statements for each new approach:

The most beneficial aspect of this new approach was . . .
Another advantage was that . . .
Parents' response to this approach was . . .
Students' response was . . .
One difficulty with this new approach was . . .
I felt more comfortable when using this method because . . .

METHODS FOR SECONDARY TEACHERS

As stated at the beginning of this chapter, secondary teachers usually have fewer direct parent contacts than their elementary school counterparts. Most secondary schools do not require parent conferences for all students, nor do they expect teachers to maintain continuing contact with their students' parents. Nevertheless, our own experience and reports from numerous teachers suggest that secondary teachers too often underestimate both the value and feasibility of steady parent contacts. Teachers who have employed the following cost-effective methods for communicating with parents report increased parental support and improved student attitudes toward academic activities.

Introductory Letters

We can provide parents with a wide range of information by sending home a form letter describing selected aspects of our learning goals, instructional methods, and classroom procedures. A letter might include a course syllabus or similar list of topics to be covered and specific skills the students will learn. We may also comment on the specific teaching methods we will use during the course. For example, if we employ group work or projects, we might describe the activities in which students will be involved as well as the educational rationale for employing these methods. We may also comment on our grading procedures and our decision on when to inform parents about lack of student progress. And we can describe the methods we will employ in responding to disruptive student behavior. When doing so, we must preface this material by suggesting that such behavior is not anticipated, because the combination of interesting and effective instruction and our commitment to assist students will make it unlikely that these methods will prove necessary.

Newsletters

A newsletter is an expedient way to keep large numbers of parents informed. Because most secondary teachers have three separate preparations, a newsletter sent every three weeks for each class requires a teacher to write one newsletter each week. The newsletter can involve less than a page, describing subjects currently being taught, projects due, films being shown and so on. We can also use this opportunity to jot a personal note on newsletters to parents whose child is experiencing noteworthy success or problems.

Progress Reports

Many schools require that teachers notify parents at midterm of each nine-week period if their child is earning lower than a C grade. You can readily develop your own form for immediately contacting parents whose children are beginning to experience academic or behavioral problems. Because this form should be sent when students are just beginning to experience a problem, you should summarize the steps you will be taking to help the student. This form need not initially require you to write; you can simply list the methods you systematically employ.

DEALING EFFECTIVELY WITH PARENTS' CRITICISM AND CONFRONTATION

Anyone who has taught for several years has had to deal with an angry or critical parent. Many teachers state that, along with classroom discipline, this type of confrontation is perhaps the least desirable aspect of teaching. Although there is no foolproof method for dealing with an angry parent, there are several strategies we can employ to cope with such situations in an effective, professional manner.

1. Greet the parent in a pleasant manner. It is more difficult for a parent to remain critical and aggressive if you seem glad to see them.
2. Employ active listening to defuse the parent's emotions. Becoming defensive or initially arguing with the parent will usually only intensify the parent's emotions. By using phrases such as "I appreciate your concern . . . ," or "I can see that you are really concerned about this," you can help the parent to feel understood. This tactic will gradually enable the parent to calm down and replace angry or frightened feelings with more positive and productive feelings.
3. Look genuinely interested and listen carefully. This attitude also helps the parent to feel accepted and will gradually reduce negative or intense feelings.
4. Present a calm, professional manner. Stand erect, look at the parent, and remain calm. Just as students respond more effectively to teachers who remain calm and in charge during a crisis (Brophy & Evertson, 1976; Kounin, 1970), parents need the structure provided by a calm response.
5. Ask the parent what he or she wishes to accomplish. One method of structuring a confrontation conference is by questioning the parent: "I appreciate your concern. What would you like to accomplish with our discussion today?" This approach helps to focus the parent's energy and moves the conference away from a "gripe session" into a potentially productive problem-solving conference.
6. Set a time limit if necessary. If your time is limited, it is important to inform the parent. Do so by stating, "I have twenty minutes before I have to be back with my class. Let's see how far we can get in solving the problem in that time. If we need more time, I will be glad to schedule a conference as soon as possible."

7. Ask the parent whether the student is aware of the problem. Because the student is the most important person involved, it is important to clarify how they feel about the issue being raised by the parent. This question also slows the parent down and creates a more productive focus for the conference. Furthermore, the question helps to introduce the issue of the student's responsibility for any problem that may exist.

8. Be honest. When confronted by parents, it is easy to understate the seriousness of a problem or to accept too much responsibility for a problem that is largely something the child must work on. We must maintain our professional integrity and set the stage for future conferences by initially presenting an honest and clear statement of the problem.

9. Emphasize specific data. Data are simultaneously one of your best professional tools and your best defense. If a parent angrily states that his daughter did well in math last year but is having difficulty this year, the most logical and effective approach is to examine data on the student's math skills.

10. Tell the parent specifically what will be done to deal with the problem. Parents have a right to know what the teacher will do to alleviate a difficulty. Furthermore, critical parents can often become strong supporters if they learn that they will be listened to, confronted with data, and presented with a plan. If the parent's worry was not justified, the plan may simply involve a follow-up conference to examine the results of the current program. If, however, the parent highlighted an area that required attention, developing a plan shows respect for the parent's concern and competence on your part.

INVOLVEMENT WITH PARENTS OF HANDICAPPED CHILDREN

With the passage of PL 94–142, teachers became more frequently and formally involved in working with parents of handicapped students. As awareness about various handicapping conditions increased, more handicapped students were placed in public schools, more services became available to help them, and teachers found themselves referring more students for these services. Referral forms vary from district to district, but usually include requests for this information:

> date of referral
> name of person making referral
> parent's name, address, and phone number
> student's current placement
> reason for referral
> examples of attempts to correct problem
> responses of student to such efforts. [Meyan 1982, p. 69]

Although parents need not be contacted until their permission is required for the educational evaluation, they should be notified as soon as we perceive a problem, so that teacher–parent communication will be open throughout our efforts to assist the student and during the referral process. Steady communication with the parents better prepares them to productively participate in the decision on placement and in creating an individualized education program (IEP).

> They are also able to share information that can be of value, and can allow insight into any cultural and language differences that may be contributing to the student's difficulty. Effective communication between home and school is an effective way to help gain a total picture of the child's needs and to prevent disagreements and misunderstandings that too often have led to delays in needed services. [Meyer, 1982, p. 70]

In addition to involvement in the referral process, PL 94–142, Section 121a. 344) states that the student's teacher(s) will, along with the parents, other school personnel, and, when appropriate, the student, be involved in an IEP conference to determine the specific special services needed to assist the student. The formats employed vary from state to state, but most IEPs include:

1. a statement of the child's present levels of educational performance, including academic achievement, social adaptation, prevocational and vocational skills, psychomotor skills and self-help skills;
2. a statement of annual goals which describes the educational performance to be achieved by the end of the school year under the child's individualized education program;
3. a statement of short-term instructional objectives, which must be measurable, intermediate steps between the present level of educational performance and the annual goals;
4. a statement of specific educational services needed by the child (determined without regard to the availability of services), including a description of:
   a. all special education and related services needed to meet the unique needs of the child, including the type of physical education program of the child, and
   b. any special instructional media and materials which are needed;
5. the date when those services will begin and length of time the services will be given;
6. a description of the extent to which the child will participate in regular education programs;
7. objective criteria, evaluation procedures, and schedules for determining, at least annually, whether the short-term instructional objectives are being achieved;
8. a justification for the type of educational placement that the child will have; and
9. a list of the individuals who are responsible for implementing the individualized education program. [Heward & Orlansky, 1980, pp. 20, 21]

Our involvement does not end with participation in developing an IEP. In many cases a portion of the student's special educational program will be carried out in the regular classroom. It is likely that this placement will involve us in periodic contacts with the student's parents and school support personnel. Although we need to be aware of these requirements, we need not be intimidated by them. If you employ the skills presented in this chapter, you will find most relationships with parents to be a positive and productive aspect of your professional role.

RECOMMENDED READING

Books on Teacher-Parent Contacts

Bailard, V., and Strang, R. (1964). *Parent–teacher conferences.* New York: McGraw-Hill.

Gordon, I., and Breivogel, W. (1976). *Building effective home–school relationships.* Boston: Allyn and Bacon.

Heffernan, H., and Todd, V. (1969). *Elementary teachers' guide to working with parents.* West Nyack, N.Y.: Parker.

Jones, V. (1980). *Adolescents with behavior problems: Strategies for teaching, counseling, and parent involvement.* Boston: Allyn and Bacon.

Kelley, E. (1974). *Parent–teacher interaction: A special education perspective.* Seattle, Wash.: Special Child Publications. A Division of Bernie Straub Publishing Company, Inc.

Losen, S., and Diament, B. (1979). *Parent conferences in the schools: Procedures for developing effective partnership.* Boston: Allyn and Bacon.

Rutherford, R., and Edgar, E. (1979). *Teachers and parents: A guide to interaction and cooperation.* Boston: Allyn and Bacon.

Wilson, G., and Wingate, B. (1974). *Parents and teachers: Humanistic educational techniques to facilitate communication between parents and staff of educational programs.* Atlanta, Ga.: Humanities Press.

Books that Teachers May Provide Parents as References for Parenting Skills

Faber, A., and Mazlish, E. (1980). *How to talk so kids will listen and listen so kids will talk.* New York: Rawson, Wade.

Ginott, H. (1965). *Between parent and child: New solutions to old problems.* New York: Macmillan.

Gordon, T. (1970). *Parent effectiveness training: The tested way to raise responsible children.* New York: Wyden.

Pogrebin, L. (1980). *Growing up free: Raising your child in the 80s.* New York: Bantam Books.

Swick, K., and Duff, E. (1979). *Parenting.* Washington, D.C.: National Education Association.

Wagonseller, B., and McDowell, R. (1979). *You and your child: A common sense approach to successful parenting.* Champaign, Ill.: Research Press.

MINIMIZING DISRUPTIVE BEHAVIOR AND INCREASING LEARNING BY EFFECTIVE CLASSROOM ORGANIZATION AND INSTRUCTION

During the late 1970s and the first half of the 1980s, the major research efforts in classroom management were focused on discovering instructional behaviors that would prevent disruptive student behavior and facilitate increased student achievement. As presented in Chapter 1, researchers have discovered three categories of instructional behavior that influence students' behavior and achievement. In the three chapters in Part III, we examine the specific teaching methods suggested by research in one of the three categories.

Chapter 7 presents the methods effective teachers use at the beginning of the school year. We emphasize strategies for teaching classroom rules and ensuring that all students learn such key classroom procedures as what to do during the first few minutes of class, how to request assistance with seatwork, when it is appropriate to talk, and how to request permission to leave the room. In this chapter we also examine methods effective teachers use when students fail to follow accepted rules or procedures.

Chapter 8 lists in detail strategies that effective teachers use when presenting material to students and monitoring students' seatwork. Researchers have demonstrated that use of these strategies is associated with higher rates of on-task student behavior and greater academic achievement.

Chapter 9 responds to the large and growing body of data indicating that many students find schools to be confusing, boring, meaningless places. We examine the instructional factors that contribute to low student motivation and provide a variety of specific teaching methods for clarifying instruction, increasing meaningful student involvement in the learning process, and employing teaching methods that respond to individual students' needs. Ideas for teaching young adolescents and gifted students are included in this chapter.

In Part III we summarize much research and offer numerous organizational and instructional strategies that have proven effective in many types of instructional settings. We have intentionally shied away from suggesting a uniformly prescribed method. Classroom settings vary markedly in such variables as students' age and socioeconomic status, instructional goals, students' values, and teachers' style. Consequently, teachers must become knowledgeable in the many teaching methods associated with reduced disruptive behavior and higher student achievement. Each teacher must intelligently and thoughtfully consider these research findings and selectively implement new methods in his or her classroom. Finally, the teacher should collect data to ascertain whether use of these new methods is in fact associated with improved behavior and higher achievement in his or her own classroom.

CHAPTER 7

Developing Productive Student Behavior by Effectively Teaching Rules and Procedures

Although the rules and procedures used by effective classroom man-agers vary from teacher to teacher, we do not find effectively managed classrooms operating without them.

Edmand Emmer, Carolyn Evertson, Julie Sanford,
Barbara Clements and Murray Worsham, (1982),
Organizing and Managing the Junior High School Classroom

And teachers can't expect students to follow rules they perceive only as arbitrary challenges to their freedom and dignity. When teachers take the time to explain the rationale underlying rules, student compliance increases.

Today's Education, 1983–84 Annual Edition

Teaching is a demanding, fast-paced job. Each day the typical elementary school teacher has more than a thousand teacher-student interactions and teaches ten subjects. Secondary teachers often teach 150 or more students with only four minutes between classes. These demanding working conditions can cause confusion and frustration and limit students' learning time. Research indicates that effective teachers take time early in the school year to develop classroom rules and procedures that help their classrooms run smoothly, minimize disruptions, and thus maximize students' learning time.

Research in teacher effectiveness has increasingly stressed that effective teachers organize their classrooms so as to prevent disruptive behavior.
More than ten years ago Good and Brophy (1973) wrote:

> Teachers who take time early in the year to listen to students and to explain care-
> fully the rationales underlying rules and assignments are making a wise invest-
> ment. This ultimately will establish teacher credibility and reduce the students'
> tendencies to continue to test the teacher throughout the year. [p. 168]

Three years later Brophy and Evertson (1976) reported a similar result:

> Much of the behavior that distinguished the most effective teachers from the less
> effective ones was behavior that could be called "proactive." That is, it was be-
> havior initiated by the teachers themselves, often prior to the beginning of the
> school year or the beginning of a particular school day. [p. 142]

Research reviews by Soar and Soar (1979, 1983) also suggest that students'
learning is enhanced by teachers' developing basic classroom structure. Soar
and Soar (1979) write that research indicates that, ". . . unless a teacher has established a minimum of structure, relatively strong interactions that are not
functional for pupil learning are likely to occur" (p. 117).

Research conducted at the Research and Development Center for Teacher
Education at the University of Texas at Austin (Emmer, Evertson, & Anderson, 1980; Evertson & Emmer, 1982a, 1982b) provides specific information on
techniques that effective teachers employ during the first few weeks of
school. Effective classroom managers at both the elementary and junior high
school level spend time teaching students classroom rules and procedures.
Emmer and Evertson and their colleagues (1981) describe *rules* as ". . . written rules which are either posted in the classroom, given to students on ditto
or other copy, or copied by students into their notebooks" (pp. 18, 19). *Procedures* are defined as, "Procedures, like rules, are expectations for behavior.
They usually apply to a *specific* activity, and they usually are directed at accomplishing, rather than forbidding some behavior" (p. 19). Effective teachers
do more than post rules or present procedures. Especially in elementary
classrooms, teachers work with students to ensure that they understand and
can demonstrate rules and procedures. This is an important point. Students'
behavior needs to be dealt with much like their academic skills. Teachers
spend considerable time during the first few weeks of school assessing students' knowledge, reviewing material, and reteaching academic skills students
have forgotten. Similarly, when effective teachers first introduce important
academic material, they attempt to provide clear instruction, carefully monitor
students' progress, and provide immediate corrective feedback if a student or
group of students are having difficulty with the material. In the same manner,
teachers must begin the school year by teaching the classroom rules and procedures, carefully monitoring students' behavior, informing students of mistakes, and reteaching rules or procedures that students are frequently failing
to follow.

We must keep in mind that many behaviors that are undesirable in the classroom are not inherently bad, and in fact may be encouraged in other settings. For example, neither student chatter nor attention-seeking behavior are bad or destructive in themselves. We would expect thirty children placed in close quarters to make a considerable amount of noise. Similarly, children often show off in front of adults or their peers. In fact, adults encourage children to actively seek the limelight in sporting events or other competitive activities. Therefore, we should not be surprised when we discover that we must help children develop attitudes and skills that support behavioral norms that are most adaptive in a school environment.

We offer several words of caution before discussing approaches to establishing productive classroom rules and procedures. Rules and procedures should be developed in conjunction with teaching strategies that help students meet their personal and academic needs. In his *Culture Against Man*, Jules Henry (1963) vividly depicts an example of a classroom procedure that violates students' personal needs.

> Boris had trouble reducing "12/16" to the lowest terms, and could only get as far as "6/8". The teacher asked him quietly if that was as far as he could reduce it. She suggested he "think." Much heaving up and down and waving of hands by the other children, all frantic to correct him. . . . She then turns to the class and says, "Well, who can tell Boris what the number is?" A forest of hands appears, and the teacher calls Peggy. Peggy says that four may be divided into the numerator and the denominator.
>
> Thus Boris' failure has made it possible for Peggy to succeed; his depression is the price of her exhilaration; his misery the occasion for her rejoicing. This is the standard condition of the American elementary school, and is why so many of us feel a contraction of the heart even if someone we never knew succeeds merely at garnering plankton in the Thames: because so often somebody's success has been bought at the cost of our failure. [pp. 295, 296]

Unfortunately, students are often expected to behave in compliance with rules and procedures even though the learning environment does not respond sensitively to their needs and interests. When we find this condition in a classroom, it is understandable that students' behavior begins to oppose the classroom rules. The educational exchange must function effectively in both directions. Students can be expected to support rules and procedures that enhance learning only if the learning process shows respect for students and their needs.

Another concept that will help you thoughtfully develop classroom rules is that rules should not be designed to catch children misbehaving so that they can be punished. Instead, rules should provide guidelines or benchmarks that help children examine their behavior considering its effects on themselves and others. Consequently, behavior that violates accepted rules should be dealt with by discussing the matter with the child. This does not mean that reasonable punishments should not be employed, but when dealing with unproductive behavior, we must help children examine both their motivations and the consequences of their actions. Overemphasis on punishment often obscures the issue of motivation and attitude, and simultaneously limits the child's attention to the immediate negative consequences of his or her behavior. This pressure tends to limit thoughtful consideration of either the effect the behavior has on others or the long-term consequences associated with continuing the behavior. In a very real sense, a punishment orientation reinforces a low level of moral development and does not help children develop a higher, more socially valuable level of morality.

DEVELOPING CLASSROOM RULES

Thoughtful, reasonable rules that are stated clearly help individuals behave in a manner that is beneficial to themselves and those around them. Most adults have at some time had a desire to drive 50 miles an hour in a 35-mph zone in order to be on time for an appointment. The concern over being late may momentarily impair judgment, and may cause the driver to ignore the fact that children are playing on the street or that cars may enter from side streets and driveways. The existence of rules and signs to serve as a reminder provides an important and reasonable structure. Like adults, children need rules that assist them in adhering to behaviors that, though occasionally difficult or frustrating, serve their own and their classmates' best interests. We must, however, realize that rules are not universally beneficial. You may recall feeling anger and frustration when confronted with an unnecessary speed trap in a small town. Rules should be carefully examined to ensure that they are necessary and beneficial to students and teacher alike.

Rules are fairer and more readily accepted when they are stated clearly. You may recall having been involved in a situation where traffic signs were either intentionally or accidentally obscured or placed too far apart. It is frustrating and anxiety-provoking to drive through a small town on the highway without being certain of the acceptable speed limit. Even if the limit is ridiculously slow and should be changed, it is helpful to know what it is so that we can abide by it and avoid the negative consequences.

Rules are also more readily obeyed when students are involved in their development. It is an accepted principle in organizational psychology that individuals will support and implement decisions they have helped make, but they will frequently resist obeying rules or implementing decisions that have been imposed upon them. The concept of democracy is based on participation in the decision-making process. Many state constitutions acknowledge the right of the voters to initiate legislation and to become involved in recalls and referendums. Most teachers believe strongly in being involved in making decisions that affect their professional behavior. Therefore, we should expect that children will better understand and be more likely to abide by rules that they have helped to make.

Research on parenting styles provides useful information on the advantages of employing an authoritative approach, in which children are involved in discussing issues that directly affect them. Authoritative parenting assumes that children will be involved in making decisions, although parents do not abdicate their responsibility, and the final decision must meet with parent approval. Studies indicate that, compared to autocratic or permissive parenting, the authoritative model is associated with closer parent-child relationships, less rebellion against the parents' views and rules, and more likelihood that children will model their parents and associate with peers approved of by their parents (Bell & Ericksen, 1976; Elder, 1963; Enright et al., 1980; Middleton & Snell, 1963). These results have obvious meaning for teachers. Because a classroom will function much more effectively when children feel close to us, accept our views and norms, model themselves on us, and are influenced by peers whose behavior we accept, we will want to seriously consider employing an authoritative approach in our classroom. Involving students in discussion and development of classroom rules is a large step toward employing a cooperative classroom structure as a means of creating positive, mutually accepted classroom rules.

Several factors increase the likelihood that students will accept and consistently follow classroom rules. First, students need to be involved in developing the rules that will apply in the classroom. Second, rules need to be clearly stated. Students have difficulty responding to glittering generalities such as "behave appropriately". Third, although it is important to state expectations clearly, it is just as important to keep the rules as few as possible. Fourth, students must clearly indicate their acceptance of the rules agreed upon by the classroom group. Fifth, because rules established in the school setting may conflict with rules children experience outside of school, it is important that student behavior be monitored and frequently discussed to ensure that it is consistent with the classroom rules. Finally, students will be more likely to behave in accordance with rules if they know that the rules are accepted by significant others such as their parents and peers.

The specific methods presented in the remainder of this chapter apply most directly to elementary school classrooms or other relatively small, self-contained settings, such as a special education class or a small alternative school. The basic ideas, however, describe the essential ingredients in establishing classroom rules and responsibilities. Whenever significant variations are needed for secondary classrooms, they are included.

Discussing the Value of Rules

The first step in developing classroom rules is to help students discuss why it is important to develop rules that all members of the class agree to follow. We may want to introduce or stimulate the discussion by asking students why adults have rules such as obeying traffic signals, paying their taxes, or not crowding in lines. Throughout this discussion, we will want to reinforce the concept that the classroom group and the school are a society; and like larger societal groups, they will function more effectively when people decide to create and follow rules. We can help students consider how rules benefit people who must work together. This topic places the focus clearly on the advantages each child derives from class members' accepting the rules. For example, students may state that rules are important because if everyone did whatever they wanted, the classroom might become too disruptive for effective studying.

Students' statements on why it is important to develop classroom rules can be written on the blackboard or a large piece of butcher paper. The latter approach has the advantage of making the list easier to save and discuss later should the group have difficulty in following its rules. Secondary teachers will generally employ a less elaborate discussion of why rules are needed. Nevertheless, we should elicit students' comments about why rules are needed when a group of people work for some time together in a relatively small space.

Developing a List

The next step in developing functional classroom rules is to have the students list all rules they believe are important. These should include rules related to academic as well as behavioral expectations. An academic rule might include working quietly during study periods or attempting to complete all homework on time. During this stage, we should assist the students in stating all rules in a positive manner. If a student states, "Don't talk while others are talking," we will help the student phrase this rule thus: "Each student should listen quietly while other people are talking." Similarly, the rule: "Students should not steal from each other, the teacher, or the school," could be stated as: "If anyone needs something he or she will ask to borrow it." Once the students and you have completed their list of rules, help them cross out any that do not apply and combine as many as possible.

Secondary teachers may not want to develop a separate list for each of five or six classes; two optional strategies are available. First, we know teachers who have each class select one rule. These rules are combined to form the teacher's class rules. Second, we may wish to present our own rules and ask each class if they believe one or two additional rules might help their class.

ACTIVITY 7.1   Selecting your classroom rules

List five classroom rules you would choose for your class. When you are satisfied with the rules, discuss them with a colleague who teaches or has recently taught at your grade level.

Getting a Commitment

When the final list has been developed, lead a discussion to clarify each rule and ask students to state whether they can accept each rule. During this important stage several students may state that they do not believe they can abide by a particular rule. You can then ask the students whether the rule seems to be one that does not help people or whether they agree that it is a good rule, but do not believe they can consistently act in accordance with it. If they express the latter, you can explain that they are not expected to be able to act perfectly all the time. Just as they will learn how to solve new math problems and read more efficiently, they will also learn how to behave in ways that are more effective. The initial question is not whether the students can already solve all their math problems or consistently behave appropriately, but whether they believe that these skills are helpful to them and if they will attempt to improve these skills. If the students state that a rule is not acceptable, you can help them clarify why they believe it to be undesirable. In most cases, students will quickly acknowledge the basic value of the rule. If one or more students persist in stating that a rule is unacceptable, however, you have the option of deleting the rule, asking to postpone further discussion of the item until you have had an opportunity to discuss it with the small group of students who disagree, or stating that the class will vote on the rule and that the majority opinion will stand.

If the issue is relatively unimportant, you may want to simply delete the rule by stating that because some students disagree, the issue can be dismissed unless it becomes a problem in the future. But, if the rule involves a major issue such as borrowing items or solving problems by discussion, you will want to start with the second option. The advantage of this procedure is that it includes the possibility of obtaining a consensus decision in which all parties feel that they have been listened to and understood. Students will most often readily agree to accept a rule once they have been given an opportunity to express their reservations.

There are several disadvantages to voting on rules that several students believe are unacceptable. First, the losers are likely to feel resentful and may respond by disrupting the class. It is a bad policy to begin a school year by alienating disruptive students by making them feel insignificant and powerless. A second disadvantage is that this process suggests that the students have the final decision. It would therefore be possible for a class to reject all reasonable rules.

Once the class has discussed all the rules, you have several options for solidifying their commitment to these rules. If the rules have been unanimously accepted by the end of the discussion period, you may simply want to have the students vote to accept the entire list of classroom rules. If they do, you have the advantage of referring to the classroom rules as "Those the class developed and voted to accept." If several students have expressed reluctance to accept various rules, though, it is more effective to express the rules in the form of a contract and print a copy for each student to sign. This agreement not only creates individual accountability but also gives you an opportunity to work individually with any student who refuses to sign the agreeemnt. Even though this task may appear somewhat distasteful, it is much more desirable to attend to this issue early in the year than to wait until serious problems have arisen. Early intervention enables you to better understand the student's needs and to consider options for meeting these needs. If the student consistently refuses to accept the rules or accepts them but demonstrates unwillingness to behave in accordance with them, you may want to involve the parents. Again, early intervention before resentments or frustrations have become serious is always the most productive approach and clearly places you in the role of a concerned, competent professional.

Monitoring Classroom Rules

Once students have developed reasonable rules and agreed to behave in accordance with them, the next step is to help them recognize and monitor their behavior. One approach that is especially helpful with primary-age children is to have them take turns acting out the rules. Each child can be asked to role-play both the appropriate and inappropriate behavior, and you can ask their peers to raise their hands whenever the student is behaving appropriately and place their hands in their lap when the student is behaving inappropriately. This activity is helpful in ensuring that every child clearly understands the rules.

At all grade levels it is important to frequently review the rules for several weeks. A good approach is to review them every day for the first week, three times a week during the second week, and once a week thereafter. It is also helpful to have the rules displayed in a prominent place in the classroom. During the first week it is desirable to discuss them briefly at the beginning of each day and to end the day by having the class evaluate their behavior and consider whether improvement in any area is needed. If the entire class consistently displays appropriate behavior or shows considerable improvement over the previous day, you may want to send a positive note or award home with each student. Significant individual improvements can be similarly rewarded.

For students beyond the third grade, it is often useful to periodically give a quiz on the classroom and school rules. You can ask students to list the rules and write a description for each. You can also ask them to rate themselves on how consistently they follow the rules.

After the first month of school, there are two occasions on which the rules should be brought to the class's attention. First, it is a good idea to review these rules every two weeks to determine whether they are still meaningful and whether any rules need to be added or deleted. Not only does this refresher provide a helpful review of the rules, but it also acknowledges that students' needs and skills change; and therefore students may be allowed more freedom as the year progresses. For example, if an initial rule was for students to remain seated unless given permission to leave their seats, you may decide after several weeks that they have demonstrated enough responsibility that this rule can be altered or eliminated.

Rules should also be discussed when a student or the teacher indicates that violation of one or more of the rules is detracting from learning or infringing on a student's rights. One of us recently found that her classroom was becoming quite noisy during an afternoon study period. Despite several clear "I" messages from the teacher as well as several students, the classroom continued to be unproductively loud during this time. Consequently, at the beginning of the study period the next day, the teacher asked the class to discuss the rule of maintaining a noise level that was conducive to studying. The class decided that they often became too loud and agreed to reduce their noise level. At the end of the period the teacher asked the students to examine the amount of work they had completed. Most students acknowledged that they had accomplished much more work. We brought the issue to their attention again the next day and every other day for six days. Because the noise level appeared to maintain an acceptable level the discussions were terminated. The rule had been reestablished.

The situation just described is an excellent example of the major advantage of creating clearly defined classroom rules. Individual or group misbehavior is often accompanied by statements indicating that the students did not think they were behaving inappropriately. Clearly defined rules that have been agreed upon by the students reduce the arguing that occurs when students are asked to examine their behavior. Problem solving can immediately focus on whether the students failed to meet their responsibilities and what can be done to assist them in meeting these in the future.

The benefits accrued from reviewing classroom rules can also be seen in association with school-wide rules. Anyone who has taught for even one year is aware that students become restless and tend to lapse into unacceptable behavior near the end of the school year. We have worked with several school staffs who have dealt with this problem by meeting during the latter part of the school year to review the school rules. The teachers then set a time when all discuss the school rules with their classes. Finally, the teachers agree to monitor the rules in a uniform manner. The clarity and structure provided by this uniform approach help students behave more productively and make the final weeks of the year more enjoyable for everyone.

WHAT TO DO WHEN A RULE IS NOT FOLLOWED

One of the questions we are most frequently asked during workshops and classes is "What do I do when students misbehave?" Our first response is to ask teachers to consider their goals related to classroom management. Hosford (1984) reports that when hundreds of teachers and administrators were asked to rate the most important objectives of education they consistently listed as the top four objectives.

1. desire for learning,
2. improved self-concept,
3. basic skill acquisition, and
4. respect for others

Similarly, in collecting data for *A Place Called School*, Goodlad (1984) and his colleagues examined educational goal statements from every state and interviewed 8,600 parents. Statewide statements consistently included numerous goals related to personal and civic skills, and parents voiced their support for these goals. Therefore, it seems ironic that teachers so often accept classroom-management methods such as Assertive Discipline (Canter, 1976) that emphasize immediate control and order but fail to provide children with skills needed to become responsible citizens. These control-oriented solutions also fail to help teachers examine the possible causes of misbehavior or to adjust the learning environment so as to prevent future student failure and misbehavior. If we sincerely wish to help students become motivated learners and responsible citizens, we must respond to their misbehavior in a manner that encourages students' participation and responsibility.

Before discussing a specific approach to handling student violations of rules, we stress that students should be clearly informed about any approach you select. Students do not respond well to surprises. They rebel against arbitrary, unexpected consequences. The teacher must take time to discuss and even practice with students his or her response to disruptive student behavior. This is particularly true for middle school and high school teachers. Adolescents are sensitive to issues of equality and justice. They are experiencing the developmental task of becoming responsible for their own behavior and demonstrating their competence. When approaches to classroom management directly conflict with these needs, they will be met with varying degrees of resistance.

If our goal is to develop positive student attitudes toward school and improved student self-responsibility, we can implement a graduated five-step response to student violations of rules (Figure 7.1). First, we should simply use a predetermined signal to help the student become aware of his or her behavior:

FIGURE 7.1   Steps in responding to students' violation of rules

Step	Procedure	Example
1.	Nonverbal cue	Raised index finger
2.	Verbal cue	"John, check yourself"
3.	Focus on the rule or procedure	"John, what rule or procedure are you violating?"
4.	Student moves to a designated area in the room to develop a solution	"John, you have chosen to take time to work out a plan."
5.	Student is required to go somewhere else to develop a plan	"John, because you cannot quietly develop a plan here, you will need to see Mrs. Johnson to develop a plan."

we might raise an index finger. If the student does not see this action or fails to respond to it, we can say the student's name, followed by the words "check yourself." This signal will get the student's attention and focus it on his or her behavior. If this checking and awareness step fails, we can ask the student to state which rule (or procedure) he or she is violating. Most students will respond to this third step by acknowledging their behavior and returning to acceptable behavior. If the student continues to ignore the teacher or begins to argue, however, the next step is to inform the student that he or she has chosen to take some time to develop a solution to the problem. Ideally this work can occur within the classroom. We can select a place in the classroom where students can go to develop a plan for improving their behavior. For students who have adequate writing skills, this area should include the materials necessary for the student to write out a solution. This provision may include a form specifically designed for this purpose. If a student will not accept this consequence, we will need the support of another teacher or administrator so that the student can go elsewhere to deal with the problem before returning to the class. In Chapter 10 we provide a thorough discussion of this type of support for teachers and forms you can use to implement it.

As we mentioned earlier, it is essential that we instruct students in problem solving. One method is to role-play each of the five steps and then ask a student to violate a classroom rule (such as talking to a neighbor while you are talking). You could then ask the student to stop the inappropriate behavior when you employ the second step. This procedure could be continued until several students had been involved in responding to each of the first three steps. You could then instruct the students in writing solutions and plans. Each student could write a plan, you could check these, and you would subsequently discuss them with the class.

We have ourselves used this procedure and have taught it to hundreds of teachers. Several years ago during a graduate seminar one of us commented that it was probably not necessary to teach the problem-solving step to students in college preparatory junior and senior high school classes. A seminar participant who had been in a course we taught five years earlier disagreed with this statement. He said that he role-played the procedures described above with all his juniors and seniors in chemistry and physics. He noted that students and parents frequently commented on the value of this process. This teacher was convinced that despite needing to employ the fourth step only about a dozen times each year, it was a vital aspect of an effective classroom-management program.

As with all methods suggested in this book, you should carefully consider its applicability to your own teaching setting, and should critically assess results when you use the new method. Should you choose to implement the method above for responding to rule violations, it is critical to ensure that it is not used in a manner unduly emphasizing disruptive behavior. Studies show that teachers often attend more frequently to disruptive than on-task behavior, and that this action tends to increase off-task student behavior (Becker, Engelmann & Thomas; Mordock, 1975; Walker, Hops, & Fiegenbaum, 1976).

Therefore, when implementing this method, attend to desired student behavior frequently, and monitor behavior to assess whether the new approach was indeed associated with an increase in on-task behavior.

CLASSROOM PROCEDURES

As we mentioned earlier in this chapter, research by Evertson and Emmer (1982b) indicates that effective teachers not only work with students to develop classroom rules, but also teach the procedures they expect students to follow during specific classroom activities. This research also provides specific information on the types of classroom activities for which effective teachers develop procedures. In their research in elementary classrooms, Evertson and Emmer found five general areas in which effective teachers taught students how to act:

1. students' use of classroom space and facilities;
2. students' behavior in areas outside the classroom, such as the bathroom, lunchroom, drinking fountain, and playgrounds;
3. procedures to follow during whole-class activities, such as whether to raise a hand to speak, where to turn in work, or how to get help during seatwork;
4. procedures during small-group work; and
5. additional procedures such as how to behave at the beginning and end of the school day, or when a visitor arrives.

For junior high school classrooms these researchers found four key areas in which effective teachers developed procedures:

1. beginning the class;
2. whole-class activities;
3. student assignments; and
4. other activities such as the end of the class period, interruptions in the class, and fire drills.

An example from our experience teaching in junior high school will help to clarify the concept of procedures. Most junior high school students have only four or five minutes between classes. Therefore, they usually enter the classroom excited or agitated, having had little time to review what they learned in their previous class or to get mentally prepared for the coming class. I discussed this problem with the students in my class and worked with them to develop procedures for making a smooth transition when entering the classroom. First, the class and I listed warmup activities for the first four minutes of class. These changed every month, but they included:

1. an instructional warmup activity,
2. sharing something you had learned in school during the past day,

3. a relaxation activity,
4. listening to music selected by the teacher, and
5. listening to music selected by the students.

Students daily selected the transition activity, each activity being used once each week. I also developed a procedure for tardy students to report to class, a procedure for taking roll, and a signal for gaining the students' attention at the end of the transition activity. Similar procedures were developed for summarizing the day's lesson and leaving the classroom. Activity 7.2 gives you an opportunity to consider the procedures you wish to establish in your classroom.

ACTIVITY 7.2   Deciding on your key classroom procedures

For each of these areas in which Evertson and Emmer (1982b) found effective teachers to establish procedures, list the key area in which you will need to teach a procedure and the specific procedure you will teach. If you have difficulty, consult a colleague or refer to Evertson and Emmer's (1984) *Classroom Management for Elementary Teachers* or Emmer and Evertson's (1984) *Classroom Management for Secondary Teachers.*

General area	Needed procedures	Specific procedure
Beginning the class	1. Getting students' attention 2. Entering the class 3. Obtaining materials 4. What to do if tardy 5. Where to put slips that need signing 6. 7.	Students determine a signal
Whole-class activities	1. How to leave the room 2. What to do when work is completed 3. Voice level 4. How to get help on an assignment 5. Using the pencil sharpener 6. When students can leave their seats 7. 8. 9.	Take the hall pass

continued

Student assignments	1. How to find work missed while absent 2. How late work will be handled 3. Heading papers 4. Where to hand in work 5. Credit for late work 6. 7.	Notebook on the back table.
Other activities	1. Dismissing 2. Public address-system announcements 3. Fire drill 4. Guest entering the class 5. 6. 7.	Everyone must be seated and quiet.

Teaching and Monitoring Classroom Procedures

A procedure is best taught by:

1.   discussing the need for the procedure,
2.   possibly eliciting student ideas,
3.   having students practice the procedure until it is performed correctly, and
4.   reinforcing the correct behavior.

When introducing the procedure of developing a signal to obtain students' attention, you might work with the class to develop the signal, set a goal (everyone facing the teacher and quiet within five seconds), employ the procedure while students are engaged in an activity, and reinforce them when they respond within the determined time limit. For a procedure such as lining up, you might elicit ideas for behaviors students display when lining up, practice lining up, and reinforce the class when they line up in the desired manner.

Classroom procedures must be carefully monitored during their initial acquisition. Early in the school year, teachers should respond to almost every violation of a rule or procedure. When you notice that the class or an individual student is not correctly following a procedure, the best approach is to simply ask the student to state the correct procedure and then to demonstrate it. If a class lines up poorly after having once demonstrated the correct procedure, you should politely comment that you know the class can line up more effectively and ask them to return to their seats so that they can practice the procedure. You might then ask students to describe the behaviors associated with lining up correctly. The class could then be asked to demonstrate their skill and be reinforced for their improved effort. Effectively teaching procedures to students is similar to good athletic coaching. The skilled coach first demonstrates the new procedure—often having the athlete perform the maneuver in slow motion. The athlete is then asked to perform the task and receives feedback on the performance, sometimes in the form of videotape replay. The coach will have the athlete practice until the feat is performed satisfactorily. Later, perhaps under game conditions, if the athlete incorrectly performs the task, the coach will reteach it in a subsequent practice session.

There are situations in which you will need to do more than provide additional instruction to ensure that an individual or class follows a procedure. The key concept to keep in mind is that your response should help students take responsibility for their behavior. Generally, the initial approach would be to follow the five-step procedure (Figure 7.1) described for responding to violations of classroom rules. To assist students in developing greater self-responsibility, you may wish to employ the goal-setting methods described in the following section. Finally, in Chapter 11 we offer suggestions for working with students who require a highly concrete, structured approach to changing their behavior.

Setting Individual Goals
Although it is important to teach students classroom rules and procedures, it may also be necessary to involve individual students in setting goals that support these rules. Children who have experienced difficulties in learning or behaving appropriately require assistance in developing behaviors that enable them to follow classroom rules and procedures. It is simply not enough to assist these children in understanding and agreeing to abide by these rules.

Employing individual goal setting as an approach to creating positive behavior is effective when it actively involves the student in establishing the goals, monitoring progress, and evaluating results. Compare your own response to goals that you established with those set by others. It is very likely that in almost all situations you were more committed to goals you established for yourself even if they were identical to those which might have been set for you. Students respond in a similar manner. Students' involvement in individual goal setting teaches them to be responsible for their own behavior. This responsibility enhances motivation and almost inevitably reduces the need for external consequences to control behavior.

Teaching Goal Setting
It is relatively easy to teach students how to set appropriate goals. All students have experience in goal setting. Their simple commitments not to repeat a behavior or to perform a task more effectively are examples of simple, informal goals. Furthermore, students generally enjoy setting goals because the activ-

ity is "grown-up" and provides them with a sense of competence and power. Nevertheless, students do need assistance to understand the value of goals, learn how to develop specific goal statements, and evaluate their progress.

One approach to teaching goal setting is to begin by asking youngsters whether they have ever heard of New Year's resolutions. We can help students develop the concept that New Year's resolutions are goals aimed at changing behavior. Students can also be asked why these resolutions are so often broken, and can usually develop the concept that the goals are too grand. They can then be asked to discuss goals they have set for themselves. During this stage we should reinforce all responses indicating that a goal was set. Following this sharing we should ask each student to set a goal for that day relating to one of the classroom rules or procedures. Focusing on classroom rules or procedures ensures that pupils will choose a reasonably specific goal that is associated with a behavior they understand. This activity also provides an opportunity for reinforcing classroom rules and procedures. At the end of the day we should lead a discussion in which the students relate whether or not they have met their goal. We should be completely positive during this discussion, so that goal setting is viewed as an enjoyable, reinforcing activity. If some pupils respond that they did not meet their goal, we can simply mention that an important aspect of goal setting is to become more aware of one's behavior and that now they know one rule or procedure they may need to work harder to follow.

The next day we can reinforce the previous day's lesson by creating a lesson in which students learn to write specific goal statements. One method for beginning this lesson is to involve them in listing factors associated with "goals that work" and "goals that are hard to keep." Students may state that useful goals focus on specific behavior, involve a relatively short time span, and that efforts at reaching the goal are reinforced by others. After the class has developed these lists, we can ask them to list possible goals that individuals might make about classroom behavior. This activity provides the students with practice, while allowing us to instruct the students by helping them write each goal in accordance with the previously completed rules for writing useful goals.

The next step is to have each student choose a goal and write a daily goal statement. This statement includes the student's name, the goal, and how the student will determine whether the goal was met. At this stage in the learning process it is helpful for us to provide the students with a simple form on which they can write their goals (Figure 7.2).

We should initially check each student's goal statement and provide individual assistance to students who are having difficulty writing useful goals. At the end of the day the class should again be given time to discuss their specific goals and indicate whether they were able to meet them. They should have ample time to discuss their goals, and their efforts need reinforcing. Further reinforcement can be provided by sending positive notes home to parents.

An activity that supports goal setting is centered around a sport, for example soccer. Of course, use any sport that is particularly interesting to the

FIGURE 7.2

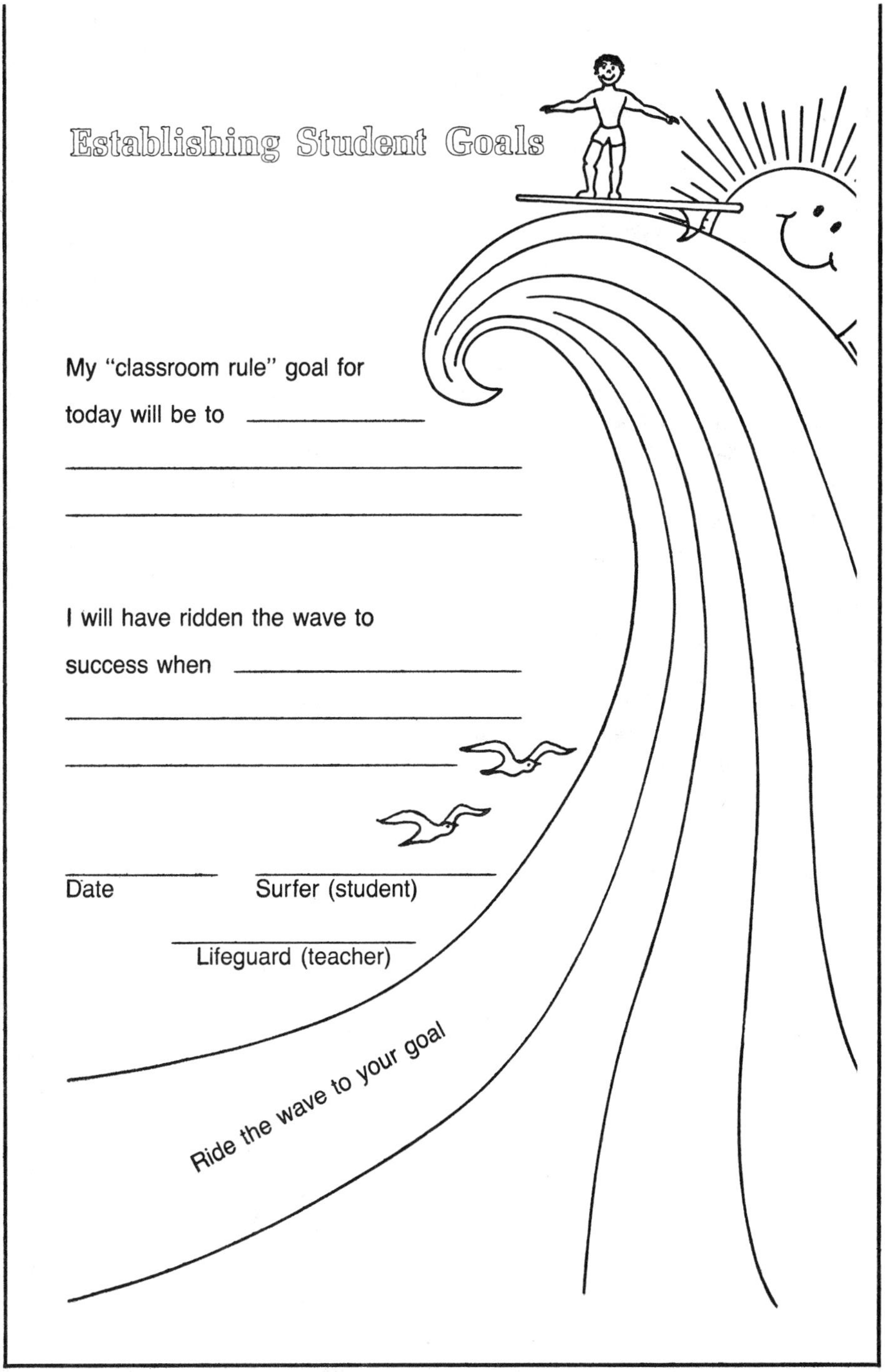

Establishing Student Goals

My "classroom rule" goal for
today will be to _____

_____

_____

I will have ridden the wave to

success when _____

_____

_____

_____   _____
Date   Surfer (student)
                  _____
                  Lifeguard (teacher)

Ride the wave to your goal

class. Students are asked to set a goal for the day. The goals are written on soccer balls and placed in the center of the field on a bulletin board. At the end of the day, ask students to move their soccer balls into the net if they have succeeded in achieving their goal for the day. Allow time for students to share their methods for accomplishing their goals. Students who reach their goal should be praised for their effort. Ask those who fail to meet their goals to leave the soccer balls in the center of the field and try to achieve their goals the next day. It is useful to have the students write and discuss daily goals for several days. Continue to monitor these to ensure that students have mastered the skill of writing useful goal statements.

The next step is to have the students write weekly goals. Because it is obviously more difficult to maintain a behavior for a week, it is helpful to have students work in pairs. Each student can write a goal statement that includes at least one prearranged time when partners can meet to discuss how effectively they are meeting their goals. When first implementing peer sharing, we will want to set a designated time for this discussion so that we can facilitate it and be available to respond to any problems that arise. A time should be set aside at the end of the week for students to discuss their results. Once again the focus should be on reinforcing students' attempts rather than on criticizing failures. Students who are unsuccessful can simply be encouraged to carry the goal over into the next week or write a goal that is slightly less demanding. Because of the difficulty in keeping track of goals for thirty students, it is helpful to employ a form similar to that shown in Figure 7.3. This form allows us to systematically monitor students' progress toward their goals.

Goal setting as described in this section can be effectively used with the entire class in grades 1–5. With middle school or high school students, this form of behavioral goal setting will generally be used with students expe-

FIGURE 7.3   Chart for monitoring students' goals

Student	Goal	Target date	Date checked by teacher

riencing consistent problems and will often be associated with the behavioristic methods presented in Chapter 11.

EXAMINING YOUR METHODS OF ESTABLISHING CLASSROOM RULES AND PROCEDURES

With any textbook it is tempting to complete a chapter and either set the book aside or move on to the next chapter. It is extremely important, however, to slow down and assess one's current behavior and consider methods presented in the chapter that might prove useful. A few minutes spent on the activity that follows could stimulate some productive changes that will improve student behavior.

ACTIVITY 7.3   Examining your methods of establishing rules and procedures

Evaluate your use of various methods of developing classroom rules and procedures by completing the following form. If you are not currently teaching, respond by recalling a classroom in which you previously taught or observed.

	Yes	Somewhat	No
1. Do clear classroom rules apply in your class?			
2. Are the rules listed in the form of positive statements?			
3. Are there five or fewer rules?			
4. Can every student list these rules from memory?			
5. Are the rules clearly displayed in your room?			
6. Are students involved in developing the rules?			
7. Does each student make a clear commitment to follow these rules?			
8. Do you discuss these rules frequently when they are first developed?			
9. Do you review the rules every three weeks?			
10. Do you employ individual behavior goal setting to reinforce the concept of student responsibility?			
11. Do students clearly understand your approach to handling rule violations?			
12. Do you teach students the important procedures related to classroom activities?			
13. Do you teach students the major procedures related to behaviors outside the classroom?			

continued

	Yes	Somewhat	No

14. When students fail to follow a procedure do you immediately reteach the procedure?
15. Does every parent know the classroom rules that apply in your class?
16. Does every parent know your methods of handling discipline problems?

Carefully examine your responses to the above questions and then complete the following statements:

I learned that....
I am pleased that I....

Three approaches I will implement in order to develop more productive classroom rules and procedures are:

1.
2.
3.

I will also consider the possibility that next year I could....

RECOMMENDED READING

Emmer, E., Evertson, C., Sanford, J., Clements, B., & Worsham, M. (1984). *Classroom management for secondary teachers.* Englewood Cliffs, N.J.: Prentice-Hall.

Evertson, C., Emmer, E., Clements, B., Sanford, J., & Worsham, M. (1984). *Classroom management for elementary teachers.* Englewood Cliffs, N.J.: Prentice Hall.

Fox, R., Luszki, M., & Schmuck, R. (1966). *Diagnosing classroom learning environments.* Chicago: Science Research Associates.

Henry, J. (1963). *Culture against man.* New York: Vintage Books.

Jones, V. (1980). *Adolescents with behavior problems: Strategies for teaching, counseling, and parent involvement.* Boston: Allyn and Bacon.

Schmuck, R., & Schmuck, P. (1983). *Group processes in the classroom.* Dubuque, Iowa: William C. Brown.

CHAPTER 8

Teaching Methods That Increase Learning by Maximizing On-Task Behavior

> *We also found that student engagement in lessons and activities was the key to successful classroom management. The successful teachers ran smooth, well paced lessons with few interruptions, and their students worked consistently at their seatwork.*
>
> Jere Brophy and Carolyn Evertson, (1976),
> *Learning From Teaching*

More than a decade and a half ago, Jacob Kounin discovered that effective teachers could be distinguished not by their way of dealing with students' misbehavior but by the teaching strategies they employed to prevent classroom disruptions. Subsequent studies have reinforced and elaborated upon Kounin's findings. To increase students on-task behavior and achievement and minimize disruptive behavior, you can consider implementing many proven methods of classroom management discussed in this chapter.

The importance of teachers' employing the skills described in this chapter was emphasized by Kounin's (1970) research on classroom discipline. Kounin began his study by collecting several thousand hours of videotapes, both from classrooms of teachers who were acknowledged to be extremely effective in managing their classes, and from classrooms of teachers who had serious, continuing management problems. Kounin expected to find significant differences in the manner in which teachers from these two groups handled discipline problems that occurred in their classrooms. Surprisingly, the results indicated that the successful teachers responded to control problems in much the same manner as did the teachers whose classrooms were often disorderly.

Based on these findings, Kounin and his colleagues reexamined the tapes, seeking any real differences between the teaching methods of teachers who were successful and those who experienced major management problems. They discovered that the differences lay in the successful teachers' ability to prevent discipline problems. These teachers employed many types of management skills to ensure that students were more consistently and actively engaged in instructional activities. Successful teachers were better prepared and organized and moved smoothly from one activity to another. These teachers also maintained students' involvement in instructional activities by initially stimulating the students' interest and effectively holding their attention throughout the lesson. Similarly, successful teachers employed seatwork that was individualized and interesting. Kounin also discovered that the more effective teachers had greater classroom awareness, constantly scanning the classroom so that they were aware of potential problems and could deal with these before any real difficulties arose. These teachers anticipated students' needs, organized their classrooms to minimize restlessness and boredom, and effectively coped with the multiple and often overlapping demands associated with teaching.

Research on teachers' effectiveness in producing gains in students' learning (Brophy & Evertson, 1976) indicates that the same teacher behaviors that reduce classroom disruption are also associated with increased student learning. In describing the findings of the two-year Teacher Effectiveness Project, which examined the relationship between various teacher behaviors and gains in students' learning, Brophy and Evertson (1976) stated: ". . . our data strongly support the findings of Kounin (1970). . . . That is, the key to successful classroom management is prevention of problems before they start, not knowing how to deal with problems after they have begun (p. 127)." Brophy and Evertson also wrote that:

> Of the process behaviors measured through classroom observation in our study, the group that had the strongest and most consistent relationships with student learning gains dealt with the classroom management skills of the teachers. By "classroom management," we mean planning and conducting activities in an orderly fashion; keeping students actively engaged in lessons and seatwork activities; and minimizing disruptions and discipline problems. [p. 51]

In their study of twelve inner-London secondary schools reported in *Fifteen Thousand Hours,* Rutter et al. (1979) found teachers' classroom-management skills to be a key factor influencing students' achievement and behavior. They write that:

> The measures we used touched on only a few aspects of classroom management and there are innumerable ways in which good management may be achieved. What is important is that teachers learn the skills involved. [p. 186]

The research on academic learning time (ALT) supports the idea that teachers should incorporate teaching methods that increase on-task student behavior. "If 50 minutes of reading instruction per day is allocated to a student who pays attention about one-third of the time, and only one-fourth of the student's reading time is a high level of success, the student will experience only about four minutes of ALT-engaged reading time at a high success level" (Berliner, 1984, p. 62).

Barak Rosenshine (1983) summarizes specific teacher behaviors found to be associated with students' achievement gains and includes many of the skills presented in this chapter. Research demonstrates that we can now provide teachers with training in specific instructional procedures and know that if these procedures are implemented, students will behave in more acceptable ways and learn more effectively (Anderson, Evertson, & Brophy, 1979; Borg & Ascione, 1982; Good & Grouws, 1979; Tharp, 1982).

METHODS FOR IMPLEMENTING DISRUPTION-FREE LESSONS

Our purpose in this chapter is to provide you with a wide variety of effective teaching methods that prevent students' misbehavior. If you are an experienced teacher you will undoubtedly find that many of these methods are already a part of your teaching behavior. Probably, however, many new methods can easily be added to this repertoire. These additions can be expected to significantly reduce disruptive student behavior and thereby make teaching more enjoyable while increasing students' achievement.

The chapter is organized around the nine general instructional management skills listed in Figure 8.1. Following a brief statement about each skill, we present numerous specific teaching strategies that will help improve your classroom management.

It is critical to appreciate how to employ the methods presented in this chapter. They are not offered as "gimmicks" for increasing students' time on-task or your control. Instead, they are methods that can assist you in helping students better understand their schoolwork and enhance the quality of learning time. Neither are these methods offered as a cookbook of behaviors to be routinely followed. Like the neophyte cook, the beginning teacher may choose to implement many of these methods. Much as a cook alters and dis-

FIGURE 8.1   Instructional management skills that facilitate on-task behavior and academic achievement

1. Giving clear instructions
2. Beginning a lesson
3. Maintaining attention
4. Pacing
5. Using seatwork effectively
6. Summarizing
7. Providing useful feedback and evaluation
8. Making smooth transitions
9. Handling minor disruptions

cards recipes depending upon the outcome, the skilled teacher seasons standard methods with understanding of how children develop and learn. We need to constantly monitor our own behavior and its relationship to students' learning in order to develop teaching methods that are maximally effective in our classrooms. In addition to the ideas and activities presented in this book, you will find Good and Brophy's (1984) *Looking in Classrooms* and Jane Stalling's (1983) work particularly useful in helping to monitor and adjust classroom organization and management behavior.

Giving Clear Instructions

A key step in presenting a lesson is to provide clear instructions for the activities in which students will be engaged. A significant amount of disruptive student behavior stems from students' not knowing how they are to proceed or what they are to do when they require assistance or complete their work. Students are often poorly prepared for seatwork assignments. Teachers frequently fail to provide adequate information on why assignments are given or how work relates to past or future learning. Students often do not get enough procedural directions. Because seatwork accounts for nearly 70 percent of students' time in class (Doyle, 1983; Good, 1983), and students tend to take seriously only work for which they believe they will be held accountable (Doyle, 1983), it is critical that we improve our skill in providing students with clear directions on academic work. The methods that follow suggest ways of eliminating disruptions caused by lack of clear instructions.

Methods

1. Instructions should include statements about: (a) what students will be doing, (b) why they are doing it, (c) how they can obtain assistance, (d) what to do with completed work, and (e) what to do when they finish. It

is also helpful to clearly indicate how much time they will be spending on the task. This direction may include a statement about when the work can be completed if it cannot be finished within the designated time limits. Research (Brophy & Evertson, 1976, Kounin, 1970) clearly indicates that a significant amount of disruptive student behavior stems from students not having enough information on these matters. Students respond to this uncertainty by interrupting us with multiple requests for information or by expressing their boredom or anxiety by acting out. We should specify too the aspects of the assignment that are most important, and we may even want to post these factors where students can refer to them. This information is valuable in reducing students' anxiety and helps them pace themselves. Some of these instructions are best taught as continuing procedures. For example, students should understand the procedure for obtaining assistance, handing in work, and selecting alternative activities after they complete seatwork.

2.   To increase students' sense of accountability and decrease their anxiety, we should describe the desired quality of the work. Students tend to take seriously only that work for which they are held accountable (Doyle, 1983; Good, 1983). Accountability without clarity, however, is often confusing and anxiety-provoking, and it is important to provide specific guidance on our expectations. A teacher of talented and gifted students recently told us that she tells students that there are three types of work: (1) "throwaway"—material that is for practice only and not to be handed in; (2) "everyday learning"—work that should be neat because it will be graded by the teacher, but not a perfect copy because the main purpose is to check students' understanding; and (3) "keepers"—work which will be displayed or which the student may wish to keep.

3.   Vary your approach to giving instructions. Though we must consistently provide clear instructions, it is useful to employ different approaches in giving them. For example, changing one's voice from a soft to an excited tone (or vice versa) can heighten students' attention. We can also employ different media such as the blackboard, overhead projector, or butcher paper for writing instructions.

4.   Employ attending and listening games to improve students' receiving skills. They must have clear instructions, but it is equally important that students develop skill in listening to and understanding instructions. Figures 8.2 and 8.3 provide two skill-building activities that students enjoy.

5.   *After giving instructions, have students paraphrase the directions, state any problems that might occur to them, and make a commitment.* After giving instructions, ask such questions as, "What is one thing you will be doing?" "What will you do if you finish early?" or "What do I want you to do?" It is often useful to ask key questions of several students who normally have difficulty in following instructions. This tactic not only increases the likelihood that they will listen to instructions, but also provides reinforcement for their attending skills. The next step is to ask students whether they see any problems that might arise. Students are very

FIGURE 8.2   Activity for improving students' listening skills

Can you follow directions?

1. Read everything carefully before doing anything.
2. Put your name in the upper right-hand corner of this paper.
3. Circle the word "name" in the second sentence.
4. Draw five small squares in the upper left-hand corner of this paper.
5. Put an X in each square mentioned in number 4.
6. Put a circle around each square.
7. Sign your name under the title of this page.
8. After the title write "YES, YES, YES."
9. Put a circle around sentence 7.
10. Put an X in the lower left-hand corner of this page.
11. Draw a triangle around the X you just made.
12. On the back of this page multiply 70 by 30.
13. Draw a circle around the word "paper" in sentence 4.
14. On the reverse side of this paper add 10 to 278.
15. Put a circle around the answer to this problem.
16. Count in your normal speaking voice backward from 1 to 10.
17. Punch three small holes in your paper with your pencil here: _____
18. Underline all even numbers on the left side of this page.
19. Now that you have finished reading carefully, do only sentences one, two, and three.
20. Turn your paper over and sit quietly until the time is up.

FIGURE 8.3   Activity for improving students' listening skills

Directions: I will say each direction only once, and so listen very carefully.

1. Draw a picture of a small round ball about one inch in diameter.
2. Make the ball you just drew look like a shining sun by drawing lines around the outside of the ball.
3. Draw a pumpkin on your paper.
4. Turn the pumpkin into a jack-o'-lantern by drawing a face on it.
5. Draw a Christmas tree and put a star on the top.
6. Print your name in the upper right-hand corner of your paper.
7. Put three Xs under your name.
8. Draw a circle around the middle X.
9. I will say three words. Write down each word. The words are dog, bed, cat.
10. I will say six words. Write down only the words that name colors. The words are: red, table, green, pink, food, and blue.

11. I will say a sentence. Write only the last word of the sentence. A great big bumble bee buzzed briefly in the breeze.

12. I will say a sentence. Listen carefully and write just the last two words in the sentence. We attend the greatest school on earth.

13. Write the name of a city in the United States and circle all the vowel letters.

14. Write the entire sentence on your paper. My friend worked very hard to become a doctor.

15. Listen to these words and name only those which name a fruit. The words are: apple, peach, rug, pear, telephone, and plum.

16. Listen to these words and write down only the words that begin with the letter "d." The words are down, ball, dentist, umbrella, doorbell, dip, flower, and desk.

---

adept at listing potential difficulties, which can then be alleviated. Finally, we can look at various groups of students and ask, "Are you ready to start and follow these directions?" By obtaining a nod or verbal commitment from each student, we increase the likelihood that they will attempt to satisfactorily complete the activity. If a student indicates that he or she is not interested in attempting the task, we can simply accept this statement and indicate that they will need to meet briefly after the class has begun their work. We can then proceed to obtain a commitment from the remaining students.

6. *Positively accept students' questions about directions.* Employing the strategies described in this section will vastly reduce the number of questions about directions, but situations will arise in which students have questions. To create a safe, supportive atmosphere it is important to respond positively to student questions. Reprimanding students in front of the class only creates a negative atmosphere. If one or more students consistently ask questions about directions that have already been clearly stated, we should discuss this problem privately with the student(s). This discussion should employ the problem-solving approaches described in Chapter 10. Examples of solutions that might result from discussing the problem include having the student write the directions, having the student choose a classmate to assist in clarifying directions, or calling on the student to paraphrase a portion of the directions.

7. *Place directions where they can be seen and referred to by students.* Accessibility is particularly useful when directions are complicated, when students will be working on an assignment over an extended period, or when students frequently repeat an activity. For nonreaders we can use pictures to describe the directions.

8. *Have students write out instructions before beginning an activity.* This method provides students with much-needed practice in thinking through the steps they should take before they begin their work. Students can be told that their directions must be checked by the teacher or

aide before they begin the assignment. Though checking requires time and effort and should not be employed with every lesson, it is especially useful when students will be working on a long-term project.

9. *When students seem to be having difficulty following directions, consider breaking tasks down into smaller segments.* Young children often have difficulty following a series of directions. Therefore, it is often necessary to give only one or two directions at a time or to have students complete one portion of a task before going on to the next activity.

10. *Give directions immediately prior to the activity they describe.* One of us recently observed a student-teacher give excellent directions about seatwork, then proceed to present fifteen minutes of direct instruction. By the time students were released for seatwork, most of them had forgotten the directions.

11. *Model the correct behavior.* If students have been asked to raise their hand before answering, we can raise our hand while asking the question.

12. *Hand out worksheets or outlines before taking a field trip.* Anyone who has visited British schools has seen excellent examples of this strategy. British children are frequently provided with worksheets to complete during a field trip. By helping students focus on relevant materials, this method reduces acting-out behavior and simultaneously helps students understand what they can learn from the activity.

Beginning a Lesson

Teachers frequently have difficulty in attracting students' attention and getting a lesson started. The reason is at least partly that students often attempt to postpone the beginning of a lesson by socializing or moving about the room. Students quite accurately realize that the best time for "buying time" is before the lesson begins. The material presented in this section suggests approaches you can employ to reduce disruptions that occur while you are introducing a lesson. Before implementing any of these methods, however, you should carefully examine such factors as whether the previous lesson has been satisfactorily summarized so that students are ready to move on to a new lesson, and whether the problem may lie more in the transition between lessons than in the beginning of the new lesson. We refer you to sections later in this chapter for suggestions in summarizing lessons and facilitating smooth transitions.

Methods

1. Select and teach a "cue" for getting students' attention. Students benefit from having a consistent cue indicating that it is time to focus their attention. Students hear standard phrases such as "Okay, we are ready to begin" so often that these statements are often ineffective for eliciting attention. One of us has her class select a new cue each month. Students enjoy being involved and choose catchy phrases. During a recent year

students chose "Boo" for October, "Gobble Gobble" for November, and "Ho Ho Ho" for December. While teaching a summer institute on classroom management, we demonstrated the value of using a "catchy" phrase by recording the time it took forty teachers to quietly pay attention following the phrase "May I please have your attention?" The average time for five such requests was nearly two minutes (in each instance, students were involved in group work). The class was presented with this figure and asked to develop a less common phrase. They chose "Rain Rain Go Away." This phrase was practiced until the class could attend within ten seconds. Follow-up data gathered during the next two weeks showed that the group never took more than ten seconds to become completely quiet.

2. *Do not begin until everyone is paying attention.* Almost every teacher has heard this suggestion, and yet most teachers find it very difficult to follow. Worried about "wasting time," we often begin a lesson even though we do not have several students' attention. Unfortunately, numerous disadvantages are associated with this decision. First, teachers inevitably spend much more time reprimanding students or repeating directions than they would waiting for students to be quiet. Second, it is impolite to talk over other people even if they are talking when they should be listening. Third, talking over students is poor modeling because it suggests that this is an acceptable method of gaining attention. Fourth, by beginning a lesson while students are talking or not paying attention, we indicate that we are not in control of the class. Finally, both we and the students who are behaving appropriately will be distracted by inappropriate student talk and consequently the lesson will be less effective. Because of these multiple disadvantages, it appears obvious that we will do well to delay our introductory comments until every student is quiet and attentive.

3. *Begin the lesson by removing distractions.* Many students—especially those with behavior problems—find it difficult to voluntarily screen out distracting stimuli. We can help students focus on the lesson by closing the door if noise is coming from the hallway or asking students to clear their desks of everything except items they will need for the assignment.

4. *Clearly describe the goals, activities, and evaluation procedures associated with the lesson being presented.* Students are more highly motivated and learn more when they are aware of the specific goals toward which they are working (Bryan & Locke, 1967; Kennedy, 1968). Clear statements about the learning process meet students' needs for safety and control over their environment. Because students are often extremely concerned about such factors as whether they can complete the work on time and how it will be evaluated, we should respond to these issues at the beginning of the lesson. If these issues are not discussed, some students will be worrying about these factors rather than devoting their attention to the lesson.

5. *Stimulate interest by relating the lesson to the students' lives or a previous lesson.* It is extremely important to place content in perspective. Students

often feel that they are simply being asked to learn a series of unrelated facts or concepts. Students' motivation can be increased dramatically by indicating why the material is being learned and suggesting ways in which the learning can influence their lives. For example, division can become much more interesting if it is viewed as a method for determining a Little League batting average. We can reduce anxiety associated with learning a new skill by relating this material or its components to skills students already possess or information that has been learned previously. This approach increases students' sense of safety and enables them to approach the new task with greater confidence.

6. *Start with a highly motivating activity in order to make the students' initial contact with the subject matter as positive as possible.* One of us begins a unit on the Lewis and Clark expedition by dressing up as Meriwether Lewis and collaborating with a colleague to present a skit summarizing the lives of these two noteworthy explorers. Students find the skit entertaining and are motivated to learn more about the expedition. Students' interest can be similarly stimulated by a good film, an experiment, or by presenting interesting questions such as "Why can birds fly though people cannot?" or "Why does rain fall while clouds remain aloft?"

7. *Hand out an outline, definitions, or study guide to help students organize their thoughts and focus their attention.* This material can be made more interesting by embellishing it with humorous cartoons or scattering thought-provoking questions or comments throughout.

8. *Challenging students to minimize their transition time.* Children enjoy games and are impressed by data. We can draw upon this knowledge by presenting students with data indicating the amount of time it requires them to "settle down" and asking them to try to reduce this time. There are six basic steps to implementing this approach. First, we must collect baseline data (see Chapter 11) and record them on a large and easy-to-read chart. Second, the data should be discussed with the students and their assistance requested. Third, we must assist the students in choosing an appropriate and reasonable goal. Fourth, it is necessary to define exactly what we mean by "being ready for class." Fifth, the class must develop a system for collecting and recording data. Finally, it may be necessary to determine a reward for reaching the stated goal.

Maintaining Attention

The amount of time students spend involved in instruction is significantly related to their achievement (Denham & Lieberman, 1980; Fisher & others, 1978; Rossmiller, 1982). Classes vary dramatically in the percentage of time students are engaged in instructional tasks, with rates ranging from consistently less than 50 percent to 90 percent (Fisher & others, 1978).

Many teachers state that one of the most frustrating tasks associated with teaching is maintaining students' attention during group instruction.

Although children and young adolescents do in fact have a somewhat shorter attention span than adults, their ability to attend quietly to an interesting television program or video game suggests that the skilled teacher can stimulate more consistent attention to task than is seen in most classrooms.

Methods

1. *Arrange the classroom so that students do not have their backs to the speaker.* When a lesson involves the teacher as the center of attention, students should be seated so that everyone is facing the teacher. This arrangement can be accomplished using rows, a circle, or a U shape. When students are seated in small groups, we should request that all students face us before beginning a lesson. Similarly, if we wish students to talk to each other, desks must be arranged in a circle, square, or U shape so that students can comfortabl see and hear each speaker. Teachers who employ a variety of instructional activities should consider teaching students a procedure for quickly and quietly moving desks. We have found that with a small amount of instruction, students in all grades can learn to rearrange desks in approximately one minute. Figure 8.4 presents a seating arrangement we have found particularly useful in elementary school classrooms because it allows for easy monitoring of seatwork as well as effective group discussion.

2. *Employ a seating arrangement that does not discriminate against some students.* Teachers spend nearly 70 percent of their time in front of the

FIGURE 8.4   Classroom arrangement

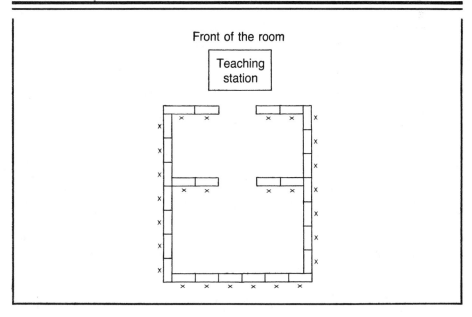

classroom (Adams & Biddle, 1970). Therefore, it is no surprise that students at the back of the room contribute less to class discussions (Adams & Biddle, 1970; Delefes & Jackson, 1972), are less attentive and on-task (Schwebel & Cherlin, 1972), and achieve less (Daum, 1972) than students seated near the front of the class.

Considering these findings, it is interesting that teachers tend to place higher-achieving students nearer the teacher and provide them with more contact (Rist, 1970). Fortunately, research also indicates that teachers can encourage more evenly distributed student responding. Daum (1972) demonstrated that when low-ability students were moved to the front of the room, their achievement improved more than that of low-ability students who remained at the back of the room. Interestingly, the high-achieving students' achievement did not suffer when they were moved farther from the teacher. Similarly, Adams and Biddle (1970) discovered that students' involvement is more evenly distributed when high- and low-achieving students are interspersed throughout the room. These studies suggest that teachers can increase on-task student responses by adjusting seating arrangements and moving around the room so that all students become actively involved in meaningful classroom interaction.

3. *Employ random selection in calling on students.* When we call on students by simply progressing up and down rows or around a circle, students who have just responded or who know they will not have to respond for several minutes often become bored and disruptive. Students can be kept attentive if we select them randomly and occasionally return to a student who has recently answered a question. When employing random selection we must be careful not to unintentionally provide significantly more response opportunities to high-achieving students. Research (Brophy & Good, 1974; Cooper & Good, 1983) indicates that teachers provide high-achieving students with more response opportunities than their low-achieving peers. One strategy for preventing this bias is simply to place a tally beside each child's name as he or she is called upon. It is a good idea to periodically explain to students why we choose to call on every student. Students who always volunteer answers have probably received numerous response opportunities during their school career and may become frustrated when these opportunities are distributed more equally. We can reduce this frustration by informing the class that calling on all students allows us to find out whether most people understand the material and helps everyone to learn by giving everyone a chance to respond. One danger in involving all students is that we are less likely to receive an immediate correct answer to every question. Studies (Brophy & Evertson, 1976; Stallings, 1976; Ward & Tikunoff, 1976) indicate that, especially in the primary grades and when working with children from lower socioeconomic classes, students' achievement is enhanced when we provide information, ask focused questions, and receive correct answers from students. Therefore, we should carefully consider when to involve lower-achieving students. For example, these

students might be called upon when they raise their hands during skill-acquisition lessons and might be encouraged to become actively involved during lessons that involve personal issues or opinions.

4. *Ask the question before calling on a student.* When we select the student before asking the question, other students may become less interested in the question. By asking the question, looking around the room, and providing students with an opportunity to consider the question, we create greater interest and anticipation and thereby increase attending behavior. We can also take this opportunity to reinforce the procedure of students' raising their hands to answer questions. We might say, "Raise your hand if you can answer this question," or, "John, you have your hand raised. What is the answer?"

5. *Wait at least five seconds before answering a question or calling on another student.* Most teachers are surprised to learn that research (Rowe, 1974) indicates that, on the average, teachers wait only one second for a student to respond before answering a question themselves or calling on another student. To make this finding more believable and relevant, consider a typical question you might employ in your classroom and silently count to ten in order to experience a ten-second wait. You may be surprised at how long ten seconds seems. Consider, however, the process students must go through when asked a question. First, they must hear the question and decide whether or not they understand it. Second, they must search for the information. Third, they must consider whether the answer they believe is correct will be accepted. Fourth, they must decide whether or not they will receive reinforcement or rebuke for their response (in some situations a correct response will be reinforced by the teacher, but punished by peers). This process may occur very rapidly for bright students, but most students require considerably longer than one second to complete it.

Perhaps the main reason we fail to wait following a question is that many students' hands are raised before we complete the question and the class moves along smoothly if we simply call on a student whose hand is raised.

Research (Rosenthal, 1973) indicates that teachers tend to wait longer for answers from students they view as brighter. The study also suggests, though, that when teachers do wait longer for lower-achieving students, they are rewarded with greater responsiveness from the students. Rowe (1978) reported that when teachers increase their waiting time, a variety of positive things occur. Figure 8.5 summarizes her findings.

If we wish to maintain students' attention and increase their willingness and ability to answer questions, we must provide all students adequate time to answer. When we fail to provide this time, students soon learn that they can maintain their uninvolvement simply by failing to respond immediately.

6. *Employ games that encourage attentive listening.* Children often find it difficult to sit quietly and listen when the teacher or their peers are talk-

FIGURE 8.5   Advantages of increasing teachers' wait time

1. Length of students' responses increases
2. Number of unsolicited but appropriate answers increases
3. Failure to obtain a response decreases
4. Children's confidence increases
5. Teacher-centered teaching decreases
6. Students' questions increase
7. Lower-achieving students contribute more
8. Students' proposals increase
9. Students give more evidence to support their answers
10. The variety of students' responses increases

ing. This important skill can be taught by involving students in activities that encourage listening. One strategy that students enjoy is the yarn activity. Before leading a group discussion, we inform the class that they will use a ball of yarn to facilitate the discussion. The students are told that only the person holding the ball of yarn can speak. When a student finishes speaking, he or she is to roll the yarn to another student who has raised his or her hand. Before releasing the ball, the speaker holds on to the yarn. This act indicates that he or she has been involved in the discussion; as the yarn is passed from student to student a sociogram-like matrix is created by the yarn. Another good activity is to employ paraphrasing during a group discussion. Before stating their point, each speaker must accurately paraphrase the point made by the previous speaker. Students quickly learn that they are often thinking about their response rather than listening to the speaker, and they quickly learn to become better listeners.

7. *Ask students to respond to their classmates' answers.* We often inadvertently reinforce the idea that students do not need to listen to their classmates' answers. By asking students a series of independent (though often related) questions, we create a situation in which students can, with no immediate consequences to themselves, become inattentive to their peers' responses. We can alleviate this problem by occasionally asking students to comment on an answer provided by a classmate. It is important, however, that we not employ this approach as a method for catching and embarrassing inattentive students. When calling on such a student, we should ask a question that he or she can answer. You might say, "John says that when we do not give this plant any light it will die. Do you agree, Bill?"

8. *Do not consistently repeat students' answers.* Many teachers parrot nearly every answer provided by a student. This practice is intended to ensure that all students hear the correct answer. But it also teaches students that: (1) they do not need to speak loudly because the teacher is the only

one who needs to hear their answer, (2) they do not need to listen to their peers because the teacher will repeat the answer, and (3) the teacher is the source of all learning in the classroom. All these negative side-effects reduce students' motivation, involvement, and attention.

9. *Model listening skills by paying close attention when students speak.* Children model their behavior after adults who have a significant role in their lives. If we want students to listen attentively to their peers, we must model good listening skills. We should concentrate on looking at the speaker and employing nonverbal cues that indicate sincere interest. Unfortunately, teachers often find that their attention is distracted by disruptive student behavior. We should initially attempt to deal with this distraction by simply employing a quick glance or gesture to indicate displeasure. If the behavior requires a more extensive diversion of attention from the speaker, we may wish to apologize to the speaker by making a statement such as, "I'm sorry that I did not hear the last part of your answer, John, but I had to ask several students to check themselves. Would you mind repeating your answer?"

10. *Be animated.* In his classic work on classroom discipline, Kounin (1970) writes, "... teachers who maintain a group focus by engaging in behaviors that keep children alert and on their toes are more successful in inducing work involvement and preventing deviancy than are teachers who do not" (p. 123). Studies indicate not only that students like enthusiastic teachers (Conger, 1977), but that our enthusiasm facilitates students' achievement (Coats & Smidchens, 1966; Mastin, 1963; Rosenshine & Furst, 1973). We can demonstrate enthusiasm and animation by moving around the room, varying our voice level, using interested facial expressions, and maintaining a high energy level. If we wish to periodically examine our behavior to see whether it appears animated we can employ audio or videotape recordings of our teaching. Though every teacher must develop his or her own style and few teachers want to put on a performance all day every day, some animation is extremely helpful in keeping students' attention.

11. *Reinforce students' efforts and maintain a high ratio of positive to negative verbal statements.* Students will feel safer and more willing to be involved in a classroom characterized by warmth and support. Though they do not want overly affected or unrealistically positive feedback, they are motivated by straightforward and sincere praise. When teachers fail to provide frequent, clear, and varied reinforcement, students begin to lose interest and often attempt to acquire more interesting responses by engaging in inappropriate behavior.

12. *Vary instructional media and methods.* Anyone who has sat through a two-hour monotone lecture is aware of the need to vary the stimuli used during instruction. Because they spend a great deal of time watching television, youngsters may be particularly sensitive to changing stimuli. Though we cannot match television's diversity, we should nevertheless concentrate on adding diversity to instruction. We can employ various

media such as an overhead projector, blackboard, butcher paper, and film, as we move from lesson to lesson. Similarly, different instructional approaches can be used for different lessons. We may use seatwork for math, small groups for social studies, and a presentation during science. Teachers and students can also invite guests into their classrooms. During a recent school week one of our guests included a local folk-singing group, an ambulance driver who demonstrated the equipment in her ambulance as well as mouth-to-mouth resuscitation and cardiopulmonary resuscitation, and a mother who spoke about nutrition. Students enjoy and are almost always attentive to adults from their community. Finally, teachers can add surprises such as using different-colored chalk or writing larger and smaller in the same sentence to attract students' attention.

13. *Create anticipation.* We can create a sense of interest by making statements such as, "This is a tough one," or "I'm not sure we've talked about this but maybe someone can answer it." Anticipation can also be created by leaving an interesting lesson without attaining closure. People tend to recall unfinished tasks and are more likely to forget completed tasks. By stimulating interest but moving on to a new activity, we can increase students' interest. This increased interest may also generalize to other subjects. When using this approach, however, you will want to attain some closure by examining possible answers and will also want to assure students that they will be able to return to the subject the following day.

14. *Use silences effectively.* Research on teachers' waiting time suggests that most teachers are uncomfortable with silence: we seem to believe that silences will be filled with disruptive behavior. Silences, however, offer several advantages that enhance students' learning and may reduce disruption. Silence can create suspense and anticipation. It can also give students time to slow down and assimilate material. Similarly, silence often clarifies information by breaking it into smaller segments. Finally, it can be used to emphasize an important point or to signal students to attend to the next statement or action. If we fall into the habit of employing rapid, nonstop talking to prevent students from interrupting, they often develop strategies for taking their own breaks. Unfortunately, these strategies often include disruptive, attention-getting behavior. Students who are poor auditory learners will find rapid, uninterrupted talk frustrating and will frequently respond by tuning out or acting out. As we saw in discussing random questioning, it is helpful to inform students why silences are being used and to provide them with assistance in using silences productively. We may state, "Before answering, I would like each of you to think about the question and see if you can find the answer," or "Please sit quietly for a minute and think about the slide we just saw."

15. *Ask questions that relate to students' own lives or similar situations.* Students find learning more meaningful when it can be related to their own lives and interests. We should therefore include questions such as, "Have you ever felt this way?" "How would your parents feel about this?" or "Do you believe that it is right to. . . ?" Similarly, we can incorporate as-

pects of students' daily lives into our instruction. During creative writing, students can write stories in which others in the class are characters.

16. *Provide work of appropriate difficulty.* Students' misbehavior is often a response to work that is either too easy or too difficult. Students prefer work that is moderately difficult over tasks that are too easy (Kleinfeld, 1975; Maehr & Sjogren, 1971). When work is too difficult, though, students become discouraged. Failure also causes students to lower their expectations of their own performance.

   Research (Brophy & Evertson, 1976) suggests that when the teacher is available to provide assistance (as during monitored seatwork or recitation), students should be able to answer 70 to 80 percent of questions correctly. When students must work independently (as on independent seatwork or homework), students should be able to answer 95 percent correctly (Brophy, 1982; Fisher et al., 1980). Seatwork must not only allow for these high success rates but must also be different enough from previous work to challenge students.

17. *Provide variability and interest in seatwork.* Seatwork can be made more interesting by developing units that relate to current events such as sports or students' other interests (animals, entertainment figures, and so on), or by creating seatwork that is based on some form of board game. Students can also be involved in working cooperatively with peers or presented with a competitive situation (Johnson & Johnson, 1975, 1984).

18. *When presenting difficult material, clearly acknowledge this fact, set a time limit for the presentation, and describe the type of follow-up activities that will clarify the lesson.* Students are less likely to become discouraged and subsequently act out when we provide this type of information. Though we must not create a self-fulfilling prophecy, students benefit from knowing that the presentation involves a new and complicated concept. We can simultaneously stimulate interest and acknowledge the difficulty of the material by comments such as, "We're going to work on a new math skill today. I'll talk about it for fifteen minutes and then give you some problems. If you have difficulty, I will help you with the problems."

Pacing

Undoubtedly you have experienced numerous examples of both effective and ineffective pacing. Anyone who has sat through a dull movie or a long meeting in which they were neither interested in the topic nor asked to be involved, has experienced ineffective pacing. Conversely, teachers have all experienced lessons that presented an ideal blend of active involvement and presentation of new ideas. Take a moment and recall a specific situation in which you felt the pacing was optimal. Now, recall an instance in which the pacing was very poor. Reflect upon how you felt and behaved in each situation. If you are like most people, you were much more comfortable and attentive in the well-paced setting. Students' behavior is also dramatically influenced by the quality of their teacher's pacing. Disruptive student behavior can often be linked directly to poorly paced lessons.

Methods

1. *Develop awareness of your own teaching tempo.* Students' behavior and performance are affected by their teacher's tempo (Yando & Kagen, 1968). We can learn to effectively generate interest and enthusiasm or create a calming effect by adjusting our own personal pace in the classroom. The best method for examining your own pace is to videotape yourself during large-group instruction. As you watch the replay, ask yourself questions such as, "Did I talk to fast?" "Was I animated?" "Did I repeat myself too often?" and "Would I enjoy listening to my own presentations?"

   Another method for obtaining feedback on pacing involves incorporating questions about pacing into questionnaires given to students to assess the teacher's instruction. Students can respond to questions such as, "Do I speak slowly enough?" "Do I notice when you are not understanding the material and stop to explain?" or "Do you have time to complete the work I require?" Following a workshop presented by one of us, an experienced high school teacher decided to improve his pacing by teaching his students several signals they could use to provide him with feedback. Students were asked to make the common "chattering" movement with their hand to indicate that the teacher was repeating himself, place their hand up in a "stop" motion when he was going too fast, and make a circle with their index finger when they were confused. The teacher reported to his colleagues that students thoroughly enjoyed providing him with feedback and that he believed his teaching was more effective.

2. *Watch for nonverbal cues indicating that students are becoming confused, bored or restless.* We often become so involved in presenting our material that we fail to attend to indications that several or even many students are becoming increasingly inattentive. Kounin (1970) discovered that teachers who had fewer discipline problems effectively scanned their rooms and responded to potentially disruptive student behavior before it became a major problem. When students appear restless, we have several options. First, we can state our perception and ask the children to express their feelings. We might say, "A number of you seem to be having difficulty paying attention. Can someone tell me what is causing the problem?" If students have become accustomed to sharing feelings and solving problems, it is very likely that one or more can pinpoint the problem. Another option that may be used separately or may follow the intervention above is to speculate about the cause of the problem and change the pace accordingly. Therefore, we might decide that too much material is being covered and may shorten the lesson and incorporate several per-

sonalized questions to increase students' involvement and attention. The teacher who continues undaunted in the face of students' restlessness is inviting further disruptive behavior.

3. *Break activities up into short segments.* The use of films as instructional aids helps demonstrate this strategy. Teachers almost always allow a film to run all the way to the end before discussing its content. There are, however, several advantages to stopping the film at important points and discussing the ideas being presented. First, major points of information can be highlighted. Second, this procedure allows students to assimilate smaller amounts of information at a time. Many students simply cannot process the material offered in a half-hour film. Third, this method differentiates viewing a film at school from watching a movie or viewing television. Students can begin to learn that movies shown in school are meant to convey specific information and ideas rather than simply to entertain.

4. *Provide structured "short breaks" during lessons that last longer than 30 minutes.* Disruptive behavior is sometimes merely students' method of obtaining a short respite from the rigors of a long school day. Because many students do not have the skill to quietly and productively refresh themselves during extended periods of study, we can reduce disruptions either by providing structured breaks or by teaching children how to take their own breaks. We can provide a break by asking the class to simply put their pencils aside and take a minute to stand and stretch. We can also create a break by involving students in a short (three to five minutes is the optional length for such break activities) game such as Twenty Questions, Seven-up, or Simon Says. It is important to inform the students that this activity is being used to provide a brief break and that they will be expected to return to work as soon as the activity is completed. Students can be taught how to relax themselves using deep muscle relaxation. We can then encourage them to respond to the need to wander around the room or disrupt another student by simply taking a moment to relax themselves before continuing with their work. We can reinforce this approach by occasionally employing it as a structured break activity.

5. *Vary the style as well as the content of instruction.* Students often become restless when faced with extended instructional periods employing only one type of instruction. If students have completed a large-group discussion in social studies, it is best not to move directly to a large-group science presentation. Teachers with good classroom-management skills learn to move smoothly among a variety of instructional approaches.

6. *Do not bury students in a "purple plague."* Students' misbehavior is not infrequently an attempt to add a little entertainment and relief to a day filled with innumerable worksheets. Students may act out because they are given thirty problems to complete when only five were needed to indicate mastery of a new skill or when they are confronted with a continuous procession of worksheets.

Using Seatwork Effectively

Research in hundreds of elementary school classrooms shows that students spend more than half their time working privately at seatwork (Angus, Evans, & Parkin, 1975; Good & Beckerman, 1978; McDonald, 1976). Data from some of the classes of the Beginning Teacher Evaluation Study (Fisher & others, 1978) also show that in some classes students make nearly 100 percent errors during 14 percent of the time they are involved in seatwork. Given findings suggesting that during seatwork students learn best when experiencing approximately 90 percent success rates (Rosenshine, 1983), it is critical that we learn to effectively structure seatwork so as to ensure students' involvement and success.

During a visit to a second-grade classroom, a student in one of our courses reported observing a child who was spending most of his time staring out the window or doodling on his paper. The observer finally approached the child and asked if she could be of any assistance. Much to her surprise, the child indicated that he understood the work. When asked why he was staring out the window rather than working on his assignment, the boy pointed to a girl several rows away and said, "See her? She does all her work real fast and when she's done she just gets more work." The student obviously viewed seatwork as a never-ending task and had learned to pace himself—quite possibly to the detriment of his own learning. This incident shows that we must effectively integrate periods of seatwork with other learning activities and employ seatwork as a method for individualizing and reinforcing learning rather than for keeping students busy.

Methods

1. *Make seatwork diagnostic and prescriptive.* Seatwork should be designed to provide students with meaningful practice while enabling teacher and student to assess the student's progress. Therefore, seatwork should be checked by the teacher or student, recorded and filed by the student, monitored by the teacher, and discussed in periodic teacher-student conferences. When this procedure is followed, students view seatwork as meaningful and are much less likely to act out during instructional periods designated for seatwork.
2. *Develop a specific procedure for obtaining assistance.* Students will inevitably require assistance when engaged in seatwork assignments. Because teachers are often engaged in small-group instruction or helping other students while all are doing seatwork, it is necessary to establish a procedure whereby children can obtain assistance without interrupting the teacher. If such procedures are not established and students are instructed not to disturb the teacher, they will become frustrated when they need assistance and are very likely to respond by acting out. The most effective method of providing assistance is peer tutoring.
3. *Establish clear procedures about what to do when seatwork is completed.* It is helpful to display a poster reminding students what to do with their

completed work (for example, we may remind them to score, record, and file their work), and what alternatives are available once these tasks have been completed. Learning centers and puzzles or other challenging activities provide useful and necessary alternatives for students.

4. *Add interest to seatwork by including cartoons, puzzles, or personalized questions to worksheets.*

5. *Monitor seatwork by moving around the room systematically.* Teachers often inadvertently spend a disproportionate amount of time in one or more areas of the classroom. During seatwork instruction, it is important to monitor each student's work. We can ensure that this is done by carrying a clipboard and noting when each student's work is monitored, or by having a colleague or student draw a map of our walking pattern during a seatwork period.

   When involved with a small group, we can assign the group a task and leave briefly to monitor students involved in seatwork. By teaching a procedure for obtaining assistance, we can reduce the need to provide lengthy assistance to students involved in seatwork and can simply remind them to follow the procedure.

6. *Monitor students' seatwork and make needed adjustments.* One of us recently observed a student teacher in a fifth-grade class. Students in the class completed seatwork at varying rates and the teacher's failure to adjust seatwork or provide optional learning activities ensured that many students were free to wander and disrupt the class. To bring out this point for the teacher, I coded at five-minute intervals the number of students who had completed a quarter, half, three-quarters, or all their work. The results (Figure 8.6) clearly indicate the inappropriateness of giving all students the same seatwork task.

   In addition to monitoring the time required to complete seatwork, we should monitor the percentage of students who complete their work with at least 75 percent accuracy (a higher percentage should be selected if we are not available to monitor the seatwork). This information as well as a group average score should be recorded as a basis for determining future seatwork assignments for individual students or the class as a whole.

FIGURE 8.6   Number of students who had completed various amounts of seatwork at five-minute intervals.

	Percentage of work complete			
	0–25%	*26–50%*	*51–75%*	*76–100%*
5 minute	11	12	8	2
10 minute	6	10	10	7
15 minute	4	6	13	10
20 minute	3	4	7	19

7. *Work through the first several seatwork problems with the students.* All students will then understand the procedure to be followed and will be able to ask questions if they do not understand the work.
8. *Spend considerable time in presentation and discussion before assigning seatwork.* Students learn more effectively when they have been well prepared for this work.
9. *Relate seatwork directly to material presented immediately prior to it.* Students will have more difficulty with seatwork assignments related to material discussed on the previous day or stemming from individualized work.
10. *Keep contacts with individual students relatively short (30 seconds or less).* Longer contacts minimize your ability to scan the room or to provide assistance to all students.
11. *Provide short segments of seatwork.* Rather than making one long presentation followed by an extended period of seatwork, break the instruction into smaller segments and follow each with a short period of seatwork.
12. *Have students work together during seatwork.* Students can jointly develop solutions or can cooperatively prepare for group competition.

Summarizing

Many children view the school day as a series of tasks to be completed and do not understand what they have learned or how the learning relates to specific learning goals or their own lives. Try to recall a course you found particularly difficult. Take a moment to consider how you went about studying for the course and how well you understood the material. It is quite likely that you studied specific facts and that you did not fully understand the central concepts of the discipline or the relationship between what you were studying and your own life. It is also very likely that you found the course to be quite frustrating and confusing. Unfortunately, many students experience similar feelings about much of the school day. We should not be surprised that acting-out behavior replaces appropriate on-task behavior. Many of the methods presented in this chapter are effective in producing more positive student behavior precisely because they reduce students' frustration. Helping students understand what they have learned is a key factor in clarifying the school experience. When combined with clearly stated goals and useful feedback, the methods presented in this section provide students with a sense of accomplishment and meaning in their school experience.

Methods

1. *At the end of a lesson or a school day, ask students to state or write in a journal one thing they have learned.* Not only does this activity help clarify what they have learned, but it provides each student with a sense of accomplishment. Students should be informed that if they have difficulty

stating what they have learned, they can seek assistance from the teacher or a peer.

2. *Have students play the role of a reporter and summarize what has been learned.* We can introduce a student as a news reporter who will highlight the information from a lesson. We might say, "This is NBC reporter Billy Williams, who will report on the Nez Perce conflict that caused the tribe's flight to Canada. Come in Billy."

3. *Have students create a skit to act out what they have learned.* In a unit on fur trappers, students can play the role of trappers building a bull boat. During their work the trappers can discuss how the boat is built and how it applies to their livelihood. Similarly, when studying parts of speech, students can be given cards listing various parts of speech and asked to organize themselves into meaningful sentences.

4. *Ask students to create learning displays.* Students can develop a collage, outline, newspaper article, and so on, to display their learning. They might write an article reporting on how plants grow. Students could also draw a chart that demonstrates this process.

5. *Encourage students to present their learning to others.* Students can share what they have learned with their classmates, other classes, or their parents. This sharing can take the form of reporting results of science experiments, performing skits, or showing the results of art projects, and so on. Students can also share their learning by actually teaching their newly acquired information to other students.

6. *Display students' work.* Displaying students' work not only provides students with a sense of pride and accomplishment but also provides closure to an activity. Students can view the end result of a unit or lesson, which reinforces the fact that the various steps led to an observable final product.

7. *Relate material to students' lives and interests.* An effective summary involves clarifying how the new material relates to students' lives or can be useful to students. When completing a unit on division, students can be asked to calculate their Little League batting averages, their teams' won–lost percentages, or whether they would save money on certain items by purchasing them in larger quantities. Similarly, at the completion of a unit on how plants grow, students could be asked to list the ways in which their new knowledge will help them to grow a better garden or keep their house plants alive longer.

8. *Provide frequent review sessions.* It is helpful to frequently review previous learning and relate this information to current or future lessons. When presenting a daily, continuing lesson, we should begin the day's lesson with a brief review of the material covered on the previous day. This refresher not only enhances retention but also reinforces the concept that learning builds upon previous learning. Students all too often perceive each lesson as an isolated hurdle to be jumped rather than a step in a sequential learning process. Frequent reviews increase the likelihood that learning will be seen as a connected series of events.

9. *Use tests as tools for summarizing learning.* Teachers should treat tests like any other summary or learning experience. Students need to be informed that tests are a means for discovering how much they have learned and what material may need to be covered more thoroughly. When they have completed a test, answers should be discussed so that students receive a review of the correct answers.

Providing Useful Feedback and Evaluation

Evaluation of students' performance is an area that causes much worry among students, teachers, and parents. Teachers worry about their ability to accurately evaluate students and whether their feedback is fair and helpful. Students worry not only about what evaluations indicate about their own competence, but about their parents' reactions to teachers' evaluations. Finally, parents worry about reports on their child's performance, not only because they hope their child will be successful and happy and because a good evaluation reflects favorably upon them, but also because consistently poor evaluations may suggest either poor parenting or poor inherited abilities. Because of the interest and potential anxiety associated with evaluation, it is clear that by employing effective methods in this area we can create greater clarity and safety and thereby reduce disruptive behavior. Many years ago Regan (1966) wrote in his *Modern Elementary Curriculum* that the six basic purposes of evaluation were:

1. To reveal to teachers what is happening to each child.
2. To motivate learning through furnishing pupils with information concerning success in various areas of the curriculum.
3. To furnish teachers with a means of appraising teaching methods, textbook, and other instrumentalities of the educative process.
4. To provide a basis for continuous improvement of the curriculum.
5. To give pupils experience in evaluating their own progress.
6. To reveal the progress the school program is making toward the achievement of the accepted objectives.[p. 452]

The methods presented below reinforce these purposes and offer practical ideas for effectively using evaluation in the classroom.

Methods

1. *Help students view evaluation as part of the learning process.* We need to place no greater emphasis on tests or report cards than on any other instructional activity. Children should be encouraged to view evaluation as simply an integral part of learning. This understanding can be enhanced by employing many of the methods described in this section.
2. *Tell students the criteria by which they will be evaluated.* When working with specific skills, students should know what they are to learn and

what level of performance is acceptable. Similarly, when they are assigned projects in subjects from art to social studies, they should be informed about the specific goals for the lesson; and, if their work will be evaluated, what specific criteria will be used. The importance of sharing information with children was powerfully stated by Herbert Kohl (1967):

> The easiest way to bring this up in class was to tell the children exactly where they stood. I braced myself, and defying all precedent as well as my own misgivings, I performed the unforgivable act of showing the children what their reading and IQ scores were according to the record cards. I also taught a lesson on the definition of IQ and of achievement scores. The children were angry and shocked; no one had ever come right out and told them they were failing. It was always put so nicely and evasively that the children never knew where they stood. [Kohl, 1967, p. 176]

3. *Relate feedback directly to individual or teacher goals.* Feedback should help students understand how effectively they are progressing toward clearly specified goals. This clarification makes the learning process much more concrete and clear. Studies (Burrows, 1973; Collins, 1971) indicate that providing students with the results of diagnostic tests and then providing instruction aimed at achieving mastery of specific objectives leads to dramatic increases in learning.

4. *Record data so that students can monitor their progress.* Students can benefit immensely from the realization that they are able to learn. One of us once worked with a seventh-grade boy who viewed himself as a totally inept learner. One day while the boy was working in a room that included a two-way mirror, the boy was videotaped during a period in which he worked diligently for fifty consecutive minutes. When the videotape was shown to the student he responded with disbelief. He simply could not believe that he could study for fifty minutes. The student asked to have the principal and his own mother view the tape. This incident proved to be a watershed in the boy's school life. Students should be taught how to record their academic progress. We can do so by teaching simple graphing skills. We may also wish to provide interesting data displays such as a football field with strings to which cardboard football players are attached. The players can be moved down the field to represent individual or group acquisition of skills. Chapter 10 provides specific techniques for employing academic goal setting and student self-monitoring.

5. *Provide immediate and specific feedback.* Page (1958) found that students' learning was enhanced when they were provided with specific positive and negative information about their performance. Generalized feedback such as a grade or comments such as "Good" or "Nice work" do not tend to improve students' performance on subsequent tests.

6. *Attempt to focus on positive accomplishments.* Whenever possible, we should assist students in recording their accomplishments rather than focusing on their failures. We can initially focus on the items students have answered correctly and then help them correct mistakes. Effective

feedback encourages students to describe both the strengths and weaknesses of their work.

7. *Provide honest feedback.* It is important to focus on students' success, but students' performance is not aided by feedback that is inaccurately positive. Students resent feedback they perceive as fake (Travers, 1967). Furthermore, providing students with too much praise for work that does not meet acceptable standards only confuses them and reduces their motivation and performance (Fernandez, Espinoza, & Dornbush, 1977).

8. *Ask students to list factors that contributed to their success.* Students need assistance in specifying behaviors that enabled them to succeed. Low-achieving students often view their successes as based on luck or outside forces rather than their own efforts. Helping children focus on the relationship between their effort and performance can help them in feeling a greater sense of competence and power. This confidence will in turn increase the likelihood that they will begin to accept greater responsibility for their own behavior. Figure 8.7 provides a form you can employ to help students analyze the relationship between their behavior and performance.

9. *Deemphasize comparisons between students and their peers.* Though it is helpful for students to know how they stand in relation to grade-level norms, we should not evaluate how well they perform in relation to their peers. In addition to placing some children in a no-win situation, comparative evaluations suggest that the goal of learning is to outperform one's peers rather than master the material. Students should be evaluated on criterion-referenced tests and their performance compared to their own earlier work.

10. *Deemphasize grades as feedback on students' work.* Grades by themselves provide almost no useful information. When it is important or necessary to provide students with information about the quality of their performance as compared to an external criterion such as grade-level norms, it is best to have a teacher-student conference and outline specific skills the student will need to improve in order to score at grade level. Detailed teacher's comments and supportive statements are much more effective than grades in motivating students' performance.

Grades tend to motivate those students who least need it; that is, those who are already successful; while, perversely, the very students who need motivating the most (poor students) are most put off and threatened by grades. . . .

When it comes to motivating school achievement, it appears that the type of learning structure is by far the more important factor, with grades playing a secondary, even negligible, role. [Covington & Beery, 1976, pp. 116, 117]

Making Smooth Transitions

A surprisingly large amount of classroom time is spent in transition from one activity to another. The approximately thirty major transitions each day in ele-

FIGURE 8.7   Looking at me

	Always	Usually	Sometimes	Seldom	Never
1. I do my best to learn new skills.					
2. I plan my work well.					
3. I am proud of the work I do.					
4. I try to get my work in on time.					
5. I listen carefully to others.					
6. I am ready to begin my work on time.					
7. I can make choices when I need to.					
8. I can admit when I am wrong.					
9. I take part in discussion groups.					
10. I cooperate with other students.					
11. I am polite.					
12. I keep my desk neat.					
13. I respect other students' property.					
14. I always bring my materials.					
15. I follow classroom and school rules.					
16. I accept responsibilities without being reminded.					
17. I help people.					
18. I can accept changes and disappointments.					

mentary classrooms account for nearly 15 percent of classroom time (Gump, 1967; Rosenshine, 1980). Most experienced teachers acknowledge that the beginning and end of class periods, or the transition between subjects or activities during the period, are the times when students are most likely to be disruptive. Therefore, as we would expect, the handling of transitions distinguishes skilled from less-skilled classroom managers (Arlin, 1979; Doyle, 1984).

Students' disruption during transitions often leads to extended periods of off-task behavior, which drains teachers' energies and reduces students' achievement. Because students' learning is directly related to the amount of time they spend studying a subject (Borg, 1980; Rosenshine, 1976; Sirotnik, 1982), we must develop skill in making smooth transitions. It is equally important, however, that we realize that the quality of learning time is more important than time itself (Berliner, 1979; Doyle, 1983; Good, 1983; Peterson & Swing, 1982). Therefore, the goal of an effective transition is not so much getting students immediately on task as it is preparing students to be productively involved in the coming instruction.

Methods

1. *Arrange the classroom for efficient movement.* The classroom should be arranged so that areas through which students move frequently are wide and cleared of materials. Desks should be arranged so that students and teacher can move around the room without disturbing students who are working. We encourage you to make a detailed map of your classroom and mark areas where students frequently move or congregate. Are these large enough to prevent overcrowding and its accompanying disruption? Are pathways clear and wide? Is space used so that the classroom has a sense of openness?

2. *Create and post a daily schedule and discuss any changes in schedule each morning.* Numerous low-level discipline problems arise when students are confused over scheduling issues such as a change in their violin lesson or not attending reading due to the specialist's absence. These difficulties can be minimized by discussing the classroom schedule each morning. This activity also provides a clear and task-oriented transition into the school day.

3. *Have material ready for the next lesson.* It is often helpful to have an outline of the lesson written on the blackboard or on butcher paper. Similarly, having a filmstrip or film set up and ready to go or having materials ready for distribution allow us to make a smooth transition rather than attempting to prepare materials while monitoring students' behavior and dealing with disruptions that often occur during transition periods. Students' behavior is dramatically affected by our behavior. If we are well prepared, relaxed, and make smooth transitions, students will almost always follow by moving calmly from one activity to the next. Conversely, when we become frustrated or anxious while attempting to arrange an activity, students inevitably follow suit.

4. *Do not relinquish students' attention until you have given clear instructions for the following activity.* We can prevent numerous problems by moving from a summary of one lesson immediately into a transition activity (such as a brief game of 7-up) or the next lesson. All too often, we allow the class to become disruptive while we prepare for the next lesson, only to find that it requires considerable time and energy to regain the students' attention.

5. *Do not do tasks that can be done by students.* We can free ourselves to monitor the class and can reduce the demands upon our own time and energy by having students do a wide variety of tasks such as handing out and collecting materials, running filmstrips, and taking the roll. In addition to freeing us for more important instructional and management tasks, involving students in organizational tasks can provide them with a sense of competence and power.

6. *Move around the room and attend to individual needs.* Being prepared and allowing students to handle many small tasks can free us to more effectively scan the classroom and handle any minor problems that, if ignored, could expand into major disruptions. Having a moment to notice and say a few words to a student who is frustrated by his or her inability to complete the previous activity may prevent a major disruption by that student during the next lesson.

7. *Provide students with simple, step-by-step directions.* Younger students especially benefit from being given specific directions asking them to do one thing at a time. Rather than asking students to "get ready for lunch," we might break this task into the smaller steps of clearing their desks, sitting quietly, one group at a time getting their lunches, and so forth.

8. *Remind students of key procedures associated with the upcoming lesson.* If the next lesson requires some students to work independently while you instruct a small group or have conferences with students, remind students of the procedures they should follow during this type of activity. This is best handled by first describing the learning activity and its goal and then asking students to describe the procedures they are to follow during this type of activity.

9. *Employ group competition to stimulate more orderly transitions.* We can involve the class in attempting to reduce the amount of time required to make a transition. Similarly, small groups or rows of students can be involved in competition to see who can make the quietest and fastest preparation for the next lesson.

10. *Develop transition activities.* Students often find it difficult to make the transition from home to school or from lunch or physical education back to a quieter setting. We can facilitate smooth transitions by implementing structured activities that help students make these transitions. We can ask them to begin the school day by writing in their journals or by discussing the daily schedule. Transitions from active periods such as lunch into quieter learning activities can be facilitated by transition activities such as our reading to the students or leading students in deep

muscle relaxation. When these activities are used consistently, students not only find safety and comfort in this structure, but also can learn how to monitor transitions for themselves.

Handling Minor Disruptions

Misbehavior often occurs because students find acting out to be more interesting than a boring lesson or a better option than yet another failure experience. Similarly, unproductive student behavior often occurs because students do not understand a task, are not involved in the learning activity, or are unable to obtain assistance when it is needed. Therefore, most minor discipline problems can be alleviated by implementing the instructional methods discussed throughout Part III of this book. Nevertheless, when thirty people are required to work for approximately six hours a day in a thirty-by-thirty-foot area, minor problems will inevitably occur. As Kounin (1970) discovered, a major factor in effective classroom management is teachers' ability to deal with minor disruptions before they become major problems.

Figure 7.3 and the associated narrative in Chapter 7 provide a systematic procedure for responding to minor disruptions that violate classroom rules or procedures. The methods described below can effectively supplement the more formal approach presented in Chapter 7.

Methods

1. *Arrange seating patterns so that you can see and easily move to be near all students.* During small-group work the students should have their back to the class and you should face the class. By maintaining awareness of what is going on and being able to move around the room without disturbing children, you can solve minor problems more quickly.

2. *Scan the class frequently in order to notice and respond to potential problems or minor disruptions.* One of the most difficult tasks for beginning teachers to learn is how to attend to more than one thing at a time. Teachers frequently become so engrossed in working with a group or an individual student that they fail to notice potential problems stemming from a frustrated student or a minor argument. Though it is important to thoughtfully attend to the student(s) being taught, we can learn to quickly scan the room.

3. *The disruptive influence of the teacher's intervention should not be greater than the disruption it is intended to reduce.* Teachers often create more disruptions with their attempts to discipline students than the students are causing themselves. We should, whenever possible, ignore such minor disruptions as a dropped book or overuse of a pencil sharpener. If an individual student continually creates minor disruptions, this problem can be dealt with more effectively by discussing the issue privately with

the student. If a large number of class members are involved in low-key disruptive behavior, the behavior should be discussed during a class meeting.

4. *An inappropriately angry teacher response creates tension and increases disobedience and disruptive behavior.* Both Kounin (1970) and Brophy and Evertson (1976) found evidence of a "negative ripple effect" associated with harsh teacher criticism. Rather than improving student behavior, students tend to become more anxious and disruptive in classes characterized by overly harsh discipline. Therefore, though firmness can have a positive effect on classroom behavior, it should be associated with teacher warmth, politeness, and explanations.

5. *A "positive ripple effect" is associated with a calm and immediate response to a problem.* When teachers react calmly and quickly to a student's disruptive behavior, other students respond by improving their own behavior.

6. *When misbehavior occurs, the first step is to quietly make contact with the student.* We can do so with a glance, by moving close to the student, by touching the student on the shoulder, or by asking the student for an on-task response. When asking the student to respond, we should always ask a question the student can answer. If the student has obviously not been listening to the discussion, we will embarrass the student by asking "Sam, what do you think about Tom's answer?" Asking Sam a new question, however, or paraphrasing Tom's statement and asking Sam for his opinion can productively reintegrate Sam into the mainstream of the classroom activity. Another approach to making a positive initial contact with the student is to praise a positive behavior that competes with the negative behavior. Rather than criticize a student's off-task behavior, we can praise the student the moment he or she begins to work on his or her assignment or focus on the class discussion.

7. *Employ effective communication skills when resolving conflicts.* Rather than criticizing students, use paraphrasing to defuse their anger and anxiety. If a student states angrily, "This work is stupid!" we can respond by paraphrasing, "The work doesn't seem to make any sense. Would you like some help with it?" Similarly, if a student is off-task, rather than criticize, simply describe the student's behavior and offer assistance. We might say, "Pat, you seem to be wandering around the room a lot during this math assignment. Would you like someone to help you with the work?" Another communication skill involves sending an "I" message rather than criticizing a student. When a student consistently interrupts during a lesson, we can say, "Excuse me Bill, but when you interrupt without raising your hand, I get distracted and it is harder for me to teach. Would you please raise your hand next time?"

Teachers should also avoid threats and appeals to authority when stopping misbehavior through direct intervention. By simply stating how they want the student to behave, teachers communicate the expectation that they will be obeyed. However, if they add a threat ("Do it or else . . ."), they place themselves in a position of conflict with the student, and at the same time, they indirectly suggest that they are not sure he is going to obey. [Good & Brophy, 1973, p. 204]

It is often difficult to remember to use these skills when confronted with annoying or aggressive student behavior. When we can train ourselves to employ these skills, however, we model appropriate behavior for our students, create a calmer, more positive classroom environment, and feel considerably more positive about ourselves and less resentful toward our students.

8. *Remind students of the classroom rule or procedure they are not demonstrating.* Rather than yelling, "Chris, stop bothering Mary while she is working!" we can simply walk over to Chris and ask quietly, "Chris, do you know which rule you are not following?" Similarly, if an entire class is becoming disruptive or lining up without having cleared their desks, we can ask the class to describe their behavior and mention any classroom procedures that are being neglected.

9. *When one or two students are being extremely disruptive it is best to focus the other students' attention on their task and then talk privately with the disruptive student(s).* We could say, "Would you all please help me by working quietly on your spelling sentences while I help Tom and Bob solve their problems?" By handling the situation calmly and positively, we indicate our competence, which in turn will have a calming effect on the other students.

Implementing and Assessing New Teaching Methods

A major problem associated with reading a long list of methods is the tendency to acknowledge their value but not slow down long enough to systematically implement any one method. You may feel stimulated or overwhelmed by the many methods presented in the previous section. Unfortunately, neither of these feelings has a direct, positive effect upon students' behavior. To improve students' learning and behavior, you must take time to thoughtfully employ several of these methods in the classroom.

ACTIVITY 8.1   Implementing and assessing new teaching methods

Label each of nine sheets of paper with one of the nine approaches to reducing disruptions during a lesson (see Figure 8.1). Next, under each topic write one specific method you do not currently employ and which you believe would help you reduce classroom disruptions. On the page labeled Giving Clear Instructions, you might write: Place directions where they can be seen and referred to by students. The next step involves writing and completing these statements on each page:

I will begin using this method (give a specific date) _____.
I will know that I have implemented this method when I have. . .
After _____ days I will evaluate this method by. . . .

After thoughtfully and specifically completing these statements for each
of the nine methods, write the following statement near the bottom of
each page and complete it after you have implemented and evaluated the
new method.

Based on my evaluation, I believe the new method. . . .

In addition to selecting specific methods that will help improve students' learning and behavior, you will develop professionally by attempting the following activity that helps to demonstrate the value of collecting data on your use of new teaching methods.

ACTIVITY 8.2   Monitoring students' hand raising

Part I: During a question-and-answer period, select five questions varying in difficulty. When asking these, stop approximately two-thirds of the way through each question and quickly count the number of hands that are raised. Also, try to notice which students have their hands up. It may help to involve a colleague or parent in collecting these data. After the lesson, complete these questions:

How many students had their hands raised when you stopped during
    each question?
Were considerably more hands raised for the less difficult question?
What did you notice about the students whose hands were raised? Did
    they tend to be your higher-achieving students?

Part II: During a question-and-answer period in the same subject with the same students, select five questions varying in difficulty. Wait five full seconds after completing each question. Count the number of hands that were raised to answer each of these questions. Again, try to notice which students raised their hands.
    After the lesson, complete these questions:

How many students had their hands raised to answer each question?
Were considerably more hands raised for the less difficult questions?
What did you notice about students who raised their hands?

Now compare the results of your two experiments. Make the task easier by completing this form for each set of questions.

continued

Question	Number of students' hands raised	Type of student raising hand
1. Most difficult		
2.		
3.		
4.		
5. Least difficult		

Finally, answer these questions.

I learned that . . .
I was surprised that . . .
When I waited longer . . .

This is only one example of the manner in which you can collect data to assess the results obtained by implementing new teaching methods. Whenever possible, we encourage you to generate some form of evaluation to assess the results of employing new methods.

RECOMMENDED READING

Brophy, J., & Evertson, C. (1976). *Learning from teaching*. Boston: Allyn and Bacon.

Good, T., & Brophy, J. (1984). *Looking in classrooms*. (3rd ed.). New York: Harper and Row.

Hosford, P. (1984). *Using what we know about teaching*. Alexandria, Va.: Association for Supervision and Curriculum Development.

Kounin, J. (1970). *Discipline and group management in classrooms*. New York: Holt, Rinehart and Winston.

Smith, D. (1984). *Essential knowledge for beginning educators*. Washington, D.C.: American Association of Colleges for Teacher Education.

Squires, D., Huitt, W., & Segars, J. (1984). *Effective schools and classrooms. A research-based perspective*. Alexandria, Va.: Association for Supervision and Curriculum Development.

Wlodkowski, R. (1978). *Motivation and teaching: A practical guide*. Washington, D.C.: National Education Association.

CHAPTER 9

Instructional Methods That Motivate Students and Increase Learning

Certain skills or abilities are also essential to the educated man: the ability to learn for himself, to take hold of a subject and 'work it up' for himself, so that he is not dependent upon his teacher's direction. ...

Charles E. Silberman, (1970),
Crisis in the Classroom: The Remaking of American Education

This important work of several decades ago, as well as much of what has since been in the forefront of educational thought, stresses the importance of teachers finding ways to make subject matter relevant to students, to involve students in setting their own goals, to vary the ways of learning to use approaches that employ all of the senses, and to be sure that there are opportunities for relating the knowledge to experiences or actually using it.

John I. Goodlad, (1984),
A Place Called School: Prospects for the Future

All genuine learning is active, not passive. It involves the use of the mind, not just the memory. It is a process of discovery in which the student is the main agent, not the teacher.

Mortimer J. Adler, (1982),
The Paideia Proposal: An Educational Manifesto

A self-propelled learner is the goal of a school, and teachers should insist that students habitually learn on their own. Teacher-delivered knowledge that is never used is temporary.

Theodore Sizer, (1984),
Horace's Compromise: The Dilemma of the American High School

It is difficult to separate effective classroom management from effective instruction. Students learn more and behave better in classrooms where teachers employ instructional methods appropriate to the learning goals and students' learning needs. At all grade levels, effective teachers are skilled in providing direct instruction to large and small groups. Effective teachers also incorporate methods that help students become actively involved in the learning process and develop skill in taking responsibility for their own learning.

The past several years have seen leading educators increasingly emphasizing the idea that the quality of instruction is a key factor influencing students' behavior and achievement. Research and practice focusing on the quality of instruction has followed two general paths. First, a group of researchers (Anderson, Evertson, & Brophy, 1979; Good & Grouws, 1979, 1981; Stallings, Needels, & Stayrook, 1979) have examined the specific instructional skills and amounts of time spent on various instructional tasks displayed by teachers whose students achieved higher scores on standardized tests. Stimulated by these process-product studies relating students' acquisition of basic skills to a variety of teacher behaviors that increase students' engaged learning time, several leading educators including Thomas Good (1979), Madeline Hunter (1981), and Jane Stallings (1984) have developed teacher-training programs aimed at increasing students' achievement by improving teachers' skills in providing direct instruction to students. Because recent national studies indicate that many students are not mastering fundamental knowledge in basic skills, it is imperative that teachers learn instructional skills that will increase students' gains in acquiring basic skills. Furthermore, attainment of higher-level cognitive goals depends heavily upon students' having mastered basic skills.

Another group of educators, including John Goodlad (1984), David and Roger Johnson (1975; 1983; 1984), Bruce Joyce and Marsha Weil (1980), Vern Jones (1980), Bernice McCarthy (1980, 1983), Robert Slavin (1983), and Robert Soar (1983) emphasize instructional approaches that actively involve students in instructional activities aimed not only at acquiring important basic skills but also higher level cognitive skills and interpersonal skills. This work seems to coincide with increasing interest in student responsibility and self-control (Brophy, 1983; Duke & Jones, 1985; Good, 1983). Research (DeCharms, 1972; Johnson & Johnson, 1984; Lepper & Greene, 1975; Maehr, 1974; Mahoney, 1974) supports the concept that increased choice and feelings of personal responsibility enhance academic achievement. Thomas Good (1983b) summarizes the focus on students' involvement:

> In particular, researchers should examine how teachers' classroom management styles influence student initiative and self-control. Students need structure and purposeful direction, but they must also have opportunities to learn to deter-

mine their own objectives and to develop strategies for evaluating progress in self-chosen goals. Such abilities become increasingly important as students get older. [p. 63]

Taken together, the research described above suggests that teachers must possess the skills (outlined in Chapters 7 and 8) for organizing and managing classrooms and for systematically presenting material to students. Teachers must also, however, have skill in helping students establish learning goals, initiate and evaluate their own learning, work cooperatively in the learning process, and develop skills in higher-level cognitive processes such as analysis, synthesis, and research methodology. "Since no single teaching strategy can accomplish every purpose, the wise teacher will master a sufficient repertoire of strategies to deal with the specific kinds of learning problems he or she faces" (Joyce & Weil, 1980, p. 19). This concept is echoed by Thomas Good (1983b, p. 62): ". . . effective managers in the research reviewed here thought about the needs of their students and adjusted their teaching to particular classes. These teachers appeared to be good decision makers." We believe that, as professionals, teachers must be introduced to a broad range of knowledge and be provided with assistance in learning to make thoughtful decisions about how to integrate various methods of instruction and classroom management. Joyce and Weil (1980) say in their *Models of Teaching* that a wide range of instructional methods is available to teachers.

This chapter provides a practical overview of many instructional skills (Figure 9.1) that can improve students' acquisition of basic skills and increase their motivation, interest, and higher-level cognitive skills. It is obviously not possible in one chapter to describe in detail the increasing amount of excellent work available for helping teachers improve and diversify the quality of their instruction. Therefore, although we refer to much available literature and materials, we have focused on the aspects we have found most useful in our own teaching and our work with teachers. This chapter should help you

FIGURE 9.1   Instructional methods for improving students' motivation and achievement

1. Improving the quality of direct and active instruction
2. Teaching more than facts
3. Incorporating students' interests
4. Responding to students' individual learning styles
5. Taking into account students' level of cognitive development
6. Involving students in academic goal setting
7. Employing learning centers
8. Implementing self-evaluation
9. Employing group work
10. Using peer tutoring

develop a variety of practical skills as well as directions for further professional growth.

EFFECTIVE DIRECT INSTRUCTION

Barak Rosenshine (1978) describes direct instruction as "Teaching activities focused on academic matters, where goals are clear to students; time allotted for instruction is sufficient; content coverage is extensive; student performance is monitored; questions are at a low cognitive level and produce many correct responses; and feedback is immediate and academically oriented" (p. 46). Numerous studies have found that students learn basic skills more rapidly when they receive a greater portion of their instruction directly from the teacher (Brophy, 1979; Evertson, Emmer, & Brophy, 1980; Fisher, Berliner, Filby, Marliave, Cohen, & Dishaw, 1980; Good, 1979; Good & Grouws, 1979; Rosenshine, 1976; Stallings et al., 1978). These studies reinforce the value of teachers working directly with the entire class and with small groups of five or more students rather than assigning large amounts of seatwork and assisting individual students. This research also indicates that students learn best when teachers actively engage them by asking questions, expecting responses, and increasing accountability by calling on all students and frequently monitoring completed work.

We believe direct instruction involves four key components: (1) clear determination and articulation of goals, (2) teacher-directed instruction, (3) careful monitoring of students' outcomes, and (4) consistent use of effective classroom organization and management methods. During classroom supervision and consultation with more than two hundred pre-service and experienced teachers over fifteen years, we have consistently found failure to implement effective, direct instruction to be a major cause of classroom-management problems. Likewise, every skilled classroom manager with whom we have worked has possessed good skills in direct instruction. Madeline Hunter and Jane Stallings are two researchers who have been particularly successful in devising in-service training programs aimed at assisting teachers at all grade levels in improving their direct instruction.

Madeline Hunter's Instructional Theory into Practice (ITIP)

Madeline Hunter and her associates at the University Elementary School at the University of California at Los Angeles have spent two decades analyzing educational research and specifying the instructional skills possessed by effective teachers. This work has led to the finding that, to be effective, teachers need skill in seven basic areas:

1. content,
2. materials,

3.   planning,
4.   classroom management,
5.   human relations,
6.   human growth and devlopment, and
7.   instructional methods.

Acknowledging the value of the first six areas, Hunter's work nonetheless has focused primarily on the elements of effective instruction. Hunter describes four of these elements:

1.   teaching to an objective,
2.   selecting an objective at the correct level of difficulty,
3.   monitoring and adjusting, and
4.   employing principles of learning.

It is beyond the scope of this book to describe the four elements of instruction. More nearly complete descriptions of these skills can be found in teacher-training material developed by Madeline Hunter (1976, 1981), Carol Cumming's (1980) *Teaching Makes a Difference*, and an article by Barak Rosenshine (1983).

These instructional elements have been incorporated into a lesson design teachers can use for presenting almost any type of lesson (Figure 9.2). Our experience strongly supports the value of developing lessons organized around this design. Students find lessons that follow this format to be clear and respond by demonstrating high rates of on-task behavior during these lessons. A sample lesson will help you understand and implement this lesson design.

The lesson, taught by one of us, involved teaching the water cycle to fourth-grade students. As an anticipatory set, the teacher asked the class, "Why does rain fall though clouds do not?" After soliciting answers from the class, the objective and purpose was provided by informing the students that when they went home in the evening, they would be able to tell the adult(s) at home how rain was formed and how water was recycled. The teacher then asked students to list any specific questions they wished answered about rain and water. The instructional input and modeling involved presenting the information with a model prepared on a felt board. A film, filmstrip, or overhead projector could also have been used. Monitoring was accomplished by several methods. Students were periodically asked to orally summarize points the teacher had made. On several occasions students were asked to tell an answer to the student next to them and, after the teacher gave the answer, students whose partner had answered correctly raised their hands. Guided practice had students label and describe phases in the water cycle presented on a worksheet. Independent practice was accomplished by having students work in groups to research specific problems associated with the water cycle.

Research (Goodlad, 1984) supports what Madeline Hunter has said for many years. Most teaching involves only steps three and six in the eight-step lesson design presented in Figure 9.2. Teachers all too often merely present

FIGURE 9.2   Lesson design

1. Anticipatory set
   a. Focus the students' attention
   b. Provide tie with prior learnings
   c. Develop readiness for instruction
2. The objective and its purpose: What the learner will be doing and why they will be doing it.
3. Instructional input (sometimes called direct or active instruction)
   a. Present material in small steps
   b. Focus on one point at a time
   c. Present varied and specific examples
4. Modeling
   a. Visual input accompanied by verbal input
   b. Criteria for a correct performance are known
5. Monitoring to check for understanding
   a. Sampling: Question whole group and take responses from individuals
   b. Signaled responses: Thumbs up if you agree
   c. Private response: Written or whispered to teacher
6. Guided practice: The initial practice stage in which the response of the learner must be monitored by the teacher to make certain it is accurate.
7. Summary
   a. Students state or write what they have learned from the lesson
   b. Students record their progress toward a learning goal
8. Independent practice: The student can perform the task without major errors, discomfort, or confusion, with a minimum of teacher supervision.

information and then assign individual seatwork. Furthermore, research (Anderson, 1981; Doyle, Sanford & Emmer, 1982) suggests that teachers who employ large amounts of seatwork often fail to provide students with adequate procedures and assign tasks that are poorly matched with student ability. This instructional approach fails to provide students with a sense of purpose or direction, ignores the reality that a significant number of students do not understand the material, and does not provide for students' involvement in using the information they have acquired.

Many school districts across the country have trained teachers in Madeline Hunter's procedures. One of us recently observed a creative supplement to this type of staff training. The staff at a middle school nationally recognized for its excellence taught students a variation of the eight elements in an effective lesson (Figure 9.2). These elements were then posted on the front wall of each classroom and students were asked to inform the teachers any time they omitted a step. This procedure not only ensured consistently more effective teaching, but also provided students with a sense of meaningful involvement in the instructional process.

ACTIVITY 9.1   Designing a lesson

Select a lesson you plan to teach in the next few days. Using the outline in Figure 9.2, develop a lesson design. When teaching the lesson, make sure to employ all eight steps. After the lesson is complete, answer these questions:

Compared to recent lessons I have taught, students were more. . . .
Compared to recent lessons I have taught, students were less. . . .
The element I think helped make the lesson go well was. . . .
One thing I would do differently if I taught this lesson again is. . . .
Compared to recent lessons, during this lesson I felt more. . . .
One thing I learned from this activity is. . . .

Jane Stallings's Staff Development Work

Jane Stallings (1983) of Vanderbilt University provides another model of in-service teacher training. Like Madeline Hunter's work, Stallings's approach is based on teacher-effectiveness research, including her own work on the amounts of time effective teachers spend on various instructional behaviors. Stallings's program involves providing teachers with training units on such key topics as research on teaching, classroom management, motivation, questioning and feedback techniques, and structuring information. Teachers are observed by peers who provide them with specific data on the quality of their interactions with various students; their questioning strategies; and the amount of time they engage in such teaching activities as organizing, reviewing, instructing, checking for understanding, providing guidance during discussion, monitoring seatwork, reteaching material, and summarizing. These data are compared to data collected on teachers whose students have made significant academic gains, and particular adjustments are suggested for the in-service teacher. Like Madeline Hunter, Jane Stallings has developed an in-service training program in which educators skilled in her methods work directly with teachers and other school-district personnel.

Lecture and Question and Answer

Teacher presentation (lecturing), or demonstration followed by or interspersed with questions to students, is the primary mode of direct instruction. Teacher presentation has been heavily criticized (Goodlad, 1984), primarily because of its overuse and teachers' lack of skill in incorporating questioning strategies that actively engage students and encourage higher-level thinking. The lecture method is appropriate, however, in several situations. Hoover (1968) stated that lectures are an appropriate form of instruction:

1. When needed background information is not readily accessible to students.
2. When facts conflict.
3. When unique experiences enable a teacher, student, or resource person to give a lecture that contributes substantially to the clarification of issues.
4. When time is of the essence and data sources are scattered.
5. When a change of pace or variety is needed (oral reports and demonstrations fall into this category).
6. When the presentation of data is likely to result in greater understanding than would occur otherwise.

In addition to their value when used in appropriate situations, lectures can be incorporated with effective question-and-answer strategies in a manner that actively engages students in analyzing and synthesizing information. Groisser (1964) states that effective questions are: (1) clear, (2) purposeful, (3) brief, (4) natural and adaptable to the level of the class, and (5) thought-provoking. He further says that questions should be balanced between factual and thought questions, planned and sequential, widely distributed, and should periodically involve asking students to respond to their peers' answers. When we incorporate effective questioning with clear lectures, this technique can be an effective instructional method for accomplishing several learning objectives. Especially past the primary grades, though, it should not be overused. We must realize that ". . . research on teaching reveals that variety (along with clarity and enthusiasm) is important for maintaining student interest and attention, and ultimately for producing higher achievement . . ." (Good & Brophy, 1984, p. 342).

EFFECTIVE ACTIVE INSTRUCTION

Tom Good (1983) has suggested that the term "active instruction" is preferable to direct instruction because it is broader and less tied to one set of research findings. Good states that active instruction includes many of the key instructional factors associated with direct instruction, but that active instruction encompasses more diverse instructional methods. Thomas Good (1983b) summarizes this research:

Teachers who present information accurately, pay attention to the meaning and conceptual development of content, look for signs of student comprehension and confusion, and provide successful practice opportunities appear to have more achievement gains than do teachers who are less active and who rely more upon seatwork and other classroom activities. . . . In active teaching, the initial style may be inductive or deductive, student learning may be self-initiated or teacher-initiated (especially if thorough critique and synthesis activities follow students' learning attempts). Active teaching also connotes a broader philosophical base (it may occur in classrooms using a variety of organizational structures) and should become somewhat less direct as students become more mature and instructional goals more focused on affective and process outcomes. . . . [p. 59]

We strongly support the training of teachers to provide effective direct instruction and believe that it provides the foundation for effective teaching, and yet we also believe that Good's conceptualization of the difference between direct and active instruction exposes an important issue. Like most of the methods presented throughout this book, direct instruction has too often been presented in isolation and offered as the solution to teachers' instructional and management problems. Instead, research consistently indicates that the choice of most effective teaching method varies according to such context variables as student's age, student's ability, instructional goals, and student's personal characteristics. Some teachers' behaviors such as giving clear instructions seem to be desirable in all settings, but our choice of teaching methods will vary considerably depending on the context variables.

In his work on the quality of academic tasks, Walter Doyle (1983) helps clarify the relationship among curriculum, instruction, and classroom management. He writes that teachers often fail to effectively match instructional tasks with the cognitive outcomes they desire. Doyle suggests that teachers must become more skilled in understanding the cognitive skills they wish students to develop and to assign academic tasks that help students obtain and demonstrate these skills. Instructional methods should never be viewed as ends in themselves, but as means to obtain clearly defined educational outcomes. We must consider our instructional approaches in light of students' cognitive development, our long-term educational objectives, and our understanding of learning theory and research. The primary-grade teacher teaching basic mathematics and reading will want to employ a high rate of teacher-directed instruction, involving a limited amount of student interaction and a high percentage of correct answers. Even primary grade teachers, however, should keep in mind that in the learning process, active involvement is necessary if students are to become competent learners who, as they grow older, can take responsibility for increasing amounts of their own learning. In his *Freedom to Learn*, Carl Rogers (1969) defined significant learning as including four components: (1) personal involvement, (2) self-initiation, (3) pervasiveness—making a difference in the learner's life, and (4) self-evaluation. Piaget's theoretical work on the learning process also points to the importance of actively involving the child in the learning process.

Thus Piaget's theory and research encourage inquiry, discovery, and inductive approaches to learning in which students acquire an understanding of concepts and principles through personal activity. He emphasizes the importance of such teaching procedures, especially at the preschool and early elementary levels. [Johnson, 1979, p. 80]

Teachers of middle school and high school students will often find that even basic facts are better learned by actively involving students in games, group work, or discovery learning.

Unfortunately, too few teachers actively involve students in learning either basic facts or higher-level cognitive skills. In lamenting the lack of exciting instruction taking place in American schools, Theodore Sizer wrote:

> No more important finding has emerged from the inquiries of our study than that the American high school student, as student, is too often docile, compliant, and without initiative (p. 54).

He goes on to note that " . . . most high school students perceive the course of study to be a large collection of unambiguously specific data to be memorized and sometimes manipulated" (p. 93). In *High School: A Report on Secondary Education in America*, Ernest Boyer (1983) wrote, "Classes are at times inspired, occasionally dreadful, and most often routine" (pp. 15,16). Many instructional activities are ignored because they are more difficult for most teachers to manage than are teacher presentation or seatwork. Although high rates of student engagement can occur during instructional activities involving extensive student input and interaction (Johnson & Johnson, 1975; Jones, 1980; Silverstein, 1979), this technique appears to require greater classroom management skills than obtaining on-task behavior during teacher-dominated lessons. Teachers are also reinforced by students for offering high rates of teacher presentation. Even in first grade, students tend not to take risks and instead employ strategies that encourage teachers to provide the answer (Mehan, 1974). To no one's surprise, studies with high school students also suggest that students are hesitant to shift away from teacher-directed learning focusing on memory of basic facts (Brause & Mayher, 1982; Davis & McKnight, 1976; Wilson, 1974). In fact, in secondary schools where students are developmentally more capable of benefiting from active involvement and cooperative work, classes are characterized by less instructional variety than elementary classes (Rounds, Ward, Mergendoller, & Tikunoff, 1982).

In middle schools, teachers' beliefs about students' cognitive limitations combine with teachers' worries about classroom management to increase the likelihood that teacher-controlled direct instruction will be the preferred instructional mode. In her *Successful Schools for Young Adolescents*, Joan Lipsitz (1984) discusses this issue:

> The quality of discourse in the classrooms is characterized by a surprising lack of intellectual rigor. While school administrators stress inquiry into ideas, teachers for the most part stress the transmission of facts. There is relatively little inquiry. The tone of classroom discussion reflects an assumption that young adolescents are developmentally incapable of grappling with concepts. . . . However, two points are being overlooked in the stampede to concrete thinking and learning for all students. First, it is as much a failure to deny the diversity of development during early adolescence by making teaching predominantly concrete and atheoretical as by making it predominantly abstract. Second, sensitivity to the major-

ity of students' limited capacity for theoretical ideation does not preclude the teacher from extracting general principles from the factual, making connections among concrete examples, or encouraging preliminary examination of ideas and values. [pp. 189, 190]

From an instructional point of view, the problem with overemphasis on control-oriented teaching is that it often (although not necessarily) emphasizes passive student behavior and acquisition of factual knowledge at the expense of students' creativity, responsibility, and comprehension. In an analysis of case studies in science education, Stake and Easley (1978) observed that students seemed primarily interested in grades. "They did not think of themselves as mastering a certain body of knowledge, but more of mastering (or not mastering) those things being required by the teacher or the test" (Ch. 15, p. 29). Studies in elementary schools indicate a similar trend for students to complete work without concern for understanding what the content means (Anderson, 1981; Blumenfeld, Pintrich, Meece, & Wessels, 1982).

These studies should not be interpreted as suggesting that teachers should dramatically reduce the amount of time during which they present information to students. Research (Brophy & Evertson, 1976; Good, 1979; Medley, 1977) suggests that active student involvement in the learning process may, especially during the early elementary years, be less effective than more structured, didactic instruction in increasing children's scores on standardized tests. To react to such findings by focusing exclusively (or even primarily) on instruction that minimizes active student involvement, however, means failing to respond to students' needs and thereby increasing unproductive behavior for a significant number of students. Therefore, though the ideas presented in these pages should not necessarily become the focus of every lesson, they should be systematically incorporated into every learning environment. In the sections that follow we offer specific suggestions for using nine approaches (see items 2 to 10 in Figure 9.1) for more actively and effectively involving students in learning activities.

PLANNING INTERESTING LESSONS THAT ACTIVELY INVOLVE STUDENTS

Almost everyone involved in education would agree with the idea that children should find learning to be an interesting process. As an adult who has spent between fourteen and twenty years as a student, you can certainly appreciate how important this concept is. Take a moment to consider how your reactions differ when confronted with learning tasks you find meaningful and interesting, compared to those you find tedious and uninteresting. If you are like most learners, you face interesting tasks with enthusiasm and a positive attitude, but approach uninteresting tasks somewhat begrudgingly. Students also learn best material that interests them and can be related to their own experiences.

Relating children's interests and ideas to classroom activities is probably a useful procedure for all children. However, for inattentive youngsters such an interplay of interest and classroom is paramount for decreasing the distraction caused by preoccupation with thoughts, ideas, interests, or activities which pull their attention away from the classroom. [Swift & Spivack, 1975, p. 21]

When considering the issue of increasing students' involvement in the classroom, it is interesting how limited this involvement actually is. Summarizing his findings on classroom interactions, Flanders (1963) presented the law often called "the rule of two-thirds." His findings indicate that someone is talking during approximately two-thirds of class time, about two-thirds of the talking is done by the teacher, and nearly two-thirds of the talk is spent giving directions, expressing opinions and facts, and criticizing students. Numerous research studies have supported Flanders's finding that the teachers monopolize verbal interchanges in the classroom. Based on observations of first-, sixth-, and eleventh-grade teachers, Adams and Biddle (1970) report that teachers were the dominant factor in 84 percent of classroom interactions. Hudgins and Ahlbrand (1969) report similar findings based on their work in seventh- and ninth-grade classrooms. Studies in both elementary schools (Flanders, 1963) and secondary schools (Bellack et al., 1966; Gallagher, 1965) indicate that students often do little more than respond to teachers' factual questions. More recently, Goodlad's (1984) Study of Schooling found that, across all grade levels, teachers talked three times as much as students. Goodlad's study paints a clear picture of uninvolved students sitting listening to the teacher or involved in seatwork.

Although studies suggest that teachers tend to monopolize classroom interactions, research also indicates that students' feelings are seldom dealt with in classroom settings. Adams and Biddle (1970) reported that less than .5 percent of verbalizations in the classrooms they studied focused on feelings or interpersonal relations. Similarly, after collecting data in a large number of classrooms, Flanders and Amidon (1967) reported that the acceptance of feelings accounted for only .005 percent of the verbal exchanges in classrooms. Goodlad's (1983a) data support these findings. He concluded that, ". . . affect—either positive or negative—was virtually absent. What we observed could only be described as neutral, or perhaps 'flat' is a better adjective" (p. 467).

As indicated by the emphasis on relationships and students' needs that you saw in earlier chapters, our experience suggests that the issue of students' motivation is much broader than students' interest and involvement in their studies. Whether or not students find schools exciting, safe, interesting places depends on many interpersonal and emotional factors as well as on what and how they study. Nevertheless, though it is difficult if not impossible to separate the variable of interesting lessons from other classroom-management and instructional skills, our willingness to create interesting lessons does significantly affect students' feelings about school and subsequently their behavior and achievement. As we saw in Chapter 1, children's interest in school and feelings of successful achievement appear to decline as they progress through school. Uninteresting work may be only one cause of this change, yet it is certainly a factor worth considering. When discussing children's decreasing interest in school, Morris (1978) provides a similar analysis:

> The reasons for this are complex. However, the drop might be minimized by a careful examination and involvement of children's interests (not what teachers think children's interests are) in the curriculum. [Morris, 1978, p. 242]

William Glasser (1969) reflected this view of school instruction and its influence on students' motivation and behavior: ". . . both excess memorization and increasing irrelevance cause them to withdraw into failure or strike out in delinquent acts" (p. 30).

It is interesting to note that during the 1930's a team of educators and psychologists carried out a major study to assess the value of active student involvement in the learning process (Aikin, 1942; Chamberlain, 1942). The program, called The Eight Year Study, involved working with thirty secondary schools to dramatically increase interdisciplinary study and the use of diverse teaching methods such as small groups, cooperative learning, and simulation. The results of the comparison showed that, in college, students from the experimental schools:

1. earned a slightly higher total grade average;
2. earned higher grade averages in all subject fields except foreign language;
3. specialized in the same academic fields as did the comparison students;
4. did not differ from the comparison group in the number of times they were placed on probation;
5. received slightly more academic honors in each year;
6. were more often judged to possess a high degree of intellectual curiosity and drive;
7. were more often judged to be precise, systematic, and objective in their thinking;
8. were more often judged to have developed clear or well-formulated ideas concerning the meaning of education— especially in the first two years in college;
9. more often demonstrated a high degree of resourcefulness in meeting new situations;
10. did not differ from the comparison group in ability to plan their time effectively;
11. had about the same problems of adjustment as the comparison group, but approached their solutions with greater effectiveness;
12. participated somewhat more frequently, and more often enjoyed appreciative experiences in the arts;
13. participated more in all organized student groups except religious and "service" activities;
14. earned in each college year a higher percentage of non-academic honors (officeship in organizations, election to managerial societies, athletic insignia, leading roles in dramatic and musical presentations);
15. did not differ from the comparison group in the quality of adjustment to their contemporaries;
16. differed only slightly from the comparison group in the kinds of judgments about their schooling;

17.   had a somewhat better orientation toward the choice of a vocation;
18.   demonstrated a more active concern for what was going on in the world.
       (Aikin, 1942, pp. 111–112)

One of the realities of modern living is that children spend an incredible amount of time watching television. Preschool children watch television for nearly four hours a day, and elementary school children often watch as much as six hours a day (Friedrich & Stein, 1973).

> By the time a child is 18, he or she has spent 11,000 hours in school—and 15,000 hours watching television. The average 18-year-old has used up the equivalent of more than two full years of his life mummified in front of the TV set. [Torgerson, 1977, p. 4]

This extensive television viewing strongly influences teachers and the educational process. During their many hours in front of the television set, children are passive recipients of information. The medium provides a colorful, diverse, entertaining array of programs aimed at holding children's interest. It is therefore no surprise that we often find it difficult to hold students' attention during passive learning activities. Most teachers simply do not have the flair, energy, or diversity to match the motivational/entertainment quality to which students have become accustomed. Therefore, it is not surprising that students often "tune out" while we present material to them. Students have learned by years of turning the channel during boring programs or advertisements that it is possible to tune out less-than-interesting input.

Television does provide passive entertainment, but it is not capable of meeting children's needs to be actively and personally involved in the learning process. Students may often become bored and restless during periods of passive learning; conversely, they can become stimulated and intense when actively and emotionally involved in their own learning. When lessons require passive learning, they should be short and interesting. Misbehavior is also significantly less during lessons that involve students in employing higher levels of cognitive skills, incorporate students' feelings, and relate material to their own lives.

> The curriculum can be a positive force in classroom control. As a matter of fact the most constructive approach to discipline is through the curriculum. Learning that is interesting and provides a sense of growing power and accomplishment is the best means of classroom control. [Tanner, 1978, p. 43]

We cannot here present an indepth, theoretical examination of the various levels at which material can be presented to children, but in the following section we do provide a general outline of instructional levels as well as examples from each level.

Teaching More Than Facts

The teaching of factual material is a major function of the public schools. Schools serve society by transmitting information and providing children with basic skills in reading, writing, and arithmetic. The acquisition of basic factual information and skills is, especially in the primary grades, a very important component of a child's learning. This issue is emphasized by studies such as *A Nation at Risk: The Report of the National Commission on Excellence·· in Education*, by facts indicating that average test scores on the Scholastic Aptitude Test (SAT) declined steadily from 1963 to 1980, and that approximately 13 percent of American teenagers (and between 30 and 40 percent of minority adolescents) are functionally illiterate (Goldberg and Harvey, 1983).

It is certainly important that schools assist children in acquiring basic factual information, but it is equally true that children increasingly need skills in analyzing their environment and making important personal decisions. Between 1981 and 1982, the National Assessment of Educational Progress examined the reading, mathematical, and writing skills of 106,000 nine-, thirteen-, and seventeen-year-olds. In a report presented in November 1982, the agency concluded that even though American schools have been quite successful at teaching basic facts, students could not write statements to explain or defend their answers. Students' work was described as generally shallow and superficial.

In a society characterized by rapid changes in technology and information processing, the acquisition of facts is increasingly a means to an end rather than an end in itself. Schools must begin early to assist children in using their basic skills for more analytic and creative purposes. Basic skills are important prerequisites to higher-level cognitive functioning. Especially at the secondary level, though, curriculum and instructional techniques employed with students who possess basic skills too often focus on memorization and low-level cognitive skills.

Respondents to the 1984 Gallup Poll of the Public's Attitudes Toward the Public Schools (Gallup, 1984), gave high rankings to numerous goals other than acquisition of basic skills. Slightly more than half of the respondents gave a 10 (the highest rating) to the education goal: "to develop the ability to live in a complex and changing world." John Goodlad reported similar findings from his Study of Schooling (1983a):

> Second, analysis of documents regarding goals for U.S. schools reveals a steady evolution from narrow academic skills to a far wider array of concerns—and to citizenship, vocational, and personal goals as well. All 50 states endorse them, as did most of the 8,600 parents surveyed in A Study of Schooling. Are we to brush these aside as impractical idealism simply because, for the most part, they elude our ability to measure them? [p. 553]

Incorporating material that goes beyond the factual level also greatly influences students' motivation and behavior. Students enjoy acquiring factual information; they also have a strong need to become emotionally involved in the learning process.

Levels of Instruction
In their *Clarifying Values Through Subject Matter*, Harmin, Kirschenbaum, and Simon (1973) suggest that instruction can take place at the fact, concept,

or values level. Additional models were presented by Bloom (1956) in his *Taxonomy of Educational Objectives Handbook I: Cognitive Domain* and Krathwohl, Bloom, and Masia (1964) in their *Taxonomy of Educational Objectives Handbook II: Affective Domain*. In developing curricula, we have found it most helpful to categorize instruction into the four levels: facts, concepts, generalizations, and values.

The facts level involves providing students with basic information. When developing a unit on ecology, we would include information on the chemicals that are associated with pollution, what causes pollution, and the effects various pollutants have upon the human body. This level is similar to the knowledge level described by Bloom (1956).

The concept level focuses upon the relationships between facts and examines major themes that are associated with facts. An ecology unit might examine the concept of people's relationship to their environment, the benefits and costs associated with progress, or our responsibility to future generations. This level incorporates what Bloom describes as comprehension and analysis.

The generalization level provides students with an opportunity to use the information they have obtained and the concepts they have developed to solve problems or interpret situations. In the context of an ecology unit, students might be asked to write legislative proposals dealing with ecology or to develop a model city. The educational objectives associated with these activities are similar to those Bloom labels application, synthesis, and evaluation.

At the final level is values. Here, students are asked to relate their learning to their own beliefs, feelings, and behaviors. In an ecology unit we might ask them to discuss their own behavior regarding such topics as litter, recycling, or water usage. This level relates to the learning objectives in the affective domain described by Krathwohl et al. (1964). Because it is at this level that students relate learning directly to their own lives, we should, whenever possible, incorporate this level into our instruction. No other level has greater potential for stimulating students' interest and increasing on-task behavior.

It is obvious that older students will be better able to become involved in instruction associated with higher levels. Nevertheless, primary teachers should attempt to help children develop simple concepts, think creatively about generalizations and applications, and, most important, view learning as something that relates to their own lives. Though this approach may not be the major emphasis during the primary grades, failure to incorporate higher levels indicates to children that learning is merely the acquisition of often unrelated facts. When this failure occurs, it is more difficult for teachers in subsequent grades to introduce higher levels of instruction.

An Example

An example of a lesson employed by one of us in a fourth-grade class will help to clarify how each of the levels can be incorporated into an instructional unit. The example involves a unit on the Northwest Indians. The unit begins with students learning numerous *facts* about the lives and history of these Indians.

Individual student interests are accommodated by having each student choose a topic of special interest, obtain relevant material, and make a presentation to the class. As students learn about the beliefs Indians held and how their lives have changed over the years, we incorporate discussions of such *concepts* as prejudice, progress, and "might makes right." In this lesson, instruction at the *generalization* level takes two forms. First, students are asked to discuss topics such as what legislators could do to assist the Indians, how society should handle current problems such as salmon-fishing rights, and whether Indians should live their own life-style separately or be integrated into society. Second, students design and perform a Potlatch. This performance involves creating costumes, learning authentic songs and dances, making dried food, and decorating the room. One of us and one of our colleagues have also developed a method for incorporating the values level by providing students with an intense personal experience related to this unit. The activity has one class move out of their classroom on the pretext that the other class needs the room to complete some useful research. The displaced class is placed in a corner in the hall behind a blackboard. When students become uncomfortable and complain, it is suggested that they petition the principal to change the situation. The principal's refusal almost inevitably provokes anger associated with a sense of impotence. Once students have been allowed to experience these feelings, they return to their classroom and are assisted in sharing their feelings with the class that displaced them. The teachers then help the students draw the analogy between their experience and that of the American Indian. The activity ends by the two classes having a short party to reduce any negative feelings that may have been created by the experience.

It is likely that students will remember this activity and the basic concept taught. Although this example provides a rather dramatic approach to incorporating students' feelings into a lesson, there are numerous less time-consuming approaches. Figures 9.3 and 9.4 provide outlines of high school units that incorporate all four levels. If you are interested in obtaining additional suggestions, you may consult Harmin, Kirschenbaum, and Simon's (1973) *Clarifying Values Through Subject Matter.*

FIGURE 9.3   Teaching more than facts: Sample unit

Factual level
Activities: Read the newspaper article titled ". . . Man Given Five-year Sentence," which describes a local man being charged with manslaughter in the death of a teacher from our school.

In small groups, list the five major facts presented in the article.

List the facts on the board and come to a consensus as to the five major facts.

continued

Conceptual level

Again in small groups, outline and be prepared to discuss, the relationship of this incident to students of our school establishing a chapter of SADD (Students Against Drunk Drivers).

Activities: Discuss these questions:
1. Why did they set up this group?
2. What did they hope to accomplish?
3. What effect could a group of students have?
4. What is the main issue or problem on which they would focus?
5. What principles of citizenship are represented by these students' actions?

Generalization level

Drunk driving has become a very emotional public issue. The legislature recently passed even more stringent laws designating the blood alcohol level that is considered legally intoxicated, and they also increased the consequences for driving while intoxicated.

Activities: Discuss these questions in your small groups:
1. Do you think that these measures will solve the problem? Why or why not?
2. What other alternatives would you suggest, pro or con?

Value level

The convicted man's wife has filed a $100,000 lawsuit against the restaurant that served her husband alcoholic beverages.

Activities: Write a three-paragraph essay answering these questions:
1. Is the restaurant liable?
2. Is the lawsuit fair?
3. If you were on the jury, whose side would you favor? Why? Conduct a debate between the people on opposite sides.

FIGURE 9.4   Teaching more than facts: A lesson design for teaching
Romeo and Juliet

Factual Level

Activities
1. Read the play orally with students taking parts and the teacher reading the more difficult parts and explaining as they progress through the play.
2. Discuss what happens in each act, using a guide sheet.
3. Introduce students to the structure of a Shakespearean tragedy.
4. Introduce major themes and elements of a Shakespearean tragedy.
5. Give quizzes after the completion of each act and at the end of the play.

Concept Level

Activities

1. Relate the plot of Romeo and Juliet to other movies they have seen or books they have read. (A shortened version of West Side Story might be taught at the end of this unit in which a character-by-character and scene comparison is done.)
2. Discuss the problems Romeo and Juliet had in communicating with their parents. (Relate to Romeo's tragic flaw—impetuousness.)
3. Discuss the effects of hate and prejudice.
4. Discuss the concept of fate.
5. Introduce students to Elizabethan concepts relevant to a greater understanding of the play.
6. Point out universality of themes, characters and situations to show their relevancy to students.
7. By reading the play in class students will study it as a literary work and dramatic performance but they also will be viewing the Franco Zephrelli's version of "Romeo and Juliet" to analyze his interpretation.
8. Discuss the plot complication of Juliet's impending marriage to Paris.

Generalization Level

Activities

1. Relate the specific problem of Romeo and Juliet to adolescents to-day.
2. Discuss alternatives to the outcome of Romeo and Juliet.
3. Discuss examples of hate and prejudice today.
4. Help students realize that reading Shakespeare's plays, like reading any great works of literature, is both a demanding and a rewarding experience.
5. Do environmental situations influence prejudice? Would there be more prejudice against gays in a small rural town or San Francisco?
6. How does nationalism cause prejudice?
7. Give examples of prejudice against nationalities, beliefs, appearance and values.

Value Level

Activities

1. What could Romeo and Juliet have done differently?
2. Do you think their death justifies the ending of the feud? (Does the means justify the end?)
3. Are Juliet's parents hypocrites?
4. How do you view the nurse's relationship to Juliet and did she betray Juliet?
5. Has the Friar done the right thing for Romeo and Juliet?
6. What prejudices do you think you have?
7. How did you arrive at those prejudices? Did anyone or any situation influence you?
8. What can you and society do to help eliminate or lessen prejudice?

Informing Students About the Learning Process

Regardless of what or how one is teaching, we must consider whether students understand why they are studying the material and why the instructional method has been selected. Many, if not most students do not really understand the learning process. They study to obtain good grades, please their parents or teacher, or avoid punishment. For many students, school simply becomes a game. As one adolescent stated:

> School is just like roulette or something. You can't just ask: Well, what's the point · of it? . . . The point of it is to do it, to get through and get into college. But you have to figure the system or you can't win, because the odds are all on the house's side. [Silberman, 1970, pp. 146–147]

It is really no surprise that 55 percent of a sample of 160,000 teenagers sampled by Norman and Harris for their *The Private Life of the American Teen-Ager* stated that they cheated in school.

Students' motivation can be increased dramatically by providing them with information about the learning process. Students can learn how individuals differ in their preferred learning style, that different learning tasks are conducive to certain learning outcomes, and that, ideally, teachers select instructional activities to support specific learning outcomes and student learning styles. Following a recent presentation, a veteran high school teacher commented that within one class period it was difficult to employ different instructional activities and assignments with students varying in ability because the students complained about doing different work. When asked if he had discussed his thinking and decision about instructional methods with his students, he responded rather pensively that he had not. The teacher followed the suggestion that he discuss his instructional goals and decisions with the students. Several weeks later he commented that it felt like he had a "new class." He reported that students were more positive and were turning in more work. Furthermore, he reported that students were enthusiastic about his attempts to provide varied instructional methods with different student groups.

In addition to increasing students' motivation, the act of instructing students about the learning process can help teachers improve their instruction. In order to inform students about instructional decisions, we must be clear about these choices. Because many teachers are not skilled at correctly matching instructional methods to learning outcomes (Doyle, 1983), attempting to give students explanations for such choices will provide us with important motivation to develop, and practice in, a critical teaching skill. When working with a beginning high school English teacher recently, one of us noticed that the teacher seemed to focus exclusively on factual-level questions. Although students in the upper middle-class school were generally well behaved, students in this class were only moderately attentive and were frequently observed completing work other than English. When asked to describe her learning goals, the teacher listed several higher-level concepts, and she seemed surprised to hear that her instructional methods were not those which could be expected to reach these goals. The teacher was encouraged first to clarify her goals; second to consider learning activities (including altering her questioning strategies) that would facilitate this learning; and finally to share her goals and instructional decisions with students. This procedure proved very helpful to the teacher, and her sophomore students responded enthusiastically to the increased clarity.

In addition to increasing the clarity of learning goals and their relationship to instructional methods, teaching students about the learning process helps teachers more effectively evaluate learning. When students know what and how they will learn, they can better understand how their work will be evaluated. Also, teachers are both clearer about and more accountable for their evaluation procedures. If we select one learning goal as being able to list concepts from Greek mythology that describe universal human flaws and their influence on history, students know they must go beyond basic story-line facts and incorporate ideas generated in class. We know that evaluation of student learning must involve questions aimed at the concept and generalization level, although these need to be supported by specific facts from the material students have read. This clarity of goals, teaching methods, and the evaluation process make learning less a game of student versus teacher. This cooperation in turn increases students' motivation, reduces students' frustration, and enhances achievement.

Incorporating Students' Interests

Children are incredibly curious. Anyone who has raised or taught children has variously been exhilarated, exhausted, and annoyed by their frequent "Why?" questions. Likewise, as they become able to examine abstract concepts and develop new skills in taking different perspectives (Selman, 1980), adolescents are, when given the opportunity, inquisitive, challenging learners. We are making a major mistake and creating numerous problems for ourselves when we fail to provide productive outlets for students' interests. Although teaching at more than the facts level will stimulate students' interest and involvement in the learning process, we can increase their motivation and learning by employing a wide range of strategies that directly incorporate students' interests into the curriculum. The following eleven ideas suggest various approaches to incorporating students' interests.

Methods

1. *Early in the school year, have students build a list of things they would like to learn.* This activity provides you with valuable information and stimulates students' interest by showing that some of their learning will relate directly to their interests. You may choose to create a unit on one or

more topics that received widespread interest. Topics of interest can also be incorporated into the regular school curriculum. Finally, you may integrate these interests into several of the other strategies presented in this section.

2. *When introducing a unit, have the students list questions they have about the topics that will be covered.* In addition to providing you with useful information, this activity creates for the students an association (often lacking) between their interests and the material they are asked to learn.

3. *Teach students how to order films so that they can order films on topics that interest them.* Students can watch these films during study times when they have completed their work, in place of recess, or when you structure time for exploring individual interests. If a film is of particular interest because it relates to a topic being examined by the entire class or because many students share an interest, the film can be shown to the entire class.

4. *Teach students how to invite guest speakers (including parents) to discuss a topic of interest to students.* You will of course always want to confirm younger students' contacts, but they can learn to take major responsibility for obtaining interesting guests.

5. *Create a unit on biographies.* Students can be asked to choose a person about whom they would like to know more and acquire information about this person. Each student can then dress up like the person they have researched and present themselves to the class as that person.

6. *Allow individual students to choose special topics they would like to study.* When presenting a unit, have students choose different aspects of the topic and report their findings to the class.

7. *Create opportunities for structured sharing.* Each day of the week can be designated as a time for sharing what students have read or accomplished in a particular area. Monday might be set aside for sharing written compositions, Tuesday for newspaper articles, Wednesday for something positive students did for someone else, and so on.

8. *Have students develop special-interest days or weeks.* Students can decide upon a topic they would like to study. All subject matter for the day (or week) can be related to this topic. If they selected whales, lessons in math, reading, creative writing, science, and social studies could be constructed around whales.

9. *When involving students in creative writing, do not always assign topics.* Instead, allow them to write stories related to experiences that have been meaningful to them.

10. *Utilize "learning logs," in which students write in their own words what they are learning, what it means to them, and how it relates to their own life.*

11. *Begin a unit by having students write what they already know about the topic.* In addition to providing diagnostic information, you can use these data to actively involve students who have special interest and knowledge in instructing small groups or the entire class.

Responding to Students' Individual Learning Styles

A less obvious and relatively new approach to inolving students in the learning process is to allow students to employ an approach to learning that they find most beneficial. As we mentioned in Chapter 3, individual students vary considerably in the manner in which they learn most effectively, and several authors have attempted to list the factors that influence students' learning and to categorize individual learning styles.

Writers disagree on how effectively teachers can diagnose students' learning styles. Knowing the quality of knowledge available in this area and the demands individualization places upon teachers, it seems reasonable that rather than attempt to individualize according to each student's preferred learning style, we should employ instructional methods that respond to rather obvious differences in students' learning styles. Although teachers often view this as a herculean task, there are two very reasonable and realistic approaches to accommodating various student learning styles.

Adjusting Environmental Factors to Meet Students' Learning Needs

One approach to responding to students' learning styles has been developed by Rita and Kenneth Dunn (see Chapter 3). Research (Dunn, 1983) indicates that most students are significantly affected by approximately six of the twenty-six factors that influence students' learning (Figure 3.2). By adjusting the classroom environment and some instructional methods, we can quite easily create a learning environment more conducive to many students' unique learning needs.

The following methods have been implemented by ourselves and by numerous teachers with whom we work.

Methods

1. *When presenting material, use visual displays, such as writing on the overhead projector, to assist students who are visual learners.* Dunn (1983) states that approximately 40 percent of students learn more effectively when they can read or see something. Interestingly, Price (1980) suggests that most children are not good visual learners until they reach third or fourth grade.
2. *Allow students to select where they will sit.* Students vary in the amount of light, sound, and temperature they prefer and may in fact self-select seats that provide more productive learning environments for them. Teachers often comment that, especially during junior high school, some students may abuse this privilege. We have found that they seldom do so if they are taught the concept of learning styles and if classroom procedures such as allowing students to select their own seats are presented as part of a procedure to make learning more personalized and effective for all students.

3. *Permit students to choose where they wish to study.* Some students work most effectively at a table, others in a soft chair, and still others seated at a traditional school desk. We have taught children who worked best when they could move around the room and do their work on a clipboard.

4. *Be sensitive to individual student's needs to block out sound or visual distractions.* Discuss differences in learning style with the class and allow students to select a quiet study carrel. Also observe students to see whether they appear easily distracted during seatwork. We have observed that teachers frequently move easily distracted students nearer to the teacher's desk. Because this is often the busiest place in the classroom, however, this move may aggravate the problem by creating even more distractions for the student to cope with.

5. *Make healthy snacks available to students or allow them to bring their own.* Because many students fail to eat an adequate breakfast, midmorning is a key time for allowing them to have a snack. Teachers who try this tactic generally find that initially all students take a cracker, carrot, or celery stick. Soon, however, only students who are hungry or who work best when they can eat will choose to eat.

6. *Provide opportunities for students to select whether they will work alone, in pairs, or with a small group.* Students can work with peers to complete assignments, study for tests, work on long-term projects, or critique each other's work.

7. *Provide adequate structure for both short-term and long-range assignments.* Students learn more effectively when seatwork is preceded by substantial direct instruction. Likewise, students need the structure provided by periodic conferences with the teacher or an assignment checklist and timetable for longer assignments.

8. *Give students instruction in study skills.* Both reflective and impulsive learners can benefit from learning to organize material prior to writing a formal paper. Some students organize material best using an outline format. More right hemisphere-oriented students may prefer to organize by mapping—a process of making connections in nonlinear fashion. Likewise, visual and kinesthetic learners profit from learning how to take notes.

9. *Provide learning activities that require use of both sides of the brain.* Figure 9.5 lists a variety of traditional instructional activities that emphasize use of either the right or left hemisphere as well as activities that tend to require use of both hemispheres.

10. *Employ individual goal setting, self-monitoring, and contracts to assist students who require structure and concrete evidence to enhance motivation.*

11. *Realize that some students require more frequent breaks than others.* Teach students how to take short breaks without disrupting the class.

12. *Consider the possibility that students doing poorly in a subject might perform better if that subject were taught at a different time of day.* It is somewhat difficult to make this adjustment, but we have worked with several teachers who have had dramatic results by switching a student's basic-skill lesson from morning to afternoon. Secondary school schedules that

FIGURE 9.5 Learning activities related to the right and left hemispheres of the brain

workbooks, worksheets	creative art activities
drill and repetition	boundary breakers
repetitive learning games	guided imagery
demonstrations	creative writing
copying	values clarification
following directions	use of metaphors
collecting facts	designing
computations	solving old problems new ways
record keeping	mythology
making displays	open-ended discussions
making scrapbooks	self-expressive activities

LEFT / RIGHT

INTEGRATIVE

directed art activities	group sharing
brainstorming	writing essays
oral reports	being read to
independent research	reading aloud
word problems	designing an experiment
research methods	personal journals, logs

problems of logic	role-plays
acting	evaluating alternatives
interpreting data	"show and tell"
hypothesizing	developing plans
simulation games	group projects
dramatic presentations	organizing and directing

rotate the periods at which classes are taught allow students to study all subjects at a time when they work best.

13. *Increase the length of time you wait before calling on a student to answer a question.* This time assists more reflective learners. Again, it is important to explain and teach this procedure to the class before implementing it.

14. *Consider using the four-by-four plan in your classroom.* This idea suggests that each of four types of classroom activity should be used one-fourth of the time in the classroom. The activities that should be present in equal amounts are: (1) teacher talking to students, (2) student talking to teacher, (3) students talking to students, and (4) quiet study time.

Incorporating a Variety of Instructional Techniques

A second approach to accommodating various student learning styles has focused on training teachers to employ a wide range of instructional methods when presenting information to students. A number of models have been developed to help us create more diverse instructional methods; of these, we have found three approaches most useful. Before presenting these methods, we offer a word of caution. The methods described in the remainder of this section are quite complex, and it is likely that only the experienced teacher will be able to incorporate them from the limited exposure that can be provided here. These methods are offered because our experience clearly indicates that their use can increase students' motivation and learning. Most readers, however, will want to consult the original source material or take a workshop on these methods to consistently and effectively incorporate them into their instructional repertoire. First, in their book, *Models of Teaching,* Bruce Joyce and Marsha Weil (1980) present twenty-two models of teaching. The presentation of each model includes a description of the instructional goals the model is best suited to meet, the student and teacher roles and relationships encouraged by the model, and the special conditions and materials needed to implement the model. Teachers with whom we have worked state that the addition of several models to their repertoire has had dramatic effects on their enjoyment of teaching as well as on students' motivation and behavior.

Second, Anthony Gregorc describes four types of learners. His work suggests that students learn best when teachers include optional approaches that students can select for practicing material or demonstrating their understanding. Figure 9.6 provides a lesson plan with options for students who have each of the learning-style preferences described by Gregorc (see Chapter 3). If you are interested in additional ideas, you can consult work by Kathleen Butler (1984).

Like Gregorc, Bernice McCarthy (1980, 1983) states that students' learning styles can be described by four categories (see Chapter 3). Rather than emphasizing the importance of determining each student's preferred category, McCarthy encourages teachers to develop lesson plans that include learning activities that systematically respond to all four student learning styles. In each unit, this approach provides some instruction matched to each students'

FIGURE 9.6   Adjusting to students' learning styles

Unit: Advertising
Goals: Students will:
1.   Become aware of propaganda techniques.
2.   Learn how to introduce and market an item.
3.   Understand the five myths of advertising.
4.   Become more aware of consumerism.
5.   Become aware of careers in the field of advertising.

Possible learning activities for each learning style presented by Anthony Gregorc

Abstract sequential
1. Describe the history and growth of the advertising field in the past fifty years.
2. Interpret the meaning of the phrase "honesty in advertising."
3. List myths about advertising.
4. Devise a theory for the recent changes in commercials that are viewed during prime time.
5. Research each advertising technique.
6. List careers in the field of advertising.

Abstract random
1. Create a taste test for the public on a new product.
2. Devise and conduct a survey about what consumers want in a fast-food restaurant.
3. Write a "jingle" for a product.
4. Write, then role play a commercial.
5. Design a bulletin board about advertising.

Concrete random
1. Brainstorm many ways in which advertising influences people in their daily lives.
2. Create and design a new product and its logotype.
3. In the year 2000, describe the types of products consumers might buy.
4. Write a poem or story about how toothpaste became popular.
5. Design a board game to teach facts and information about advertising.
6. Identify twenty-five products by their logotypes.

Concrete sequential
1. Design a storyboard using sequential procedures.
2. Write a computer game about advertising.
3. Design a wall display showing a past advertisement for a product, a current advertisement, and a future advertisement for the same product.
4. Make a collage of advertisements from various magazines by classifying them according to an advertising technique.
5. Take a field trip to an advertising agency.

preferred approach to learning, but it also requires that students experience and hopefully develop further skills in the other three styles of learning. If you are interested in considering this approach, Figure 9.7 offers activities for each of the four quadrants or learning styles as well as for right and left brain-dominated learners within each style.

ACTIVITY 9.2   Responding to variations in learning styles

Create a chart like the one presented below. List the instructional activities you have used (or those you have seen employed if you are currently observing a classroom rather than teaching) during the past two days. Behind each activity indicate the type of cognitive skill it emphasizes.

Instructional activity	Right brain (RB) Left brain (LB) Integrative (I)	Abstract sequential (AS) Abstract random (AR) Concrete sequential (CS) Concrete random (CR)
1.		
2.		
3.		
4.		
5.		
6.		
7.		

Tally the responses to provide yourself with an indication of the number of activities that fell into each category (e.g., 10 left-brain activities, 2 right-brain, and 7 integrative).

Within the lessons you have planned (if you are not in a classroom, design a set of lesson plans), attempt for two days to use instructional activities that fall into each category. You may also wish to design a lesson that incorporates Bernice McCarthy's four learning-style types.

After teaching these lessons, answer these questions:

Did you notice any differences in students' behavior during the two days in which the lessons were more balanced? Describe these differences.

Were any particular students noticeably more involved or better behaved or both during these two days? If so, which students were they?

How did you feel during these two days?

Complete these sentences:

I learned that. . . .
I was surprised that. . . .
In the future I will try to. . . .

FIGURE 9.7 Sample activities for a unit on water supply

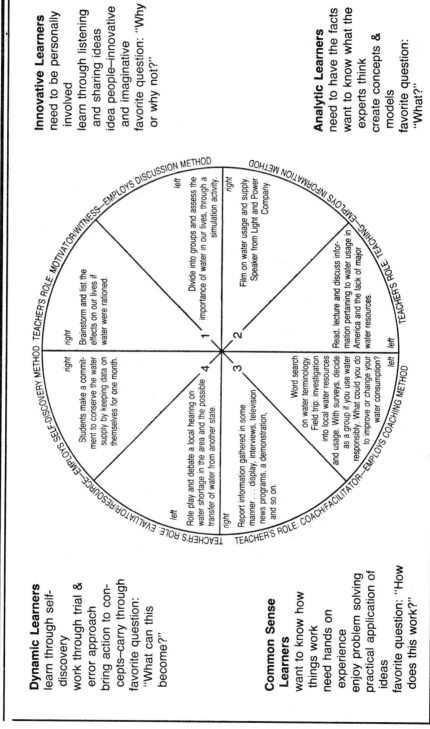

Innovative Learners
need to be personally involved
learn through listening and sharing ideas
idea people–innovative and imaginative
favorite question: "Why or why not?"

Analytic Learners
need to have the facts
want to know what the experts think
create concepts & models
favorite question: "What?"

Dynamic Learners
learn through self-discovery
work through trial & error approach
bring action to concepts–carry through
favorite question: "What can this become?"

Common Sense Learners
want to know how things work
need hands on experience
enjoy problem solving
practical application of ideas
favorite question: "How does this work?"

TEACHER'S ROLE: MOTIVATOR/WITNESS—EMPLOYS DISCUSSION METHOD

TEACHER'S ROLE: RESOURCE—EMPLOYS SELF-DISCOVERY METHOD

TEACHER'S ROLE: TEACHING—EMPLOYS INFORMATION METHOD

TEACHER'S ROLE: COACH/FACILITATOR—EMPLOYS COACHING METHOD

TEACHER'S ROLE: EVALUATOR/RESOURCE—EMPLOYS SELF-DISCOVERY METHOD

left Divide into groups and assess the importance of water in our lives, through a simulation activity.

right Brainstorm and list the effects on our lives if water were rationed.

right Film on water usage and supply. Speaker from Light and Power Company.

left Read, lecture and discuss information pertaining to water usage in America and the lack of major water resources.

left Word search on water terminology. Field trip: investigation into local water resources and usage. With surveys, decide as a group if you use water responsibly. What could you do to improve or change your water consumption?

right Report information gathered in some manner . . . display, interviews, television news programs, a demonstration, and so on.

right Students make a commitment to conserve the water supply by keeping data on themselves for one month.

left Role play and debate a local hearing on water shortage in the area and the possible transfer of water from another state.

1

2

3

4

277

Taking into Account Students' Level of Cognitive Development

We cannot in this book provide a comprehensive discussion of the relationship between instructional strategies and students' level of cognitive development, but we emphasize two key points. First, research (Rosenshine, 1983) indicates that many of the strategies associated with direct instruction are particularly important when teaching primary students. Specifically, instruction should be broken into small segments with frequent practice and the goal of overlearning; discussions should be teacher-led with an attempt to elicit primarily correct answers; material should be reviewed frequently; and we should present most material and ask numerous questions to monitor students' understanding.

Second, early adolescence is another stage that has received considerable attention in terms of desired instructional strategies. Many writers have shown that early adolescents have unique learning needs (Elkind, 1981; Dorman, 1981; Horst & Johnson, 1981; Jones & McEwin, 1980; Martorella, 1980; Toepfer, 1979; 1980). Specifically, these writers point to the need for young adolescents to deal with concete material, be actively involved in the learning process, study high-interest material they can relate to their own lives, work cooperatively with peers, investigate information outside the school environment, and be allowed to learn in ways congruent with their preferred learning styles.

Several examples from our experience will help to display and clarify these concepts. Several years ago, I visited a sophomore history class for low-achieving students. Three of the students were labeled "emotionally disturbed" and spent much of the school day in a resource room. The class also included a large number of behavior-problem students. The lesson being presented was on the League of Nations. The class had previously studied the history of this organization. The teacher began his lesson by dividing the class into groups of five. Each group was then given the five-square game, which provides each group with a variety of puzzle pieces. When distributed properly, the pieces can be arranged so that each group member has a square in front of him or her. The pieces are designed, however, so that there is only one combination that enables all five members to make a square. A variety of other combinations will allow several members to make a square, but will prevent all members from building a square. The goal of the game is for each group to arrive at the situation where each group member has a perfect square in front of him or her. The major rules of the game are that no talking is allowed and that although a group member can give away one or more pieces, no one can take a piece or signal to have a piece given to them. These rules are intended to put a premium on observing others' needs and being willing to give up something of value for the eventual greater good of the group.

The students worked feverishly at this task for approximately half the period. By that time, several groups had finished and two other groups were blocked by members' refusing to break up their square in order to open new combinations for the group. At that time, the teacher asked the students to put aside their task and form one large circle. He began the discussion by asking students to discuss how they felt about the activity and to examine their own behavior during the exercise. Students listened carefully as their peers talked about their experiences. After approximately fifteen minutes of discussion, the teacher asked the class how this activity related to the League of Nations. A number of students offered the idea that when individuals or nations protect their private interests, this act adversely affects the goals of the larger group. Students were then asked to list specific instances in which this blocking had occurred both in the League of Nations and at their school.

The student on-task level throughout the class period was nearly 100 percent. This example is not meant to imply that in every case students will respond positively to this form of classroom instruction. It does, however, indicate that behavior problems can often be prevented by actively involving students in lessons that they can relate to their own experience.

Effective junior high and middle school teachers employ teaching methods that allow students to deal with concrete and practical aspects of what they are learning. Too often, young adolescents are required to do work that is simply too abstract for them to understand. Recently a young man who lived with us brought home an assignment dealing with adverb phrases. Despite being an "A" student, the boy struggled with the material all evening. After he had correctly completed the task, one of us asked him to explain what he had learned. The young man had no idea. He had simply studied the example in the book and consistently replicated it.

A final example of the value of matching teachers' instructional styles to students' cognitive level occurred during our year-long involvement in a project to study effective instruction for early adolescence. When presenting the findings of a committee report to his colleagues, a junior high school teacher, who was well regarded by his colleagues, said that he wished to make a personal comment. He informed his colleagues that he had discovered he was a "closet elementary teacher." He proceeded by saying that for years he had proudly kept his door open while lecturing to students. Whenever students worked in groups, were involved in game-like activities, or in other ways studied using an active, experiential approach, though, he had closed his door. The teacher reported that over the years he had observed that students were happier and learned best when involved in the more active learning. He also commented that he went home more satisfied and relaxed on days when students had been actively involved. He reported, however, that prior to being involved in the District's study, he had always been embarrassed to admit that he taught in a mode other than lecture followed by seatwork. He concluded by stating that he would now proudly open his door during lessons in which students were actively involved in the learning process.

Young adolescents enjoy games, their peers, and activity. They need material to be concrete and need to see its usefulness. A significant portion of disruptive behavior (Jones, 1980) and failure (Toepfer, 1979) in secondary schools is caused by instruction that is too abstract and teacher-dominated. The following methods suggest ways in which we can adjust instruction to meet the developmental and cognitive needs of early adolescence.

Methods

1. *Increase active student participation.* Students should be involved in co-operative group work (Johnson & Johnson, 1975, 1984); competitive teams (Slavin, 1983), group discussions, debates, and role playing.
2. *Learning should be concrete.* When abstract concepts are presented, use concrete activities to develop the concepts. The example of using student participation in five-square presented earlier in this chapter used a personalized, experiential, concrete activity to teach an abstract concept. You can also make your presentations more concrete by following the lesson design shown in Figure 8.2. Students need clear statements about goals as well as frequent summaries that help them understand the purpose of what they are learning.
3. *Use games whenever possible.* Young people are avid game players. The use of computers is successful partially because students enjoy the graphics and gamelike quality of the experience. We know a highly successful eighth-grade social studies teacher who teaches her subject by incorporating material into many types of television games.
4. *Whenever possible, relate material to students' lives.* Because they are just developing a sense of past and future, young adolescents are very here-and-now oriented. They are motivated by seeing how what they learn can help solve real problems. They will neither benefit from nor be excited about learning, in isolation, three causes of the civil war, the leading export of Australia, or adverb phrases.
5. *Bring community resources into the school and allow students to collect information in the community.* A ninth-grade teacher with twenty years of experience recently told us that if someone wanted to see his students at their best, they should observe them during field work in the community. He reported his constant amazement at the difference in energy, attitude, and behavior displayed by his fifteen-year-olds in class compared to the amount they showed in the community.
6. *Allow students to teach their peers.* Young adolescents are extremely peer oriented, and much positive behavior can be generated by involving them in goal-directed peer activities.
7. *Involve students in evaluating their own work as well as your instruction.* Young adolescents have a strong developmental need to experience a sense of responsibility and control over their environment. They are motivated by sincere and consistent efforts to involve them in goal setting and evaluation.
8. *Provide adequate structure for learning activities.* Because early adolescents are experiencing extreme physical, personal, and cognitive changes in their lives, they need structure in their school experience. Assignments should be clear and must be frequently checked by the teacher. Students should know exactly how they will be graded and they benefit by regularly keeping records of their assignments and grades. We can also instruct students on taking notes and other key study skills.

Involving Students in Academic Goal Setting

Students need to experience a sense of control over their environment and to acquire the feeling of competence associated with accomplishing a task they set for themselves. DeCharms (1968, 1971, 1976) has applied White's (1959) theory of competence motivation to education and found that students who view themselves as directing their own learning will achieve more and experience greater satisfaction than will students who are working primarily for externally controlled rewards. DeCharms (1971) cites several studies indicating that students who perceive themselves as directing their own learning work harder and take greater pride in the outcome than do students who are less involved in decision making.

Individual goal setting is perhaps the most effective method for enabling students to experience a sense of understanding and controlling their own learning while incorporating their own interests. This method also has potential for helping students select learning activities that are congruent with their learning style.

Wlodkowski (1978) mentions several benefits associated with academic goal setting.

> The advantage of this method is that it brings the future into the present and allows the student to become aware of what it is necessary to do in order to have a successful learning experience. . . . With the goal-setting model, the student knows that she/he is in command and can calculate what to do to avoid wasting time or experiencing self-defeat. Thus, before even beginning the learning task, the student knows that her/his effort will be worthwhile and has an actual sense that there is a good probability for success. [p. 54]

Teachers need to help students develop goals that are both realistic and directed at improving skill deficits revealed by diagnostic testing and observation, but students' involvement in establishing goals and recording progress can also significantly enhance their motivation and reduce acting-out or withdrawal behavior.

An academic goal statement or contract should include: (1) what material the student plans to learn, (2) what activities the student will engage in to develop these skills, (3) the degree of proficiency the student will reach, and (4) how the student will demonstrate that the learning has occurred. We can employ several approaches when implementing academic goals. Each student can be involved in working toward one or more academic goals associated with a skill deficit or interest he or she experiences. This emphasis on goals can be expanded to incorporate term-length goal statements. Because most schools provide an academic report to parents (and we hope students) following a nine-week term, students can be aided in setting several academic goals on a term basis. Nine weeks will be too long for primary children, but most intermediate-grade and secondary students with whom we have worked say they find nine-week goal setting provides a sense of direction and commitment. At the beginning of each term you and the student can examine the student's current performance level and the material he or she will study during the term. The student can be assisted in writing several goals for the term, perhaps stating that by the end of the term he or she will be able to solve two-place multiplication problems with 80 percent accuracy. It is obviously important that we help each student choose goals which are attainable but which will require some additional effort by the child. Although children are motivated to achieve goals that require some real effort, they are also frequently intimidated by goals that seem impossible to reach. Furthermore, continued failure only tends to reduce students' achievement orientation and self-concept.

Figure 9.8 is an example of a high-interest form an elementary or middle school teacher could use to help students commit themselves to specific academic goals. Figure 9.9 is an example of a form a teacher could use to reinforce goal attainment. Secondary teachers will generally want to use less detailed goal setting forms. At the beginning of each unit, students might be asked to list such things as the grade they wish to earn, the percentage of assignments they plan to complete on time, and specific new information they wish to possess following the lessons. It is important that teachers support this process by clearly stating their goals in terms of student learning outcomes. Teachers can also help by providing students with forms that ask specific questions about students' learning goals. Student responses should be collected, responded to and returned to students as soon as possible. Teachers should confer with students whose goals seem unrealistically high or low.

Another approach to employing academic goal setting involves designing assignments that allow students to choose the type of work they will complete, and, if appropriate, the grade they will earn for completing the designated amount of work. The most common format for employing this method involves listing assignments for earning each grade and having students sign a contract indicating which assignment they plan to complete. This approach is particularly effective when we wish to involve all students in an assignment on which lower-achieving students might experience considerable difficulty with more complex aspects of the assignment. A contractual approach enables each student to choose an appropriate level of difficulty, and we can ensure that the basic concepts are learned by incorporating them within the lowest acceptable level. Students respond positively to this approach because it is a clear statement of what they will learn and what they must accomplish.

Employing Learning Centers

Although the use of learning centers as a primary instructional approach may not facilitate learning as well as a blend of teacher-directed and self-initiated instruction, these centers can serve several very important purposes. They give us an excellent opportunity to respond to students' individual learning styles and interests. They also provide a valuable opportunity for children to learn how to make choices and to experience a sense of competence and power. Finally the centers can be used as constructive alternatives for children who

FIGURE 9.8 Goal-setting form

My Goal in _____ for
(subject)

today is to _____

_____

I will have my goal completed

by _____ with _____ %
(time)

accuracy.

_____
student

_____
date

_____
teacher

HEAR
YE
HEAR
YE

FIGURE 9.9   Goal-completion award

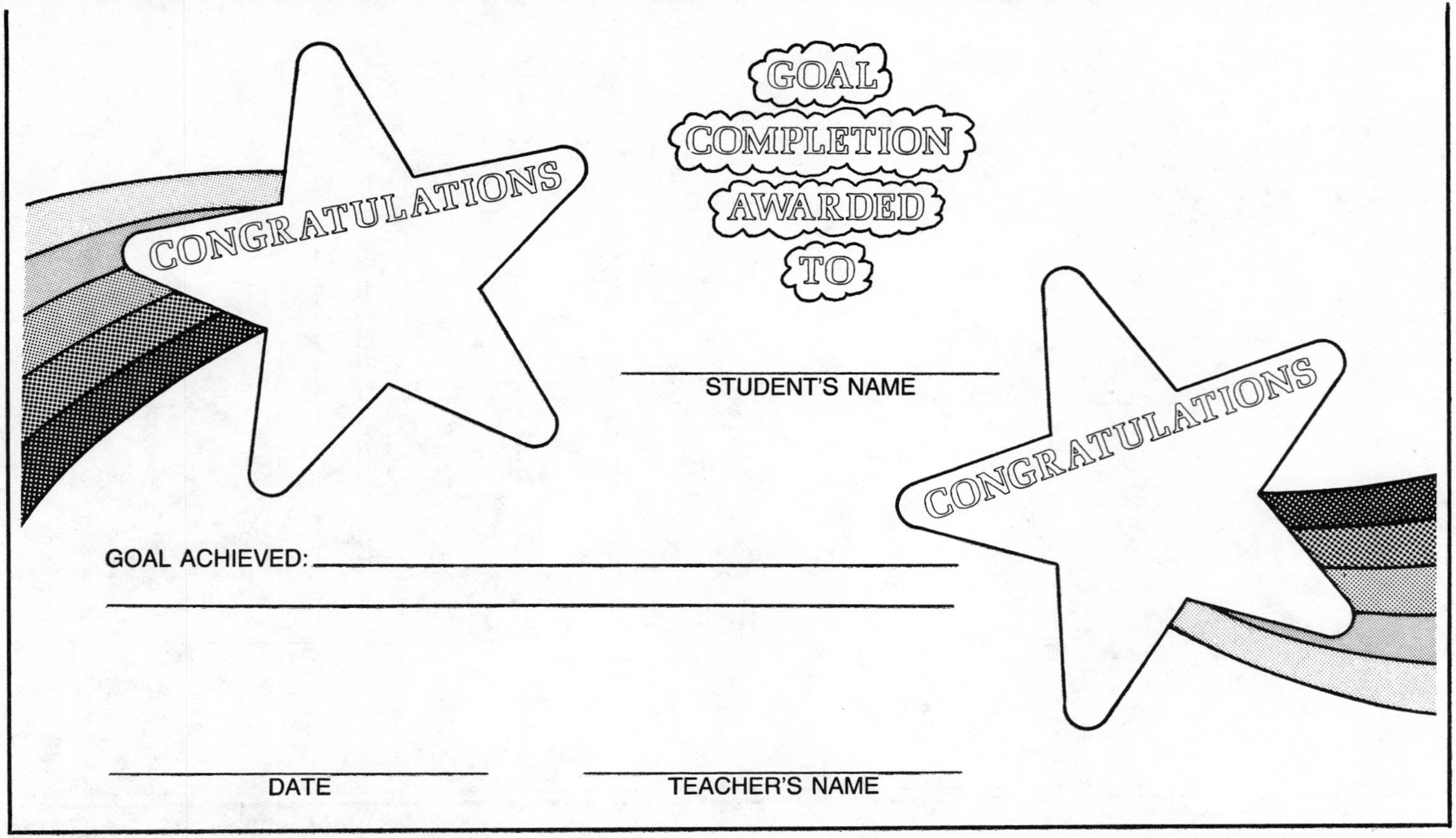

GOAL COMPLETION AWARDED TO

CONGRATULATIONS

CONGRATULATIONS

STUDENT'S NAME

GOAL ACHIEVED: _____

DATE _____

TEACHER'S NAME

have completed their seatwork or who have mastered concepts that we are presenting to the class. Although developing learning centers requires that we invest much time, the benefits of increased student motivation, reduced time in responding to individual students' needs, and decreased acting-out behavior far outweigh the initial investment. If you are interested in exploring this approach further, we encourage you to examine the references at the end of this chapter and to seek the assistance of colleagues and specialists who have experience in this area.

Implementing Self-Evaluation

Involving students in self-evaluation not only saves us much time and energy, but also provides students with an opportunity to better understand their academic performance and to experience a sense of personal responsibility. When students evaluate and record their own work, they are more likely to develop an internal locus of control and view their progress as based on their own efforts. Similarly, self-evaluation enables students to acknowledge areas that need improvement. In working with third-grade students from an inner-city public school, Klein and Schuler (1974) found that when students were allowed to evaluate their own performance contingent upon passing skill texts in math, their performance improved markedly. Apparently the ability to be autonomous was motivating to these students. Allowing students to score their own work also demonstrates our respect for them, which in turn enhances students' sense of significance and competence and the associated increase in self-esteem often has a positive effect on students' behavior.

Students are impressed with displays of data, especially when the data deal with their own performance. Data provide immediate, concrete reinforcement for learning. Students often fail to associate their seemingly herculean efforts with actual increased knowledge or changes in behavior. Data make the learning or behavior change a concrete experience, which alone often provides more reinforcement than any free time or praise from us. Surprisingly, the benefits associated with monitoring progress may be particularly great for students who are progressing slowly. These students often view themselves as making no progress whatsoever or actually falling behind (as indeed they may be when the basis of comparison is their peers' work). Providing these students with specific data that demonstrate their progress is perhaps the most effective and honest motivational strategy.

Student goal setting provides an ideal opportunity for introducing regular data collection into the classroom. Students need periodic checks to determine how they are progressing toward their goals. One method for monitoring students' progress is to teach them to chart their own improvements. We can do so by instructing them in using graph paper to display results. Because bar graphs involve simple counting, students will have little difficulty in acquiring this skill. In fact, one of us worked with a teacher who successfully taught primary grade, emotionally disturbed children to use six-cycle graph paper.

Once students have learned how to chart data, they can begin to monitor their own progress. The graphs can be kept in their desk or notebook and should be attached to the associated contract or statement of goals. Students can be asked to contact the teacher or a peer with whom they are working if their graph suggests that they are having difficulty reaching their goal. We should of course periodically check students' results to see whether they are making satisfactory progress in reaching their goals. Figures 9.10 and 9.11 are examples of charts students can use to record their academic progress.

Because students' behavior clearly influences their academic performance, a valuable approach related to academic self-evaluation involves students in assessing their own school behavior. Anyone who is serious about teaching responsibility and about helping students see the relationship between their efforts and success should consider having them periodically assess their learning behaviors (see Figure 8.7). When students have completed the form, we should discuss it individually with each of them. This type of self-assessment can also be incorporated into students' citizenship grades or be discussed with students during parent conferences.

Another approach to student self-evaluation is to involve students either in pre-parent conferences or to include students in parent–teacher conferences. Teacher–student conferences held prior to parent–teacher conferences can be a chance for students to evaluate their own behavior and academic performance and compare this to the marks we have prepared. Teacher and student can discuss any differences, which can lead either to a compromise or to our helping the student to better understand his or her marks and setting specific goals for obtaining the desired marks during the next marking period. Another obvious advantage to this type of teacher–student conference is that it can reduce the anxiety many students experience in parent–teacher conferences. The fear of the unknown is eliminated when students know their marks and the issues we plan to discuss with their parents.

Although many parents and teachers hesitate to involve students in parent–teacher conferences, this procedure seems to be particularly valuable with upper elementary and middle school students. These students are able to understand much of the information discussed during parent–teacher conferences, and older students need to be involved in decisions that directly affect them. Therefore, though the teacher and parent may choose to meet privately during a portion of the conference, adults provide students with valuable information and demonstrate respect for them when they involve students in discussions about progress in their academic and social skills.

Employing Group Work

As children become less egocentric and more social, they increasingly enjoy and benefit from working with their peers to achieve learning goals. Consid-

FIGURE 9.10   Self-feedback form

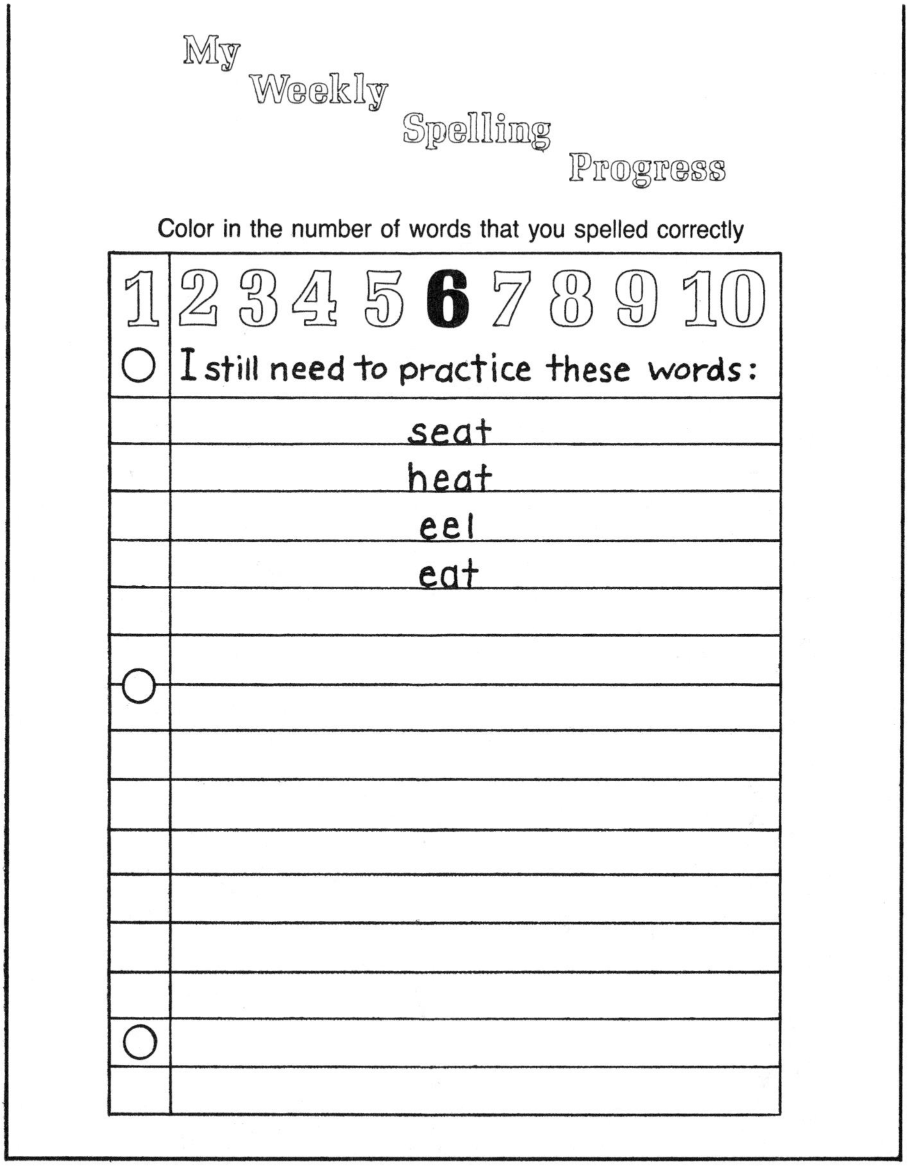

My
Weekly
Spelling
Progress

Color in the number of words that you spelled correctly

1 2 3 4 5 6 7 8 9 10

○ I still need to practice these words:

seat

heat

eel

eat

erable research evidence indicates the value of students' working in groups. David Johnson discusses this work:

> The successful mastery, retention, and transfer of concepts, rules, and principles is higher in cooperatively structured learning than in competitive or individualistic learning. . . . Members of cooperative groups evolve superior strategies

FIGURE 9.11   Monitoring acquisition of skills

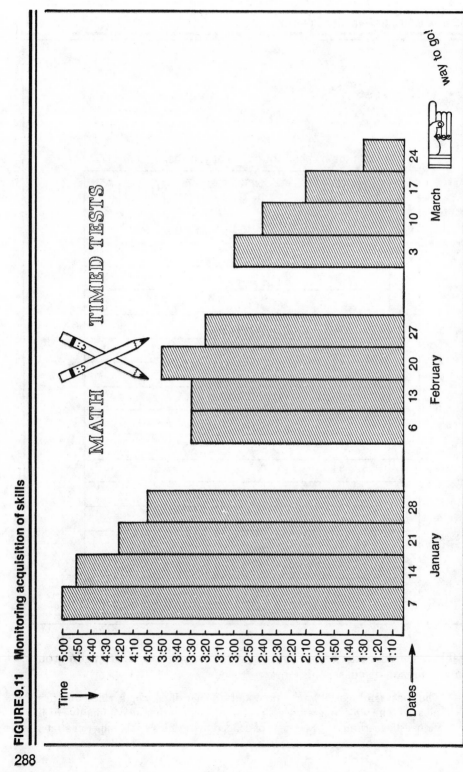

for conceptual learning, seek and utilize others' information more effectively, cognitively rehearse and formulate in their own words the material being learned, and cover more material in a shorter period of time. . . .

The more cooperative students' attitudes and experiences, the more they see themselves as being intrinsically motivated, persevering in pursuit of clearly defined learning goals, believing it is their own efforts that determine school success, wanting to be good students and get good grades, and believing that ideas, feelings and learning new ideas are important and positive . . . students experiencing cooperative instruction like the teacher better and perceive the teacher as being more supportive and accepting (academically and personally) than do students experiencing competitive or individualistic instruction. [Johnson, 1979, pp. 149–151]

As mentioned in Chapter 5, working cooperatively with peers not only enhances learning and positive attitudes toward school, but also creates positive peer relationships (DeVries & Edwards, 1973; Johnson & Johnson, 1975b, 1983), and enhances students' self-esteem (Johnson & Johnson, 1978, 1983).

If we accept the multiple advantages asociated with having at least some instruction occur in groups where children work cooperatively to reach a goal, the question becomes how to create these groups in the classroom. First, cooperative group work will be accomplished more smoothly and will have more positive results when it occurs in classrooms in which children feel positive about their peers. In Chapter 5, we offer activities for creating positive peer relations. Second, we must decide when to employ cooperative group work in the classroom.

When deciding whether to employ individualized, competitive, or cooperative learning activities, we should consider the learning outcomes we are seeking. In their *Learning Together and Alone*, David and Roger Johnson describe the relationship between three learning activities or goal structures and cognitive outcomes (Figure 9.12). Third, we must help children develop the specific skills necessary for working effectively in groups. We can do so by providing children with group decision or problem-solving tasks followed by discussions about which behaviors facilitated and blocked each group completing their task. A number of books with group skill-building activities include: Stanford and Stanford's (1969) *Learning Discussion Skills Through Games*; Johnson and Johnson's (1975) *Joining Together: Group Theory and Group Skills*; and Castillo's (1974) *Left-Handed Teaching: Lessons in Affective Education*. As students begin to understand individual behaviors that help groups complete their tasks, we can instruct children in becoming process observers who provide feedback to their groups on how the group is functioning. Teachers are often surprised at how easily elementary school-aged children can learn to function effectively in groups and to analyze group processes.

The fourth and final step in effectively employing group work in the classroom is to provide the groups with clear instructions and ensure that students are aware of how to solve problems that may arise. In this list we suggest several issues that teachers need to clarify if group work is to function smoothly:

FIGURE 9.12   Goal structures and cognitive outcomes

Cognitive outcome	Cooperative	Competitive	Individualistic
Mastery of factual information			x
Retention, application, and transfer of factual information, concepts, principles	x		
Mastery of concepts and principles	x		
Verbal abilities	x		
Problem-solving ability and success	x		
Cooperative skills	x		
Creative ability: divergent and risktaking thinking, productive controversy	x		
Awareness and utilization of one's capabilities	x		
Perspective- (role-) taking abilities	x		
Speed and quantity of work on simple drill activities		x	
Competitive skills		x	
Individualistic skills			x
Simple mechanical skills			x

D.W. Johnson and R.T. Johnson, *Learning Together and Alone: Cooperation, Competition, and Individualization,* © 1975, p. 32. Reprinted by permission of Prentice-Hall, Inc., Englewood Cliffs, N.J.

1. Do the groups clearly understand their task and the associated learning goals?
2. Do the students possess the skills necessary to complete the task, e.g., do they know how to use the materials and can at least several students in each group read any written material associated with the task?
3. Do the students know how much time they have to complete the task?
4. Do the students know what to do if they finish early or what options are available if they cannot complete the task in the allotted time?
5. Are all materials readily available, and has a procedure been established so that these can be easily obtained?

6. Have we established a method for gaining the class' attention should it be necessary in order for us to add an instruction, clarify a problem, or ask the groups to stop their work?
7. Do the students know what they should do if they require assistance?

Another approach to cooperative learning was devised by Robert Slavin (1978, 1980, 1983) at the Center for Social Organization of Schools at Johns Hopkins University. Slavin's best-known method, "Teams-Games-Tournament," has students work in groups of four or five to help peers learn material presented by the teacher. At the end of a lesson or a week, members from the various groups compete with one another to earn points for their team. If you are interested in expanding your repertoire in this area, we encourage you to subscribe to the newsletter, "Reporting on Cooperative Learning" (J & J Book Company, 162 Windsor Lane, New Brighton, Minnesota 55221).

Using Peer Tutoring

A number of benefits can be derived from implementing peer tutoring in a classroom. First, tutoring fosters the concept that asking for and offering help are positive behaviors. This act encourages cooperation and concern for peers and thereby creates a more supportive, safe learning environment. Second, the opportunity to instruct another child can provide a student with a sense of competence and personal worth. Third, in assisting another student, the student frequently learns the material more thoroughly. The combination of increased understanding and the act of instructing another student frequently makes a student a more excited and confident learner. Finally, peer tutoring helps the teacher monitor and individualize instruction. By allowing students to serve as resources for other students, we increase the availability of individual attention and thereby reduce students' frustration and the accompanying acting-out behavior.

Although peer tutoring has may benefits, it can become a frustrating and counterproductive activity if students are not provided with skills in how to assist each other. Therefore, it is important that if we plan to implement peer tutoring we then provide our students with instruction in how to assist another student. We can do so by listing and discussing the do's and don'ts of helping someone with their work. We can then model appropriate behavior and we should allow students to practice this behavior and receive feedback from us. If the equipment is available, students can be videotaped while assisting other students and the tape can be viewed and discussed. An exciting aspect of providing students with instruction in how to teach another student is that this activity helps them to better understand the learning process.

There are numerous approaches to implementing peer tutoring. Students can be provided with green and red 8½-inch-square cards that are attached to their desks so that they can be displayed in front of the desk. Students who need help during seatwork can display a red card, and students who understand the material and are willing to assist other students can display a green card. This procedure can be particularly helpful when we are busy working with a small group and are not available to assist students. A similar approach involves our listing on the board the names of students who are able to assist their peers on a project.

Assigning individual students to work with a student who needs assistance is another common approach to peer tutoring. This activity may involve students in the same class or students from higher grades. Another method involves arranging students' desks in groups of four and informing students that they may assist their peers as long as they follow previously learned procedures for effective teaching.

Recently one of us observed a young teacher presenting an art lesson to a group of eighth-grade students. The teacher was working with a particularly difficult class. The class included several students whom the school had characterized as behavior problems, as well as a very withdrawn, emotionally handicapped boy. The teacher indicated that she was somewhat concerned about the day's lesson because she had a very limited background in the material she was presenting. She also said that the last period of the day on a particularly nice spring day was not the ideal time to be teaching eighth graders a concept as difficult as depth perception. With this introduction, I was prepared to observe chaos and to have numerous opportunities for observing the teacher's skills in dealing with behavior problems.

The teacher began the lesson by briefly reviewing the material she had presented on the previous day. She appeared comfortable responding to a variety of students' questions. On one occasion, a student pointed out a major flaw in something she had presented. The teacher indicated that she did not see his point and asked the student if he would be willing to come up to the board and clarify his point for both her and the class. The student did so, and the class responded politely to his brief instruction.

After perhaps ten minutes of instruction, the teacher indicated that the students should continue working on their assignments. She commented that some students were finding the tasks more difficult than others and suggested that when they had a problem, they find another student to help them. As students began working on their projects, the teacher circulated around the room answering students' questions and reinforcing students' work. It soon became apparent, however, that she could not possibly answer all the questions that were being fired at her. Her interventions then changed from direct work with students to serving as a clearing center for resources available within the classroom. As she moved around the room, she made comments such as "Why don't you ask John? He does a real good job with two-point perspective." "It might help, Bill, if you could explain to him why you. . . ." "I really appreciated your helping, Sue. You did a really good job of teaching because you helped him to discover the answer for himself."

As I observed the class, I was impressed with the extremely high percentage of on-task behavior displayed by the students. In addition, the teacher's role as facilitator freed her to spend much time with her most severely disturbed student. Because she had structured students' responses to be positive and supportive, students' interactions throughout the class period were extremely positive. In addition to assisting each other, students frequently showed their work to their peers and almost always received either compliments or constructive suggestions.

In examining the dynamics of this class period, it is interesting to recall Postman and Weingartner's (1969) statement that teachers should perhaps teach subjects outside of their area of academic preparation. When teaching subjects they understand extremely well, teachers often do all the teaching, while the students are forced into the role of passive learner. On the other hand, when teachers are learning the material or are somewhat unsure of the content, it may be easier to allow students to become involved as co-learners and team teachers. It may appear that material is being covered more slowly (and perhaps more noisily) when using this format, but the theoretical considerations and research results presented earlier in this section point to many advantages associated with this form of instruction.

IMPLEMENTATION ACTIVITIES

A major problem with listing numerous teaching methods is that you will feel overwhelmed and will respond by failing to implement or even consider any of the methods. Activity 9.3 will help you in making a commitment to attempt at least one teaching method aimed at increasing students' involvement in the learning process. If you cannot implement a method at this time, try to write a specific statement about a method you will employ when an opportunity arises.

ACTIVITY 9.3   Implementing methods for increasing students' involvement in the learning process

1. List two additional methods you can employ to increase students' involvement in the learning process.
   a.
   b.
2. Select one of the methods discussed in this section and incorporate it into your classroom. After completing the activity or implementing it for several weeks, answer these questions:
   a. How have students responded to the activity?
   b. Has any student become particularly involved in the activity?
   c. Has involvement in the activity seemed to bring about a more positive attitude for any student(s)?
3. Develop a short form on which students can express their reaction to the new activity.

ACTIVITY 9.4   Analyzing students' behavior problems

If you are having problems with the behavior of a student or group of students, it is important to consider instructional factors that may be causing the problem. First, write the name of the student or students who are creating the most difficulty for you in a class. Next, complete the form in Figure 9.13 for each student you have listed. After carefully examining your responses, answer these questions:

One reason this student(s) may be acting out in my class is. . . .
This activity made me realize that. . . .
In order to help this student(s) behave more appropriately in this class, I
    will need to. . . .
Two specific things I will change in this class or with this specific student
    are. . . .

FIGURE 9.13   Analyzing the classroom environment

As you present your next lesson or assignment in an area in which a student or group of students has had trouble, notice:

	Almost always	Sometimes	Almost never
1. Is the subject area one in which the student has always failed?			
2. Can the student read at whatever level the material is presented?			
3. Is the assignment clear enough so the student knows exactly what is expected?			
4. Is the task at a level of difficulty that is challenging but which offers a chance of successful completion for the individual (rather than for the class average)?			
5. Is the material presented in a manner which seems to interest the student: written, lecture, audio-visual, programmed workbook, independent work, group assignments, etc? Is the material content of interest?			
6. Is enough time allowed to get into the assignment and develop an interest and complete the task satisfactorily?			

	Almost always	Sometimes	Almost never
7. Will the student be graded on an individual basis so that successful completion will get a good grade?			
8. Is there a pleasant consequence that you know appeals to the student (possibly chosen by the student) that will follow successful completion of the task?			
9. Is there some motivating consequence to at least complete part of the assignment, even if the student cannot complete all of it?			
10. Do you give the student another chance to do the assignment correctly and to improve the grade?			
11. Do you give more attention to the student when he tries a task than you do when he refuses to try?			

From *Developing Student Discipline and Motivation.* Martin, R. & Lauridsen, D. © 1974 by Research Press, Champaign, Ill. Reprinted by permission.

A Case Study

This case study, taken verbatim from a project completed by a high school English teacher as part of her work in a graduate education course, typifies the manner in which you can incorporate ideas found throughout this book to help individual students reach their potential. We chose this example because:

1. It was carried out and written by a teacher who deals with 140 students each day.
2. The teacher developed and carried out the project with no assistance.
3. The teacher had just completed a course utilizing this text as the major sourcebook.

At first I didn't take much notice of Bill in my freshman and sophomore-level writing class. He's one of those quiet, unobtrusive students, the kind you love to use in a seating chart as a barrier between the class clown and a social butterfly. Rarely, if ever, did he call attention to himself. He never raised his hand to volunteer an answer, and when called on, would struggle so to come up with an appropriate response that I would too frequently—to avoid his obvious embarrassment—cut short his efforts and recognize one of the hands waving excitedly around him. He is never late to class; he has never asked for a hall pass; he never questions directions or instructions for an assignment; he seldom visits in class with his neighbors; he always appears to listen attentively to lectures. Therefore, next to the 140 other students who come to me daily with varying levels of ability and enthusiasm for "creative writing," Bill, at first, didn't demand a lot of my attention.

A couple of weeks into the term, however, I began to notice that in fact Bill was becoming a problem of the subtler type: he was not doing his assignments. In fact, his pattern of behavior seemed suspiciously close to what has been categorized as "failure syndrome"—a feeling of defeatism and helplessness resulting from repeated failure. Therefore, after three weeks of inconsistent, below-class-average performance, I decided to investigate Bill's history as a student in our district.

I discovered that in his elementary years he was apparently a pleasure to his teachers. Their comments on his conduct and citizenship grades suggested he was a model of exemplary behavior, and his academic marks were "satisfactory" or better. In junior high school, however, his grades began to slip; notably, those earned in English dropped to a "D" average throughout his seventh and eighth grades. As a result, his junior high English teachers recommended that he be placed in Sentences (our low-level remedial-writing class) during the first term of his freshman year in high school. Let there be no doubt that, as well-intentioned as this program may be, a stigma is attached to this placement as surely as if these students wore a badge that proclaimed their lack of proficiency and their below-average performance. At any rate, in Sentences he earned a term grade of "C minus" and was promoted the next year to Paragraphs. That is where our paths crossed.

Next, I checked into Bill's current C.A.T. scores. The grade-level score for overall comprehension for his age group is 9.7; Bill's score was 7.7—two years below grade level. On the Gates Reading Test he had scored 8.3 on comprehension; the grade-level score is 9.3. He scored about a year below grade level, no small consideration in a class such as writing, which is a complex activity requiring mature, advanced mental operations. Therefore, his scores indicated that many of the writing tasks I required of him were quite possibly beyond his level of competence.

I wondered about his other classes. So I sent a Progress Report form to his other teachers to determine how successful he was in his other courses. The results were that in classes requiring incremental, concrete, mechanical exercises he was doing above-average work. But in the majority of his classes—those requiring more abstract, complex cognitive processes—his grades were below average. Unfortunately, the beginnings of a pattern seemed to be developing that, without intervention, sooner or later would probably lead to resignation on his part.

Glasser's theory indicated what my first move should be: provide a caring atmosphere. I decided to make a point of casually noticing him, smiling and saying hello as he entered the classroom daily. I routinely do this to my students at random, and so this notice didn't cause him to be unduly curious. But each day I made sure I spoke to *him* until it became a habit for both of us. The next step he provided. He received the "Outstanding Athlete of the Week" award, for which I, of course, complimented him and placed his newspaper picture on a bulletin board in my room where "Class Heroes" who have received such an honor get recognition of some sort. On seeing his picture in this spot and receiving accolades from his classmates, I believe his chest size must have expanded three inches.

While he was feeling more comfortable and "invited" in the classroom, he seemed to be gaining confidence in himself, which was reflected in his assignments. (And was I also—albeit unconsciously—giving him more credit as a struggling student who deserved the benefit of the doubt?) I used as many opportunities as possible to reaffirm these signs of success—praised his improved writing, included a well-written narrative paper (on soccer, naturally) as a class model for effective writing. As research on attribution theory suggests, low-achieving students need to be reminded that their success is due to their efforts. A "Happy-Gram" sent home mentioning specifically his particularly good narrative paragraph, followed two weeks later by his "Goal Completion Award" seemed to be the turning points that altered his downward slide in my class.

During this intervention I made some academic changes as well as the social ones. First, I allowed more flexibility in the topics I assigned for writing projects so that Bill (and the other students) had more options to choose from. The more interested he was in a topic, the more knowledgeable he was about it, and the more motivated he became to write. I also began to assess his learning style—both by analyzing the type of assignments he did well on and by conversations with him when I asked for feedback. As a result, after giving directions for an assignment, I used my "roaming" time for private contact with him to clarify his understanding and review his independent work, making solicited suggestions so that I could spot misunderstandings and frustrations and offer follow-up assistance. I also began to use a different approach to grading his writing. Martin and Lauridsen (1974) suggest in *Developing Student Discipline and Motivation* that students need to be graded on an individual basis. Consequently, I allowed him to compete against himself and not his more academically mature classmates, so that his continuous progress merited praise. Then, because he was growing in confidence and self-esteem, the next step seemed to be to try the suggestions of Johnson and Johnson (1975, 1984) and allow Bill to work in a group. Their research suggests that successfully orchestrated group work increases confidence in one's ability. And so I arranged for Bill to participate in a peer editing group in which he was both academically and socially compatible. In this setting, a feeling of interdependence grew between him and members of the group, fostering sociability, responsibility, and self-esteem.

Meanwhile, research by Jones (1980) suggests that students should share the responsibility in behavior modification by some type of self-monitoring. Therefore, it became Bill's responsibility to keep personal records on a weekly Progress Report form I filled out. He also continued to keep a class notebook in which he copied daily assignments from the board and kept them in front of his notebook as a type of table of contents. The completed assignment then, after it was graded and returned, was kept chronologically in his notebook and a check mark was made on the assignment page. As a back-up reminder, in case an assignment did not get turned in by the deadline, we agreed that a "Homework Alert" notice was to be sent home, signed by his parent, and returned to me within two days. If the card was not returned within the time limit, Bill was aware I would be calling home to discuss the situation with his parent. This back-up strategy was never necessary, however. In fact, during the past five weeks, Bill has missed only one assignment (because of a late soccer game and a long bus ride home).

A statement by Jere Brophy (1982) summarizes my intervention best:

For example, in dealing with failure-syndrome students who have essentially given up attempts to cope with classroom demands, effective teachers refuse to cave in by reducing task demands and treating these students as if they are really unable to succeed in the classroom. Instead, they approach such students with a mixture of sympathy, encouragement, and demands. These teachers reassure the students that they do have ability and that work given will not be too difficult for them. Then, the teachers help them to get started when they are discouraged or need some support, reinforce their progress, and perhaps offer contracts providing rewards for accomplishments and allowing opportunities for students to set goals. In general, the emphasis is on encouragement and help rather than prodding through threat of punishment. Failure-syndrome students are not merely *told* that they can succeed, but *shown* convincingly that they can, and helped to do so. [p. 23]

These suggestions seemed to have worked in providing more realistic expectations, building self-confidence, and in creating a more comfortable classroom in which Bill could become the student he can be.

ACTIVITY 9.5   Student feedback to the teacher

As suggested throughout this book, students can provide teachers with useful feedback on how consistently they are implementing effective teaching methods. Figure 9.14 is a sample form that you can administer to students to assess how effectively you are using many of the methods presented in this chapter.

FIGURE 9.14   Student's assessment of teacher's instructional skills

I believe students are knowledgeable both about how they learn best and in describing effective teaching. Therefore, I am asking you to give me some feedback on what I believe to be important aspects of my teaching. Please be serious, fair, and honest when completing this form. Also, please do not put your name on the form. Place an X in the box that best describes the question.

What's the Score?

FORE!

	Hole in one	Birdie	Par	Bogey	Out of bounds
1. Are the goals and objectives for each lesson clear?					
2. Do you value what you are learning in this class?					
3. Do I use different ways to teach lessons (films, projects, discussions, guest speakers, and so on)?					
4. Do you get to study subjects or ideas that interest you?					
5. Is there a good balance for you in the amount of time spent in large- and small-group activities?					
6. Do you think the skills taught in this class are useful in some other areas of your life?					
7. Do you accomplish goals you set in this class?					
8. Do tests give you information about what you have learned?					
9. Do tests help you to see what skills still need to be practiced?					
10. Do you feel pressured to finish work in this class?					

continued

	Hole in one	Birdie	Par	Bogey	Out of bounds
11. Are you comfortable sharing your ideas with other students in this class?					
12. Are the goals of each new assignment clear?					
13. Are you aware of how you are doing in this class?					
14. Are most of the assignments challenging but not too hard for you?					
15. Do I allow enough time for questions and discussion?					
16. Does the class allow you to express yourself creatively?					
17. Do you think the grading is fair?					
18. Do you feel you have a chance to be actively involved in learning?					
19. The best thing about this class is. . . .					
20. The thing I like least about this class is. . . .					
21. If I were teaching this class I would. . . .					
22. The way I learn best is to. . . .					

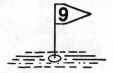

Administer Figure 9.14 (or a revision you develop) to at least two of your classes. Tally the results as suggested in Figure 2.2. After carefully examining this tally, answer these questions:

Students rate me very highly on my ability to. . . .
Students' feedback suggests that I may need to. . . .

I was pleasantly surprised to find that students believe I. . . .
I was disappointed that students rated me somewhat low on. . . .
One specific change I will make in my teaching is. . . .

RECOMMENDED READING

Carin, A., & Sund, R. (1978). *Creative questioning and sensitive listening techniques*. Columbus, Ohio: Charles E. Merrill.

Cummings, C. (1980). *Teaching makes a difference*. Edmonds, Wash.: Teaching.

Dunn, R., & Dunn, K. (1972). *Practical approaches to individualizing instruction: Contracts and other effective teaching strategies*. West Nyack, N.Y.: Parker.

Dunn, R., & Dunn, K. (1978). *Teaching students through their individual learning styles: A practical approach*. Reston, Va: Reston.

Harmin, M., Kirschenbaum, H., & Simon, S. (1973). *Clarifying values through subject matter*. Minneapolis, Minn.: Winston Press.

Hunter, M. (1976). *Improved instruction*. El Segundo, Calif.: TIP.

Johnson, D., & Johnson, R. (1975). *Learning together and alone: Cooperation, competition, and individualization*. Englewood Cliffs, N.J.: Prentice-Hall.

Johnson, D., Johnson, R., Hohnson Holubec, E., & Roy, P. (1984). *Circles of learning: Cooperation in the classroom*. Alexandria, Va.: Association for Supervision and Curriculum Development.

Jones, V. (1980). *Adolescents with behavior problems: Strategies for teaching, counseling, and parent involvement*. Boston: Allyn and Bacon.

Joyce, B., & Weil, M. (1980). *Models of teaching* (2nd ed.). Englewood Cliffs, N.J.: Prentice-Hall.

Lemleck, J. (1979). *Classroom management*. New York: Harper and Row.

Postman, N., & Weingartner, C. (1969). *Teaching as a subversive activity*. New York: Delacorte.

Rogers, C. (1969). *Freedom to learn*. Columbus, Ohio: Charles E. Merrill.

Slavin, R. (1983). *Cooperative learning*. New York: Longman.

Stanish, B. (1981). *Hippogriff feathers: Encounters with creative thinking*. Carthage, Ill.: Good Apple.

PART IV

WHEN PREVENTION FAILS: METHODS FOR ALTERING UNPRODUCTIVE STUDENT BEHAVIOR

When sensitively and consistently employed, the methods presented in Parts II and III increase students' achievement and eliminate a significant amount of disruptive student behavior. A few students, however, will cause major or consistent behavior problems despite our efforts to create positive, supportive, well-organized, and stimulating learning environments. Furthermore, the pressures and inevitable frustrations of learning and working in a relatively small area with thirty or so classmates create a situation in which some students will occasionally misbehave and require assistance in controlling and improving their behavior.

In Part IV, we present many types of intervention strategies that teachers, counselors, child development specialists, and administrators can use to help pupils better understand and control their behavior. When examining and implementing these strategies, educators should keep in mind that these methods will be more effective when employed in conjunction with the methods discussed in the previous chapters. In fact, we believe that adults harm youngsters by implementing behavior-control strategies to ensure that young people act passively and positively in environments that do not meet their basic psychological and academic needs.

Underlying the behavior-change interventions presented in Part IV is the belief that students should be actively involved in all attempts to alter their behavior. Students should be involved in solving problems, helped to collect and understand data about their own behavior, and be instrumental in developing contracts aimed at altering their behavior. Finally, although it may not be desirable to have students present during all discussions of their behavior, they should be included in many such discussions and should always be aware of the problems being discussed and the programs being implemented.

When you use the methods presented in Chapters 10 and 11, be careful not to view problem-solving and behavioristic interventions as mutually exclusive. Problem-solving approaches do emphasize students' involvement in the behavior-change process, but we should recognize that the final solution may, in fact, incorporate a behavioristic approach such as self-observation or the creation of a contract. Consistent with our belief that educational interventions should meet students' needs, maintain their integrity, and teach them to control their own behavior, Part IV begins with a chapter about helping students solve their own problems.

CHAPTER 10

Reducing Unproductive Student Behavior with Problem Solving

Philosophically, there is little question about the desirability of extending autonomy and freedom of choice to everyone; the problem is determining when and how much. The ability to act independently and make wise and appropriate choices is learned just like any other facet of behavior. . . . A child needs not only experience but the right kind of experience. And he needs a wise guide who can steer him clear of danger and who encourages, prompts, and reinforces behavior that is adaptive and successful.

Garth Blackham and Adolf Silberman, (1975),
Modification of Child and Adolescent Behavior

Regardless of how effectively we create positive learning environments and implement varied instructional methods, some disruptive student behavior is almost inevitable. At all grade levels, students' developmental needs conflict with an environment that requires large groups of students to engage in learning new skills for an extended time. Skilled teachers prevent most disruptions by employing methods of classroom management and instruction that encourage positive interpersonal relationships and academic success. They also, however, possess a repertoire of methods for helping students responsibly solve minor conflicts that arise.

The ultimate goals of implementing methods to reduce unproductive or disruptive student behavior are: (1) to increase the achievement of both the individual student and his and her classmates, and (2) to help youngsters develop positive social skills. As stated in the introduction to Part IV, the very fact that schools group twenty or more students for instruction creates a situation in which some minor conflicts are likely to occur. Unfortunately, many teachers lack training and skill in helping students solve their problems (Brophy & Rohrkemper, 1981; Brown, 1975). Teacher-training programs have frequently failed to provide teachers with either prerequisite communication skills or specific methods for involving students in solving problems. Consequently, teachers all too often find themselves resorting to the authoritarian models they experienced as students. This point was brought home recently when a young teacher told one of us, "My voice is one octave lower than it was at the beginning of the year. I really hate myself for yelling at the students, but I don't know what else to do."

Regardless of the approach we take, working with students whose behavior is disruptive requires time and energy. Research (Walker & Buckley, 1973; Walker, Hops, & Fiegenbaum, 1976) indicates that teachers spend a large amount of time attempting to control acting-out students. Teachers often, however, misdirect their energies:

> It often appears that the harder a teacher tries to control an acting-out child's behavior, the less effective she/he is. This process can be physically draining and emotionally exhausting. [Walker, 1979, p. 18]

Teachers will generally be more effective if they spend less energy attending to and trying to control disruptive behavior and considerably more energy implementing the methods described in Parts II and III. When disruptions occur in spite of our employing effective interpersonal, organizational, and instructional strategies, we should focus our energies on involving students in examining their behavior and developing mutually agreed-upon methods for changing the behavior.

Whenever confronted with the decision to use an authoritarian or problem-solving approach to discipline, one of us is reminded of a comment made by a veteran junior high school teacher with whom he taught. When talking to a group of young teachers about the teaching profession, the teacher stated that it was impossible to be a teacher and not go home tired every night. The teacher said, however, that there were two ways to go home tired. The first was to leave the school building and sigh with relief that another day was over and the students had been kept in line relatively well. He stated that this feeling usually stemmed from teachers' taking an authoritarian, power-oriented approach to discipline; this type of teacher frequently spent evenings worrying about whether the students would behave the next day and what could be done if they did not. The second type of fatigue, he stated, was based on employing a problem-solving approach to discipline. He described it as caused by having interacted openly with students all day. Because he experienced the latter type of fatigue, he almost always felt good about his work and generally looked forward to seeing the children the next day.

In his *Teacher Effectiveness Training*, Gordon (1974) stated the issue in a similar manner in discussing the problems associated with teachers' attempting to control students by using power methods of influence:

> Teacher-student relationships at the upper-elementary and secondary levels are much more strained and stressful because teachers relied so heavily upon power (backed up by rewards and punishment) when the children were younger. Then, when students are older, they begin to react to these techniques to an ever-increasing degree with anger, hostility, rebellion, resistance, and retaliation. . . .
> Students do not naturally have to rebel against adults in the schools. But they will rebel against the adults' use of teacher power. Drop the use of teacher power, and much of the student rebellion in schools disappears. [Gordon, 1974, p. 198]

A basic assumption that teachers must accept before employing a problem-solving approach is that they can reduce their authoritarian control and replace it with natural authority. Natural authority is the logical and readily accepted leadership associated with obvious competence, interest, and concern. Anyone who has attended a summer basketball camp run by professional athletes has observed natural authority. Young people listen attentively to these athletes because they are competent at something the learner finds interesting. In the school setting, natural authority can be based upon the teacher's knowledge of subject matter, ability to develop interesting lessons, or skill in solving problems.

An important point to consider when deciding whether or not to give up authoritarian control is that this approach becomes noticeably less effective as students become older. Authoritarian control can be effectively employed in the primary grades (although the effects on children are often destructive), but it is less effective with older students who are beginning to enter a developmental stage whose main task is developing an individual identity and sense of independence.

As suggested by the teacher who discussed the two ways in which teachers can go home tired, giving up authoritarian control can have benefits for teachers as well as students. As teachers begin to involve students in solving classroom problems, the teacher's role changes from that of an all-knowing, totally responsible adult to that of an effective facilitator. Although teachers cannot abdicate their ultimate responsibility, they can create classroom settings in which they do not have to be constantly and totally in charge of every decision. The difficulty of maintaining an authoritarian role and the number of teachers who continue to accept it is one reason why teacher turnover continues to be extremely high.

Even when teachers are skilled in involving students in solving their own problems, they often find that these skills are relatively ineffective in working with seriously acting-out students. Some severely disruptive students experience major personality disorders that prevent them from responding to interventions that require establishment of a trusting relationship and ability to evaluate one's behavior in light of its effect on others. Nevertheless, it is important to initially employ methods that involve students in controlling their own behavior. There are several advantages to initially employing less teacher-directed, behavioristic interventions. First, though some young people will, in fact, respond only to very structured, controlling interventions, others will respond surprisingly well to effective problem-solving approaches presented in a safe, caring environment characterized by effective teaching. Because it is impossible to determine which students will respond to less control-oriented methods, it is always desirable to try these first. Second, students know when they are being singled out from their peers. Students view adults as powerful and knowledgeable, and so they internalize much of what adults' words and actions say about them. Consequently, when adults employ behavioristic methods for controlling a student's behavior, students may learn that they are different from and less capable than their peers. Although this situation is sometimes inevitable, its influence can be reduced by initially employing problem-solving interventions with all students. Students who perceive that a more behavioristic intervention is a response to their inability to respond to a problem-solving approach will understand more clearly why they are being provided with a structured program than will students who are initially confronted with such a program. Third, by providing acting-out students with an introduction to problem-solving approaches, educators increase the likelihood that the youngster who must be temporarily removed or controlled by a structured behavioristic program will be more knowledgeable about and able to adjust to less controlled methods when these become appropriate. Finally, because they are quite effective in controlling behavior, teachers sometimes use behavioristic interventions without first examining such important variables as the quality of teacher–student and peer relationships or the instructional materials and techniques being employed in the classroom. Therefore, behavioristic approaches are sometimes used to manipulate pupils into behaving passively in environments that are not meeting their basic needs. Because problem-solving approaches give students an opportunity to discuss the environment, they are an important precursor to behavioristic interventions.

BASIC ISSUES AND ASSUMPTIONS UNDERLYING EFFECTIVE PROBLEM SOLVING

The comments in the previous section are based on several fundamental beliefs about working with young people. These basic beliefs or assumptions must be accepted by anyone who plans to sincerely and effectively employ a problem-solving approach to resolve conflicts and reduce inappropriate student behavior.

Importance of the Teacher–Student Relationship

Just as the quality of teacher–student relationships is a major factor in preventing discipline problems and improving students' motivation (Chapter 4), positive teacher–student relationships are a prerequisite to effective problem solving. Teachers who wish to employ problem solving as a method for dealing with disruptive student behavior must first create a classroom atmosphere characterized by warmth, openness, and safety. Students will honestly examine their own behavior and sincerely attempt to change only in an atmosphere where they are cared for and where their input is consistently valued.

The importance of the teacher–student relationship in facilitating responsibility and effective problem solving has been expressed by numerous well-known educators and therapists. Virginia Axline wrote:

> When a teacher respects the dignity of a child, whether he be six or sixteen, and treats the child with understanding, kindliness, and constructive help, she is developing in him an ability to look within himself for the answers to his problems, and become responsible for himself as an independent individual in his own right. [Axline, 1947, p. 156]

William Glasser presented a similar picture of the importance of a warm, positive teacher—student relationship:

> . . . they can't make better choices, more responsible choices, unless they are strongly and emotionally involved with those who can . . . teachers and therapists too often stand aloof from children; they do not get emotionally involved; they are not warm, personal and interested; they do not reveal themselves as human beings so that the children can identify with them. Thus they fail to alleviate the loneliness of the many children who need human warmth so desperately. Only in a school where a teacher and student are involved with each other and equally involved with the curriculum through thinking and problem solving does education flourish—an education that prepares students to live successfully in the world. [Glasser, 1969, p. 19]

Respect for Students' Abilities

Closely related in importance to the teacher–student relationship is the fact that the implementation of individual and group problem-solving methods is based on the assumption that young people want to control their own behavior and experience a sense of competence. Not that youngsters have the skill to solve all their own problems. Rather, youths are seen as having the potential and desire to be involved in solving their own problems and therefore can be expected to respond enthusiastically to teachers' sincere efforts to involve them in this process.

Unfortunately, teachers often give up after one or two attempts at problem solving have failed to bring about a satisfactory solution. Before rejecting this approach, we should first consider whether students have really been involved in the procedure or whether the problem-solving intervention was, in reality, a disguised teacher's solution. Furthermore, even when we effectively employ problem-solving approaches, students cannot be expected to immediately resolve all conflicts effectively. Not only do students need to learn problem-solving skills or begin to apply these skills in a new setting, but students who have experienced several years of teacher-dominated solutions may initially be skeptical of our sincerity in involving students. We frequently need to prove that we respect young people and their abilities before students will apply themselves in helping to solve problems.

The extensive research on the powerful effect of teachers' expectations (Brophy, 1983; Good & Grouws, 1983) indicates that pupils' behavior is influenced by the expectations adults communicate to them. Therefore, when we express our respect for students' ability to solve their own problems, students will often respond by living up to these expectations. It appears that students would benefit more from our erring slightly in the direction of expecting too much in this area than expecting too little.

Desire to Help Students Learn Responsibility

A frequent complaint heard in school staff rooms is, "Students simply are not responsible. They must be constantly reminded and cannot do things on their own. I have to tell them what to do every step of the way." Teachers understandably bemoan this situation, and yet it is one they have often inadvertently created or reinforced. It is unrealistic to expect students to be independent and responsible learners when they have received limited assistance in developing problem-solving skills and few opportunities to display their independence.

Students need problem-solving skills if they are to become productive members of society. Ruth Benedict (1954) presented the concept that societies should provide young people with gradually increasing amounts of responsibility rather than suddenly inundating young adults with new responsibilities. Schools should make a concerted effort to teach students how to solve their problems and to provide them with opportunities to practice these skills. When teachers implement this approach they are usually surprised to find that it significantly reduces the amount of negative discipline they employ in the classroom. Thomas Gordon placed the relationship between discipline and responsibility in an interesting perspective:

> When teachers say, "I don't have enough authority in the classroom," they mean they need more power to reward and punish. When teachers complain, "Kids these days have no respect for authority," they mean that the rewards and punishments are too few or too ineffective.
>
> Paradoxically, most teachers genuinely reject dependence and fear as desired traits in the students in their classes. Here is their dilemma. Teachers say they want unafraid, independent, self-reliant, self-disciplined students, but when they have students with those qualities they find that power will not work well with such students. [Gordon, 1974, pp. 195–196]

The work on attribution theory referred to in Chapter 4 has important implications about methods required to help students develop responsibility. Skinner (1971) stated that individuals will feel accountable for their behavior only if they are not being controlled by external factors. Attribution theory states that individuals will be more likely to make a continued personal effort when they believe results are attributable to their effort rather than to luck, basic ability, or the difficulty of the task. Harter and Connell (1981) found that students' sense of understanding of whether control was internal or external was an important factor influencing their achievement, self-concept, and intrinsic motivation. If we want students to have a sense of controlling and taking responsibility for their own behavior, it is critical that we involve students in discussing and actively resolving individual and classroom problems. A problem-solving approach facilitates this process.

METHODS FOR SOLVING PROBLEMS

Several writers have developed methods for helping students resolve problems and take responsibility for their own behavior. In his *Teacher Effectiveness Training*, Tom Gordon (1974) offers a six-step approach to problem solving. Frank Maple's (1977) *Shared Decision Making* describes a variety of skills needed to effectively resolve problems. For teachers working with students who have serious problems, the method of Life Space Interviewing developed by Fritz Redl and expanded by William Morse and Nicholas Long (Long, Morse, & Newman, 1971) provides a method for helping the student understand and resolve conflicts within a structured, supportive approach. Similarly, Mary Wood's (1975) *Developmental Therapy* and Betty Epanchin and James Paul's (1982) *Casebook for Educating the Emotionally Disturbed* offer methods for working with seriously disturbed students.

Although we have at various times employed each of the methods described above, in the remainder of this chapter we present the approaches we have found most useful in our own teaching and counseling experience. If you are interested in examining other methods, we refer you to the recommended readings at the end of this chapter.

Allowing Students to Solve Their Own Problems

Teachers too seldom allow students to work out their own solutions to conflicts involving two or more students. By the third or fourth grade most children have considerable experience in resolving interpersonal conflicts. Furthermore, students' disagreements are often short-lived. It is not unusual to see younger children who were fighting one minute, playing happily together several minutes later. Indeed, adults' attempts to involve children in extensive problem solving about peer conflicts often tend to extend, compound, and intensify the problem. Similarly, when adults punish children for peer conflicts, they often inadvertently intensify the conflict. Rather than being forgotten, conflicts may linger on as students recall the punishment they received.

Teachers' involvement in solving peer conflicts may also reinforce the undesirable behavior. Students often enjoy the attention they receive when the teacher or counselor spends time helping them solve a peer conflict. This reinforcement may be especially powerful if the discussion takes place during time the students would normally be involved in academic tasks.

Excessive teacher involvement in resolving peer conflicts also suggests that students are unable to resolve their own conflicts. By reinforcing the concept that teachers alone possess the knowledge and skill for solving problems, we inadvertently encourage students to be more dependent. This situation affects both teacher and student negatively. Students are prevented from developing a sense of industry, competence, and power. This interference negatively affects their self-esteem, and students will often find less productive means of demonstrating their power. The effect on teachers is less pronounced but nevertheless notable. Teachers who attempt to solve every minor problem are often inundated with student concerns. This flood not only drains energy but also detracts from the teacher's ability to assist children with their academic tasks.

Knowing the considerable disadvantages associated with teachers' too frequently intervening in peer conflicts, it is useful to examine how we can go about increasing students' involvement in this process. The first factor to consider before encouraging students to solve their own conflicts is the degree to which students in the classroom know and like one another. If we have employed a variety of activities such as those discussed in Chapter 5, students will be much more likely to work together to solve their own problems. If students are highly competitive, however, or have not been assisted in establishing a positive peer culture, they will normally be much less effective in solving their own problems. Similarly, even when positive peer relations have been established, we should be careful about having two students resolve a conflict if one student has considerably more power or prestige than the other. Unless the more powerful student is very sensitive and willing to use his or her power to help facilitate a positive solution, the situation may be characterized by negative manipulation. When we have good reason to question the students' ability to obtain a positive resolution, it may be best for us to serve as a third-party facilitator during the discussion.

The actual process of involving students in solving their own conflicts is quite simple. The first step is to discuss the procedure with the class. We may introduce the topic by asking students how they think problems are solved most effectively. When working with older students, we may wish to incorporate a brief discussion of the ways in which nations or individuals in the larger society solve their differences of opinion. The purpose of a discussion is to increase students' involvement in the process while making the point that disagreements are usually most effectively solved by direct communication between the parties. Even when a third party is involved, this person's role is simply to facilitate a productive dialogue between the disagreeing parties. Once the students have discussed this issue, we should inform them that whenever a student comes to us with a problem or we are required to temporarily intervene in an angry interchange between students, they will be asked to set a time to meet to resolve their differences.

It is important that we provide adequate structure for these student meetings. We should designate an area of the room where such meetings will take place. We know a teacher who tapes two lines on the floor so that students will discuss their differences while remaining far enough apart so that physical contact is discouraged. We may also wish to designate a time when conflict-resolution conferences will take place. Students can be informed that these will occur during recess periods, lunch breaks, or after school. Similarly, especially if students are allowed to meet during classroom activities, we may wish to set a time limit for such meetings. We can also provide students with a worksheet that helps them structure their meeting and clearly report their solution. Figure 10.1 is a form we have used with children in grades four through eight. Finally, we can help students develop the skills necessary for productive conflict resolution. Students can be taught to use "I" messages and active listening. We can also model an effective conflict resolution and can involve the class in role playing several typical conflicts. This skill building takes very little time, is an enjoyable activity for students, and significantly increases the percentage of conflict-resolution meetings that result in two happy students and a positive solution.

Though it is often possible for students to resolve their own conflicts, we can serve as a facilitator. This example was taped in a fourth-grade classroom:

Teacher facilitating a student problem

Peter:	I did not cheat!
Tom:	You did too and you always cheat.
Peter:	I do not always cheat. You always have such a loud mouth and you are a tattletale.
Tom:	I am not a tattletale, you dummy!
Teacher:	Boys, you seem upset. Did a problem at recess start all this?
Peter:	Yes!
Teacher:	Would you both be willing to talk about the problem?
Tom:	Well, okay.
Teacher:	Peter, is that okay with you?
Peter:	Yeah! Tom and I were playing wallball together. The ball bounced just inside the line of the square but Tom called me out. I said that I wasn't out so Tom called me a cheater and another name.
Teacher:	So you felt that you weren't cheating.
Peter:	Yeah, the ball hit the line.
Teacher:	Tom, would you like to tell us what you think happened?
Tom:	Yeah, well, Peter was cheating. The kids in the line all voted him out and he wouldn't go out. This happens all the time when Peter plays in a group game.
Peter:	It does not!
Teacher:	You sound frustrated, Tom.

FIGURE 10.1   **Problem solving form**

WORKING

TOGETHER

to

Solve

Problems

1. What happened that caused the other person to become upset?

    Before   During   After

_____   _____   _____

_____   _____   _____

_____   _____   _____

_____   _____   _____

2. Did the behaviors described above violate a school or classroom rule?

_____   _____ if so which one _____
     no   yes

_____

3. Did the behaviors help you to positively resolve the problem?

   _____   _____
    no   yes

4. What agreement or plan can you create to resolve the problem? Complete the sentence.

   We have decided that we will _____

   _____

   _____

5. What plan can you develop for preventing future problems? Complete the sentence.

   The next time one of us does something that bothers the other we will

   _____

   _____

_____   _____   _____
Student #1 signature   Student # 2 signature   Date

Tom:	This happens all the time and I get really tired of it.
Teacher:	Tom, can you send Peter an "I" message?
Tom:	Peter, I want to play with you and be your friend, but I get really mad when you always have to have your own way. It wastes our recess.
Peter:	Nobody likes me.
Teacher:	Peter, did you listen to what Tom just said? Can you tell me what Tom just said?
Peter:	He said that he wants to play with me but that he doesn't like me because I have to have my own way.
Teacher:	Peter, he didn't say that he did not like you. He said that he gets frustrated when you won't follow the rules at recess.
Peter:	Okay, but he calls me names all the time.
Teacher:	Peter, you seem hurt that Tom called you a name.
Tom:	Well, I was angry.
Teacher:	How do you feel, Tom, when someone calls you a name?
Tom:	Not very good.
Teacher:	How do you think Peter felt when you called him a name?
Tom:	It probably made him feel bad.
Teacher:	I think you're right, Tom. I know I feel bad when I get called a name. Peter, how do you think Tom feels when you argue with the rules?
Peter:	Not very good.
Teacher:	Yes, it sounds like he gets pretty frustrated. Would you two be willing to talk this out and see if you can come up with a plan so that you can play together without Peter being hurt and Tom being frustrated?
Boys:	Okay.
Teacher:	All right then, I'd like you to take three minutes to think up a plan to help you when you play wallball.

Three minutes later . . .

Teacher:	Did you decide on a plan?
Peter:	Yes, if the line of kids vote me out when I play wallball, I will go out without making a big deal and Tom will try not to call me names.
Teacher:	That sounds like a good plan. Would you boys please write your plan down on paper and sign and date the plan. I'll check back with you to see how the plan is working after the next recess and again tomorrow.

Allowing students to resolve their own interpersonal conflicts will not work every time. It will, however, reduce or eliminate the need for your involvement in a surprising number of minor classroom and playground problems.

Glasser's Seven Steps to Effective Discipline

Many behavior problems that occur in schools are not directly related to peer conflicts. Furthermore, regardless of the type of problem, teachers must often help individual students solve a problem or change their behavior. Many teachers find this task one of the most frustrating and time-consuming aspects of teaching. Though most of us are trained in subject matter methods, many of us are untrained or feel uncomfortable with the role of counselor and disciplinarian. Furthermore, with the increased emphasis on competencies and achievement-test scores, we frequently feel anxious about time spent solving problems. Therefore, we need to develop skills in solving problems in a positive yet rapid manner. Most teachers have neither the inclination nor the expertise to become involved in extensive counseling with their students. We are, however, confronted daily with individual problems that must be resolved in order for students to benefit from our instruction.

The simplest and most effective method of helping children solve their problems and alter their behavior was described by William Glasser (1965, 1969) in his *Reality Therapy* and *Schools Without Failure*. Though Glasser provided several step-by-step approaches to discipline, the method we have found most effective involves these seven steps: (1) be warm and personal and willing to get emotionally involved; (2) deal with specific, current behavior; (3) help the youngster make a value judgment about his or her behavior; (4) work out a plan for changing the behavior; (5) get a commitment from the student to carry out the plan; (6) follow up by checking to see how the plan is working; (7) do not punish the student be being negative or sarcastic, and do not accept excuses if the inappropriate behavior continues.

Advantages of Glasser's Method

Four factors make Glasser's model extremely useful for school personnel. First, the problem solving can be accomplished in a short time. Most conflicts can be resolved in less than five minutes and frequently a solution can be developed in only a minute or two. Therefore, though it is often desirable to remove the student from the group so that the discussion can take place privately, you do not need to become involved in a lengthy discussion that diverts your attention from other instructional or supervisory duties. Second, because the model employs a step-by-step procedure, it is easy to learn. Furthermore, if a problem-solving session does not go well, you can analyze each step and discover what needs to be improved to make the session more effective. Third, by actively involving the student in the problem-solving process, the model responds to a variety of students' needs. Rather than establishing a teacher versus student debate or a situation in which you manipulate the student by offering rewards for changed behavior, the student is meaningfully involved in examining his or her behavior and developing a plan for changing the behavior. Finally, because the model focuses on specific, observable behavior, data can be collected and the student is accountable for the results. The focus on observable behavior also enables you and the student to realistically analyze the effectiveness of the plan. To become competent at employing Glasser's approach, you will need to clearly understand each step and then frequently use the approach with students.

Step One
The first step is presented in Chapter 5. If we employ the communication skills and other strategies for improving teacher–student relationships described in Chapter 5, students will sense that we care and will almost always be willing to examine and attempt to change their behavior.

Step Two
The second step is to ask the student to describe his or her behavior. Awareness of actions is an important component in any behavior-change program. Indeed, a simple increase in children's awareness of their behavior is often accompanied by major changes in their behavior. We can help students describe their behavior by asking questions such as, "What did you do that upset Sally?" It is important to focus the student's attention on what he or she did, not on what the other person did. The emphasis should be placed on specific, observable behavior. If a student states that he or she was bad or didn't obey us, we should help the child specify how he or she was bad or what request he or she did not obey and what he or she said or did when rejecting the request. If the student begins to answer the question by discussing what the other person did, we should indicate that, although this subject can be discussed later and the other person may even become involved, the student knows what he or she did and we would like to discuss this act.

Students will sometimes respond to our question about what they did by saying "nothing" or "I don't know." Then we have several options. First, we can respond by stating, "John, I'm not trying to blame you or get you in trouble. What I want to do is help you solve the problem, and I need to know what you did so I understand what happened." When we focus on the problem rather than threatening the student or focusing on the punishment, students will often be willing to discuss their behavior. A second approach is to ask if the student would be willing to hear what we observed or, if we were not present, to have someone else share what they saw. It is important that this option be presented positively and not as a threat. When confronted with this option, students will normally discuss their behavior. If a student does not respond positively to either of these options, it usually means that they are quite emotional and may need time to calm down and think about the problem. We can deal with this situation by saying, "John, it seems you don't feel comfortable talking about the problem right now. Why don't we talk about it during recess." Providing the student with time to relax often facilitates a positive resolution of the problem.

Step Three
Once the student has described his or her behavior, we should help him or her determine whether or not the behavior is desirable. Students will not make

meaningful, lasting changes in a behavior unless they decide that the behavior should be altered, particularly older students. When directing a program for seventh- and eighth-grade students who exhibited serious behavior problems, one of us was surprised when a number of the students stated that when they changed their behavior to earn the rewards offered by a contract, they thought they were being bribed and earned the rewards only to "play the system." The students resented not being involved in assessing their behavior. Consequently, behavior changes occurred only as long as the staff could devise adequate rewards or punishments. Based on this information subsequent behavior-change interventions employed more dialogue and a less unilateral approach to solving problems. Research results (Jones, 1973) indicate that this approach was more successful.

Glasser suggests that, when helping youngsters to make a value judgment about their behavior, we ask them: "Is the behavior helping you? Is it helping me? Is it helping the other students?" When children are involved in obviously unproductive behaviors, they will almost always answer "no" to these questions. If they answer, "yes," we can ask, "How is it helping you?" or "How is it helping the others?" Finally, if the student insists that the behavior is helping him or her and his or her peers, we can describe how the behavior is causing problems for him or her. If we have established a positive relationship with the student, this will often provide the impetus for the student to acknowledge that the behavior needs to be changed.

Another approach to helping youngsters make a value judgment is to have them list the advantages and disadvantages or payoffs and costs of their behavior. When working with older students, we may ask them to put the payoffs and costs in writing. Figure 10.2 provides a form that can be used to facilitate this process.

If a student continues to state that an unproductive behavior is helping him or her and that he or she wishes to continue the behavior, it is likely that he or she is feeling backed into a corner or is testing our resolve. It is usually best to postpone the discussion for a short time. If a student continues to insist that an unproductive behavior is acceptable, we may need to confront the student with the logical consequences of the behavior. We should be very careful not to rush to this point without exhausting all possible approaches to helping the student decide to alter the behavior. If it is necessary to employ this intervention, however, it should be discussed in a matter-of-fact, nonthreatening manner, and we should clearly explain to the student why the behavior must be altered. We might say, "I am sorry that you do not see the behavior as harmful. It is my job, though, to make sure that students follow school rules. Therefore, if you do not choose to be responsible for your behavior, I must take responsibility." If the student continues to insist that his or her behavior does not need to change, we should inform the student of the specific consequences that will occur if the behavior continues.

Step Four

After the student has decided that the behavior really does need to be changed, the next step is to help him or her develop a workable plan for mak-

FIGURE 10.2   Payoff-cost model of behavioral counseling[a]

	Short term	Long term
Payoffs		
Costs		

[a]From Vernon F. Jones, *Adolescents with Behavior Problems: Strategies for Teaching, Counseling, and Parent Involvement.* © 1980. Reprinted by permission of Allyn and Bacon, Inc.

ing the change. We should start by asking the student a question such as, "What do you think you can do so that you can study without bothering other students?" or "What kind of plan could you work out so that you don't get in trouble in music?" We must not accept a superficial plan such as the statement, "I won't do it again" or "I'll try harder." We might be relieved to hear these promises, but they do not provide the student with a specific approach for dealing more effectively with the situation. Consequently, we can respond to promises by saying, "I'm glad that you are going to try not to do it. That will certainly help. But what else can you do? What can you do when you start to get frustrated with your work?"

Students are refreshingly creative at devising useful plans for solving their own problems. Nevertheless, students sometimes state that they cannot think of a solution. Our first response should be to encourage them to think about the situation and report back to us at a designated time. Students have frequently become so accustomed to having adults provide answers that at first they are confused by having the burden placed on them. When given time to think about the situation, though, they often devise thoughtful plans. If the student is unable to develop a workable plan, we can offer several ideas for the student to consider. We must offer several suggestions so that the student will make the final decision. This involvement in choosing the solution increases the likelihood that the student will accept and follow through on the plan.

Plans should initially be relatively simple and unstructured, such as a student's deciding to work with another student in order to stay on task and complete his or her work. Plans may, however, involve a somewhat more structured approach. In fact, when less structured solutions have failed, many of the procedures described in Chapter 11 can serve as methods for implementing a plan to help a child alter his or her behavior. For example, students might be involved in writing a formal contract or self-monitoring their behavior.

Step Five

The next step is to ensure that both we and the student clearly understand the plan and ask the student to make a commitment to the plan. We can say, "All right, that seems like a good plan. Now, just to be sure that we both understand it, what are you going to do when you become frustrated with your work?" After the student describes the plan we can paraphrase the student's decision, and acknowledge our role in the plan. We might say, "Okay, whenever you get frustrated you're going to raise your hand. If I'm busy and can't help you, you're going to quietly walk over and ask Sally for help. Then, it is my responsibility to come over and check your work as soon as I get a chance." Although it is often adequate to simply obtain an oral agreement, it is sometimes helpful to put the plan in writing. This contract is especially valuable when students are first introduced to problem solving or when the final plan is developed in the form of a contract in which both parties agree to behave in a specified manner.

Once the plan has been clarified, the student should make a commitment to try the plan. This compact can be accomplished by asking, "Do you believe this is a good plan? Will you give it a try?" Although this step is often part of the final negotiation of a plan, it is important to elicit a clear commitment to the plan.

Step Six

The sixth and seventh steps involve our follow-up. In devising a workable solution to a problem it is necessary to designate a time when the two parties will meet to discuss how the plan is working. This step provides us with an opportunity to reinforce the student's efforts and to discuss any problems that might arise. If the plan involves a behavior that occurs frequently throughout the day, we should meet briefly with the student on the same day as the plan is made. Furthermore, if we see the student successfully implementing the plan, we should praise the student for his or her efforts. If the plan involves a behavior that occurs only occasionally—as during the student's music class—we can agree to meet the student as soon as possible following the class. Follow-up sessions need not take long. We can simply ask, "How did your plan work?" If the plan worked well, we should express our excitement and ask the student how he or she felt about the results. If it would reinforce the student, we may choose to provide additional follow-up by asking the principal to praise the student or by sending a positive note home with the student.

Step Seven

The final step in Glasser's plan deals with what we should do if a plan does not work. First, we should not be critical or sarcastic or punish the student. A major assumption underlying the use of a problem-solving approach is that in a positive, supportive environment students will want to be responsible and behave appropriately. Therefore, the student's inability to carry out a plan should not be punished. At the same time, we should not accept excuses. Students often defend their failure to change their behavior by blaming other people. Rather than allowing the student to describe what other people did that caused her or his failure to follow her or his plan, we should begin another problem-solving conference. Because the student will already have examined the behavior and made a decision to change it, the first three steps will usually take only a minute or two to complete. The conference should then focus on asking the student to consider why the plan did not work and assisting her or him to develop another plan. If the behavior is one that is harmful to other students, such as pushing children on the playground, we may need to inform the student of the consequences that will be incurred should the behavior continue. Although the emphasis should always be on devising a plan rather than punishing the student, situations in which it is necessary to incorporate a punishment into a plan do occur.

Examples
The following examples of first an upper elementary and then a middle school teacher employing Glasser's model with one of the students indicates how effective communication skills can be combined with Glasser's step-by-step procedure to create a positive resolution to a problem.

Example 1

Step 1.	*Teacher:*	Darby, can I talk to you by my desk for a little bit?
	Darby:	Okay.
Step 2.	*Teacher:*	After we corrected math today, I went over everyone's paper. Can you tell me what I found on your paper?
	Darby:	I didn't get finished.
Step 3.	*Teacher:*	That's right. Is it helping you to not get your work done on time?
	Darby:	I guess not.
	Teacher:	What happens when you don't have your work ready?
	Darby:	Jon doesn't have a paper to correct.
	Teacher:	Yes, can you think of any other things that happen.
	Darby:	I'll get a bad grade and have to do my work again.
	Teacher:	Okay, and does it make it even harder for you to have to complete this assignment and then begin working on the one for tomorrow?
	Darby:	Yeah.
	Teacher:	Well, Darby, would you like to start having your work done on time, so that you don't get behind,

		and so that you can feel good about giving Jon a completed paper to correct?
	Darby:	Yeah.
Step 4.	Teacher:	All right. Can you think of a plan that can help you get your work done on time?
	Darby:	No—I'll just try to get it done.
	Teacher:	Well, that's super to hear, but can you think of some way to really succeed in getting this work completed?
	Darby:	Oh, I guess I could do it after I get home from school, before my mom gets home from the beauty shop each night. But I like to play, too.
	Teacher:	Well, let's plan it out. What time does your mother get home?
	Darby:	5:30.
	Teacher:	And what time do you get home from school?
	Darby:	3:15.
	Teacher:	Now, do you think you can play for a while . . .
	Darby:	Oh, I know. I'll play until 4:30 and then do my work from 4:30 to 5:30!
Step 5.	Teacher:	Darby, that sounds like a great idea! I'm sure that most days you won't even need a whole hour to finish your work, especially when you get into such a good habit! And won't it be nice to be all done when your mother gets home! How long do you think you could make this plan work?
	Darby:	Forever!
	Teacher:	Oh, whoa!! I'm excited, too, but let's take it a little at a time!
	Darby:	Okay. I will do it tonight and tomorrow night.
	Teacher:	Great! Then Jon and I can expect to see completed assignments on Thursday and Friday!
	Thursday	
Step 6.	Darby:	It worked! I played, got my math done in 30 minutes (it was easy!) and was watching TV when Mom got home. Boy, was she surprised when I showed her my work!
	Teacher:	Oh, Darby. I knew you could do it! I really am proud of you! Keep up the good plan!

Example 2

Step 1.	Teacher:	Horace, may I please speak with you for a few minutes?
	Horace:	Okay.
Step 2.	Teacher:	What did you do that upset Larry?

	Horace:	I didn't do anything.
	Teacher:	Horace, I'm not trying to blame you or get you in trouble. What I want to do is try to help you solve the problem. But before we can solve it, I need to know what you did so that I understand what happened.
	Horace:	Well, I pushed Larry's books off his desk and onto the floor and his papers got all messed up.
Step 3.	Teacher:	Thank you for being honest with me. It sounds like you are really making an attempt to try to figure this problem out. Is this helping you or Larry in any way?
	Horace:	No, but he marked in ink on my assignment sheet that I was just about to hand in, and he ruined it. And so, now I have to do it all over again.
Step 4.	Teacher:	I will talk to Larry about this problem after we get finished dealing with your part of the problem. What kind of plan do you think you could work out so that you won't retaliate against anyone the next time something like this happens to you?
	Horace:	I won't do it again?
	Teacher:	I'm glad that you are going to try to not do it again. That will certainly help. But what else can we do?
	Horace:	I don't know.
	Teacher:	Well, how about if I make a few suggestions and you pick one of my plans to try to work with?
	Horace:	Well, okay.
	Teacher:	How about sending that person an "I" message telling them how you feel. Like, "It angers me when you ruin my homework and I have to do it over again." Or you could just get up and move away from that person, showing them that you don't appreciate what they've done. Do you like either one of these plans, Horace?
	Horace:	Well, because we've worked on "I" messages and you want us to work out our own problems, I will try an "I" message next time.
Step 5.	Teacher:	Great, now, just to be sure we both understand, what are you doing to do the next time somebody bothers you and your work?
	Horace:	Send that person an "I" message.
	Teacher:	Good, I'll check back with you in a couple of days to see how your plan is working.

A couple of days later:

Step 6. *Horace:*   It worked!! Gary ripped one of my papers yesterday and I sent him an "I" message, and he actually apologized to me. I couldn't believe it.

Teacher: I'm proud of you for working out your plan. I can see by your reaction that you are happy with your results.

Implementation Activity

As we mentioned earlier, one advantage to employing a systematic approach to solving problems is that the adults can evaluate their use of the process. Activity 10.1 is designed to help you analyze your effectiveness in employing Glasser's model.

ACTIVITY 10.1   Analyzing a Glasser problem-solving dialogue

Choose a student who is acting inappropriately in the classroom and solve the problem using Glasser's model. Do not choose the most disruptive student, for the model will be learned more effectively if it is initially used to solve less serious problems. At a later time it may be useful to employ this approach with an extremely disruptive youngster and incorporate one or more of the strategies presented in Chapter 11 into the plan.

Analyze your problem-solving interaction by answering the questions listed below. This examination will help to clarify exactly how the interchange progressed. Although it will be impossible to report the dialogue verbatim, summarize the essence of each stage as specifically and accurately as possible.

Step 1   What activities or approaches have you used to help the student feel that you care about him or her?

Step 2   Record the dialogue that occurred as you attempted to help the student describe his or her behavior. Try to accurately recall the questions you asked and the answers you received.

Step 3   Record the dialogue that occurred as you attempted to help the student make a value judgment.

Step 4   Record the dialogue that took place while you helped the student make a plan, and write the plan that was finally developed.

Step 5   Record the manner in which you asked the student to make a commitment to the plan. Was the student's agreement enthusiastic? Why or why not?

Step 6   How soon after the plan was made did you follow up? Record the interaction that took place during the follow up.

Step 7   Did you use sarcasm or punish the student? If so, explain the circumstances. If the plan was not effective, record the dialogue that occurred when you confronted the student with the problem. Did you start at step 1? Were you nonpunitive?

If your intervention was successful, write three reasons why you think the model worked for you and the student.

If the use of this method was not effective, carefully examine your analysis of each step. Also, ask yourself these questions:

Do you accept the basic assumptions presented at the beginning of this chapter?

Were you helping the student solve the problem or were you solving the problem for them?

Were you positive and nonpunitive?

Having analyzed the dialogue and answered these questions, list three reasons why the approach did not work for you in this case. Do not list factors involving the student; focus on your own behavior.

Implementing Glasser's Model on a Schoolwide Basis

Glasser (1977) expanded his seven steps to reality therapy into a ten-step approach to school discipline (Figure 10.3). This approach incorporates the major aspects of reality therapy while providing school personnel with a systematic, hierarchic series of responses to student misbehavior.

FIGURE 10.3   Glasser's ten steps to discipline

1. What have I been doing when Johnny misbehaves?
2. Resolved: that whatever I've been doing I'm going to stop doing it.
3. Make at least one positive contact a day with the problem student.
4. Tell the student to stop his inappropriate behavior. Use variety and humor.
5. What are you doing? Is it against the rules?
   a. If you get no response, then you have to tell him what you saw him doing.
   b. If he doesn't answer the question, you have to answer it for him.
6. We've got to talk this over—develop a plan.
7. Teacher establishes a place where the student can go to develop the plan.
8. School establishes a place and a person to assist students who cannot develop a plan while in the classroom.
9. Send him home.
10. Referral to a community agency.

The procedure for implementing Glasser's model on a schoolwide basis is quite simple. The entire staff is introduced to this approach and is asked to agree to employ the model as the primary method for handling discipline. The staff then develops a form for recording plans made with students. This form not only encourages a uniform approach to problem solving but also allows plans to be clearly communicated.

If a teacher or aide working on the playground makes a plan with a child from another class, the teacher or aide who makes the plan is responsible for following through on it. The student's classroom teacher, however, should receive a copy of it.

An important aspect of implementing Glasser's model on a schoolwide basis is that if a student refuses to develop a plan or if several plans have failed, the student is sent to the principal's office to work out a plan. Because a record is kept of every plan, the principal knows what plans have failed. This information aids the principal in helping the student devise a successful plan. The principal keeps a copy of the plan he or she makes with the student, gives the student a copy, and has the student take a copy to the teacher. Students are informed that, should the plan they make with the principal fail, the principal will schedule a conference with the student, his or her parents, and his or her teacher to discuss the problem. This approach provides the principal with a positive role in handling discipline problems. School staffs with whom we have worked to develop such a program indicate that this procedure reduces acting-out behavior and is well received by parents.

We recently observed a related approach to employing problem solving on a schoolwide basis in an inner-city middle school. The school had a high suspension rate and had been informed by the central office that they were to suspend fewer students. Investigating the reasons for suspensions, the principal discovered that most were for fighting. Further analysis showed that most fights stemmed from name calling or other minor peer conflicts. Based on these data, the school decided to systematically train all students and staff in communication skills and conflict-resolution methods. Students learned a clear, effective, and acceptable procedure for handling critical comments from peers. Faculty and staff supported students using these nonviolent alternative methods of conflict resolution, and students developed pride in their school's way of handling situations. Results showed a reduction in office referrals and suspensions following the training sessions.

Helping Students Assume Responsibility for Their Behavior

Students, especially those experiencing problems, tend to blame others for their difficulties. Schools often inadvertently reinforce this unproductive attitude by employing discipline policies and ways of talking to students that fail to emphasize students' responsibility for their own behavior. In our work with disruptive youth, we have found it useful to teach students a conceptual framework upon which they can base their own decision-making and responsibility. This conceptual framework includes five factors: (1) knowledge, (2) limits, (3) options, (4) choices and (5) consequences.

Students need to realize that in order to make good decisions, we need to understand our environment. We need to know ourselves and factors that tend to influence our behavior. Likewise, we need to know how those around us wish to be treated, what behaviors they value and their expectations regarding our behavior. Although we may not be able to change other people, understanding their wants and needs can help us make informed, productive decisions.

Individuals also need to know the limits that exist regarding behavior. In a school setting this means knowing the rules and consequences associated with rule violation. It also means knowing the personal limits of those with whom we interact. Teachers vary in the degree to which they will permit certain types of student behavior before invoking consequences.

Students should be helped to understand the various options available to them. Many behavior problem youngsters feel almost totally controlled by external factors, and their acting out is to some extent an attempt to gain or demonstrate their control. With these students it is particularly useful to point out that they have options. For example, the student who is frustrated in class has, among others, the option to discuss the problem with the teacher, talk to a counselor, passively accept the frustration or disrupt the class.

Students need to constantly be reminded that they make their own choices about their behavior. Within the context of a situation with varying options, *they* make the choice to act. The student who is frustrated in class makes the decision to seek help, suffer silently or respond disruptively.

Finally, adults need to help students understand that individuals choose the consequences they receive. Because students have the opportunity and responsibility to understand their environment and the limits involved, and because they always have options available to them, their behavior indicates their choice of positive or negative consequences.

It is critical that adults help students understand these issues. Just as they require assistance in learning mathematical and reading skills, students need instruction in and reinforcement of the skills in taking responsibility for their own behavior. When adults respond with simple punishment, young people may develop the incorrect idea that adults are responsible for student behavior. When adults talk to young people in terms of the youngsters' options and choices, students learn responsibility.

The example that follows describes a situation in which a counselor helped a young woman better understand her options and the consequences of her behavior.

Example

This case involved a thirteen-year-old girl, named Kathy, who was seen in individual therapy at a private counseling center. Kathy was referred to the center because of her extensive truancy, school failure, and consistently being "beyond parental control." Results of testing at school and the clinic showed that Kathy scored slightly below average in intelligence, and that she scored nearly three years below grade level in reading.

Early counseling sessions with Kathy indicated that she was experiencing a strong need to be accepted. Unfortunately, the group of boys with whom she was spending much of her time were not attending school and were quite heavily involved in drug usage and petty theft. While she had not yet become involved in these behaviors, Kathy was missing numerous classes to be with these boys. Furthermore, Kathy's desire to be with her delinquent friends was causing serious family problems. Kathy frequently became involved in heated arguments with her parents concerning what she considered to be unreasonably restrictive curfew hours. This situation had been intensified by the fact that Kathy had on several occasions remained out several hours past the designated curfew. Her parents had responded to these violations by strongly suggesting that Kathy might have to leave home and live with relatives in a town several hundred miles away.

In analyzing her behavior using the model presented in this section, Kathy listed the payoffs and costs shown in Figure 10.4. An examination of Figure 10.4 highlights several recurring themes found when working with adolescents.

First, adolescents frequently focus on short-term effects to the almost complete exclusion of long-term effects. Second, adolescents often appear to ignore the short-term costs connected with their behavior. This denial of short-term costs is often accomplished by projecting the blame for any such costs upon another agent. In the case under consideration, Kathy blamed her parents' lack of concern and love for the most powerful short-term cost associated with her behavior. By blaming her parents for the fact that she might be asked to leave home, she successfully denied her responsibility for the short-term negative consequences. A final concept highlighted by this case is the tendency for payoffs to include both direct payoffs and payoffs that are based upon the avoidance of an undesirable situation or task. For example, in this case, having friends and being in exciting situations were the direct short-term payoffs while avoidance of a difficult school experience was the avoidance-based, short-term payoff. When working with adolescents, it is important to help them identify and discuss both types of payoff. Only in this way can adults assist them in developing a complete picture of their behavior and its consequences.

Returning to Kathy's specific case, the cost/payoff model was employed as a means to motivate Kathy to work with her parents. Kathy had been focusing almost exclusively on the short-term payoffs and had denied the short-term costs by blaming her parents for her problem. Therefore, in order to convince Kathy that compromises with her parents might benefit her, it was necessary that she take a more realistic look at the costs and payoffs connected with her behavior.

After working separately with Kathy for several sessions, Kathy agreed that she was ready to meet with her parents to discuss possible agreements that could lead to a reduction in their conflicts. After several sessions the family agreed that Kathy could go out after dinner on weeknights until nine o'clock twice a week. It was also agreed that she could go out until 10:30 P.M.

FIGURE 10.4   Payoff/cost list developed by Kathy

	Short term	Long term
Payoffs	1. Getting out of boring classes 2. Doing something exciting 3. Having friends 4. Feeling important	1. Becoming an independent person
Costs	1. Parents are angry 2. Having to leave home 3. Being' "hassled" by teachers 4. Flunking classes 5. Losing some friends from school 6. Possibility of getting caught 7. Developing a "bad" reputation	1. Not graduating from high school 2. Getting caught and having that on her record 3. Getting "hooked" on drugs 4. Ruining her relationship with her parents

on Friday and Saturday nights as long as she informed her parents where she was going. In turn, Kathy agreed that she would stay home after dinner for three nights a week and either work on homework or participate in family activities. Kathy further agreed that if she was not home on time or if she left home after dinner more than twice a week, she would lose the privilege of going out the following weekend.

The results of this intervention were somewhat surprising. Kathy's behavior improved dramatically over the next two months. She began to attend school more regularly, her schoolwork improved, and she did not break her contract with her parents. These results appear to be due to two major factors. First, like so many adolescents, Kathy's attraction to a destructive peer group was more a response to the lack of a relationship at home than the positive draw of the peer group. Second, Kathy learned that she could serve her own purposes more effectively by interacting openly with her parents than by rebelling against them.

Clarifying Expectations: A Model for Mainstreaming or Readmitting Behavior-Problem Students

Acting-out students frequently require a more structured environment than their peers. These disruptive students often need assistance in clarifying expectations about their behavior as well as the consequences of failing to meet these expectations. Similarly, teachers often require assistance in clarifying their expectations for acting-out students. As teachers become increasingly frustrated with a student's behavior, they often lose their objectivity about expectations and consequences.

Although it is difficult to involve young children in the clarifying of expectations and in developing a plan in response to negotiated expectations, this procedure can be extremely effective with youngsters in intermediate grades and junior high schools. Figure 10.5 presents a model described by Jones (1980) for involving a teacher and student in this procedure. Though this plan is quite self-explanatory, you may wish to refer to Jones' (1980) *Adolescents with Behavior Problems: Strategies for Teaching, Counseling, and Parent Involvement*, for an extensive discussion of this model.

FIGURE 10.5 A model for clarifying expectations and procedures as a means for mainstreaming or readmitting the behavior-problem student[a]

Step 1: Teacher lists the problems as she or he perceives them.
  a. problems should be stated in terms of specific observable behaviors
  b. if possible, data should be collected
    (1) data help determine if the behavior requires intervention
    (2) data provide a base from which to determine if an intervention is effective
Step 2: Teacher lists expectations.
  a. stated positively
  b. includes 1–5 goals
  c. goals are observable and measurable
  d. goals include the minimum level of acceptable behavior
Step 3: Teacher lists what she or he is willing to do in order to enhance the likelihood that the expectations can be met.
Step 4: Student lists the problems as he or she perceives them.
  a. problems should be stated in terms of specific observable behaviors
Step 5: Student examines the teacher's list of problems and determines what behaviors do in fact occur and create a problem.
Step 6: Student examines the teacher's list of expectations and indicates those which he or she can and cannot meet.
Step 7: The student lists what he or she needs in the class in order to meet the teacher's expectations.
  a. needs must be stated in terms of specific observable behaviors
  b. stated positively
  c. include 1–5 needs
  d. include the minimum level of acceptable behavior

Step 8:   Student lists what he or she is willing to do in order to enhance the likelihood that the teacher's expectations can be met.
Step 9:   Teacher examines the student's statements about:
    a. which teacher expectations can be met
    b. what needs the student has
    c. what the student is willing do to
Step 10:   Student and teacher meet and develop a plan stating each party's responsibilities.
    a. responsibilities are listed in terms of specific observable behaviors
    b. responsibilities are stated positively
    c. responsibilities include a mimimum level of acceptable behavior
Step 11:   Teacher and student develop a safety-net plan.
    a. plan lists what each party will do if one believes the other has violated the agreement
Step 12:   Evaluation
    a. includes periodic conferences to examine the program's progress
    b. includes specific data collection when possible

---

[a]From Vernon F. Jones, *Adolescents with Behavior Problems: Strategies for Teaching, Counseling, and Parent Involvement.* © 1980. Reprinted by permission of Allyn and Bacon, Inc.

Class Meetings

Class meetings allow both teacher and students to resolve problems openly and before they become major issues that negatively affect learning. Whenever people live close together for numerous hours every day, it is mandatory that time be taken to openly resolve minor conflicts. Like an automobile engine that may appear to run smoothly but will suddenly boil over unless properly lubricated, classrooms require proper maintenance checks and minor tune-ups. When implemented in a positive, supportive atmosphere, class meetings serve as the lubricant for a smoothly running classroom.

Class meetings are an integral part of a program designed to involve students in solving their own problems. By implementing these meetings, we clearly acknowledge our respect for students' ability to solve their own problems. Class meetings not only support the use of individual problem-solving conferences but can also provide students with opportunities for improving their social and problem-solving skills. When a youngster is positively reinforced for a behavior, another student is more likely to model the behavior (Bandura, 1968; Kazdin, 1973). Class meetings provide a setting in which this type of positive modeling can be encouraged.

Parents and educators frequently state that schools should do more to teach students to be responsible. Teachers often bemoan the fact that students cannot take responsibility for their own learning and behavior. This situation will not and cannot be changed unless students are meaningfully and consistently involved in monitoring their own behavior and solving their own problems. Responsible problem solving is as much a teachable skill as is math or reading, but it will not be learned unless we take time to thoughtfully and skillfully facilitate the learning of the skills.

The use of class meetings will vary with grade level. The ideas presented in the following section are most appropriate for relatively self-contained classrooms in which teachers have major responsibility for the social and academic skill development of twenty-five to thirty-five students. Class meetings can also be an important component in middle and high school classrooms. Because students at this age spend less time with one group of students, however, and are more sensitive to peer responses, it is generally best to focus on instructional or behavioral matters affecting the entire class, while handling individual student problems in private meetings with the teacher and one or a few students. Class meetings will generally be held less often in secondary classrooms and the agenda will normally be presented by the teacher. Students can be encouraged, though, to bring problems to our attention and request that the problem be discussed by the class.

General Guidelines for Implementing a Class Meeting

The first step in implementing class meetings is to discuss the concept with students. Students should be informed that class meetings will provide them with an opportunity to discuss things they like about the class as well as things that may need to be changed in order for the class to run more smoothly. We can ask students to develop their own list of reasons meetings are important. It is important now for us to display enthusiasm and express interest in holding class meetings.

Once students have discussed why class meetings are helpful and are excited about holding their first meeting, we should present the general guidelines for class meetings. You may add your own guidelines, but we have found the following guidelines to be useful for elementary and middle school class meetings.

1. Class meetings will be held in a tight circle with all participants (including the teacher) seated in the circle. The circle must not be too large or it will detract from students' involvement and encourage off-task behavior.
2. All problems relating to the class as a group can be discussed. Problems between two or three individuals, however, will be resolved outside the class meeting unless this problem has an effect on the class.
3. An agenda will be created prior to every class meeting. The agenda is created by students writing the topic on the chalkboard. Students must sign their name behind the agenda item. (If the children cannot write, they can tell us the item and we can place it on the board.) The items will be discussed in the order in which they appear on the board. If an agenda

item no longer applies when the meeting is held, however, it will be scratched from the list.

4. Discussions during class meetings are always directed toward arriving at a solution that is not a punishment. The goal of class meetings is to find positive solutions to problems and not to criticize people or occurrences in the classroom.

5. If an individual student's behavior is listed on the agenda, the item will not be discussed without the student's permission. If the student agrees to have his or her behavior discussed, we should emphasize that the goal of the meeting is to help the student. We must be sure that students' statements focus on the youngster's behavior and are presented as "I" messages rather than judgmental statements about the youngster or his or her behavior. The focus should always be on providing the student with sensitive, thoughtful feedback and positive suggestions for altering his or her behavior.

Students should be informed that several options are available to those who choose not to have their behavior discussed at a class meeting. First, the student may leave the room while the other students attempt to devise an approach for helping the student. We may then wish to tape- record the discussion and share it with the student during an individual conference. Second, the student may choose to discuss the problem with us and a small group of concerned students. With the student's permission the results of this discussion can be shared with the entire class at the next class meeting. Finally, the student can discuss the problem with us and design a plan for alleviating the problem.

6. Students' responsibilities during class meetings include: (1) raising hands and being called on to speak, (2) listening to the speaker and not talking while someone else is speaking, (3) staying on the topic until it has been completed, and (4) being involved by sharing ideas that will help the group.

7. The teacher will initially serve as facilitator for the class meetings.

Meeting frequency and length.   It is best to hold class meetings whenever the agenda indicates that a meeting is necessary. Students should be assisted in listing only issues that are important to the smooth functioning of the classroom. Nevertheless, it is possible that a class meeting may be held every day. Because unresolved issues will only create problems that will significantly detract from students' learning, time spent in class meetings is usually rewarded with increased on-task behavior and the associated academic gains. A class meeting should be held at least once a week regardless of whether an agenda exists. A weekly meeting is necessary to maintain students' interest and skills as well as to reinforce the concept that the group is a valuable source of ideas and solutions. If no agenda exists, we can involve the class in a discussion of the positive aspects of the week. Similarly, we may wish to instigate a positive sharing activity and praise the class for having a positive, problem-free week.

The length of class meetings will vary according to the students' attention spans, but most primary-grade teachers find that their meetings can last between ten and thirty minutes, and intermediate-grade teachers find between thirty and forty-five minutes optimal. Middle school teachers or specialists in elementary schools who meet with a class five hours or less a week often choose to hold class meetings on a bi-weekly basis or limit weekly meetings to fifteen minutes so that meetings will not take up a significant portion of instructional time.

Starting class meetings.   Begin the first class meeting by reviewing the purpose and general guidelines for class meetings.

During the initial meetings it is very important to carefully monitor students' behavior to ensure that general procedures and responsibilities are followed so that meetings run smoothly and students develop good habits. In order to ensure that initial meetings are viewed as positive and useful, ensure that each agenda item is clearly resolved. Do so by asking several students to paraphrase the solution and ask for the group's commitment to carry out any plans that are developed. You may even initially wish to record each decision and post it in a prominent place in the room so that the class is reminded of their decision. A positive feeling can also be enhanced by closing each meeting on a positive note. You can do so by asking each student to state one nice thing that has happened to them or that they did for someone since the last meeting. Similarly, the group can be asked to say one nice thing about each member of the group.

Reinforce the value of students' solutions by beginning each meeting with a discussion on the results of solutions developed at the previous meeting. Unless students feel that their solutions are useful, they will understandably soon lose interest in class meetings. Furthermore, because class meetings are designed to teach problem-solving skills, it is important to reinforce students' successful efforts, analyze their failures, and help them develop increasingly effective solutions.

Increasing students' involvement in class meetings.   Because a major goal in implementing class meetings is to teach students skills involved in functioning effectively in a problem-solving group, it is desirable to gradually increase their responsibility for facilitating class meetings. It is difficult to do with primary-grade children, but third-grade students can be taught to run their own class meetings. We have found that these steps provide a successful approach to having students take over the class meeting:

1.   After leading approximately ten class meetings, present students with a handout describing the major functions a leader serves when facilitating a group meeting (Figure 10.6). Discuss each of the functions and behaviors with the class and inform them that they will soon be asked to lead their own meetings by having students serve these important functions.

FIGURE 10.6   Class-meeting jobs

Discussion Leader
1.   Make sure everyone is comfortable and all distracting things are out of the way.
2.   Make sure everyone can see all others in the circle.
3.   Give the speaker time to get his or her point across.
4.   Give the speaker a nod or a smile.
5.   Ask clarifying questions:
     a.   Are you saying that. . . ?
     b.   Do you feel that. . . ?
6.   Summarize:
     a.   Is there anything else you would like to say?
     b.   Would someone briefly summarize what has been said?

Task Observer
1.   Make sure the task gets finished on time.
2.   Watch the time.
3.   Make suggestions of alternatives to solve the problem.
4.   Point out behaviors that don't help in solving a problem.
5.   Listen carefully and understand what the discussion leader is doing.
6.   Understand the agenda and call out each agenda item.

Behavior and Feeling Observer
1.   How did this discussion make you feel?
2.   What could we do now? What might help us?
3.   Was anything asked that caused you _____ (name of person) to be concerned?
     Can you tell us what it was and how you felt about it?
4.   _____ (person's name) you usually help us out. Do you have any ideas for this problem?
5.   Has anyone thought of new ideas for improving our discussions?
6.   How many of you feel that the discussion was of value to you? Why?

---

2.   Introduce an agenda item or classroom problem. While the class discusses this situation, point out and define each intervention you make. Because you continue to serve all three functions, the discussion will be interrupted on numerous occasions. Students are usually excited about learning the new skills, however, and enjoy your instructional interventions.
3.   After running three or four actual class meetings by consistently pointing out the function being served by each intervention, meet with and teach one student the role of discussion leader. At the next meeting this student serves as the discussion leader while you maintain the other

roles. Prior to the following meeting you meet with another student who learns the role of task observer. At the next meeting the student serves this function. Following this meeting, you instruct a third student in the role of behavior and feeling observer, and at the following meeting you become a group member who abides by the group responsibilities while the students run the meeting.

4.   Each student should function in a role for five or six meetings so that he or she can master the skills associated with the role and effectively model it for other students. If a student has difficulty with a role, take time between meetings to instruct the student in the skills associated with the role. Providing students with this type of experience requires a small amount of time and considerable restraint and patience, but students respond to their new skills by becoming more positive, productive class members. Indeed, behavior-problem children often respond especially well, for they gain self-esteem and peer acceptance when serving as productive participants in class meetings.

Examples of problems resolved during class meetings.   The two problems described in the following paragraphs were solved during class meetings held in a fourth-grade classroom. They show the types of problems that can be solved in class meetings and the manner in which problem solving occurs.

The first problem occurred because the class was having difficulty lining up to enter the building following recess and lunch. Consequently, the class was nearly always the last one allowed to enter the school. As the students discussed the problem it became clear that the trouble occurred at the end of the line. Because a line leader (a classroom job) helped to remind students near the front of the line to settle down, problems seldom occurred among students near the front. After discussing several suggestions, the class decided to establish the job of second line leader for the end of the line. The students agreed to set aside several minutes following the next four recess periods to discuss how their solution was working. The discussions indicated that it was working well and the students decided to maintain the new position of line leader. They appeared pleased with both their solution and the subsequent improvement in their behavior.

You may wonder what would happen if a line leader became domineering. First, this is less likely to happen when students determine that the job is necessary, agree to respond positively to the line leader's reminders, and elect the person who will serve as line leader. If a problem does arise, however, a student can simply place the issue on the agenda for discussion at the next class meeting.

The second example occurred in a class meeting held two months after the beginning of school. Several students placed a classmate's eating habits on the agenda for a class meeting. When asked whether he would be willing to allow the class to discuss the topic, the boy consented. The meeting began with several students stating that even though they had politely asked the boy not to mix his food together, play with his food, and put it into his milk carton, he continued this behavior. The teacher asked whether any other students were bothered by Jim's behavior and several students sent Jim "I" messages about their reaction to his lunchroom manners. The teacher then asked Jim how he felt about the problem. He stated that he felt bad because he did not realize that so many students were bothered by his behavior. He indicated that he would try to change his behavior. The students then agreed to show their appreciation if he would eat more neatly. The following day after lunch several students raised their hands and reported that Jim had been very neat at lunch and that they appreciated the change. Jim's manners remained improved and at the next class meeting students again shared their appreciation. The students did not complain about Jim's eating habits for the remainder of the school year. The clear but thoughtfully presented information from his peers was adequate input to change Jim's behavior.

ACTIVITY 10.2 Assessing your classroom meetings

If you currently employ class meetings, complete these evaluation items. If you do not currently employ class meetings, use the general guidelines presented above to implement class meetings in your classroom. Hold at least five class meetings before evaluating the results.

List two classroom problems that have been positively resolved using this approach.
List two ways in which class meetings have helped to improve students' attitudes or behavior in your classroom.
Write a brief statement about how your students have responded to or feel about class meetings.
Write a brief statement about your reactions to class meetings.
List two problems you see associated with class meetings.
List two things you could do to improve your class meetings.
If you are having difficulty with class meetings, ask a colleague who uses them effectively to observe at least one meeting and give you suggestions.

RECOMMENDED READING

Dreikurs, R., Grunwald, B., & Pepper, F. (1982). *Maintaining sanity in the classroom: Classroom management techniques* (2nd ed.). New York: Harper and Row.

Duke, D., & Meckel, A. (1984). *Teacher's Guide to Classroom Management.* New York: Random House.

Fagan, S., Long, N., & Stevens, D. (1975). *Teaching children self-control: Preventing emotional and learning problems in the elementary school.* Columbus, Ohio: Charles Merrill.

Glasser, W. (1965). *Reality therapy.* New York: Harper and Row.

Glasser, W. (1969). *Schools without failure.* New York: Harper and Row.

Gordon, T. (1974). *T.E.T.: Teacher effectiveness training.* New York: Wyden.

Jones, V. (1980). *Adolescents with behavior problems: Strategies for teaching, counseling, and parent involvement.* Boston: Allyn and Bacon.

Knause, W. (1974). *Rational-emotive education: A manual for elementary school teachers.* New York: Institute for Rational Living.

Kraft, A. (1975). *The living classroom: Putting humanistic education into practice.* New York: Harper and Row.

Maple, F. (1977). *Shared decision making.* Beverly Hills, Calif.: Sage.

O'Leary, D., & Wilson, G. (1975). *Behavior therapy: Application and outcome.* Englewood Cliffs, N.J.: Prentice-Hall.

Wood, M. (1975). *Developmental therapy.* Baltimore: University Park Press.

CHAPTER 11

Behavioristic Management Procedures

The classroom teacher is the most powerful influence in any classroom. One reason for this is that the teacher has such direct control of the antecedents and consequences that precede and follow child behavior... Further, the more deviant and disruptive a child's behavior, the more likely it is that reinforcement and punishment will be required to effectively change the child's overall behavior.

Hill Walker, (1979),
The Acting-Out Child: Coping with Classroom Disruption

Students occasionally need highly structured programs to help them change specific behaviors. A few students require our continuing efforts to help them acquire and demonstrate acceptable behavior. We cannot be expected to spend large amounts of time implementing behavior-change programs, but to be effective, we must be able to implement behavior-management methods that have proven effective in the classroom. When implemented in classroom settings characterized by supportive interpersonal relationships and instruction matched to students' needs, these methods frequently have dramatic effects on students' behavior.

The first response to unproductive student behavior should be to examine the learning environment and attempt to alter the student's behavior by creating an environment that more effectively meets the students' personal and learning needs. When children behave unproductively in positive learning environments, adults should first help them examine their behavior and solve their problems. Unfortunately, a few children continue to behave in ways that harm themselves and others despite our efforts to create positive learning environments and effectively employ problem-solving strategies. These children require special assistance in controlling their behavior so that they can take advantage of the positive school environment that has been created for them.

Public Law 94–142, with its emphasis on mainstreaming exceptional children, combined with the fact that many children come from families that are experiencing serious turmoil or adjustment problems, has created a situation in which teachers are faced with an increasing number of children who require considerable help in developing appropriate behaviors. Therefore, we need the skills described in this chapter. Teachers should not, however, use these methods unless they have first created a classroom in which all students are accepted by the teacher and their peers, classroom rules and procedures have been carefully taught and consistently monitored, effective instructional methods are being employed, and students are involved in interesting work at which they can succeed. Employing behavioristic interventions to manipulate students into behaving docilely in an environment that does not meet their personal-psychological and academic needs is morally wrong. Employing behavioristic interventions to help students adjust to a positive learning environment, on the other hand, is an important part of being a competent teacher.

We begin this chapter with a brief presentation of the key assumptions associated with behavior modification and a discussion of the advantages and disadvantages of using behavioristic methods. In the remainder of the chapter we offer specific techniques for collecting and recording data, involving young people in monitoring their own behavior, writing contracts with pupils, and involving parents in a program to change their youngster's behavior.

BEHAVIOR MANAGEMENT IN PERSPECTIVE

Behavioristic interventions have, in many ways, been misunderstood by teachers. On the one hand, some teachers have viewed behavioristic methods as a complex, time-consuming approach that nevertheless held the answer to all their discipline problems. Conversely, many teachers have viewed behaviorism as a manipulative, overly repressive approach to working with students. As we often find, the answer lies somewhere between these extremes. Behavioristic methods cannot and should not solve all discipline problems. There is no substitute for effective teaching in a caring environment. Behaviorism, though, is also not necessarily a mechanistic, manipulative science. Rather, it can be used to help teachers better understand students' behavior and improve it by applying consistent positive and logical consequences to students' behavior. Furthermore, many behavioristic interventions are relatively simple and can be applied quickly and comfortably in a classroom setting.

Keep in mind that the methods described in this chapter need not, and, indeed, should not be employed with most students. Most teachers will find that at any given time these methods will be used with only 5 to 10 percent of their students. Moreover, most teachers indicate that these techniques are extremely helpful in assisting students with serious or persistent discipline problems to positively alter their behavior. The time spent in developing an effective behavioristic intervention is almost always repaid many times over by reduction in the student's disruptive behavior.

Basic Assumptions Underlying Behavioristic Interventions

Behaviorism is really more a rationale and a methodology than a specific set of procedures. It is based on examining specific data and applying experimentally validated procedures in order to alter behavior. Quite simply, behaviorism is a scientific approach to changing behavior. This approach is based on three major assumptions: (1) behavior is influenced by the consequences following the behavior; (2) behavior-change programs must be focused on specific, observable behavior; and (3) data collection is necessary in order to thoughtfully and systematically alter behavior.

Behavior Is Influenced by the Consequences Following the Behavior

Behaviorists acknowledge the importance of antecedent conditions (the stimulus), but they emphasize the consequences of a behavior. We can see this emphasis in three basic rules of behaviorism that have been developed through careful studies of human behavior: (1) a behavior that is followed immediately by a reward will occur more frequently, (2) a behavior will be extinguished when it is no longer reinforced, and (3) a behavior followed closely by a punishing consequence will occur less often. Although behavioristic interventions emphasize changing behavior by systematically influencing the rewards or punishments that follow a behavior, behaviorists do not ignore antecedent or stimulus conditions. Students cannot be reinforced for producing a behavior unless they possess the ability to emit the behavior. Therefore, we must create positive environments in which students will risk trying new behaviors, and must systematically provide children with assistance in gradually developing new skills.

Behavior-Change Programs Must Focus on Specific, Observable Behavior

If we wish to thoughtfully and systematically help students develop new skills or eliminate undesired behaviors, we must deal with specific, observable behavior. It is helpful to neither teacher nor student to state that the student is disruptive and incorrigible. It is much more helpful if we state that the student will learn more and be better liked by his or her peers if he or she can reduce the number of times he or she interrupts the teacher and other students and can decrease the number of times he or she hits others. Focusing on observable behavior that can be counted is the first step in developing a program for systematically altering a student's behavior.

Data Collection Is Necessary in Order to Thoughtfully and Systematically Alter Behavior

It is surprising that this basic approach is so often criticized by teachers who state that data collection is too time consuming. Effective teachers base their academic instructional program on pre-tests that indicate the specific skills their students possess. This step is followed by activities specifically designed to develop new skills. Finally, another test is given or an observation is made to determine how well the skill has been learned and what activities should follow. Collecting data on students' behavior serves a similar purpose. It allows us to determine whether a problem exists, how serious the problem is, and whether the interventions being employed are significantly affecting the behavior. When teachers fail to collect some form of data, they often fail to accurately assess a student's behavior. Without data, we cannot objectively determine whether a student's behavior is in reality significantly different from that of his or her peers', or what behavior most needs changing.

Data collection also allows us to evaluate a treatment designed to change a student's behavior. Unless we collect data, it is easy to become frustrated when a new program or intervention does not bring about an immediate change in the behavior. By collecting data, we can notice small but significant changes in a student's behavior. Because behaviors often change slowly, we may misinterpret the effect of our interventions. An excellent example is found in the criticism trap (Becker, Engelmann, & Thomas, 1975): Teachers employ criticism or reprimands because these cause an immediate, although usually temporary, change in students' behavior. In the long run, however, the negative behavior often increases because it is reinforced by the teacher's attention. Collecting and analyzing data can prevent teachers from continuing an ineffective behavior-change strategy or terminating an approach that is having significant but gradual success.

Perhaps the most systematic and data-based attempt to provide teachers with specific alternatives to specific types of disruptive or disfunctional student behavior was conducted by Robert Spaulding (1982, 1983). Based on observations of 1,066 K–12 students and several hundred effective teachers, Spaulding identified eight common styles of unproductive student behavior and seven treatment methods. Spaulding then described specific treatment approaches that were most effective with each of the eight types of unproductive student behavior.

Advantages of Behavioristic Interventions

There are several advantages to employing behavioristic interventions to alter students' behavior. First, some youngsters need special assistance in controlling their behavior. Anyone who has worked extensively in special education or child psychotherapy is aware that a few youngsters do not initially respond to the types of interventions that are effective in helping most children change their behaviors. Although the research suffers from failure to examine the quality of the teacher–student relationship, it does indicate that some children do not respond to adults' praise (Sgan, 1967; Thomas, Becker, & Armstrong, 1968; Walker, Hops, Greenwood, Todd, & Garrett, 1977). Similarly, though the studies have examined the presentation of rules but not students' involvement in the development or monitoring of these rules, research suggests that some students do not change their behavior when presented with rules (Madsen, Becker, & Thomas, 1968; O'Leary, Becker, Evans, & Saudargas, 1969). Therefore, research suggests that there are situations in which it is necessary to provide structured, concrete reinforcement or a systematic monitoring of behavior to help some youngsters change their behavior.

A second advantage of behavioristic interventions is that extensive research clearly demonstrates these interventions can be effective. Research shows that, when systematically applied, reinforcers ranging from simple teacher praise (Hall, Lund, & Jackson, 1968) to a combination of praise, token reinforcers, and response cost (Walker, Hops, & Fiegenbaum, 1976) can effectively alter students' behavior.

Third, although behavioristic intervention does require our time and effort, it frequently requires less time than we anticipate and less time than we currently spend attempting to control the student's behavior. Furthermore, the behavioristic intervention may have a positive effect on other students in the classroom (Drabman & Lahey, 1974; Kazdin, 1973), whereas reprimands often create a negative ripple effect that increases classroom disruption (Kounin, 1970).

Teachers who are especially worried about students' self-concepts and peer relationships often state that behavioristic interventions isolate and alienate children, but research (Drabman & Lahey, 1974) suggests that, by helping students improve their behaviors, behavioristic treatment programs may improve students' relationships with their peers.

Disadvantages of Behavioristic Interventions

The major disadvantage associated with behavioristic interventions is that, because the focus is on changing students' behavior by systematically manipulating consequences, teachers are less likely to examine their own teaching methods or other classroom factors as possible causes of students' unproductive behavior.

One of us recalls a teacher who referred seventeen of her students for special assistance because they were emotionally disturbed. Even though students were placed in classes randomly, only one student from the adjacent classroom was referred. Observations indicated that the referred children were indeed significantly more active and aggressive toward their peers than their counterparts across the hall. The observations suggested, however, that the frequency and intensity of the teacher's critical statements to students was a major factor influencing the students' behavior. Before we attempt to modify students' behavior with behavioristic methods, we should carefully examine how extensively our own teaching strategies and style of interacting with students are negatively affecting their behavior.

A second disadvantage to behavioristic strategies for changing students' behaviors is that, except for self-management interventions, behavioristic approaches emphasize external controls. This emphasis is in opposition to children's need for a sense of competence and power and dramatically conflicts with adolescents' desire to be autonomous. The use of external rewards also tends to reinforce lower levels of moral development (Kohlberg, 1970). Therefore, particularly when working with adolescents, overemphasis on behavioristic methods may detract from the important developmental task of understanding others' perspectives and learning to make decisions based on the effect one's behavior has both on oneself and on others (Selman, 1980). Working with youngsters who are experiencing serious behavior problems can be viewed as a reparenting process. These young people have not learned the social skills or acquired the positive feelings about themselves that enable them to function effectively. Like caring, effective parents, adults who work with these students need to provide them with love, self-respect, and skills in controlling their own environment. Although this may need to be supplemented by behavioristic interventions aimed at controlling the students' behavior, these interventions should never become the major treatment program. If emphasis on behavioristic interventions sidetracks us from incorporating a wide range of less-restrictive, less control-oriented treatment interventions that help students to accomplish important developmental tasks, behaviorism can have a negative effect upon students' ability to become competent and positive individuals.

A final disadvantage associated with behavioristic interventions is that they may place a negative connotation upon the very goal they are intended to make more desirable. Several studies have found that when people are offered an extrinsic reward for performing a task they view as interesting, the task soon becomes perceived as less interesting and on-task behavior and task performance decrease (Deci, 1971, 1972; Lepper & Greene, 1975). Consequently, whenever possible, we should employ the least externally control-oriented approach to changing a student's behavior. In the long run this restraint will encourage a greater sense of personal competence and a more internalized commitment to the values inherent in the desired behaviors.

Assertive Discipline

Assertive Discipline is a good example of how behavioristic methods can be misused. The technique appeared in the mid-1970s. It is a classroom-management approach that provides teachers with clear authority. The teacher states nonnegotiable rules to students and informs them that violation of these rules will result in clear, negative consequences. When a student disobeys a rule, his or her name is written on the board. If the student misbehaves again, a check is placed behind the student's name, indicating that he or she must stay after school for fifteen minutes. A second check means thirty minutes after school. A third check means thirty minutes after school and a call home. A fourth check involves removal from the room and a visit to a building administrator. In cases of serious misconduct, a *severe clause* is invoked and the student goes immediately to the office (Canter, 1976). Rewards for appropriate student behavior are also encouraged. The teacher might put a marble in a jar whenever he or she observes the entire class on task. When the jar is filled, the class receives a special activity as a reward.

Assertive Discipline has been used widely on the West Coast and is increasingly popular nationwide. It appeals to many teachers because it is easily implemented and places the teacher clearly in control. Administrators have supported the program because it requires minimal teacher training and provides a format that can be readily implemented by an entire staff.

We have worked with several large school districts and several hundred teachers who have implemented Assertive Discipline. Though the approach was initially well received, these districts have recently moved away from it. Many teachers are frustrated because problem students seem to be relatively unaffected by the procedures, and students who do not need such repressive methods tend to find the method insulting or anxiety provoking. Our own concern is that too frequently the method creates a "sit down, shut up, or get out" philosophy in classrooms where teaching methods are failing to meet students' basic personal and academic needs. Too often teachers use the Assertive Discipline procedures rather than examining their own teaching methods to consider how to prevent disruptive behavior. This issue is outlined by Sloane, Buckholdt, Jenson, and Crandall (1979) in discussing the use of token economies and similar behavioristic interventions:

> For relatively typical students the existence of problems suggests some failure in the current teaching procedures that can be remedied by the use of social reinforcement . . . the design of teaching tasks . . . or the pacing, planning, scheduling, or manner of presentation. . . . Inadequate diagnosis and prescription . . . may need attention. Adding a powerful reinforcement system may prevent the teacher from correcting these kinds of basic teaching deficiencies. Student gains are unlikely to be as great as they would be if other problems are first corrected. [p. 209]

Fortunately, with the increased emphasis on effective schools, effective teaching, and the teacher as a professionally informed decision maker, districts have begun providing teachers with more effective instructional and group-management methods rather than behavior-control strategies.

It is interesting that, unlike teacher effectiveness, no research has been provided to support the Assertive Discipline model. A review of the literature in 1984 showed only three articles on the subject, all in popular teachers' magazines and focused on selling or critiquing the method rather than reporting results. Popular books on classroom management do allude to the model (Duke & Meckel, 1984; Charles, 1981), but presentations at scholarly conventions and reviews of the research (Brophy, 1982; Good, 1983) fail to discuss this procedure. Perhaps most important, we strongly agree with the researcher, Robert Spaulding:

> . . . a classroom management scheme that relies on strict teacher direction and a high degree of structure deprives reliable and responsible students of opportunities to learn self-management and problem-solving skills and to exercise their creativity and initiative. [Spaulding, 1983, p. 48]

The real problem with Assertive Discipline is that it has been touted as a classwide management scheme. The approach is appropriate with individual students after all efforts at environmental change, problem solving, and individual contracting using positive reinforcers have failed.

DATA COLLECTION

As we have mentioned, there are numerous benefits to collecting data on students' behavior. Data enable us to determine whether a problem exists, how serious it is, and the effectiveness of any attempts to alter the behavior. Data also help us effectively and professionally discuss students' problems with parents and colleagues. Finally, clearly displayed data motivate students to change their behavior.

Despite the multiple advantages of collecting data, teachers frequently indicate that data collection is too complex and too time consuming to be employed in the classroom. In this section we will attempt to dispel these myths by describing the types of data we can collect and presenting practical methods for collecting data in the classroom.

Defining Students' Behavior

Teachers often define students' behavior in very general terms. A teacher may state that a student acts out or is unmotivated. These descriptions express the teacher's concern and suggest that a problem may exist, but they do not provide the teacher, student, parent, or consultant with any indication of the specific problem or the behaviors the teacher wants the student to change. Therefore, the first step in collecting data is to define the behavior in specific, observable terms. A specific behavioral description about an "angry" youngster might include the fact that the youngster hits other students or will not obey the teacher's requests. Similarly, behavioral descriptions about an "unmotivated" pupil might include the fact that the youngster turns in only 15 percent of his or her assignments or is on-task only 20 percent of the time during seatwork. In order to reinforce this concept, take a minute to complete activity 11.1.

ACTIVITY 11.1   Clearly defining students' behavior

For each of the five adjectives listed in the left-hand column, write three specific, observable student behaviors that might be displayed by a student described by the adjective.

General descriptor	Specific behavioral descriptor
Angry	1. 2. 3.
Unmotivated	1. 2. 3.
Hyperactive	1. 2. 3.
Uncooperative	1. 2. 3.
Lacks social skills	1. 2. 3.

When we consider collecting data on students' behavior, it is helpful to decide whether the behavior is discrete or continuous. Discrete behavior can be easily counted, and its occurrence is more important than its duration. The number of assignments handed in by a student is a discrete behavior. Likewise, though the behavior may last for a time, handraising or talk-out behavior can be defined as discrete behavior because it can be counted and we generally care more about its occurrence than its duration.

Continuous behavior is difficult to count, and the duration of the behavior is the important factor. Out-of-seat and on-task behavior are examples of continuous behavior. We can count the number of times a student leaves his or her seat, but the important factor is the amount of time the student is actually out of his or her seat. Similarly, we can count the number of times a student is off-task, but it would be a difficult chore and the data would not be very useful. It would be much more useful to know the percentage of time the student was on-task during a lesson. To determine your understanding of this concept, complete Activity 11.2.

ACTIVITY 11.2   Discriminating between discrete and continuous behavior

Determine whether each of the ten behaviors listed is a discrete or continuous behavior. Indicate your choice by placing an X under the appropriate word in the right-hand column.

	Behavior	Discrete	Continuous
Example:	On-task		X
	sharpens pencil		
	requests to go to the bathroom		
	talks out without raising hand		
	sits with chair tilted backward		
	Out-of-seat		
	refuses to obey teacher's request		
	spends time alone on playground		
	scratches arm while sitting at desk		
	hits other children		
	talks to other students during seatwork		

Some behaviors can be described as either discrete or continuous. In Activity 11.2, it would be possible to either count the number of times a student sharpened a pencil during a two-hour period (discrete behavior) or to record the number of minutes the student was out of his or her seat while sharpening the pencil (continuous behavior). In a situation such as this we should decide what aspect of the behavior is causing the problem. If the out-of-seat behavior were creating a problem for us or the student or both, we would want to define the behavior as continuous. If the loud grinding of the pencil sharpener were the major problem, though, we would choose to focus on the actual number of times the student used the pencil sharpener.

Defining a behavior as discrete or continuous helps us determine how the behavior should be counted and recorded. Discrete behavior can be counted simply by making a tally each time the behavior occurs. Continuous behavior is monitored with a stopwatch or a time sample.

Tallying Discrete Behavior

Once a behavior has been clearly defined and labeled as discrete, we need to develop a method for tallying the behavior. We can keep a tally simply by placing a mark on a chart each time the student emits the behavior being counted. Depending upon where we will be when the behavior occurs and how frequently it occurs, this chart can be placed on our desk, carried on a clipboard, or placed on the student's desk. Figure 11.1 shows a typical form we might use for tallying behavior. For situations in which marking a tally on a sheet of paper can be distracting to us or students, we can record the behavior by carrying a golf counter and simply depressing the button each time the behavior occurs.

The only difficulty we may experience when attempting to count student behavior is that it is sometimes difficult to watch a student carefully enough to record every incidence of a behavior. Though somewhat less a problem when recording discrete behavior, it often becomes a major factor when collecting data on continuous behavior. In either case, teachers can request the assistance of parents, aides, or even of older students. Because behavioral data are usually associated with programs designed for extreme acting-out children, this process will be used sparingly and most teachers will have little difficulty obtaining assistance.

Discrete data gathering can be a simple tally, but it can also be expanded to incorporate information about the antecedent conditions that precipitated the behavior. When determining how often a student hits his or her peers, we might find it useful to know what occurs immediately prior to the student's striking a peer. Similarly, it might be useful to know the time of day when each incident occurs. Does it always occur late in the morning (perhaps the student does not eat breakfast and is especially irritable by late morning) or during a specific subject? Figure 11.2 presents a form we might use to record this type of information.

FIGURE 11.1   Form for monitoring discrete behavior

Behavior: Talks without raising hand   *Time:* 9:30–10:05

Activity: Social Studies

Tally				
Monday	*Tuesday*	*Wednesday*	*Thursday*	*Friday*

FIGURE 11.2   Form for monitoring environmental factors associated with students' behavior

Behavior: Hitting other students			Date: _____	
		Occurrences		
Time	Student hit	What occurred immediately before the hitting?	Recipient's reaction	Teacher's reaction

Time Sampling: Tallying Continuous Behavior

A time sample can be obtained by employing a time-interval approach in which the coder simply records what the student is doing at designated intervals. When monitoring on-task behavior the coder could employ a form such as that shown in Figure 11.3. The coder would simply look at the student every fifteen seconds and record his or her behavior.

This method can be employed when a stopwatch is not available, but it has numerous disadvantages compared to simply timing the student's behavior. Employing a time-interval method requires the coder to look at the student at exact time intervals, which is almost impossible for a teacher to do while helping other students. This method is also less accurate than using a stopwatch, for whatever the student is doing as the coder looks up is recorded as the behavior that occurred during the entire interval. Finally, a stopwatch is somewhat less obtrusive than a coder with a pad and pencil who makes a tally every ten or fifteen seconds.

A stopwatch can be used to record any continuous behavior. The teacher or coder simply records the starting and stopping time and the behavior to be monitored. If we wish to know the percentage of time a student is out of his or her seat, we simply start the stopwatch whenever the student leaves his or her seat and stop the watch when the student is seated. At the end of the observation period we have an immediate record of the behavior we were observing. This figure can then be recorded on a chart as time out of seat or translated into a percentage by dividing the time out of seat by the total observation time and multiplying by one hundred. Figure 11.4 presents a form we might use to rec-

FIGURE 11.3   Time sample form

Look at _____ every 15 seconds and mark whether he or she is on or off task. On-task behavior involves working on the class activity or seeking assistance by quietly raising his or her hand.

	On Task	Off Task
1		
2		
3		
4		
5		
6		
7		
8		
9		
10		
11		
12		
13		
14		
15		
16		
17		
18		
19		
20		

FIGURE 11.4   Form for monitoring continuous behavior

Behavior: Out-of-seat behavior   *Observation start time:*   10:20

                                      Observation stop time: 10:45

                                      Total observation time: 25 minutes

Activity: Language arts seatwork

Out-of-seat behavior time recorded on stopwatch: 10 minutes

                                                    22 seconds

Total seconds in observation (number of minutes × 60):   1500

Total seconds recorded (number of minutes × 60   622

+ number of seconds):

Percentage of time off task: $\dfrac{\text{number of seconds recorded}}{\text{total number of seconds}} \times 100$

$$= \frac{622}{1500} \times 100 = .41 \times 100 = 41\%$$

---

ord out-of-seat behavior and translate it into the percentage of time the student was out of his or her seat.

Classwide Data

When evaluating the effects of our instructional or management methods, we may want to collect data on the behavior of an entire group rather than one student. We can do so by having a colleague, principal, or parent complete a data-collection form such as that found in Figure 11.5. This form, developed by Jane Stallings (1983), can be used to provide information on the amount and type of off-task student behavior as well as the instructional activity occurring when each student was off-task. The data are collected by having the observer make a visual sweep of the classroom at designated intervals (usually every three or five minutes) and mark the appropriate symbol to describe the type of off-task behavior, the instructional activity in which the student was expected to be engaged, and the number of the sweep. If John was negatively interacting with another child during seatwork on sweep three, the coder would mark N/S/3. These data can be used to provide an off-task percentage with this formula:

$$\frac{\textit{Sum of number of students off task for each observation sweep}}{\text{Number of students} \times \text{Number of sweeps}}$$

This type of data enables us to determine how all students were behaving during various instructional activities.

FIGURE 11.5   Student's off-task chart

Teacher's name _____   Time _____

Date _____   Number of sweeps _____

Front of classroom

Sam	Jim	Alice	Roberto
Jack	Ursula	Naomi	Bob
Sarah	Elvin	Renaldo	Katie
Ryan	Alicia	Mary	Juan
Bill	Reggie	Steve	Lionel

Student off-task codes	Time sweep	Activity codes
		(*What students should be doing*)
S = Socializing	1, 2, 3,	S = Seatwork
U = Uninvolved	4, 5, 6,	O = Organizing
N = Negative peer interaction	7, 8, 9,	L = Listening
D = Other disruptive behavior	10	R = Oral reading
		Q = Question answering
		W = Waiting quietly

J. Stallings, *Staff Development and Administrative Support.* Copyright 1983 by the Stallings Teaching and Learning Institute, George Peabody College, Nashville, Tenn.

Recording Data

Recording data is a simple task, and students can be taught to record their own data. Data can be recorded using either a bar graph or a line graph. If all the observations took place in the same setting, we simply write the behavior being recorded on the vertical axis and the day or time when the observations occurred on the horizontal axis. The data are then recorded and a line is

FIGURE 11.6   Sample line graph

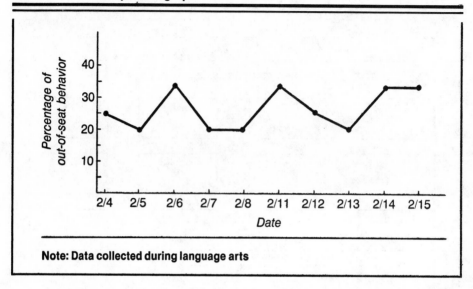

Note: Data collected during language arts

drawn to connect the points, or a bar graph is created. Figure 11.6 shows a teacher's record for percentage of out-of-seat behavior for ten days.

If we have collected data at different times of the day and during different activities, it is important to record this information so that the graph helps us determine whether the student's behavior is influenced by certain conditions. These data can be displayed by using a bar graph with different colors. The vertical axis again contains the behavior being recorded and the horizontal axis indicates the time interval or days. A code can be made to indicate the activity during which the behaviors occurred. Figure 11.7 is an example of data graphed in this manner.

One major advantage to collecting and displaying data is that it allows adults to determine whether their efforts to help a student are being successful. Therefore, the final ingredient in an effective data display is to include a record of any changes we have made to alter the student's behavior.

The most common procedure for recording our attempts to alter a student's behavior is to initially record the behavior for a time (often five days) during which no special intervention is made and we continue employing whatever approaches we have been using. The result is called baseline data and allows us to determine the effect our current method of handling classroom behavior has on the student. The next step is to implement a new approach to assist the student to change, and to record the behavior under the new conditions. The change in our approach and the subsequent student behavior can be recorded as shown in Figure 11.8. This figure presents a hypothetical case in which the teacher collected baseline data for five days, employed Glasser's model for two weeks, and then implemented a contract with the student.

FIGURE 11.7   Bar graph for recording data from observations occurring in different settings

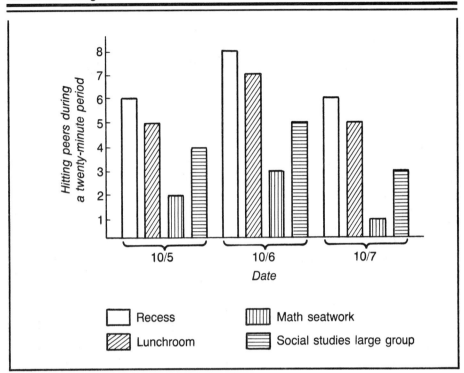

FIGURE 11.8   A complete data display

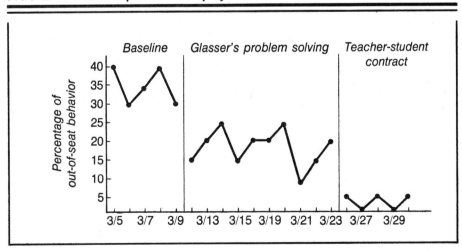

A major advantage associated with collecting data and developing con-cise data displays is that they help us determine when an intervention is nec-essary and how effectively a program is working. In addition, data clearly indicate to parents, administrators, and specialists that we are approaching the student's disruptive behavior in a conscientious and professional manner. This evidence increases parents' and administrators' willingness to accept the teacher's judgments and become involved in helping us work with the stu-dent. In an age characterized by increasing emphasis on accountability, col-lecting and displaying data is an important ingredient of effective teaching.

Practicing Data Collection

When asked to collect data on students' behavior, teachers frequently state that the advantages of possessing specific data are outweighed by the com-plexity of collecting them. The only way to fairly evaluate the payoffs and costs associated with collecting data is to attempt the procedure. Activity 11.3 offers a systematic approach to taking this step. When evaluating this proce-dure, keep in mind that, like most skills, data collection becomes easier and less time consuming with practice.

ACTIVITY 11.3   Practicing data collection

Select a student whose behavior in your classroom has been disruptive. Write a brief narrative statement about the extent of the student's behav-ior and its effect on the class.

After completing this statement, write a specific behavioral de-scription of the student's behavior. Categorize this behavior as discrete or continuous and write the appropriate term beside your description.

Choose a method for collecting data on the behavior and collect these data during a minimum of two one-half hour periods during which the student tends to frequently engage in the undesirable behavior.

Next, choose a student whose behavior is generally not a problem (do not choose a model student but merely an average student with few problems) and collect the same data on this student. If possible, collect the data simultaneously. If you cannot do so, collect the data during a similar activity and at the same time of day.

Record the data on a graph. Use a different color of line or bar for each student so that behaviors can be readily compared.

Based on your data, write a brief statement about the problem stu-dent's behavior.

Finally, complete these statements:

I learned that. . . .
I was surprised that. . . .
When I compared the first narrative statement to my last statement I
found that. . . .
One advantage to collecting data is. . . .

Comprehensive Data Collection

The methods discussed thus far help us pinpoint and record students' behavior. It is also helpful for us to thoughtfully and systematically analyze the classroom and school environment to consider why a student may be misbehaving. This twofold system of data collection and analysis is similar to that employed when diagnosing a student's academic deficiency. We first assess the quantitative deficit, then attempt to determine the specific areas in which deficits lie, and develop methods for alleviating the deficits.

An example of the advantage of systematic behavioral assessment appeared when one of our students presented a case study involving a physically aggressive fifth-grade girl. The teacher stated that the girl was involved in three aggressive attacks a week. To change this behavior, the teacher devised a contract that provided reinforcement to the student if she could have no aggressive attacks for three days.

We asked the teacher if she was aware of what environmental factors were eliciting the girl's outbursts. The teacher was also asked whether the outbursts occurred during the expected times; that is, when the student was involved in unstructured activities with her peers. When the teacher could not answer these questions, she was asked to complete a more comprehensive analysis of the girl's behavior (Figure 11.9).

The results showed that the girl's outbursts occurred during seatwork when the teacher was not available for assistance. The girl became frustrated, bothered other students while seeking help, was rebuked, and became aggressive. With this information, the teacher decided to help the girl develop a procedure for obtaining assistance. She found a student willing to assist the girl and taught the girl a phrase to use when asking for help. Data revealed that this intervention was much more effective than the contract had been.

SELF-MANAGEMENT

As we have discussed throughout this book, the approach that is most beneficial in helping students change their behavior is one that provides the greatest amount of student involvement and helps students develop new skills that can be transferred to other settings. The behavioristic strategies that best fulfill these criteria involve students in monitoring their own behavior. In addition to the problem-solving approaches discussed in Chapter 10, there are two basic approaches to helping students monitor and control behavior. The first method is to help them count and record their own behavior. A second approach is to implement cognitive-behavior therapy.

Self-monitoring

Students have a basic need to be viewed positively and to demonstrate their competence and power by controlling their own behavior. Often, however,

FIGURE 11.9   Analyzing environmental factors that influence students' behavior

Student _____
Date _____
Staff member _____

Part I   Student's misbehavior(s)
    1.   Describe misbehavior(s)
          a.
          b.
          c.
    2.   How frequent is each type of misbehavior?
          a.
          b.
          c.
    3.   What time of day does it occur?
          a.
          b.
          c.
    4.   In what physical surroundings?
          a.
          b.
          c.
    5.   With which peers or adults?
          a.
          b.
          c.
    6.   In what kinds of activities is student engaged before misbe-
          havior occurs?
          a.
          b.
          c.

Part II   Teacher (or other) actions
    1.   What do you do when student misbehaves?
          a.
          b.
          c.
    2.   How does student respond?
          a.
          b.
          c.
    3.   When are your actions most successful?
    4.   When are these actions least successful?

Part III   Student motivation
    1.   What responsibilities (assignments, tasks, or orders) does
          student fulfill?

2. What types of reinforcement (positive and negative) does student receive?
    a. positive (and/or encouragement)
    b. negative (and/or logical consequences)
3. How does student respond to reinforcement?
    a. positive (and/or encouragement)
    b. negative (and/or logical consequences)
4. How does student relate to the group (physical aggression, verbal aggression, passivity, or other behaviors)?

Part IV When student is not misbehaving
1. Describe positive behaviors.
    a.
    b.
    c.
2. How frequent is each type of positive behavior?
    a.
    b.
    c.
3. What time of day does each behavior occur?
    a.
    b.
    c.
4. In what physical surroundings?
    a.
    b.
    c.
5. With which peers or adults?
    a.
    b.
    c.
6. In what kinds of activities is student engaged before positive behavior occurs?
    a.
    b.
    c.

Part V Additional questions
1. What does student enjoy doing (hobbies or subjects)?
2. What does student do well (hobbies or subjects)?
3. Are there any reasons to suspect health or physical disabilities?

students are not aware of the extent of their unproductive behavior. Some youngsters have difficulty controlling their emotions and behaviors without the assistance of external cues (Patterson, 1971b). Involving students in collecting data on their own behavior can, in some instances, provide enough external structure to produce dramatic improvements in their behavior.

Students can be taught to record their own behavior (Anderson & Prawat, 1983). This procedure not only involves students in their own behavior-change program, but also significantly reduces the amount of time we must spend in collecting data. Furthermore, perhaps because self-monitoring helps to create an internalized locus of control, changes in behavior associated with this approach seem more likely to generalize both to other situations and to other behaviors (Johnson, 1970; Johnson & Martin, 1973).

Self-monitoring procedures have proven effective in a variety of settings and with both normal and exceptional children (McLaughlin & Gnagey, 1981). McKenzie and Rushal (1974) report that having youngsters record their behavior on a bulletin board was effective in improving the behaviors of those who were consistently late, absent, or uninvolved in activities at a swim club. Broden, Hall, and Mitts (1971) demonstrated that self-recording attending and nonattending behavior and receiving praise for improvement was an effective intervention with an eighth-grade girl who was failing history. The girl's attending behavior increased from 30 percent to 80 percent under this treatment condition. Hutzell, Platzek, and Logue (1974) reported similar success in reducing head jerking and distracting guttural vocal sounds in an eleven-year-old boy.

Procedures

When first instructing students in counting their own behavior, we must ensure that they can accurately describe the behavior. We can teach this skill by asking them to demonstrate the desirable and undesirable behaviors. The next step is to develop a method for tallying the data. Especially when working with young children, it is helpful to start by incorporating a visual display of the behavior being counted. A *countoon* can serve this purpose. A countoon includes a picture of the behavior being tallied and a place for the student to make a tally each time the behavior occurs. Figure 11.10 is an example of a countoon used to help a student become aware of how often he talks out without raising his hand. Older students may not be willing to make checks on a chart each time they emit inappropriate behaviors. A talented junior high school counselor who is a close friend of ours employs the form shown in Figure 11.11 to help students take more responsibility for their behavior.

Although most students will accurately monitor their own behavior after these two steps have been accomplished, seriously acting-out students will usually require more assistance. There are two additional steps that we can implement to encourage students to accurately count their own behavior.

We can start by reinforcing the student for obtaining data that closely match those we or another adult coder obtain. As they learn to accurately rec-

FIGURE 11.10 Countoon

COUNTOON

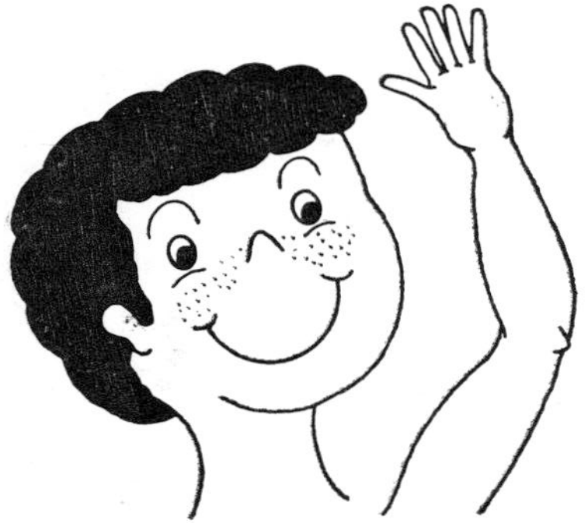

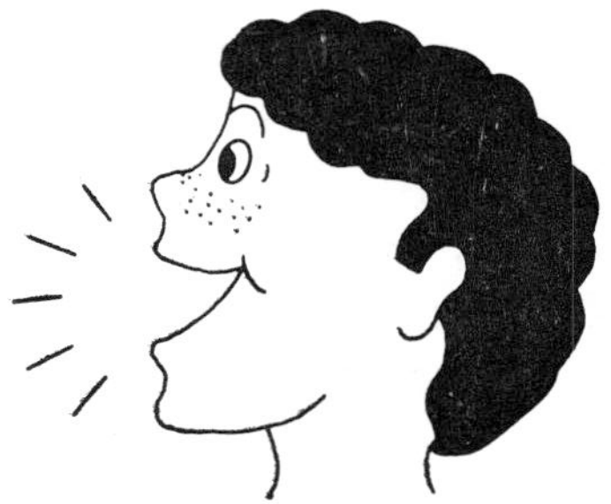

1	2	3	4	5	6	7	8	9	10
11	12	13	14	15	16	17	18	19	20
21	22	23	24	25	26	27	28	29	30
31	32	33	34	35	36	37	38	39	40
41	42	43	44	45	46	47	48	49	50

Count your hand raising

1	2	3	4	5	6	7	8	9	10
11	12	13	14	15	16	17	18	19	20
21	22	23	24	25	26	27	28	29	30
31	32	33	34	35	36	37	38	39	40
41	42	43	44	45	46	47	48	49	50

Count your talk outs

FIGURE 11.11   Student self-monitoring form

Student's Name ————————

Time	What the class is <u>supposed</u> to be doing	What good ol' (student's name) is doing . . . (+ or o)
9:55		
10:00		
10:05		
10:10		
10:15		
10:20		
10:25		
10:30		
10:35		

Teacher's signature

ord their behavior, reinforcement for accuracy can be replaced by rewarding decreases in the unproductive behavior. This procedure can be effective in reducing disruptive behavior in seriously acting-out children (Drabman, Spitalnik, & O'Leary, 1973).

Another procedure involves initially having the student receive reinforcement for improving behaviors that are being recorded by an adult. As the student's behavior improves, he or she can be allowed to monitor his or her own behavior and receive designated reinforcements for improved behavior. Finally, the reinforcement is withdrawn and the student simply receives praise for controlling and recording his or her behavior. Bolstad and Johnson (1972) demonstrated that this approach could be effectively employed with disruptive first- and second-grade children.

Regardless of the methods we employ to encourage students to accurately monitor their own behavior, the student must record his or her own data and the results must be placed where the student can refer to them. In a creative study in which emotionally disturbed junior high school students were taught to positively influence their teachers' behaviors, Gray, Graubard, and Rosenberg (1974) reported that students' involvement in collecting data was a major factor in the program's effectiveness. Youngsters who have experienced numerous failures are reinforced and motivated by data indicating that they are improving their behavior. Conversely, when these data are lacking, these students frequently become unmotivated and depressed, even though their efforts are producing meaningful results.

Case Study: Elementary

This study was conducted by a first-grade teacher who was confronted with a particularly difficult class in an inner-city school. Most of her students had been late registrants for kindergarten, and because of overcrowding, spent their kindergarten experience in an isolated room in the district's administrative office building. Consequently, the children arrived in first grade having had few interactions with older school children. In addition, their kindergarten class started nearly a month late and they had several teachers during the year. They were also generally a particularly immature, unskilled group, more than half living in broken homes. The following material is taken directly from the teacher's report of her study.

Many distractions within my classroom were caused by students who were not attending to my instructions. My students needed to learn to sit and work without talking, opening and closing their desks, walking to someone else's desk to talk, and so on. I decided to attempt a self-management technique, or a countoon, with my class. This group wanted to please me and be viewed positively by me, but they lacked the inner skills to control their behavior on their own. This technique would let them demonstrate their competence at monitoring and controlling their own behavior. I do not think they were aware of the extent of their off-task behavior. Some children have difficulty controlling their behavior without assistance from an external cue. When children are involved in collecting data on their own behavior, sometimes this act can provide enough external structure to produce dramatic results.

I started my study by collecting baseline data on five children in my group, to determine their off-task frequency. I chose five students who varied greatly in ability, behavior, background, and so forth. I recorded their behavior during seatwork three times at ten-minute intervals, and the results (Figure 11.12) showed that during a ten-minute interval, the frequency of off-task behavior averaged eight per student. I then individually informed the students that I had collected data on them and then I informed the entire group of my results without mentioning the names of the students I had observed. I tried to emphasize to them that I did not think they realized the extent of their off-task behavior. I told them I was going to set up a program whereby they would keep track of their own off-task behavior, with the hope that it would help them to increase their time on task. We then discussed, modeled, and role-played those behaviors which would be considered off-task behav-

FIGURE 11.12 Elementary classroom self-monitoring program

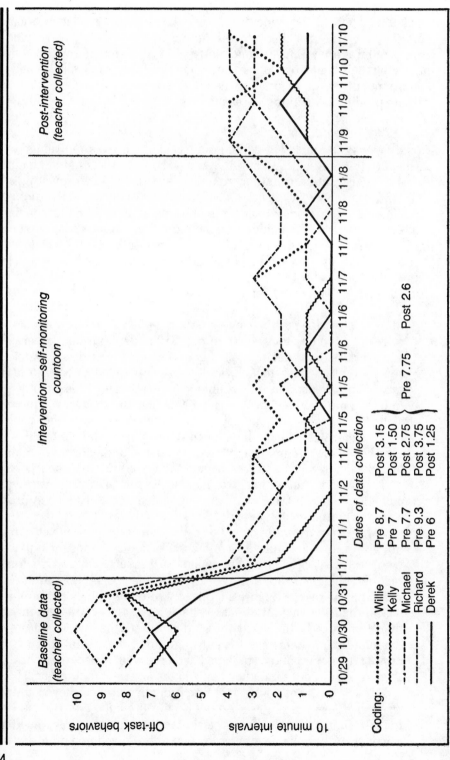

iors. This behavior included talking out loud either to oneself or to a peer; doing any other activity than what I had instructed them to do; getting up from one's desk to wander around the room; or making distracting noises, either by mouth or by opening desks, rolling pencils; and so on. They realized that if they needed assistance from me, they should raise their hand, and because I have a free bathroom-break policy, they could use the bathroom if it was necessary. Students need to be taught how to record their own behavior, and so I spent considerable time in this phase of the project. Also, with students involved in collecting their behavioral data, the time I had to spend on behavior monitoring was lessened. Self-monitoring ideally helps create an internalized source of control, and changes in behavior associated with this approach are expected to be more likely to generalize both to other situations and to other behaviors.

After we had sufficiently practiced and discussed behaviors, I gave each student a countoon. My countoon had a picture of desirable behavior on it, showing an animal deeply involved in doing a worksheet. Originally I had decided to involve only five students in the study, but after a discussion with the class, I decided to give every student a countoon. My results in this study will include only the five students described in the baseline data, but I really felt that it could not hurt to have all the students involved, making them all aware of their talking and behaviors, and keeping track of their off-task times. I then instructed the students when to keep track of their behavior. Each box on the countoon was for tallying off-task behavior. After each ten-minute interval, we circled the box with a crayon so that the children could keep track of how many intervals we had done. In that way, if a student had no off-task behavior, the box was still circled to show that we had kept track of that interval. I ran the program for six days, monitoring behavior twice each day for ten minutes each. Generally this monitoring was done during math or science, in which we were working on booklets about baby animals. Several of the children almost completely quit off-task behaviors. They were excited about the program and requested that we keep track of behaviors more often. I think they really did feel they had some control over their situation. Because the results were favorable, they also received praise and points for a class party, and the atmosphere in the room improved significantly during use of the countoons. The five students for whom I had collected baseline data went from an average of eight off-task behaviors to less than three per ten-minute interval during data collection. When I did the follow-up data collection, without their knowledge, they did regress a little, and were a little more talkative, but overall their off-task behavior was cut in half.

Case Study: Secondary

This study was conducted by a ninth-grade health teacher worried about the frequent talking out demonstrated by one of his students. The following material is taken directly from his study.

I would say my relationship before this intervention project was no different with Sam than with any other student I have this semester. With very few exceptions I think I have a good, open, honest relationship with the kids I teach. Since working on this project with him, Sam has come up to me after class and commented or asked me a question about something that happened in class that day. I don't feel communication with Sam was shut off because of this project.

I noticed that I did not see Sam with a "best buddy" or a clique of friends during passing time or at lunch. In class I think Sam might be talking to, or trying to get the attention of someone, in order to feel more accepted. By watching his relationship with peers, and watching his twin brother's relationship with peers, I would definitely say that Sam is the least popular of the two. Possibly he is acting out in this small way to gain attention and acceptance from other kids. If he wants attention badly enough, he might figure that negative attention, in the form of discipline, is still attention.

It was not difficult to pinpoint a target behavior for Sam to achieve, because it was pretty noticeable early that Sam does chatter inappropriately, turn around and bother the kid sitting behind him, or attempt to distract the kid beside him. I wanted to reduce or eliminate this behavior completely. I chose the form of self-monitoring I had researched, called frequency self-monitoring. The recording sheet I used involved simply having Sam make a mark each time he talked out without permission.

I kept track of the misbehavior on a piece of scratch paper near wherever I was in the room, and Sam kept track on his desk. I had a recording sheet taped to the top of his desk immediately before the class period when I had him. Because I had lunch right before Sam's class, it was always inconspicuously on his desk before any kids started coming into the room. As carefully as I could, I removed it right after class before the next group came in. As far as I know, Sam and I were the only people who knew an intervention program was going on.

Before the week of self-monitoring began, I talked to Sam after school one day and explained the self-monitoring sheet and the behavior I would like him to change. I also explained the type of punishment system I was going to use during the intervention. We decided together that given his age and potential, we would like to eliminate the misbehavior completely by the end of a three-week period. The reward for doing so was that Sam got to select his place in the seating chart. The type of punishment I used was a technique called verbal mediation training. Each time Sam talked out without permission, he had to make two copies of a prewritten essay by the following morning. If there was no more than one mark each period, I reduced the number of copies due to just one. If the essay was not handed to me by period six the next day, I would make a parent phone call home, explain the problem, and Sam would owe me one-half hour after school. The essay Sam copied was divided into four questions outlining the misbehavior and looked like this:

1.   WHAT DID I DO WRONG? I was talking without permission while Mr. Long was teaching class.
2.   WHAT IS WRONG WITH TALKING WITHOUT PERMISSION? Talking without permission keeps myself and other students from hearing the teacher, and I will miss out on something that might be on a test. If I miss out on one part of the class, I won't understand the rest, and I will become bored. If I talk without permission, I will have to write an essay like this or I will have to stay after school.
3.   WHAT SHOULD I HAVE BEEN DOING INSTEAD OF TALKING? Instead of talking I should have been listening to Mr. Long and following the lesson. If I wanted to say something I should have raised my hand and asked for permission.
4.   WHY SHOULD I HAVE BEEN LISTENING AND FOLLOWING THE LESSON? I should have been listening and following the lesson so that I would understand it and make a good grade on the test. I should have raised my hand for permission to speak so as not to disrupt the class. If I had obtained permission, I could have spoken without getting into trouble.

During the week that both Sam and I were monitoring his behavior he had to write only two essays (Figure 11.13). He had only one offense each period (he seemed to catch himself when he knew I was watching him closely), and so he had to write only one essay each day. Both essays came to me on time the next day. I never had to make a parent or principal contact during the monitoring time. In the week immediately following the intervention week, Sam had only one occurrence of the misbehavior on the last day of the week. The verbal mediation training was still in effect and he didn't balk at all when I handed him the essay. It came in on time the following morning.

The goals I have for my ninth-grade health students are not only to have fun and learn how to take care of their minds and bodies, but also to develop a better self-image and gain skills that will be valuable to them

FIGURE 11.13   Self-monitoring and verbal mediation training

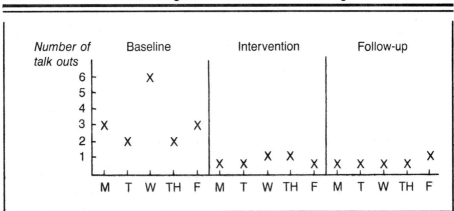

throughout life. The self-management strategies I used in trying to change Sam's behavior blended well with these goals. I feel better about creating a more positive learning environment for Sam and the rest of my class, and I think Sam feels good about the discretion I used in selecting and changing his behavior, and also about setting and accomplishing a goal for himself.

Self-instruction

Students who consistently act out in a school setting are often characterized by their inability to productively express or control their emotions. Partially because these students have had numerous failure experiences and lack confidence, they frequently respond with intense emotions when confronted by situations their peers handle quite comfortably.

One approach to helping students respond more effectively to frustration and stress is to teach them to give themselves verbal instructions that cue them to behave more appropriately. This approach is based on the concept that students who are labeled "hyperactive" or "impulsive" are less skilled than normal youngsters in using silent speech to monitor their behavior (Epstein, Hallahan, & Kauffman, 1975; Meichenbaum & Cameron, 1974). When faced with a difficult problem, a normal student might say to herself or himself, "Okay, I'll try it once more and if I can't do it I'll ask the teacher for help." Behavior-problem students may lack the ability to monitor their behavior in this manner and therefore respond actively and unproductively when faced with a frustrating task. Behavior-problem students may also employ negative silent speech. A student might say to herself or himself, "I'm stupid and I can't do this." This internalized statement simply compounds the student's problem and intensifies negative emotions.

According to the principles of rational-emotive therapy, students' behaviors can be changed by helping them make positive, thoughtful internalized statements in place of the negative, unproductive statements they often make. Research indicates that this approach can be successful in reducing students' anxiety (Warren, Deffenbacher, & Brading, 1976), improving academic performance of behavior-problem students (Lovitt & Curtiss, 1968), reducing rule-breaking behavior (Monohan & O'Leary, 1971), and responding less aggressively to oral taunts from peers (Goodwin & Mahoney, 1975).

Procedures

The basic procedure involves teaching students to employ silent statements to more effectively control their behavior. We can do so by providing students with specific statements that can be made when they are confronted with specific, frustrating situations. Students who become frustrated when attempting to solve math problems can be taught to say, "I can do this if I slow down and relax. What I have to do is first add the two numbers on the right. . . ."

Similarly, a student who becomes aggressive when he or she loses a game can be taught to say, "Okay, I didn't win this time, but that's all right. The other students will like me better if I give the ball back and go to the end of the line." We can help students develop these skills by providing them with opportunities to practice self-instruction under our supervision and on tasks they can already perform. While working on fairly simple tasks, students may initially be encouraged to make statements we provide. The students can then be asked to repeat these statements on their own. Next, they can be asked to whisper the words as they complete the task. Finally, they can be encouraged to simply say the words to themselves.

We should provide students with social reinforcement for behavior changes that accompany the use of self-instruction. When implementing this approach with a student who has had difficulty accepting losing during recess, we should attempt to monitor the student's behavior. When the student responds appropriately when confronted with the problem situation, we should immediately praise the student's efforts and discuss the process he or she employed to replace irrational, negative self-talk with more facilitative self-statements. If you are interested in examining these procedures in more detail you will find additional practical suggestions in Knaus' (1974) *Rational-Emotive Education: A Manual for Elementary School Teachers,* Kranzler's (1974), *You Can Change the Way You Feel: A Rational-Emotive Approach,* and Workman's (1982), *Teaching Behavioral Self-Control to Students.*

A similar approach focuses both on self-talk and developing alternative methods for dealing with problem situations. Students can be asked to role play situations in which they consistently respond in an inappropriate manner. As the role playing unfolds, students are encouraged to replace unproductive self-talk with statements that help them to control their behavior. Likewise, the teacher and/or other students provide alternative methods of responding. For example, a boy who consistently responds angrily to not being chosen immediately at recess may be asked to replace self-talk such as "Nobody likes me" or "I'm no good" with the statement: "I'll be chosen soon. I guess some students are a little better at this game than I am." The student may also be taught how to send an "I" message in a class meeting to express his hurt over not being chosen or given help in learning positive social skills that make it more likely that peers will choose him to be on their team.   .

A final approach to self-instruction involves teaching students skills in self-relaxation. This can be accomplished by the teacher or counselor initially providing direct instruction in how to relax. Students can learn to relax using the Jacobson (1938) method of relaxing and tensing different muscle groups. More simple and less obvious methods involve teaching youngsters yoga-like breathing skills or asking them to simply let their bodies go limp and imagine a warm, relaxing substance flowing through their body. After students have learned relaxation methods, they can be encouraged to employ these methods when they experience feelings of tension or anxiety. We can assist acting-out students by providing them with cues when it is necessary for them to employ relaxation procedures. We can reinforce use of these skills by using them with the entire class before or following tension-producing or exciting activities such as tests, recesses, or assemblies.

Relaxation can also be employed in association with cognitive rehearsal (a strategy very similar to self-talk). Before an activity that might evoke anxiety or inappropriate student behavior, we can have students close their eyes and go into a relaxed state. We then describe the upcoming situation and the desired student behavior. Before an assembly, we might have the students envision themselves walking quietly to the gymnasium, sitting quietly during the performance, and applauding at appropriate times. When students visually practice behavior in a relaxed state before performing the activity, their behavior can be significantly improved.

DEVELOPING CONTRACTS

A behavior contract is an agreement between two or more parties that indicates the manner in which one or more of the parties will behave in a given situation. Behavior contracts provide a specific, often written agreement designating the exact behavior(s) each individual will emit. Furthermore, behavior contracts frequently indicate the specific reinforcement or punishment associated with performing or failing to perform the behaviors listed in the contract. Therefore, behavior contracting is a more structured intervention than either problem solving or self-management. Behavior contracting provides students with a structure that encourages them to perform behaviors they have been unable to consistently display without some form of external, concrete payoff or negative consequences.

> Because the behavior contract . . . is definitive, interaction among the parties is highly predictable, and each person is therefore encouraged to assume his responsibilities. The specificity of the terms makes people face up to "the games they play" and prevents the conscious use of defensive posturing, such as readily invoked excuses. Since the interaction among parties is clearly structured, a sense of security and safety appears to be an important by-product of the stratagem. [Blackham & Silberman, 1975, p. 127]

Negotiating a Contract

Unless a contract is sensitively and concisely negotiated, we may find that it fails regardless of the type of consequence involved. Contracts should ideally result from a teacher–student discussion in which we help the student describe his or her behavior, decide that it needs to be changed, and suggest a plan for making the change. When a student is unable to devise a plan or previous plans have failed to bring about the desired change, we can help them develop a more structured behavior contract.

An effective behavior contract includes a statement about each of these variables.

1. What is the contract's goal? Why has the contract been developed?
2. What specific behaviors must the adolescent perform in order to receive the rewards or incur the punishment?
3. What reinforcers or punishers will be employed?
4. What are the time dimensions?
5. Who will monitor the behavior and how will it be monitored?
6. How often and with whom will the contract be evaluated? [Jones, 1980, p. 230]

Behavior contracts may be presented to students in many forms. Short-term contracts with elementary school children need not include each of the six components listed above. The important factor is that the child clearly understand the contract. Figure 11.14 is an example of a form you can use to present a contract to a primary grade child and Figures 11.15 and 11.16 are examples of forms for intermediate grade or secondary students. Though it is not necessary to develop a written contract, putting an agreement in writing tends to clarify each party's responsibilities. Whenever possible, students should be involved in determining the terms of a contract. Teachers should also help students express their feelings about a contract. Finally, once the contract has been negotiated, the student should be able to clearly paraphrase the conditions outlined in the contract.

Selecting Reinforcement Procedures and Consequences

Once we know when a contract should be employed and how to negotiate a contract with a student, the next step involves understanding the various types of consequences (reinforcers and punishers) that can be incorporated into a behavior contract.

Just as the preventive measures discussed in Parts II and III of this book should precede the corrective measures outlined in Part IV, and problem-solving approaches should be implemented before employing behavioristic methods, we should begin our contractual interventions with the least restrictive and most natural types of consequences. Figure 11.17 presents a hierarchic approach to consequences used in behavior contracts. We should start by trying to employ contractual agreements based on the types of reinforcers and controls at the bottom of the hierarchy. Only if these fail should we develop a contract based on higher-level reinforcers.

Examining Figure 11.17, we see that teachers should initially use reinforcers that are a normal part of the school day and are available to all students. Although token reinforcers may appear to be less natural than curtailment of activity, we constantly provide token reinforcers in the form of grades, points earned on tests, or promises to provide a reward if students behave appropri-

FIGURE 11.14 Primary-grade contract

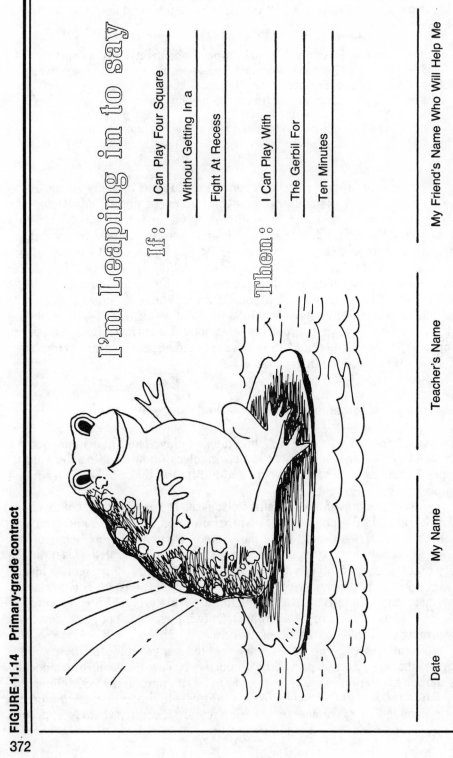

I'm Leaping in to say

If: I Can Play Four Square

Without Getting In a

Fight At Recess

Then: I Can Play With

The Gerbil For

Ten Minutes

Date | My Name | Teacher's Name | My Friend's Name Who Will Help Me

FIGURE 11.15 Upper elementary or middle school contract

I've got the POWER!

Matt

IS GREAT!
NOT LATE!

I WILL be on time to P.E. class, 11:00 a.m. sharp

FOR 5 consecutive days. Allan HAS OFFERED

TO HELP BY walking to class with Matt. MY

TEACHER WILL HELP BY telling me how well I did

each day I am on time.

TO CELEBRATE I WILL BE ABLE TO be a student

helper in P.E. and referee/umpire activities.

DATE

GREAT PERSON

HELPER

TEACHER

ately for a designated period. Furthermore, we should, whenever possible, focus on positive behavior. Punishment in the form of curtailments of activity should be used only after natural reinforcers have proven ineffective in helping a student change a behavior. Curtailment of activity is listed as more desirable than implementing a response cost (the procedure of taking away points or other rewards when a student misbehaves) primarily because response

FIGURE 11.16 Secondary school contract

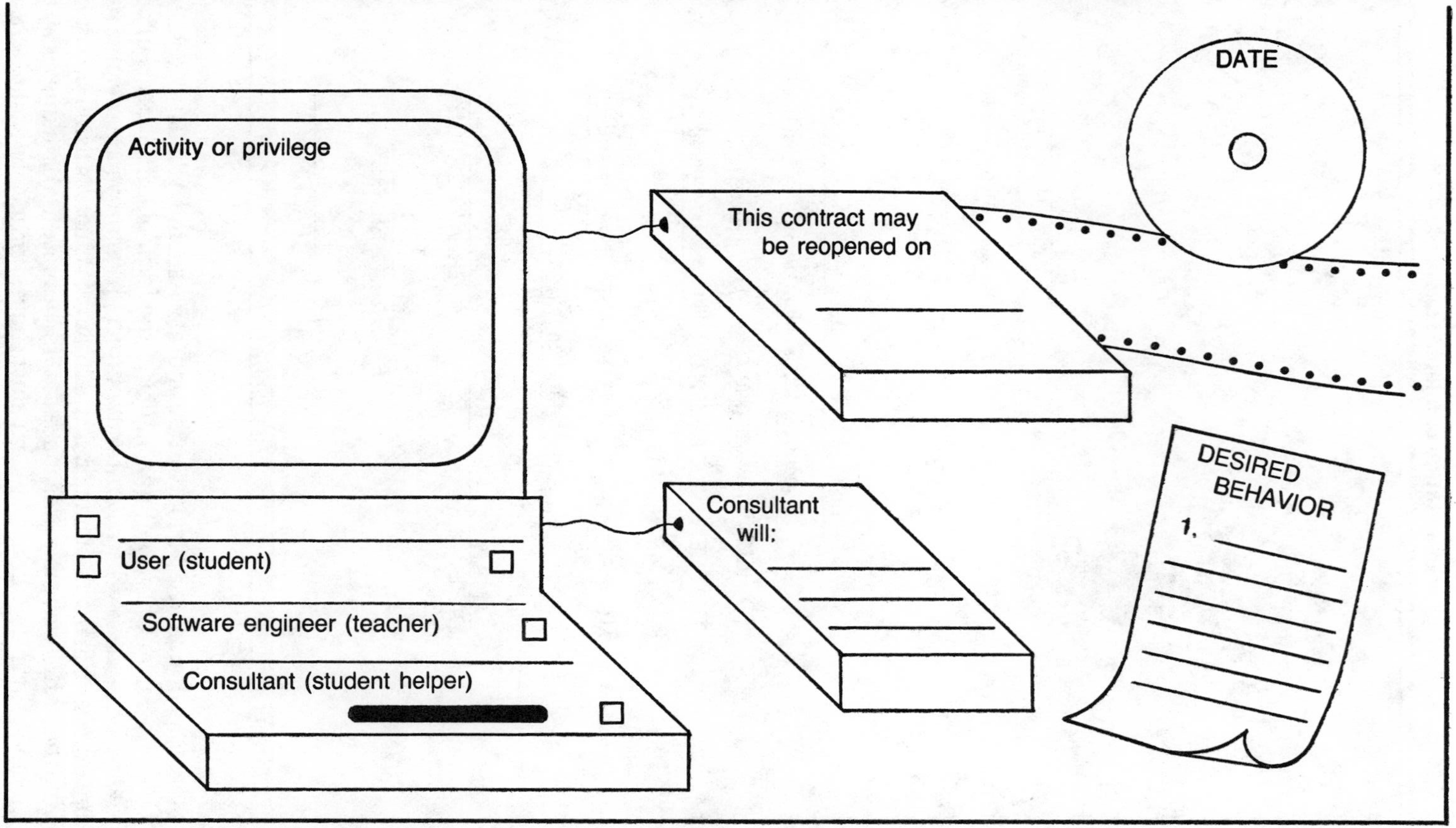

FIGURE 11.17   Behavior-contract hierarchy

Tangible reinforcement
Social, token, and activity reinforcement and response cost
Curtailment of activity
Social, token; and activity reinforcement
Activity reinforcement
Social reinforcement

cost is a complex intervention and should not be used unless simpler interventions fail. Curtailment of activity is placed lower on the hierarchy than tangible reinforcers because restricting a student's behavior by requiring that he or she stay in from recess in order to complete his or her work is a more logical intervention than providing the student with candy for completing a task. Furthermore, the use of tangible reinforcements suggests that the desired behavior is not valuable enough to warrant being displayed without a tangible payoff. This statement has subtle but potentially powerful negative consequences for long-term improvement in the student's behavior.

In the remainder of this chapter, we provide procedures for implementing the first four types of consequences listed in Figure 11.17. Because few teachers use response-cost or tangible reinforcers, these consequences are not discussed. If you are interested in these, refer to Hill Walker's (1979) book, *The Acting-Out Child,* or Vernon and Louise Jones's (1981) book, *Responsible Classroom Discipline.*

Social Reinforcement

Social reinforcement refers to behaviors of others that tend to increase the frequency with which a student emits a behavior. If a smile from us is followed by a student's continuing to work on his or her assignment, the smile has served as a social reinforcer. Similarly, if a child consistently returns to a group after having been chased away, the attention inherent in being chased may be viewed as a social reinforcer. Social reinforcement can be used either as a spontaneous teaching strategy for influencing students' behavior or as a consequence in a contract.

Procedures.   When systematically employing social reinforcement as a method for improving students' behavior, we should develop skill in employing a wide range of reinforcers, learn how to give reinforcement, and learn when to use it.

Among the many types of social reinforcement, the most obvious involves saying positive things to students. When giving social reinforcement, we should be careful not to constantly use the same word or phrase. Students appreciate different, creative expressions of encouragement and appreciation. Figure 11.18 lists social reinforcers we can use at a variety of grade levels.

FIGURE 11.18 Social reinforcers

Praising words and phrases

Good	That's interesting
That's right	That's really nice
Excellent	Wow
That's clever	Keep up the good work
Good job	Terrific
Good thinking	Beautiful
That shows a great deal of work	I appreciate your help
You really pay attention	Now you've got the hang of it
You should show this to your father	Now you've figured it out
Show Grandma your picture	Very interesting
That was very kind of you	That's an interesting point
Thank you, I'm pleased with that	Nice going
Great	You make it look easy
I like that	What neat work
Exactly	I like the way you got started on your homework

Expressions	*Nearness*	*Physical contact*
Smiling	Walking together	Touching
Winking	Sitting together	Hugging
Nodding up and down	Eating lunch together	Sitting in lap
Looking interested	Playing games with student	Shaking hand
Laughing	Working after school together	Holding hand

Words are not the only type of social reinforcement. We can employ many types of nonverbal social reinforcers. We can share our positive feelings about students' behavior by smiling, laughing, winking, or looking interested in what a youngster is doing. We can also reinforce students by spending time with them. Many behavior-problem students receive little attention and affection from adults and are starved for positive attention. We can reinforce these children by walking with them, eating lunch together, joining them in playground games, or asking them to stay after school and help us with a classroom task. Physical touch is another important and effective nonverbal social reinforcer. Research (Kazdin & Klock, 1973) has demonstrated that nonverbal reinforcement in the form of smiles and touch can positively influence students' on-task behavior.

When using social reinforcement, we must be especially careful to reinforce specific behaviors. We often use words such as "great," "good," "nice," and "super" when referring to students' work or behavior. Unfortunately, this form of reinforcement does not provide the student with specific information on which aspect of his or her behavior is being reinforced. Therefore, it is important that we describe the behavior being praised. Rather than saying, "That's nice, Bill," when Bill listens attentively, we might say, "Bill, I appreciate the way you are listening to the discussion. It should help you do well on the assignment."

Although we must develop an extensive repertoire of social reinforcers and learn to praise specific behavior, it is perhaps even more important that we learn when to reinforce students. The reason social reinforcement is frequently ineffective in changing students' behavior is that it is so often ineffectively used by teachers. Several studies have demonstrated that we often dispense social reinforcement at the wrong time. Walker, Hops, and Fiegenbaum (1976) observed the interactions between five acting-out children and their teachers. The results showed that though the five teachers praised the acting-out child's appropriate behavior about once every hour, they attended to inappropriate behavior nine times each hour. Similarly, Walker and Buckley (1973) observed an elementary classroom teacher and found that although 82 percent of the teacher's interactions with normal children followed appropriate behavior, 89 percent of the responses to acting-out children followed inappropriate behavior. Taken together, these and other studies suggest that we should attempt to increase our use of positive social reinforcement and make this reinforcement contingent upon acceptable student behavior. When an acting-out child demonstrates a positive behavior, we should try to immediately reinforce this behavior.

Social reinforcement is usually viewed as a spontaneous approach to changing students' behavior, but it can also be incorporated into behavior contracts. Because social reinforcement is inexpensive, readily available, and easy to give, we should attempt to incorporate this type of reinforcement into our initial contracts with a student. There are several approaches we can take when using social reinforcement in this manner. A contract can be developed in which a student receives social reinforcement from peers or us as a consequence for making a desirable behavior change. We can also involve parents in providing social reinforcement when their child behaves appropriately at school. A contract might indicate that if a student reaches a specified behavioral or academic goal, we will send a note home to the parent and the parents will respond by providing the student with a designated number of specific positive statements.

Activity Reinforcement
Because social reinforcement is not a powerful enough reinforcer to bring about prompt or significant change for all students, we need to employ other forms of reinforcers. Involvement in various preferred activities is another natural and easily dispensable reward for desirable behavior.

Procedures.   The first step is to list activities that students find reinforcing. Students enjoy being involved in this process and often offer creative and surprising ideas. Figure 11.19 lists classroom-activity reinforcers.

FIGURE 11.19   Activity reinforcers

Being group leader

Going first

Running errands

Collecting materials

Helping clean up

Getting to sit where he or she wants to

Taking care of class pets

Leading the flag salute

Telling a joke to the class

Being in a skit

Having a party

Making puppets and a puppet show

Doing artwork related to studies

Spending special time with the teacher

Choosing the game for recess

Getting to make puzzles

Earning an extra or longer recess

Choosing songs to sing

Work puzzle

Draw, paint, color, work with clay, and so on

Choose group activity

Take a "good" note home to mom (arrange a reward with the mother)

Extend class recess by specified number of minutes

Visit another class

Help teacher

10-minute break to choose game and play with a friend, QUIETLY

Build with construction materials

Time to read aloud

Play short game: ticktacktoe, easy puzzles, connect the dots

Performing for parents

Taking a class pet home for the weekend

Leading the songs

Being team captain

Reading to the principal

Seeing a filmstrip

Getting to read a new book

Seeing a movie

Listening to music

Playing games in class

Write on blackboard: white or colored chalk

Play with magnet or other science equipment

Solve codes and other puzzles

Listen to a song

Perform before a group: sing a song; tell a poem or riddle; do a dance, stunt, or trick

Be
   hugged
   tickled
   kissed
   patted

Choose book to review for class

Select topic for group to discuss

Read to a friend

Read with a friend

Right to tutor a slower classmate

Free time in the library

Ask child what he or she would like to do

Listen to record or radio with earphones

Plan a class trip or project

Work in school office

Work in school library

The second step is to develop a contract stipulating what the child must do to obtain the activity reinforcer. Figure 11.14 is an example of a simple contract. Whenever activity reinforcers are used, they should be paired with social reinforcement so that the social reinforcement may gradually acquire some of the reinforcing properties associated with the activity reinforcer.

The problem of delayed gratification (the student becomes frustrated because he or she must wait for the reinforcement) that is frequently associated with activity reinforcers can be dealt with by gradually extending the time a student must wait in order to receive the reward. When first implementing a contract, the student can be informed that he or she can be involved in the activity immediately after performing the desired behavior. As the student's behavior improves, he or she can be informed that he or she will have to demonstrate increasingly appropriate behavior as well as wait longer before the reinforcement is provided.

An interesting approach to using activity reinforcers involves allowing students to take home school equipment they find particularly interesting. A student's contract might indicate that he or she can take a tape recorder home for two days if he or she meets the conditions of the contract. Although this type of reinforcement may at first glance appear to be a tangible reinforcer, the student uses the borrowed item but neither consumes nor acquires permanent possession of the reinforcer. The reinforcer simply provides the student with an opportunity to reinforce himself or herself by participation in an activity involving school property. In essence the student is simply involved in the reinforcing event at home rather than at school.

Social, Token, and Activity Reinforcement

Token reinforcement refers to a system in which students receive immediate reinforcement in the form of a check, chip, or other tangible item that can be traded in for reinforcement at a future time.

Procedures.   There are seven basic steps to implementing a token reinforcement system in the classroom. Prior to introducing a token system, we should determine specifically how each step will be accomplished.

1. Determine when and with whom the program should be implemented. We might choose to employ a token system with two acting-out children whose behavior during seatwork continues to be extremely disruptive despite our attempts at instigating other types of interventions.

2. Select the specific behaviors to be reinforced. When working with an individual student, we might state that the student will receive a token for every two minutes he or she is in his or her seat, not talking to peers, and working on the assignment. When working with several students or the entire class it is desirable to generate a list of behaviors (the classroom rules may be suitable) that will be reinforced. It is desirable to involve students in determining the behaviors and to post the behaviors in a prominent place.

3.   Decide when tokens will be dispensed. When working with a seriously acting-out student you will usually have to dispense the tokens whenever the desired behavior occurs. As the student begins to gain control of his or her behavior, teacher and student can simply tally the occurrence of the desired behaviors (the tallies serve as tokens) and this total can be recorded or actual tokens can be given to the student at the end of a designated time. When employing a token system with an entire class it is best to distribute tokens randomly. Thus, as you move around the room or work with a group, you simply present tokens to students who are behaving appropriately. Though you must be careful not to overlook students or unfairly

FIGURE 11.20   Travel card

| Student _____ | Grade _____ | Date _____ |

Student _____ Grade _____ Date _____

Desired behaviors

Period	On time to class	Brought necessary materials	Handed in assignment	Obeyed class rules	Participated in class	Teacher's signature
1						
2						
3						
4						
5						
6						
7						

focus on some students, a random reinforcement schedule is easy to administer and maintains acceptable behavior at a high rate.

4.   Determine how to dispense tokens. There are numerous methods for dispensing tokens. Each student involved in the program can have a card taped on the corner of his or her desk and you can simply make a mark on the card each time the student displays the desired behavior. When working with small children, teachers occasionally choose to place a jar or box on each participant's desk so that tokens can be dropped into the container when the student behaves appropriately. When working with students who change classes or teachers during the day, a travel card (Figure 11.20) can be used. The desired behaviors are written on the card and at the end of each period the student receives a check for each desired behavior displayed throughout the period.

5.   Select a procedure for recording tokens earned. Because most token systems involve earning tokens over a specified period, it is necessary to devise a system for recording the number of tokens each child has accumulated. Likewise, because children can trade tokens in for preferred activities, a record of tokens spent and remaining must be kept. Figure 11.21 presents a form teachers or students can use to record tokens received and spent.

Curtailment of Activity

Activity curtailment refers to any situation in which inappropriate student behavior is followed by removal of a desired activity. This method of altering students' behavior has been used since time began, but it has received considerable attention with formal time-out procedures.

Procedures

1.   Students should understand the behaviors that will lead to curtailment of activity, what activities will be curtailed, and how long the restriction will be in effect. Punishment should never be presented arbitrarily.

FIGURE 11.21   Record of tokens

Name:	Teacher:
Date:	Points:
1. Points at the beginning of the day	18
2. Points earned today	15
3. Total points (add lines 1 and 2)	33
4. Points spent today	14
5. Total points at the end of the day	19

2. Rules on curtailment of activity should be employed consistently and fairly. If fighting on the playground is followed by sitting out the next recess, this restriction should be applied to all students in every instance. We should also consider, however, whether playground facilities and activities support positive play, whether rules are clearly understood, and whether students have been taught methods for resolving inevitable playground conflicts.

3. Be aware of cases in which curtailment of activity provides a more desirable alternative than the activity itself. Students may behave inappropriately in order to receive what appears to us to be a punishment but which the student views as a relatively positive consequence. A student may dawdle at work in order to stay in from recess, either because recess is perceived as undesirable or the time in the room is viewed as pleasant. Continuing to employ a curtailment of activity in this situation might prevent the child from dealing with important social skill deficits that are causing problems on the playground. Therefore, the punishment would be detrimental rather than helpful.

4. Present the negative consequences in a nonpunitive, interested manner. We should communicate sincere regret that a punishment is necessary. This attitude helps students to accept responsibility for their behavior rather than projecting the blame onto the teacher. Punishment should never be presented in anger, which only encourages the student to feel persecuted and to transfer the blame to the teacher.

5. When presenting a curtailment of activity to a student, always inform the student which specific behavior(s) were responsible for bringing about the undesirable consequence. The student should also be reminded of the desirable behaviors that could prevent the consequences.

6. When presenting a punishment, inform the student what must be done to terminate the punishment. You might inform a student that he or she can return to the class activity after he or she has quietly completed a behavior-analysis form.

7. Whenever possible, a curtailment of activity should logically relate to the behavior that necessitated the punishment. If a child could not play on the playground without fighting it is logical that he or she should miss recess until he or she can develop a plan for interacting more appropriately with his or her peers. It is not logical, though, to have children stay after school and write sentences because they fought on the playground.

8. Activity curtailment should, whenever possible, be consolidated with activities aimed at helping the student develop new skills that will prevent repeated performance of the undesirable behavior. Therefore, when being excluded from a desired activity, the student should be involved in examining the problem and developing a plan for solving it.

9. We should collect data to help us determine whether the curtailment of activity is effective in reducing the undesirable behavior or increasing the desired behavior. Because punishment in any form may have numer-

ous negative side effects, it should be discontinued if data indicate that it is ineffective.

10.   Punishment methods of changing students' behavior should be phased out as soon as possible and replaced by more positive approaches such as problem solving, self-management, or social or activity reinforcement.

Example

The following example occured when one of us was asked to assist a high school staff develop a program for a disruptive high school student. The student had received dozens of office referrals for relatively minor but persistent classroom disruptions and had finally been pulled out of two of his classes. The student was identified under P L 94–142 and had rather serious social cognition deficiencies. He demonstrated limited ability to understand others' perspectives and limited sense of his own efficacy and responsibility, and attributed his successes and failures to external factors. He also had few skills in developing specific plans to alter his behavior. Based on observations and interviews with parents, teachers, administrators, counselors, and the student, the following recommendations were made to the school staff in order to help them more productively respond to this young man. These recommendations highlight the importance of following the ten procedures for effective curtailment of activity. They also reinforce the value of collecting data, examining the learning environment, helping students become responsible for their own behavior, and systematically assessing the effectiveness of a program developed to change a student's behavior.

Recommendations

1.   The current and past IEPs available to me did not include any specific educational program that would assist Randy in remediating or circumventing his handicap. The IEP merely listed several obvious goals and an evaluation component to several but not all of the goals. Randy's school history, psychological assessment, and comments from school staff all support my belief that Randy has deficiencies in impulse control, social cognition, judgment and problem solving. It seems necessary and appropriate that an ongoing program be developed for remediating these deficiencies. A peer counseling group, focusing on social skills and conflict resolution, or at minimum, ongoing counseling, focusing on responsibility and enhancing social cognition, would seem desirable. Additionally, the school's response to Randy's behavior problems should be adjusted so that it consistently serves a behavior change function in light of Randy's handicap. (See items 3 and 5).

2.   The school staff should keep more accurate records of Randy's behavior problems. Available records are possibly acceptable for non-identified students, but are not adequate for making IEP decisions. For example, the vice principal indicated that during the past semester, Randy had been referred to his office "every other day." His records, however, were

kept on one five by seven card with no trend analysis made on an ongoing or summative basis. Additionally, I was informed that Randy had been suspended once, yet Randy stated unequivocally that he had not been suspended during the previous term. I believe it is important to have a good record concerning the behavior, the class in which it occurred (and thus time of day), the time during the class (early, middle or late), the activity in which the class was involved, preceding events, and responses by the teacher. This data can assist those involved in writing the IEP in determining the environmental factors influencing Randy's behavior.

3.   The school should develop a clear, concise policy regarding consequences for office referrals. It appears that most of the behaviors for which Randy is referred fall into the category of minor discipline problems. The student handbook is vague concerning the consequences for these behaviors. There is no indication as to how many referrals result in a Saturday school, suspension or expulsion. While this policy has the advantage of providing administrative flexibility, it creates a response that can be confusing and countertherapeutic for some students. Last semester Randy spent numerous hours sitting in the office. It is very likely that besides being moderately reinforcing, the lack of clear, precise, predictable consequences was confusing for Randy and was a factor affecting his continued disruptive behavior. Indeed, the vice principal mentioned that at one point Randy's mother was informed that ". . . Randy would be expelled if he continued to be referred." Randy continued, however, and these consequences did not follow. An expulsion certainly would not have been the correct response given the lack of a systematic program prior to this serious consequence. The point, is, however, that no predetermined guidelines were established and followed.

I recommend that a program be developed that provides Randy with a clear statement that X number of referrals will result in a Saturday school, Y number of Saturday schools will result in the next referral being a suspension, and Z number of suspensions will mean that the next referral will result in an expulsion. This consistent policy will provide clarity, limits, and structure for Randy—an important component in a responsible educational plan for him.

4.   Similar to the school-wide program, each teacher should provide Randy with a clear statement about how they will respond to his violations of classroom rules. It is important that this discussion not take place unless Randy begins to develop a pattern of disruptive behavior. At this point, Randy appears to be behaving well in all of his classes. It would be undesirable and unfair to treat him in a manner suggesting that problems are expected. However, if problems arise, Randy should have a clear understanding about how they will be handled. Generally, this should involve making a polite request to stop the behavior. If Randy continues to be disruptive, he should again politely and calmly be informed that further disruptions will mean *he is choosing* to receive an office referral. If he persists, he should be informed that he has chosen a referral.

5. If Randy receives an office referral, he should not be allowed to simply chat with the vice principal or sit in the office. Instead, he should be required to complete a worksheet in which he responds to a series of questions such as: (1) What did you do? Be specific. Describe *your* behavior, not the behavior of others. (2) Did your behavior violate a classroom rule or disrupt the class? Describe the possible negative effect your behavior might have had on the teacher and other students. (3) Do you believe this behavior needs to be changed? (4) What can you do to help prevent this from happening again? (5) Is there any way the teacher can help you prevent this behavior and have a better class? (6) Will you attempt to follow the suggestions you have made?

    Completing such a form will help Randy consider his actions in a concrete way and thus respond to the goals that should be written into his IEP. Randy needs assistance in understanding others' perspectives, taking responsibility for his own behavior, and developing plans to improve his behavior. Consequences for misbehavior should be aimed at teaching these needed skills, not merely making him sit or complete custodial work.

6. Randy needs to receive attention and praise for his positive efforts and performance. At the time of my visit, he had gone twelve days without a referral and had received only one "up slip." Staff—including the vice principal who could serve as a good model for Randy—should be encouraged to provide Randy and his mother with specific statements about Randy's improvement.

7. The change to a 2–1–2–1–2 schedule was a wise decision. Randy begins his day with two academic courses, followed by a study hall, two more courses, lunch, and completes the day with two courses. The only possible problem I envision would be the last period.

8. Randy appears to be influenced by his peers. He admits that much of his acting out involves peers who encourage and reinforce these behaviors. When planning Randy's schedule, an attempt should be made to place him in classes with students who value appropriate behavior. It may be better to err slightly in terms of placing Randy in more challenging courses than to place him in lower courses with more disruptive peers. At this point, however, I would continue on his current schedule. He seems particularly pleased with the quality and sensitivity of his current teachers.

9. Randy should be involved in a weekly monitoring of his academic and behavioral progress in each class. His assessment should be shared and discussed with a counselor with the goal of reinforcing progress and accomplishment and developing plans for dealing with any problems.

Involving parents in curtailment-of-activity contracts.   Curtailment-of-activity programs involving parents can be employed to reduce extremely disruptive student behavior. There are two basic approaches to involving parents in an activity-restriction program aimed at improving their child's school behavior. The first approach is used, in its simplest form, by many teachers. This method involves asking parents to make the availability of desirable home activities, such as watching television or playing with friends, contingent upon the child's completing a designated amount of work or behaving appropriately in school. Although these programs require considerable effort and emphasize negative consequences, they can be very effective in eliminating disruptive behavior in seriously acting-out children (Jones, 1980).

The second method of involving parents in implementing an activity-curtailment program is frequently called systematic school exclusion. In this program a student is excluded from school for one or two days if he or she emits predetermined, specific undesirable behaviors. Students' behavior can be dramatically improved following implementation of systematic school-exclusion programs (Brown & Shields, 1967; Jones, 1980; Walker & Buckley, 1974). The final section of this chapter includes a more detailed discussion of parent involvement and the steps we can take to ensure that this extreme form of activity curtailment is effectively and positively implemented.

Group Contracts

A group contract involves a situation in which the entire group earns a reward or loses previously awarded points or privileges contingent upon the entire group's behaving in a desired manner. Some writers define group contracts as including programs in which an individual student's behavior is reinforced by a desired activity for the entire group, but this technique is more accurately labeled an activity reinforcer.

Procedures.   In an attempt to reduce talking out and out-of-seat behavior in a fourth-grade class, Barrish, Saunders, and Wolf (1969) developed a group contract called the Good Behavior Game. The class was divided into two teams and students were informed that it was possible for either or both teams to win or lose. The winning team(s) received a thirty-minute free period at the end of the school day as well as an opportunity to wear victory tags and be first in line for lunch. The game was played by having the teacher make a mark on the board each time a team member talked out or was out of seat without permission. The team with the fewest points was designated the winner. Both teams could win, however, if neither team had more than five marks. Results of this activity showed marked decreases in the undesirable behavior.

Schmidt and Ulrick (1969) report successful implementation of a similar program in which a class was reinforced with free time when they maintained an acceptable noise level and remained in their seats. In their program, though, the class could also lose free time for violating these rules.

A more formal procedure for reinforcing on-task behavior involves providing a group reinforcement contingent upon the entire group's being on task for a designated percentage of the class period. A method for implementing such a procedure was reported by Packard (1970) and has been developed into a systematic program and extensively researched by Greenwood, Hops, Delquadri, and Walker (1974). This systematic program, entitled PASS (Program for Academic Survival Skills) is aimed at helping students learn and demonstrate specific skills that are necessary for academic success.

In its simplest form, the PASS Program involves these components: (1) a list of class rules (survival skills): (2) daily charting of the percentage of time these rules are followed by all class members; (3) a group reward for improvement; and (4) gradual removal of the major program components, such as the visible timing device, rules, and data display.

The PASS Program was initially designed for use with elementary school children, but it has also been successfully employed with young adolescents (Jones, 1980). The program involves the class in developing class rules stated in terms of specific, observable behaviors. The class is then informed that they will receive a group-activity reinforcement if they can improve the percentage of time during which all members of the class are obeying all the rules. The students receive feedback about their on-task behavior by means of a clock operated by the teacher. The clock shows a green light whenever the entire class is on task and the clock is recording, and a red light indicates that the clock has stopped because at least one student is violating one of the rules. As the class begins to consistently follow the rules more than 80 percent of the time, the frequency of reinforcement is systematically reduced and the clock light is replaced by a stopwatch. Eventually the reinforcement becomes entirely verbal except for periodic maintenance checks and occasional activity reinforcers associated with a particularly positive check.

Group competition and group rewards have also proved effective in reducing disruptive behavior in a school cafeteria (Sherman, 1973). In this program, rules were established and each day the class that was judged as most effectively following the rules received praise and had a star placed on a chart posted in the cafeteria. Further reinforcement was provided in the form of a special prize offered each month for the class with the most stars. Teachers on lunchroom duty were asked to ignore inappropriate behavior and praise students who followed the rules. Implementation of this program was followed by immediate reduction in disruptive behavior.

One problem that occasionally arises when implementing a group contract is that one or several students subvert the group's chance for success. When they do so, the teacher might initially implement a Glasser problem-solving discussion in order to help the student acknowledge the situation, decide whether to make a change, and develop a plan. If the student either indicates unwillingness to change or is simply unable to control his or her behavior adequately in response to a group contract, the student can be placed on an individual contract and the class can be informed that his or her behavior will not influence the class's chances of earning a reward. Although this intervention may be necessary, it tends to isolate the student. Therefore, we should periodically discuss the situation with the student with the goal of including the student in the group contract.

A final approach to devising a group contract is to develop the contract during a class meeting. An excellent example of this method occurred when one of our graduate students expressed concern because students in her eighth-grade math class were averaging nearly ten minutes before they were all seated and ready to begin the day's lesson. The teacher's initial idea was to present the students with an offer to take the entire class out for an ice cream cone on Friday if they could be ready to start class within two minutes after the bell rang for five consecutive days. We suggested, however, that students would be more likely to accomplish the goal and might need less reinforcement if they solved the problem themselves. The teacher accepted this logic and decided to present the problem to the class along with a large chart indicating the number of minutes it had taken them to settle down during the past ten days.

Because the teacher was well liked by her students and had demonstrated her competence by coming prepared with a data display, the students acknowledged that a problem existed and decided to solve it. The initial solution offered by a student and enthusiastically supported by the class was simply for everyone to be prepared every day when the bell rang. Fortunately, the teacher realized that this was an overly ambitious goal and informed the class that she would be delighted if the class could be prepared to start two minutes after the bell rang. The class then decided to clearly define the term "ready to start" and determined that it meant the entire class: (1) being in their seats, (2) having a paper and pencil on their desk, (3) being quiet, and (4) looking at the front of the room. Finally, the class decided to borrow a stopwatch from the physical education department and to allow each member of the class to time the class for one day and mark the results on the large chart the teacher had prepared.

Not surprisingly, the student involvement served as its own reinforcement and no one suggested any form of extrinsic reward. Results indicated that during the five weeks the class marked the chart, they never required more than one minute forty-five seconds to become prepared for class. Furthermore, follow-up data collected two weeks after students had ceased to mark the chart indicated that this behavior had been maintained.

The effectiveness of this group contract was based on the fact that the solution responded sensitively to students' needs for competence and power while employing a problem-solving approach that incorporated the basic components of a sound behavioristic intervention. When teachers are able to integrate these approaches, they will consistently find themselves able to work with their students to develop productive solutions to classroom problems.

IMPLEMENTING AND ASSESSING A BEHAVIORISTIC INTERVENTION

As suggested throughout this book, the only way to determine whether a procedure is effective or fits your teaching style is to systematically implement the method and evaluate the results. It is occasionally difficult to find the motivation for this process, however, when the methods appear to relate indirectly to student misbehavior. Activity 11.4 provides an opportunity to implement a method that deals directly with a specific disruptive student behavior.

ACTIVITY 11.4   Implementing and assessing a behavioristic intervention

Select an individual student's behavior that is detrimental to the student as well as the class. Describe the behavior in behavioral terms, collect baseline data for at least two one-half-hour periods, and graph the results.

Next, select one of the reinforcement procedures described in this chapter and develop a written contract with the student using this reinforcer.

Implement the contract for five days. Collect and record data during all times when the contract is in effect.

At the end of five days discuss the results with the student and determine whether to (1) continue the contract, (2) alter the contract by requiring improved behavior while reducing the reinforcement or employing a reinforcer lower on the hierarchy, or (3) discontinue the contract.

Finally, complete these statements:

The student's behavior. . . .
At the end of the five days the student said that he or she. . . .
I was surprised that. . . .
I was pleased that. . . .
I was displeased that. . . .
We changed the contract so that it. . . .
The reason for changing the contract was. . . .

INVOLVING PARENTS IN A BEHAVIOR-CHANGE PROGRAM

At times it is necessary and appropriate to work cooperatively with parents to develop an intervention program that is effective in altering a student's behavior. The necessity for parent cooperation stems from the fact that a very small percentage of students do not respond to the behavior-management methods available to schools. These students do not initially respond to a positive learning environment, problem-solving approaches, or the social, activity, or tangible reinforcers that the school can provide. Furthermore, these students may find exclusion from school to be reinforcing rather than punishing.

In such cases, it seems likely that the problem is not centered in the classroom, and a home-intervention program may be necessary to bring about meaningful change. Although the strategies presented in this section can apply to relatively minor problems, they are aimed at providing school personnel with a method for involving parents in dealing with serious, continuing problems involving students' misbehavior.

In this section we present a method for employing a cooperative parent–school approach to changing specific disruptive behavior. We should also be prepared, however, to provide parents with information about resources that will enable the parents to independently work more effectively with their child. Parents may ask us to suggest reading material that will help them develop more effective parenting skills or better understand their child. We have found that parents can enjoy and learn from a wide range of books, including Gordon's *Parent Effectiveness Training*, Ginott's *Between Parent and Child*, Satir's *Peoplemaking*, Patterson's *Living with Children and Families*, and Becker's *Parents Are Teachers*. Parents may also be interested in attending a parent group, and we should be prepared to refer parents to appropriate community resources. We may also find enough interest among parents in our school to warrant creating a parent group sponsored by the school or district.

Initial Considerations

Before attempting to involve parents in changing a student's behavior, school personnel should carefully examine the school environment to ensure that it meets the student's academic and psychological needs. If it does not, parents' involvement will merely provide a patch solution, for students will ultimately reject an environment that does not meet their needs.

Before involving parents, school personnel should also determine whether they have exhausted their repertoire of less severe behavioral interventions. Parents should not be asked to play a major role in influencing their children's school behavior when the school has not explored all possible interventions at their disposal. If educators expect to keep parents' trust and respect, they must call upon parents for assistance only when it is obvious the student cannot remain in or successfully cope with the school setting unless parental assistance is provided.

Because collaborative home–school efforts are usually necessary only when students have shown extreme inability to control their own behavior, it is unlikely that informing students about the intention to work cooperatively with their parents will significantly alter most students' behavior. Nevertheless, it is important to inform them. Because we should consistently treat youngsters with respect and provide them with a sense of understanding and controlling their environment, they should be informed of decisions that affect them in significant ways. By informing students of the intent to involve their parents and providing them with the rationale for developing a more extensive intervention program, we increase the likelihood that students will understand their world rather than feel arbitrarily manipulated. Furthermore, in some cases children may be legitimately frightened by the repercussions of their parents' being asked to help alter their child's behavior. School personnel must inform students of their intent to contact parents so that the child has an opportunity to provide us with this important information.

Steps in Negotiating a Home–School Contract

Figure 11.22 lists the major steps to follow when meeting with parents to negotiate a collaborative home–school behavior contract. The obvious first step is to reinforce the parents for expressing their concern for their son or daughter. We can accompany this message with the statement that experience indicates that when parents are willing to work with the school, it is almost always possible to develop a program that will help the student.

The second step is to briefly state the goal of the meeting. School personnel may state that the goal is to develop a behavior-management program that will allow the student to act in a manner that will allow him or her to remain in school.

The third step in negotiating a home–school contract is to describe the problem. During this step, it is important to be specific. If the problem is a student's disruptive classroom behavior, it is helpful to have specific data indicating the extent of this acting out. Similarly, it is helpful to present academic data to support the fact that the student's acting out is hindering his or her ability to perform academic tasks.

Once the problem has been clearly presented, the next step is to describe what the school has done to help the student. Again, specific data must be presented. The parents can be shown records indicating the number of times

FIGURE 11.22   Steps to follow in developing a collaborative home–school behavior-intervention program[a]

Step 1	Reinforce the parents for their willingness to attend the conference.
Step 2	Outline the goal of the conference.
Step 3	Describe the problem.
Step 4	Indicate what the school has done to alleviate the problem.
Step 5	Display the data to indicate that an additional type of intervention is needed.
Step 6	Present the anticipated consequences should the student's behavior remain unchanged.
Step 7	Indicate that the school has exhausted its resources and suggest that a collaborative home-school program appears most likely to help the student
Step 8	Outline the proposed program.
Step 9	Negotiate a final agreement.
Step 10	Plan for follow-up.

[a]From Vernon F. Jones, *Adolescents with Behavior Problems: Strategies for Teaching, Counseling, and Parent Involvement.* © 1980. Reprinted by permission of Allyn and Bacon, Inc.

teachers, counselors, and administrators have counseled the student. The parents can also be shown data indicating the type and frequency of meetings aimed at developing a productive program for their child. In addition, the parents should be shown any contracts that have been written with the student. Finally, the teacher or counselor should outline any special academic programs that have been developed to assist the student.

The fifth step is to present data indicating that the interventions previously described have not been effective in bringing about the necessary behavior changes. Ideally, the data should be in a form that includes baseline data followed by data collected during the various interventions (Figure 11.23). If such data are not available, the parents can be shown baseline data that indicate why the school staff became concerned about the student's behavior. This demonstration can be followed by data on the student's current behavior. The parents can be shown that despite all attempts to help their child change his or her behavior, the behavior has not shown the necessary improvement. The parents can be informed that the data indicate that something more extensive must be done to ensure that the student can remain in school and have a positive school experience.

The sixth step is to inform the parents of the likely consequences associated with continuation of their child's current behavior. This information should not be presented in a threatening or intimidating manner. Instead, the parents should be informed that they have been asked to attend the conference because the school staff sincerely wishes to develop a program that will prevent their child from experiencing the consequences that would be associated with continuation of the current behaviors.

Once the parents are aware of the impending consequences of their child's behavior, they should be informed that the school has exhausted its resources and that the best solution seems to be a collaborative effort between

FIGURE 11.23   Format for presenting intervention data to parents[a]

	Baseline	Intervention 1	Intervention 2	Intervention 3
Problem behavior				
			Time	

[a]From Vernon F. Jones, *Adolescents with Behavior Problems: Strategies for Teaching, Counseling, and Parent Involvement.* © 1980. Reprinted by permission of Allyn and Bacon, Inc.

the home and the school. Here it is important to assure parents that, regardless of whether or not they agree to become involved in a collaborative program, the school will continue to make every effort to assist their child. It is important to inform the parents, however, that, based on past records, it appears unlikely that these interventions will be adequate.

The eighth step is to present the parents with a proposed home–school program. When presenting the program, begin by discussing the school's role. This evidence indicates to the parents that the school is not abdicating its responsibility and that the school staff will be actively involved in the program. After the school's role has been defined, the parents' anticipated role should be clearly outlined. This role must be presented in terms of specific behaviors so that the parents know exactly what will be expected of them. Now, we must also specify the time parameters. Parents need to know how long the program will last. In addition, they should be given some information on when they can expect to see the desired changes in their child's behavior. Finally, the parents should be shown how the program will be evaluated. This explanation should include a discussion of the data-collection system as well as a tentative schedule of future conferences with both the student and the parents.

After the parents have heard the proposed program, they should be encouraged to ask questions or make suggestions about the proposal. It is also important to ask parents where they envision problems arising and whether they feel they can carry out the tasks outlined for them.

When the program has been thoroughly discussed and both parties have agreed to the solution, the final step is to determine when the two parties will meet again to discuss how the program is functioning. During the initial stages of a collaborative home–school intervention program, it will usually be necessary to include frequent correspondence with both phone calls and conferences. As the parents become comfortable with their role and the program is effective, however, the contacts can be gradually decreased.

Types of Parent Involvement

Parents' involvement can range from asking parents to dispense rewards or apply punishments based on their child's performance at school to involving parents in programs where they learn how to develop strategies for improving their child's nonschool-related behaviors. School personnel should, whenever possible, help parents to employ the most natural and least restrictive consequences when developing a behavior contract. Consequently, when working with parents to improve a student's school behavior, it is desirable to initially ask the parents to systematically praise their child's positive school behavior. They can do so by obtaining the parents' agreement to provide the youngster with a designated number of positive statements each time he or she brings home a note indicating that he or she has reached his or her goal. If a student is attempting to reduce the number of talk-outs he or she makes during social studies, we can send a note home each time the data indicate that the student reaches his or her goal. The parents can agree to make three positive statements about the child's school behavior each evening that he or she brings a note home.

When simple social reinforcement does not bring about the desired change, parents can be asked to provide the youngster with preferred activities at home when the child produces desired school behavior (Phillips, 1968). This approach will often succeed when contracts at school have failed, because usually more diverse and important activities are available at home than at school. Although activity reinforcers will usually be effective with young children, monetary reinforcement can be used when other rewards fail (McKenzie, Clark, Wolf, Kothera, & Benson, 1968).

Although it is desirable to employ positive reinforcement whenever possible, it may occasionally be necessary to control a student's school behavior by restricting privileges at home when the youngster behaves inappropriately at school (Jones, 1980). As with home activity reinforcers, restricting out-of-school activities will often change a student's school behavior when school interventions have failed. This failure occurs because parents have control over more important social and recreational activities than do teachers.

Perhaps the most dramatic method of involving parents in changing their child's behavior is what is often termed systematic school exclusion. This approach can be very effective (Brown & Shields, 1967; Jones, 1980; Keirsey, 1969; Walker & Buckley, 1974). It involves removing the student from school and should therefore be used only as a last resort. Systematic school exclusion is merely a thoughtfully employed school suspension. When a student continually exhibits seriously disruptive behavior, the student and his or her parent(s) are asked to meet with the teacher, principal, and counselor. The problem is discussed, data are presented, and the parent(s) and student are informed that the student will be suspended from school for a designated period (usually one or two days) each time the child exhibits the specific behavior. When implementing a systematic school exclusion program, it is extremely important that the program focus on a limited number of specific behaviors and that the student clearly understand the behaviors that cannot be accepted and what will occur if these behaviors are displayed.

If you are interested in a more detailed discussion of these methods or wish to examine methods for training parents to interact more effectively with children, you should refer to the recommended readings that follow.

RECOMMENDED READING

Alberto, P., & Troutman, A. (1982). *Applied behavior analysis for teachers: Influencing student performance.* Columbus, Ohio: Charles E. Merrill.

Axelrod, S. (1983). *Behavior modification for the classroom teacher.* (2nd ed.). New York: McGraw-Hill.

Becker, W., Englemann, S. & Thomas, D. (1975). *Teaching I: Classroom management.* Chicago: Research Press.

Blackham, G., & Silberman, A. (1975). *Modification of child and adolescent behavior.* Belmont, Calif.: Wadsworth.

Canter, L. (1976). *Assertive discipline: A take-charge approach for today's educator.* Los Angeles: Canter.

Duke, D., & Meckel, A. (1984). *Teacher's guide to classroom management.* New York: Random House.

Gardner, W., (1977). *Learning and behavior characteristics of exceptional children and youth: A humanistic behavioral approach.* Boston: Allyn and Bacon.

Jones, V. (1980). *Adolescents with behavior problems: Strategies for teaching, counseling, and parent involvement.* Boston: Allyn and Bacon.

Jones, V., & Jones, L. (1981). *Responsible classroom discipline.* Boston: Allyn and Bacon.

Long, J., & Frey, V. (1977). *Making it till Friday: A guide to successful classroom management.* Princeton, N.J.: Princeton Book.

O'Leary, D., & O'Leary, S. (1972). *Classroom management: The successful use of behavior modification.* New York: Pergamon Press.

Sloane, H., Buckholdt, D., Jenson, W., & Cranall, J. (1979). *Structured teaching.* Chicago: Research Press.

Spaulding, R., & Spaulding, C. (1982). *Research-based classroom management.* San Jose, Calif.: Maple Press.

Walker, H. (1979). *The acting-out child: Coping with classroom disruption.* Boston: Allyn and Bacon.

CHAPTER 12

Schoolwide Discipline Programs

Field research we have conducted suggests that educators often fail to consider all the possible control strategies available to them before they decide on a particular course of action. If failure to review alternative strategies characterizes other schools besides the ones we have investigated, it would help explain the contemporary crisis in school discipline and the seeming inability of educators to control dysfunctional behavior. The likelihood of making an effective decision is increased by expanding the number of alternatives that are considered.

Daniel L. Duke, (1980),
Managing Student Behavior Problems

Teachers need the support provided by a clear, fair, consistent, school-wide discipline policy. It is the teachers' responsibility to effectively prevent and deal with minor student misbehavior in the classroom, and they must have assistance in dealing with serious or persistent behavior problems. Students need to know that even though they have a right to attend skillfully taught classes, they will not be allowed to disrupt the learning process. School programs for handling discipline must be based on the creation of positive, productive learning environments and a commitment to helping students develop skills they need to become responsible self-managers.

As discussed in an earlier section on school climate (Chapter 5), factors out-side the classroom influence our ability to establish positive learning environ-ments and effectively respond to disruptive student behavior. What we do in classrooms cannot be considered in isolation from the values, norms, climate, and discipline procedures operating within the school at large. Research and theory on schoolwide factors that influence students' behavior have taken several directions. In an effort to determine schoolwide factors that are asso-ciated with high student achievement and low rates of disruptive behavior, re-searchers have compared schools that are more and less effective in attaining desired student outcomes, (Edmonds, 1979, 1982; Rutter et al., 1979). Based partially on findings that the quality of administrative leadership is consis-tently a significant variable affecting school effectiveness, numerous studies have examined the role administrative leadership plays in creating effective schools (Greenfield, 1982; Lipsitz, 1984; Lightfoot, 1983; Persell, Cookson, & Lyons, 1981). In addition, considerable research and prescription has focused on the quality of school climate (Anderson, 1982). Finally, work has been gen-erated on the influence associated with developing systematic schoolwide discipline systems (Duke, 1980).

Because this book is focused on classroom-management methods that influence students' behavior within classrooms, we do not examine school or-ganizational factors that influence teachers' and students' attitudes and be-havior. Because the study of classroom management involves teachers' skills in responding to disruptive student behavior, however, it is important to con-sider ways in which teachers can be supported in dealing with extreme or persistent disruptive student behavior. Therefore, in this chapter we will ex-amine major concepts and practical methods related to creating this needed support.

A CONTINUUM OF SERVICES FOR DEALING WITH DISRUPTIVE STUDENT BEHAVIOR

The passage of House Bill 94–142 placed pressure on schools to provide ade-quate services for handicapped students. Unfortunately, in many instances, teachers and schools have too hastily referred students for special education services rather than first exploring ways in which the classroom teacher and building staff could be involved in helping improve the student's achievement and behavior. Studies examining the quality of efforts made to assist students prior to referral for a special education evaluation and eligibility decision indicate that schools too seldom provide adequate services prior to placing students in special education settings (Smith, Frank, & Snider, 1985; Walker, Reavis, Rhode & Jensen, 1985).

When dealing with students who consistently disrupt the learning envi-ronment or whose withdrawn behavior prevents them from benefitting from teachers' instruction, a school must develop a systematic approach involving a continuum of services. In Figure 12.1 we present a five step continuum.

FIGURE 12.1   Continuum of services for managing student behavior

Step	Responsibility	Procedure	Resources
1	Classroom teacher	Regular classroom placement	The teacher utilizes effective instructional and classroom management methods that include posted classroom rules and consequences for behavior.
2	Classroom teacher and school staff	Regular classroom placement and referral to school resources	This involves advice and support from colleagues, involvement of the school support staff, or student referral into a systematic school discipline system.
3	Classroom teacher, school staff, and district staff	Regular classroom placement and request for district resources	The district provides consultation resources such as a special educator, school psychologist, or behavior specialist.
4	Classroom teacher, school staff, and district special education staff	Request for special education evaluation and eligibility decision. Placement in a special building program and/or regular classroom.	The multidisciplinary team determines eligibility, the IEP team determines the placement and programming, and the special education staff provides and coordinates services.

Step	Responsibility	Procedure	Resources
5	School staff, district special education, staff, and community resources	Placement within district resources and referral to community resources.	District and community resources

Most of this book has offered ideas for implementation at step one. It is also necessary for schools to provide teachers with systematic support when their best efforts fail to generate needed student behavior change. One important method for providing support involves having a procedure for holding staffings to discuss ways the teacher(s) might work more effectively with the student. These staffings will generally involve the student's teacher(s), a counselor, several additional teachers and an administrator. The goal of such staffings is to develop a clear, written statement regarding modifications in the student's academic program and the staff's interactions with the student aimed at improving the student's academic performance and behavior. A second method involves insuring that the school-wide discipline system provides a systematic, consistent and fair response to students' disruptive behavior. When these two components exist, many misbehaving students can be effectively worked with within the regular school program. The remainder of the chapter presents methods for providing support through the use of school discipline programs.

KEY ISSUES IN CREATING SCHOOLWIDE DISCIPLINE PROCEDURES

During the decade 1975 to 1985, more and more schools developed schoolwide discipline programs. By the early 1980s, it was estimated that three out of four schools had some form of printed disciplinary code (Safer, 1982). In some, teachers' organizations had worked to incorporate within their contract a statement that each school must implement a schoolwide discipline procedure (Jones, 1984). Although some schoolwide discipline programs have been developed by extensive staff involvement and critical analysis of data on patterns of disruptive student behavior, many others have been hastily conceived stopgap methods for responding to a perceived crisis or an organizational mandate.

By signaling to students and parents that students' behavior is a problem, creation of a schoolwide discipline procedure increases the visibility of student behavior problems. This process also raises teachers' expectations that they will receive the support they desire. Finally, students may get the message that their behavior is a matter of interest. If not thoughtfully handled, this awareness may create a negative self-fulfilling prophecy. Therefore, though an effective schoolwide discipline program can have numerous positive results, implementation of a poorly conceived program may have detrimental effects on students' behavior, teachers' morale, and community support for the school.

The development of an effective schoolwide discipline program must involve the entire school staff in considering a variety of critical issues. A discipline program must also meet numerous criteria if it is to respond to the learning and psychological needs of the students whose development it is intended to enhance. In this section we present our beliefs about the philosophical, organizational, and operational issues (Figure 12.2) that must be addressed if a schoolwide discipline program is to enhance students' learning and personal development.

FIGURE 12.2   Components in an effective schoolwide discipline program

Philosophical and organizational components
1.   The program is congruent with the school's stated goals on students' development of academic and personal skills.
2.   The program responds to the developmental levels and tasks of the students involved.
3.   The program's development and continuing evaluation involves representatives from the entire school community: teachers, administrators, staff, students, and parents.
4.   The program is based on data about specific factors associated with student-management problems within the building.

Operational components
5.   The program includes a positive school climate component focused on the quality of peer and teacher–student relationships.
6.   The program places initial emphasis on teachers' responsibilities for adjusting students' instructional programs and implementing productive classroom-management interventions.
7.   The program emphasizes educational activities that provide students and staff with new knowledge and skills.
8.   The program includes clear, concise school rules that are systematically communicated to students, parents, and staff.
9.   The program includes a clear statement about consequences associated with violating school rules.
10.   The program provides a consistent response to students referred by a staff member.
11.   The program includes a systematic procedure for involving parents in working with the school to alter their child's behavior.
12.   The program includes periodic analysis of data related to key outcome variables.

From "An administrator's guide to developing and evaluating a building discipline program." NASSP Bulletin, April 1984. Reprinted by permission.

Philosophical and Organizational Components

A program should be congruent with the school's stated goals on students' academic and personal skills development. Most school districts have produced thoughtful, educationally sound goals. Unfortunately, these goals too often remain locked in central-office file cabinets while building programs reflect convenience or the most recent vogue in instruction and management. Development of a schoolwide discipline program should begin with teachers, administrators, parents, and students (at least at the middle and high school level) generating a list of the schools' goals for students' learning and personal growth. Almost inevitably these statements of goals include references to developing responsibility, self-discipline, positive attitudes toward school and learning, and positive self-concepts. Having a set of program goals provides important direction and also serves as a check and balance against the authoritarianism that tends to creep into schoolwide discipline systems.

A program must be responsive to the cognitive and psychological developmental levels of the students involved. Schoolwide discipline programs too often respond to teachers' needs and wants while failing to consider students' skills and developmental tasks. Primary-grade children may not respond effectively to a model whose primary component involves group problem solving. Likewise, a program for young adolescents that employs rigid rules and consequences with no room for dialogue will consistently conflict with these students' desire for fairness, independence, and mutual respect (Jones, 1983a). When developing a schoolwide discipline program, educators must incorporate components that take advantage of students' current skills and developmental needs while challenging students by including components that encourage the use of more advanced skills. A primary-grade program should strongly emphasize helping children to: (1) learn basic school procedures; (2) follow classroom rules; and (3) develop positive attitudes about peers and self. These children, however, should also be taught basic skills for taking responsibility for their own behavior by individual and group problem solving. Likewise, middle school students need a program that provides clear guidelines and is employed with particular attention to consistency, fairness, and mutual teacher–student respect. At the same time, a program for these students should include developing skill in interpersonal relationships, decision making, and conflict resolution. These students should also be involved in the development and continuing evaluation of the program.

Program development and continuing evaluation must involve the cooperative effort of the entire staff. To be effective, a schoolwide discipline system must have widespread staff support. Consistency in staff expectations and methods of responding to students' behavior are an important factor in minimizing students' misbehavior (Rutter et al., 1979). Staff who feel uncommitted to a program can do much to minimize its effectiveness. In addition to the effect staff input has upon program consistency and staff morale, involving a wide range of staff members enhances the potential for accurate diagnosis of the problem and for creative solutions. Staff involvement can also improve the quality of staff relationships, which matter because the quality of staff relationships will affect a staff's ability and willingness to work cooperatively and creatively in planning, implementing, and adjusting a schoolwide program (Schmuck & Schmuck, 1974). Staff relationships will also influence a discipline program because students tend to model adult behavior. When staff relationships are poor, problems are more likely to occur within an institution. Studies in both general and psychiatric hospitals suggest that patients suffer when staff morale is low (Revans, 1964; Stanton & Schwarts, 1954). William Purkey's (1984) *Inviting School Success* summarizes the powerful role interpersonal relationships play in influencing behavior and performance in school settings.

During the initial stages of developing a schoolwide discipline program, all staff members should be involved in defining the problem and establishing procedures for generating solutions. In schools with more than twenty staff members, a committee can be charged with devising ideas for discussion by the whole staff. If outside consultants are involved at this stage, their role should be to help the staff obtain information and to facilitate staff discussion and organization; it is counterproductive to have consultants present solutions this early.

A program should be based on data about the specific factors associated with student management problems within the building. Student management problems are always to some degree related to factors within the school environment (Wayson & Pinnell, 1982). Just as a teacher would not prescribe an academic program for a student without examining the student's skills and deficits, discipline programs should not be developed without careful analysis of the possible causes of students' misbehavior. This examination should take two forms. First, teaching methodology, curriculum, and human relationships in the school and classroom should be systematically examined in light of current research. Recently one of us has worked with several schools that have employed this format:

1. offering a course in which teachers became familiar with current research in human development, classroom management, and teacher effectiveness;
2. developing assessment procedures to determine students' and teachers' perceptions of the school environment;
3. listing recommendations for altering curriculum, instruction, and school climate;
4. creating an implementation plan;
5. outlining a continuing assessment plan.

A second form of analysis involves collecting data on the frequency, type, location, timing, and pattern of behavior problems in the school. Schoolwide discipline programs often fail not because answers are not available, but because at first the staff asked the wrong questions. Dan Duke (1980) suggests that schools might collect these types of data:

1. average daily attendance;
2. average daily illegal absenteeism;
3. average daily referrals to office;
4. annual number of suspensions and breakdown according to reason;
5. breakdown of number and type of student behavior problems;
6. along with above breakdowns, data on race/ethnicity of students (to determine if a disproportionate number of certain groups of students are being suspended or reported for rule-breaking;
7. breakdown of punishments applied to students and rate of repeated offenses;
8. estimates by administrators, counselors, and teachers of time per day spent on discipline-related matters;
9. breakdown of student behavior problems in special programs (i.e., alternative schools, continuation schools, etc.);
10. sources of referrals to the office;
11. comparative data on school discipline from (a) previous years and (b) nearby schools;
12. number of student behavior problems occurring "in class" and "out of class" (before school, between classes, cafeteria, after school);
13. number of students in disciplinary difficulty who transferred into the school after regular fall registration. [pp. 68–69]

Most schools will not need to collect data from all thirteen areas, but it is essential that solutions stem from a solid data base. Data collected in this second area of problem analysis can provide support or clarification for ideas generated by the more theoretical approach. Furthermore, collection of concrete data provides a basis from which to assess whether program changes do in fact bring about significant changes in behavior.

Operational Components

The eight components described in this section comprise the operational aspects of a schoolwide discipline program. Once a staff has worked together to assess problems related to students' misbehavior, the operational components should be developed with a consistent effort to ensure that the philosophical and organizational issues brought up during the initial stages serve as a basis for program development.

A program must include a positive school climate component focused on the quality of peer and teacher–student relationships. Because schoolwide discipline programs often respond to a perceived or real crisis, there is a tendency to focus on punitive measures that provide immediate, albeit short-term effects while ignoring preventive measures that may respond to the cause of the problem. The greatest danger associated with developing schoolwide discipline procedures is that the procedures will be employed to instill compliance in situations where students' personal and academic needs are not being met (Jones, 1981). Except for instructional factors, interventions aimed at improving school climate are the most important ingredient in creating positive student behavior (Brookover, 1978; Edmonds, 1979). Numerous authors (Anderson, 1982; Jones, 1980; La Benne & Green, 1969; Purkey & Novak, 1984; Schmuck & Schmuck, 1983) point to the significant relationship between students' behavior and the quality of personal relationships in the school environment. Students who feel safe, accepted, cared for, and involved at school seldom exhibit consistent disruptive behavior.

Numerous instruments exist for gathering students' views about school or classroom climate (Borich & Madden, 1977; Epstein, 1981; Fox, Luszk, & Schmuck, 1966; Moos, 1979). These instruments assess students' feelings about factors such as teacher–student relationships, peer relationships, the curriculum, instructional methods, and the school physical plant. Once data have been obtained from students and staff, a group consisting of students, teachers, staff, and administration can work to implement activities aimed at creating more positive attitudes in specific areas rated as problems. A variety of sources provide creative ideas for improving school climate (Fuller & Lee, 1981; Olivero, 1977; Purkey & Novak, 1984; Robert, 1976).

Because of the high student turnover rate in many schools experiencing significant problems in student management, a positive school climate program should include methods for integrating new students into the school. This agenda should include activities for helping new students develop friendships, become familiar with school and classroom expectations and procedures, and obtain assistance with academic, peer-relationship, or other school-related problems.

A program must place the initial emphasis on teachers' responsibility for adjusting students' instructional programs and implementing productive classroom-management interventions. The effectiveness of a building-wide discipline system is based on the instructional skill and personal warmth and concern of individual teachers. The responsibility for discipline problems is too often placed almost exclusively on students and administrators. Educational leaders must resist the temptation to accept solutions that place few demands upon teachers.

When considering methods available for responding to discipline problems, educators have tended to underestimate the influence that curriculum and instructional methods have on students' behavior. Research (Block, 1978; Ellison, 1973; Jones, 1985b; Osborne, 1977) indicates that low-achieving students are more frequently involved in serious misbehavior than their higher-achieving peers. This finding suggests that any effective student discipline program must focus much time and energy on providing students with meaningful instructional activities that provide opportunities for individual success. Instructional activities must take into account the cognitive skills and learning styles of individual students and groups of students. A schoolwide discipline plan must systematically incorporate procedures for assessing whether a misbehaving student is involved in appropriate instructional activities and provide teachers with assistance in adjusting curriculum and instructional methods that are associated with students' failure and frustration. Failure to build this component into a discipline program is a clear violation of professional responsibility.

In addition to early emphasis on instructional factors, an effective program requires that, before invoking sanctions imposed by an administrator, the teacher will work with the student (and perhaps with the parents) to examine the student's misbehavior and develop a plan for improving the behavior. Because our intervention may be only the first phase of a program to help a student, forms and procedures should be devised to communicate our efforts to a counselor or building administrator (Jones, 1983a). Whenever we refer a student to an administrator, we should be expected to provide a written description of the methods employed to help the student change his or her behavior. Because we should be given major responsibility for dealing with classroom-management problems, a program must provide flexibility for us as classroom teachers to employ methods we find congruent with our personal style and instructional goals. Teachers vary tremendously in personal style and ability to effectively incorporate specific management methods. We should be provided the most recent research on effective instructional and management methods, and teacher evaluation should focus on our ability to implement methods we select that incorporate these findings. Consistency in handling discipline should be provided by consistent but not identical approaches to instructional excellence, sound management approaches employed within classrooms, and *systematic* procedures that occur *after* we have referred a student.

A program should emphasize training that provides students and staff with new personal and educational skills. Schoolwide discipline systems too often are focused on developing systematic procedures for monitoring and disciplining students. Instead, discipline should be viewed as a process for teaching students and teachers alternative methods for meeting their personal and intellectual needs (Jones, 1977). When a school accepts this definition of discipline, its student-management program is focused on training teachers and students in new methods for structuring the learning environment, presenting information, learning, interacting, and solving problems (Alschuler, 1980; Jones, 1980). The emphasis is shifted away from controlling students and toward creating methods that increasingly involve both parties in mutually positive educational and personal experiences in the school setting.

Training for students may include instruction in communication skills, study skills, or problem-solving methods. Teacher training may involve us in a review of human development theory and research, new ideas for instructional methods appropriate for the age group we instruct, curriculum-evaluation workshops, and new approaches to handling disruptive student behavior (Jones, 1982). If educational leaders wish to retain the best teachers and increase students' achievement, they must place a high priority on high-quality in-service training. This training should be provided during release time so that teachers view it as a legitimate aspect of their job. Equally important, this training must actively involve teachers in small groups in which they can share their expertise, generate new methods, and be accountable for reporting the results obtained when implementing new methods. Teaching is a highly demanding profession that requires support, skill improvement, and periodic opportunities to sit back and assess one's work.

A program must include clear, concise school rules that are systematically communicated to students, parents, and staff. Because middle school and high school students are particularly sensitive to such issues as fairness, democracy, and individual rights, an effective program involves these students in the developing of school rules. Once rules have been established, everyone involved must understand and must have had an opportunity to question and discuss the rules and procedures. Most adults would be angry if they received a ticket for speeding when the speed-limit sign was hidden behind a row of bushes. Likewise, students and parents wish to know what is expected of students.

A program should include a clear statement about consequences associated with violating school rules. Consequences for violating school rules should be communicated to students and parents. Methods of disseminating this information include printing it in a parent–student handbook, making presentations in classes attended by all students, posting it in prominent places around the school, and discussing the program's components at an evening community meeting.

A program must provide a consistent response to students referred by a staff member. A discipline program must place a premium on fairness and consistency. Most students are willing to accept a system in which reasonable rules that facilitate learning apply equally to all individuals. Consistency also meets our need to have clear support in matters involving students' misbehavior. Our morale and willingness to be productively involved in working with misbehaving students are strongly influenced by the clarity, consistency, and quality of the support we receive in dealing with consistent or serious student misbehavior. Therefore, an effective program includes written referrals from the teacher followed by written feedback from the administrator or staff member responsible for handling the referral. The response should verify that the situation was handled according to the designated procedure and inform us of additional methods being employed to assist the student, or potential sources of assistance for helping us work with the student.

A program will not work effectively if individuals responsible for dealing with consistent or serious misbehavior do not feel comfortable with the approach they must employ. Both teachers and students will become confused or angered if students referred for serious misbehavior are not dealt with skillfully within the expectations created by the school's discipline procedures. When a program is being developed, staff, students, and the administration must work together to design a program that is acceptable to all.

A program should include a systematic procedure for involving parents in working with the school to alter their child's behavior. Parents are extremely important to young people and play a significant role in influencing their behavior (Conger, 1984; Norman & Harris, 1981; Streit, 1980). To no one's surprise, studies show that parents can have a major positive influence on their children's school behavior (Jones, 1980; Walker, 1979). Therefore, an effective schoolwide discipline system that includes a component for dealing with continual or serious student misbehavior must involve parents in a consistent, predetermined manner that has been clearly articulated to staff, students, and parents. The type of parental involvement requested will differ depending on such factors as the student's age and the community in which the school is located.

A program should be periodically evaluated by collecting and analyzing data related to key outcome variables. School personnel too often spend time and money developing and implementing new procedures, yet forget to systematically assess the results. A schoolwide discipline program should be aimed at altering specific student behavior, and data are needed to assess program effectiveness. Data for evaluative purposes should consist primarily of repeated samples of the initial data. If results of a student attitude questionnaire such as the CES (Moos, 1979) were instrumental in determining the direction for change, this instrument should be readministered semiannually. Likewise, if the rate of classes being cut or the number of fights were major problems, data collected continuously should be analyzed for their relationship to the implementation of specific program components.

SCHOOLWIDE DISCIPLINE MODELS

Options for schools interested in developing a schoolwide discipline program are innumerable. These options can be broadly categorized, however, according to their degree of structure and the extent to which teachers are given responsibility for handling student discipline (Figure 12.3). In a book dedicated to a comprehensive approach to classroom management, we cannot examine many types of possible programs. Instead, in this section we will describe

FIGURE 12.3   Approaches to school discipline

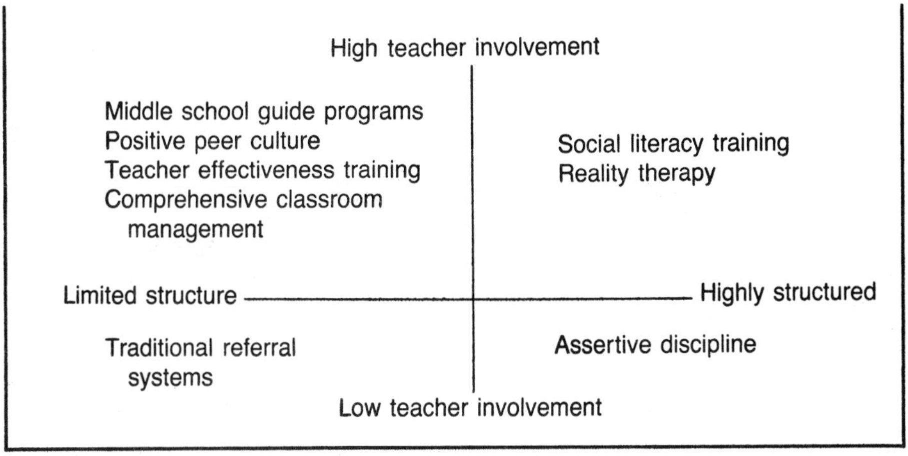

High teacher involvement

Middle school guide programs
Positive peer culture
Teacher effectiveness training
Comprehensive classroom
  management

Social literacy training
Reality therapy

Limited structure ———————————————— Highly structured

Traditional referral
  systems

Assertive discipline

Low teacher involvement

four programs ranging from low degree of structure with high teacher in-volvement to a high degree of structure with limited teacher involvement. In the latter category we have included a schoolwide policy to support substitute teachers as well as a more general schoolwide policy.

Example 1

Perhaps the best example of low-discipline structure with high teacher in-volvement is found in middle schools that implement structures to extend the time students remain with a teacher and a group of students. Specifically, middle schools that emphasize the guide or adviser program create a situa-tion in which student problems are expected to be handled by a teacher who has developed a relationship with a group of students. In her summary of four outstanding middle schools, Joan Lipsitz (1984) reinforces this point:

> The relationships students have with adults are important to the comparative calm that is characteristic of these schools. Young adolescents are not ready for the atomistic independence foisted on them in secondary schools, which is one of the causes of the behavior problems endemic in many junior high schools. [p. 181].

One of us has worked with a middle school of approximately 650 students that does not have a schoolwide discipline policy, has no locks on students' lockers, and yet has high achievement gains and minimal discipline problems. This school is in a middle and lower-middle class neighborhood and has only adequate physical facilities. The quality of instruction, teacher–student rela-tionships, and peer relationships facilitated by adults provides the basis for developing a positive school climate in which formal discipline procedures are not needed. The vice-principal employs a problem-solving approach on an individual basis and reports that this approach is consistent with the methods teachers are expected to employ before any referral is made. Students are ac-tively involved in instructional activities, frequently evaluate these activities, and are expected to work with their teachers—and with their guide teacher for a more serious or continuing problem—to resolve problems.

Example 2

Figure 12.4 shows a policy toward student conduct that was developed by a principal in an elementary school in which one of us worked. The principal's intent was to clarify the types of minor student misbehavior teachers were ex-pected to handle on their own. The principal also wanted teachers to know, however, that definite and consistent responses were expected for serious student misbehavior. Moreover, the principal intended to specify who would be responsible for handling various types of serious student misbehavior. This example presents a semistructured policy that would rate midway on teacher involvement in handling student discipline.

FIGURE 12.4   Policy on student conduct

Major offenses	*Consequences*
1. Fighting	1. Parent–teacher conference. Possible suspensions by principal.
2. Insubordination not following instructions, rude, discourteous	2. Parent–teacher conference
3. Profanity	3. Administrative discretion— notify parents for any offense. Habitual use, suspension—parents to return with student
4. Stealing (anything of substantial value)	4. Parent–teacher–principal conference
5. Truancy (willful nonattendance)	5. Notify the parents. Habitual truancy will be brought to the attention of the administrator and he shall notify the juvenile authorities
6. Vandalism	6. Suspension—parent to return with student
7. Carrying of any item that may be considered a potentially dangerous weapon.	7. Confiscate—notify parents
8. All school personnel should take appropriate action when, in their judgment, a student's behavior is not contributing to the general welfare of the school.	8. Administrative discretion

Minor offenses	*Consequences*
1. Running in the halls	1. Teacher has student sit down for one minute
2. Tardiness	
3. Teasing other students	All non-gross offenses will be
4. Boisterous behavior	handled at place and time of
5. Littering	offense by the staff members
6. Other less serious acts	or aides with the backing of the principal

From the Beaverton, Ore. School District. Reprinted by permission.

Example 3

The policy described in this section is an example of a highly structured discipline system that places a moderate amount of responsibility on teachers. This policy was implemented by one of us when he was a junior high school vice-principal. The policy was developed in response to considerable staff and community concern about the amount of disruptive behavior in the school. The policy was designed by a committee of staff, students, and administrators and was adopted by a unanimous faculty vote.

One major component of the system was a list of unacceptable behaviors and a clear statement about the consequences associated with these behaviors (Figure 12.5). This list and related policies were communicated to students and parents in several ways. The school's Student-Parent Handbook included a complete description of the new discipline procedure and a sample of all forms being used. The materials were printed in school colors, laminated, and displayed throughout the school. In addition, during the first two weeks of school the principal and vice-principal visited every English class, presented the discipline procedure, and led a discussion on students' responsibilities and rights based on the school district's Students' Responsibilities and Rights Handbook.

Consequences for students' misbehavior depended on the severity and frequency of the misbehavior. Less serious behaviors occurring in classrooms were first dealt with by the teacher. The teacher was required to confer with the student, contact the parent if the behavior occurred following a warning,

FIGURE 12.5   Discipline procedure

Step 1:   Teacher warns the student.
Step 2:   Staff member confers with student and notifies parents. In addition staff member may:
  a. refer student to counselor or other appropriate school personnel.
  b. Use classroom detention.
     Staff member should keep a record of which actions are taken in Step 2.
Step 3:   (1st Referral) Staff member sends student to office with (if possible) a completed referral form. If referral form is to follow, staff member will either send a brief note with the student or call the office.
  a. staff member completes referral before 4:00 P.M. that day.
  b. administrator will give feedback to the staff member within twenty-four hours of the referral.
  Administrative action:
  a. conference with the student and assignment of one or more of these:

       1. administrative detention

       2. essay on self-discipline

       3. cleanup detail

    b. administrator notifies parent of the incident, the punishment, and the next disciplinary action.

Step 4: (2nd Referral) Any offense warranting a second office referral (whether from the same or a different staff member, for the same or a different behavior), will result in the consequences associated with Step 4. In addition, any instance in which a student misbehaves in class after having previously been referred to Step 3 will also warrant placement at Step 4.

Step 4 involves (1) a detention (2) a required conference with the parent(s). This conference will generally involve a meeting with the parents and the student's teachers. The parents and the student will be informed that any behavior warranting an office referral (including the repeat of the behavior causing the initial referral) within six weeks of the second referral will result in a three-day suspension.

Step 5: (3rd Referral) A third Step-3 referral by any staff member within six weeks of the previous referral will result in:

    a. a three-day in-building suspension

    b. a parent conference, with the understanding that the next referral will result in a five-day suspension.

Step 6: (4th Referral) A fourth Step-3 referral by any staff member within six weeks of the previous referral will result in:

    a. a five-day in-building suspension

    b. a parent conference, with the understanding that the next action will be a seven-calendar-day out-of-building suspension.

Step 7: (5th Referral) A fifth Step-3 referral by any staff member within six weeks of the previous referral will result in:

    a. a seven-calendar-day out-of-building suspension

    b. a parent conference, with the understanding that the next action will be a recommendation for a three-week expulsion.

Use and/or possession of narcotics or other dangerous drugs or alcohol.

    a. expulsion in accordance with Beaverton School District Administrative Regulation 5000-32.

Step 8: (6th Referral) A sixth Step-3 referral by any staff member within six weeks of the previous referral will result in a three-week expulsion.

NOTE: Steps 4–8: In instances where the student receives a referral outside of the six-week limitation, the student will, at the discretion of the administrative vice-principal, either repeat the step he or she is presently at, or proceed to the next step.

Step 9: A Step-3 referral after return from an expulsion will result in:

    a. a return to Step 4

    b. if a suspendable offense—Step 5

and refer the student to the counselor if the problem involved peer conflict or other factors the teacher believed required counseling intervention. Counselors were also given copies of all referrals so that they could meet with students who were experiencing consistent difficulties.

A student who was involved in a more serious violation of school rules or repeated a lesser misbehavior despite the efforts made during Steps 1 and 2 was referred to the vice-principal (Step 3 in Figure 12.5). The student was then provided with a problem-solving counseling session aimed at helping him or her develop alternative methods for meeting his or her needs. Students were also assigned an after-school detention (staffed by administrators and teacher volunteers), in which they wrote a paper on self-discipline. The rationale for requiring a paper was that detention should be viewed both as a logical consequence and a learning experience. The staff wanted students to view discipline as a necessary part of personal growth rather than simply as arbitrary punishment. As Figure 12.5 indicates, continued violation of school rules invoked increasingly serious consequences. Consequently, a major component in the system involved an in-building suspension.

Example 4

The final example is a policy for providing support for substitute teachers working in an elementary school. The policy is an example of a highly structured discipline policy involving almost no involvement on the referring teacher's part. The policy was developed because students were acting out excessively when taught by a substitute teacher, and students frequently received limited consequences for their misbehavior in these situations. Figure 12.6 presents the policy.

We strongly support discipline systems that initially involve teachers in examining many classroom factors that may be influencing a student's behavior, but substitute teachers are in a different situation. Because they have control over far fewer classroom variables, it is fair and reasonable that they be provided with clear support and have considerably less involvement in dealing with seriously disruptive student behavior.

EFFECTIVE COMMUNICATION AMONG SCHOOL PERSONNEL

As school discipline policies have become more formal, with individuals accepting designated roles and responsibilities related to students' behavior, school personnel have developed procedures for communicating the results of their efforts. Figures 12.7 and 12.8 present two forms commonly used in schools with which we work. Figure 12.7 was developed by middle school student-management specialists in a large city school district. It emphasizes record keeping and assignment of consequences by a specialist to whom the student

FIGURE 12.6 Substitute-teacher discipline policy

1. Preparation for substitute
   Each teacher will coordinate with another to receive classroom disrupters.
   Each teacher will go over discipline procedure with all classes.
   Substitute folders will be kept in the office to be given to substitutes when they check in.
2. The plan itself:
   Two or more teachers agree to receive disruptive students from a substitute.
   A student who defies the substitute, disrupts the class, or is argumentative or otherwise uncooperative, is to be sent from the room immediately.
   The sub calls the coordinating teacher, then sends the disruptive student with the B checklist to that room.
   Disruptive student works quietly for the remainder of the class in the room.
   The student will make up all time missed from his or her regular class with regular teacher when he or she returns.
   The time is to be made up at the convenience of the regular teacher.
   If the disrupter causes any disturbance in the receiving teacher's room, then he or she calls that child's parent at home, work, or wherever and has the parent remove the child from school for the remainder of day.
   The child makes up *double* the time missed from the absent teacher's class and any other class.
   The time is to be made up at the convenience of the teachers whose classes were missed.
   The receiving teacher takes the B checklist to the office at the end of the day.
   Office sends a form letter to the parents, informing them of the child's lack of cooperation with the substitute.

From the Ainsworth Elementary School, Portland, Ore. Reprinted with permission.

has been referred. At the same time, teachers are required to provide a limited statement on their role in responding to the disruptive behavior.

Figure 12.8 was designed to help junior high and middle school staff members record their efforts to help students improve their behavior. Several schools with whom we have worked have chosen to expand teachers' involvement by requiring that Step 2 (Figure 12.8) be repeated twice before a referral could be made.

It is important for school personnel to develop clear schoolwide discipline procedures as well as forms to facilitate communication about students' behavior. As we have emphasized throughout this book, however, the critical

FIGURE 12.7   Student referral form

ROBERT GRAY MIDDLE SCHOOL
STUDENT REFERRAL FORM

Student _____   Grade _____

Referred From _____   Date _____   Time _____

REPEATED VIOLATION OF CLASSROOM RULES

A. Reason for Referral (be specific) _____
_____

B. Action taken prior to referral to Administrator/Student Management Specialist:

Date/Time	Action Taken
_____	Warning to Student
_____	Wrote Behavior Plan/Contract with Student
_____	Notified Parents
_____	Classroom Time-Out
_____	Assigned Classroom Consequences
_____	Other _____

What happened in each instance (be specific) _____
_____

C. Conference Requested: _____ None   _____ With Student Management Specialist   _____ With Parent(s)

VIOLATIONS OF SCHOOL RULES

A. Reason for Referral (be specific) _____

Date/Time		Date/Time	
_____	Chronic Tardiness	_____	Vandalism
_____	Irregular Attendance/Cutting	_____	Theft
_____	Verbal Abuse	_____	Substance Abuse
_____	Insubordination/Defiance	_____	Dangerous Instruments
_____	Use of Tobacco	_____	Physical Abuse/Fighting
_____	Unsafe Actions	_____	Assault
		_____	Other _____

What happened (be specific) _____
_____

C. Conference Requested: _____ None   _____ With Student Management Specialist   _____ With Parent(s)

ADMINISTRATIVE/SMS ACTION:

Administrative/SMS Action Taken: (Conference held with student resulting in the following action taken within 24 hours)

Date/Time		Date/Time	
_____	Conference Scheduled as Requested	_____	Held Staffing
_____	In-School Suspension	_____	Parent/Teacher Conference
_____	Student Wrote Behavior Plan/Contract	_____	Work Assigned
_____	Notified Parents (phone/sent letter)	_____	Major Suspension (home)
_____	Referred to Counselor/Social Worker/	_____	Adjusted Program
_____	BSC/Community Agency	_____	Minor Suspension
	Held Conference with Staff. Discussion	_____	Expelled
_____	Alternatives for Working With Student	_____	Exclusion From Activities
_____	Referred to Nurse	_____	Detained After School
_____	Other _____	_____	Noon Detention

Comments: _____
_____

Administrator/SMS Signature: _____

Copies could be sent to:

_____ Parent	_____ Administrator	_____ Referring Teacher
_____ Student	_____ Student Management Specialist	_____ Counselor

5/31/83

FIGURE 12.8   Student referral form

```
                                    YELLOW COPY:  GR. LEVEL COUNSELOR
                                    PINK COPY:    TEACHER
                                    GOLD COPY:    MAIN OFFICE

STUDENT _____GRADE ____ PERIOD ____ TEACHER _____

DESCRIBE THE SPECIFIC PROBLEM: _____

_____

_____

_____


STEP 2

SUMMARY OF STEP TWO CONFERENCE WITH STUDENT ____/____/____ (DATE)

_____

_____

_____


PARENT CONTACTED ____/____/____ (DATE)  AT _____ AM OR PM

RESPONSE _____

_____

_____

_____


STEP 3

REFERRED TO ADMINISTRATOR ON ____/____/____ (DATE)

ADMINISTRATIVE ACTION: ____ CONFERENCE ____ DETENTION ____ PAPER ____ SUSPENSION

____ PARENT NOTIFIED ____ PARENT CONFERENCE ____/____/____ (DATE)

_____

_____

_____

_____


COUNSELOR CONTACTS WERE MADE ON ____/____/____   ____/____/____ (DATES)

SUMMARY OF COUNSELOR CONTACT _____

_____

_____

_____

(OFFICE AND STAFF USE ONLY--NOT A PART OF STUDENT'S BEHAVIORAL OR CUMULATIVE FILES)
```

From the Glenhaven Intermediate School, Portland, Ore. Reprinted by permission.

factors in maintaining positive student behavior relate to school climate, effective classroom management, degree of instructional excellence, and quality of human relationships in the classroom and school.

Educators must respond to the increasing body of research indicating that teachers and schools do make a difference. When working as a vice-principal in a school that developed the discipline model described in Figure 12.5, one of us was impressed because, though it had a positive influence on students' behavior, implementation of the policy was not enough to bring about the desired outcomes. In response to this discovery, several teachers began creating additional strategies to improve students' behavior and achievement. A positive school climate committee was formed. A committed and concerned teacher instigated Wednesday morning training sessions to help members of the staff improve their skill in problem solving and teacher–student relationships. An administrator suggested the idea of having students who were experiencing continued discipline problems assigned to an adult mentor selected by the student. Finally, several of the staff members began working with the school counselors to develop a unit on peer relationships and problem solving to be taught to every seventh grader entering the school. These efforts suggested that staff members were aware that students' behavior is influenced by a variety of school factors and that simply providing consequences for inappropriate behavior would not help students become responsible, motivated learners. It is our sincere hope that this book provides you with an appreciation of this concept and methods for creating a classroom environment that offers students a well-organized, instructionally sound and inviting place in which to learn.

Appendix: Maps
(for real estate activities)*

Map 1: Rainfall 1

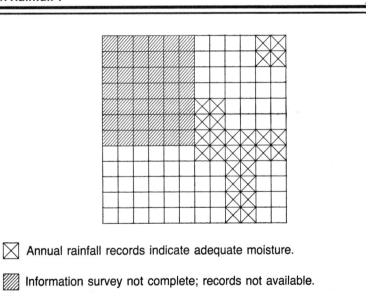

⊠ Annual rainfall records indicate adequate moisture.

▨ Information survey not complete; records not available.

*These maps are to be used with Figure 5.6, page 149.

Map 2: Rainfall 2

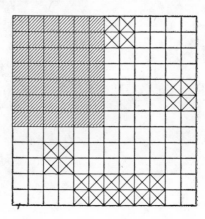

⊠ Annual rainfall records indicate adequate moisture.

▨ Information survey not complete; records not available.

Map 3: Slope 1

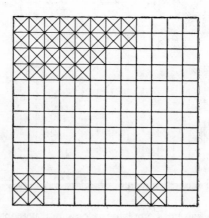

⊠ Areas where the slope of the land permits its use without terracing. Hilly areas are not mapped.

Map 4: Slope 2

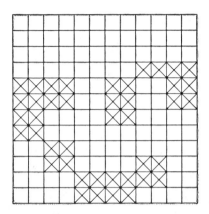

⊠ Areas where the slope of the land permits its use without terracing. Hilly areas are not mapped.

Map 5: Soil 1

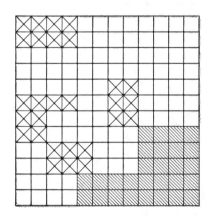

⊠ Soil has been tested, found to be suitable for vineyards.

▨ Unknown; soil not tested.

Map 6: Soil 2

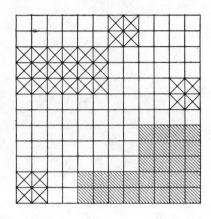

☒ Soil has been tested; found to be suitable for vineyards.

▨ Unknown; soil not tested.

Map 7: Drainage 1

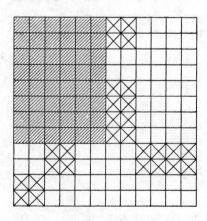

☒ Good, natural drainage.

▨ Subsoil drainage not tested at this time.

Map 8: Drainage 2

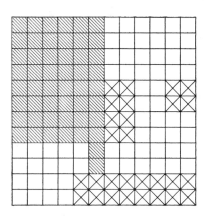

☒ Good, natural drainage.

▨ Subsoil drainage not tested at this time.

Bibliography

Adams, R., & Biddle, B. (1970). *Realities of teaching: Explorations with videotape.* New York: Holt, Rinehart and Winston.

Ahlstrom, W., & Havighurst, R. (1971). *Four hundred losers.* San Francisco: Jossey-Bass.

Aikin, M. (1942). *The story of the eight-year study, Vol. 1.* New York: Harper and Row.

Akita, J., & Mooney, C. (1982). *Natural helpers: A peer support program.* Seattle, Wash.: Roberts and Associates.

Alberto, P., & Troutman, A. (1982). *Applied behavior analysis for teachers: Influencing student performance.* Columbus, Ohio: Charles E. Merrill.

Alexander, C., & Campbell, E. (1964). Peer influences on adolescent aspirations and attainments. *American Sociological Review, 29,* 568–575.

Allen, K., Hart, B., Buell, J., Harris, F., & Wolf, M. (1964). Effects of social reinforcement on isolate behavior of a nursery school child. *Child Development, 35,* 511–518.

Allen, K., Henke, L., Harris, F., Baer, D., & Reynolds, N. (1967). Control of hyperactivity by social reinforcement of attending behavior. *Journal of Educational Psychology, 58,* 231–237.

Alschuler, A. (1980). *School discipline: A socially literate solution.* New York: McGraw-Hill.

Anderson, C. (1982). The search for school climate: A review of the research. *Review of Educational Research, 52,* 368–420.

Anderson, L. (1981, April). *Student responses to seatwork: Implications for the study of students' cognitive processing.* Paper presented at the annual meeting of the American Educational Research Association, Los Angeles.

Anderson, L., Evertson, C., & Brophy, J. (1979). An experimental study of effective teaching in first grade reading groups. *Elementary School Journal, 79,* 193–223.

Anderson, L., & Prawat, R. (1983). Responsibility in the classroom: A synthesis of research on teaching self-control. *Educational Leadership*, 62–66.

Andrews, G., & Debus, R. (1978). Persistence and the causal perception of failure: Modifying cognitive attributions. *Journal of Educational Psychology, 70*, 154–166.

Angus, M. J., Evans, K. W., & Parkin, B. (1975). *An observational study of selected pupil and teacher behavior in open plan and conventional design classrooms.* Australian Open Area Project (Tech. Rep. No. 4). Perth: Educational Department of Western Australia.

Arends, R. (1982), Beginning teachers as learners. *Journal of Educational Research, 76*, 235–242.

Arlin, M. (1979), Teacher transitions can disrupt time flow in classrooms. *American Educational Research Journal. 16*, 42–56.

Aronson, E., Blaney, N., Stephan, C., Sikes, J., & Snapp, M. (1978). *The jigsaw classroom.* Beverly Hills, Calif.: Sage.

Artley, A. (1981). Individual differences and reading instruction. *Elementary School Journal, 82*, 143–151.

Asher, S., & Markell, R. (1974). Sex differences in comprehension of high- and low-interest reading material. *Journal of Educational Psychology, 66*, 680–687.

Aspy, D. (1969). The effect of teacher-offered conditions of empathy, congruence, and positive regard upon student achievement. *Florida Journal of Educational Research, 11*, 39–48.

Aspy, D. (1972). Reaction to Carkhuff's articles. *Counseling Psychologist, 3*, 35–41.

Aspy, D., & Buhler, J. (1975). The effect of teachers' inferred self-concept upon student achievement. *Journal of Educational Research, 47*, 386–389.

Aspy, D., & Roebuck, R. (1977). *Kids don't learn from people they don't like.* Amherst, Mass.: Human Resource Development Press.

Au, K., & Kawakami, A. (1983). Vygotskian perspectives on discussion processes in small-group reading lessons. In L. C. Wilkinson, P. L. Peterson, & M. Hallinan (Eds.), *Student diversity and the organization, processes, and use of instructional groups in the classroom.* New York: Academic Press.

Ausubel, D. (1968). *Educational psychology: A cognitive view.* New York: Holt, Rinehart and Winston.

Axelrod, S. (1983). *Behavior modification for the classroom teacher* (2nd ed.). New York: McGraw-Hill.

Axline, V. (1947). *Play therapy.* Boston: Houghton Mifflin.

Bailey, R., & Kackley, J. (1980). *Positive alternatives to student suspensions: An overview.* St. Petersburg, Fla.: Pupil Personnel Services Demonstration Project, 1015 10th Ave. N.

Bandura, A. (1969). *Principles of behavior modification.* New York: Holt, Rinehart and Winston.

Bandura, A. (1977). *Social learning theory.* Englewood Cliffs, N.J.: Prentice-Hall.

Bandura, A., & Walters, R. (1963). *Social learning and personality development.* New York: Holt, Rinehart and Winston.

Barrish, H., Saunders, M., & Wolf, M. (1969). Good behavior game: Effects of individual contingencies for group consequences on disruptive behavior in a classroom. *Journal of Applied Behavior Analysis, 2*, 119–124.

Bar-Tal, D., Bar-Tal, Y., & Leinhardt, G. (1975). *The environment, locus of control and feelings of satisfaction.* University of Pittsburgh, Learning and Research Development Center (LRDC Publication 1975/27).

Bar-Tal, D., & Bar-Zohar, Y. (1977). The relationship between perception of locus of control and academic achievement: Review and some educational implications. *Contemporary Educational Psychology, 2,* 181–199.

Bash, M., & Camp, B. (1981). *Think aloud: Increasing social and cognitive skills—a problem-solving program for children.* Champaign, Ill.: Research Press.

Baumrind, D. (1968). Authoritarian vs. authoritative control. *Adolescence, 3,* 255–272.

Bebermeyer, R. (1982). *Leadership for school climate improvement.* A working paper prepared for the urban education network, St. Louis, Mo.: Cemrel.

Becker, W. (1964). Consequences of different kinds of parental discipline. In M. L. Hoffman & L. W. Hoffman (Eds.), *Review of child development (Vol. I).* New York: Russell Sage.

Becker, W. (1971). *Parents are teachers.* Champaign, Ill.: Research Press.

Becker, W., Engelmann, S., & Thomas, D. (1975). *Teaching 1: Classroom management.* Chicago: Research Press.

Becker, W., Madsen, C., Arnold, C., & Thomas, D. (1967). The contingent use of teacher attention and praise in reducing classroom behavior problems. *Journal of Special Education, 1,* 287–307.

Beilin, H. (1971). The training and acquisition of logical operations. In M. F. Rosskopf, L. P. Steffe, and S. Taback (Eds.), *Piagetian cognitive- developmental research and mathematical education.* Washington, D.C.: National Council of Teachers of Mathematics.

Belkin, G., & Gray, J. (1977). *Educational psychology: An introduction.* Dubuque, Iowa: Wm. C. Brown.

Bell, L. & Ericksen, L. (1976, September). *Family process and child development: Some preliminary findings.* Paper presented at the meeting of the American Psychological Association, Washington, D.C.

Bellack, A., Kliebard, H., Hyman, R., & Smith, F. (1966). *The language of the classroom.* New York: Columbia University Teachers College Press.

Benedict, R. (1954). Continuities and discontinuities in cultural conditioning. In W. Martin & C. Stendler (Eds.), *Readings in child development.* New York: Harcourt Brace.

Berendal, R. (1950). *The influence of the group on the judgments of children.* New York: King's Crown Press.

Berenson, D. (1971). The effects of systematic human relations training upon the classroom performance of elementary school teachers. *Journal of Research Development in Education, 4,* 70–85.

Berliner, D. (1979). Tempus educare. In P. Peterson and H. Walberg (Eds.), *Research on teaching: Concepts, findings and implications.* Berkeley, Calif.: McCutchan.

Berliner, D. (1984). The half-full glass: A review of research on teaching. In Philip Hosford (Ed.), *Using what we know about teaching.* Alexandria, Va.: Association for Supervision and Curriculum Development.

Bernard, H. (1973). *Child development and learning.* Boston: Allyn and Bacon.

Beyer, B. (1984). Improving thinking skills—defining the problem. *Phi Delta Kappan, 65,* 486–490.

Bissell, J., White, S., & Zivin, G. (1971). Sensory modalities in children's learning. In G. S. Lesser (Ed.), *Psychology and educational practice.* Glenview, Ill.: Scott, Foresman.

Blackham, G., & Silberman, A. (1975). *Modification of child and adolescent behavior.* Belmont, Calif.: Wadsworth.

Blair, J. (1972). The effects of differential reinforcement on the discrimination learning of normal and low-achieving middle-class boys. *Child Development, 43*, 251–255.

Block, E. (1978). *Failing students—failing schools: A study of dropouts and discipline in New York State.* New York: New York Civil Liberties Union.

Bloom, B. (Ed.). (1956). *Taxonomy of educational objectives, handbook I: Cognitive domain.* New York: David McKay.

Blumenfeld, P., Pintrich, P., Meece, J., & Wessels, K. (1982). The formation and role of self-perceptions of ability in elementary classrooms. *Elementary School Journal, 82*, 400–420.

Bolles, R. (1972). Reinforcement, expectancy, and learning. *Psychological Review, 79*, 394–409.

Bolstad, O., & Johnson, S. (1972). Self-regulation in the modification of disruptive classroom behavior. *Journal of Applied Behavior Analysis, 5*, 433–454.

Borda, M. and Borda, C. (1978). *Self-esteem: A classroom affair.* Minneapolis, Minn.: Winston Press.

Borg, W. (1980). Time and school learning. In C. Denham and A. Lieberman (Eds.), *Time to learn.* Washington, D.C.: National Institute of Education.

Borg, W., & Ascione, F. (1982). Classroom management in elementary mainstreaming classrooms. *Journal of Educational Psychology, 74*, 85–95.

Borich, G., & Madden, S. (1977). Evaluating classroom instruction: A sourcebook of instruments. Reading, Mass.: Addison-Wesley.

Boyer, E. (1984). *High school: A report on secondary education in America.* New York: Harper and Row.

Bozsik, B. (1982, March). *A study of teacher questioning and student response interaction during pre-story and post-story portions of reading comprehension lessons.* Paper presented at the annual meeting of the American Educational Research Association, New York.

Brainerd, C., & Allen, T. (1971). Experimental inductions of the conservation of "first order" quantitative invariants. *Psychological Bulletin, 75*, 128–144.

Branch, C., Damico, S., & Purkey, W. (1977). A comparison between the self-concepts as learner of disruptive and nondisruptive middle school students. *Middle School Journal, 7*, 15–16.

Brause, R., & Mayher, J. (1982). Teachers, students, and classroom organizations. *Research in the Teaching of English, 16*, 131–148.

Brittain, C. (1963). Adolescent choices and parent-peer cross-pressures. *American Sociological Review, 28*, 385–390.

Brittain, C. (1966). Age and sex of siblings and conformity toward parents versus peers in adolescence. *Child Development, 37*, 709–714.

Broden, M., Hall, R., Dunlap, A., & Clark, R. (1970). Effects of teacher attention and a token reinforcement system in a junior high school special education class. *Exceptional Children, 36*, 341–349.

Broden, M., Hall, R., & Mitts, B. (1971). The effect of self-recording on the classroom behavior of two eighth-grade students. *Journal of Applied Behavior Analysis, 4*, 191–199.

Bronfenbrenner, U. (1970). *Two worlds of childhood: U.S. and U.S.S.R.* New York: Russell Sage.

Bronfenbrenner, U. (1974, August). The origins of alienation. *Scientific American, 231*, 53–57.

Bronfenbrenner, U. (1977a). Disturbing changes in the American family. *Education Digest, 42*, 22–25.

Bronfenbrenner, U. (1977b, May). Nobody home: The erosion of the American family. *Psychology Today, 10,* 40–47.

Brookover, W. (1978). Elementary school climate and school achievement. *American Educational Research Journal, 15,* 301–318.

Brookover, W., Beady, C., Flood, P., Schweitzer, J., & Wisenback, J. (1979). *School social systems and student achievement: Schools can make a difference.* New York: Bergin.

Brookover, W., Patterson, A., & Thomas, S. (1965). *Self-concept of ability and school achievement.* U.S. Office of Education, Cooperative Research Project No. 845. East Lansing: Office of Research and Publications, Michigan State University.

Brookover, W., Schweitzer, J., Schneider, J., Beady, D., Flood, P., & Wisenbaker, J. (1978). Elementary school social climate and school achievement. *American Educational Research Journal, 15,* 301–318.

Brophy, J. (1979). Teacher behavior and its effects. *Journal of Educational Psychology, 71,* 733–750.

Brophy, J. (1981). Teacher praise: A functional analysis. *Review of Educational Research, 51,* 301–318.

Brophy, J. (1982a). Classroom management and learning. *American Education, 18,* 20–23.

Brophy, J. (1982b). Supplemental management techniques. In D. Duke (Ed.), *Helping teachers manage classrooms.* Alexandria, Va.: ASCD.

Brophy, J. (1982c, May). *Classroom organization and management* (Occasional Paper No. 54). East Lansing: Michigan State University, Institute for Research on Teaching.

Brophy, J. (1983a). Classroom organization and management. In David Smith (Ed.), *Essential knowledge for beginning educators.* Washington, D.C.: American Association of Colleges for Teacher Education.

Brophy, J. (1983b). Research on the self-fulfilling prophecy and teacher expectations. *Journal of Educational Psychology, 75,* 631–661.

Brophy, J., & Evertson, C. (1974). *The Texas Teacher Effectiveness Project: Presentation of Non-linear Relationships and Summary Discussion Report No. 74–6.* Austin: Research and Development Center for Teacher Education, University of Texas in Austin. (ERIC Document Reproduction Service No. ED 099 345).

Brophy, J., & Evertson, C. (1976). *Learning from teaching: A developmental perspective.* Boston: Allyn and Bacon.

Brophy, J., & Good, T. (1971). Teacher's communication of differential expectations for children's classroom performance: Some behavior data. *Journal of Educational Psychology, 61,* 365–374.

Brophy, J., & Good, T. (1974). *Teacher-student relationships: Causes and consequences.* New York: Holt, Rinehart and Winston.

Brophy, J., & Rohrkemper, M. (1981). The influence of problem ownership on teachers' perceptions of and strategies for coping with problem students. *Journal of Educational Psychology, 73,* 295–311.

Brown, E., & Shields, E. (1967). Results with systematic suspension: A guidance technique to help children develop self-control in public school classrooms. *Journal of Special Education, 1,* 425–437.

Brown, G. (1975). *The training of teachers for affective roles.* In K. Ryan (Ed.), *The seventy-fourth yearbook of the National Society for the Study of Education.* Chicago: University of Chicago Press.

Brunkan, R., & Sheni, F. (1966). Personality characteristics of ineffective, effective and efficient readers. *Personnel and Guidance Journal, 44,* 837–844.

Bryan, J., and Locke, E. (1967). Goal setting as a means of increasing motivation. *Journal of Applied Psychology, 51,* 274–277.

Bryan, J. & Walbek, N. (1970). Preaching and practicing generosity: Children's actions and reactions. *Child Development, 41,* 329–353.

Buike, S. (1981). *The shaping of classroom practices: Teacher decisions* (Research Series No. 97). East Lansing: Institute for Research on Teaching, Michigan State University.

Burrows, C. (1973). *The effects of a mastery learning strategy on the geometry achievement of fourth and fifth grade children.* Unpublished doctoral dissertation, Indiana University.

Butler, K. (1984). Working your curriculum with style. *Challenge, 2,* 38–42.

Bybee, R., & Sund, R. (1982). *Piaget for educators.* Columbus, Ohio: Charles E. Merrill.

Calhoun, J., Grotberg, E., & Rackey, W. (1980). *The status of children, youth, and families 1979.* DHHS Publication No. (OHDS) 80–30274. Washington, D.C.: U.S. Government Printing Office.

Campbell, J. (1974). Can a teacher really make the difference? *School Science and Mathematics, 74,* 657–666.

Campbell, P. (1967). School and self-concept. *Educational Leadership, 24,* 510–515.

Canter, L. (1976). *Assertive discipline.* Los Angeles: Lee Canter Associates.

Carkhuff, R. (1969). *Helping and human relations: A primer for lay and professional helpers. Vol. 2: Practice and research.* New York: Holt, Rinehart and Winston.

Carrino, C. (1966). Identifying potential dropouts in the elementary grades. *Dissertation Abstracts, 27,* 343.

Cartledge, G., & Milburn, J. (1978). The case for teaching social skills in the classroom: A review. *Review of Educational Research, 48,* 133–156.

Casler, L. (1965). The effects of extra tactile stimulation on a group of institutionalized infants. *Genetic Psychology Monographs, 71,* 137–175.

Castillo, G. (1974). *Left-handed teaching: Lessons in affective education.* New York: Praeger.

Chaikin, A., Sigler, E., & Derlega, V. (1974). Nonverbal mediators of teacher expectancy effects. *Journal of Personality and Social Psychology, 30,* 144–149.

Chamberlain, D. (1942). *Did they succeed in college? Vol. 4.* New York: Harper and Row.

Chandler, T. (1975). Locus of control: A proposal for change. *Psychology in the Schools, 12,* 334–339.

Chapin, M., & Dyck, D. (1976). Persistence in children's reading behavior as a function of N length and attribution retraining. *Journal of Abnormal Psychology, 85,* 511–515.

Cichon, D., & Koff, R. (1980). Stress and teaching. *NASSP Bulletin, 64,* 91–104.

Clark, R. (1982). Antagonism between achievement and enjoyment in ATI studies. *Educational Psychologist, 17,* 92–101.

Clements, B. (1983). *Helping experienced teachers with classroom management: An experimental study* (R & D Report No. 6155). Austin: Research and Development Center for Teacher Education, University of Texas at Austin.

Coats, W., & Smidchens, U. (1966). Audience recall as a function of speaker dynamism. *Journal of Educational Psychology, 57,* 189–191.

Coleman, J. (1966). *Equality of educational opportunity.* Washington, D.C.: U.S. Department of Health, Education, and Welfare, Office of Education.

Coleman, J. (1974). *Youth: Transition to adulthood*. Chicago: University of Chicago Press.

Collins, K. (1971). A strategy for mastery learning in modern mathematics. In J. Block (Ed.), *Mastery learning: Theory and practice*. New York: Holt, Rinehart and Winston.

Combs, A., Avila, D., & Purkey, W. (1971). *Helping relationships: Basic concepts for the helping professions*. Boston: Allyn and Bacon.

Combs, A., & Taylor, C. (1952). The effect of the perception of mild degrees of threat on performance. *Journal of Abnormal and Social Psychology, 47*, 420–424.

Comer, J. (1980). *School power: Implications of an intervention project*. New York: Free Press.

Conger, J. (1977). *Adolescence and youth: Psychological development in a changing world*. New York: Harper and Row.

Conger, J. (1977b). Parent-child relationships, social change and adolescent vulnerability. *Journal of Pediatric Psychology, 2*, 93–97.

Conger, J., Miller, W., & Walsmith, C. (1965). Antecedents of delinquency, personality, social class and intelligence. In P. Mussen, J. Conger, and J. Kagen (Eds.), *Readings in child development and personality*, New York: Harper and Row.

Conger, J., & Petersen, A. (1984). *Adolescence and youth: Psychological development in a changing world* (3rd ed.). New York: Harper and Row.

Cooper, H., & Good, T. (1983). *Pygmalion grows up*. New York: Longman.

Coopersmith, S. (1967). *The antecedents of self-esteem*. San Francisco: W. H. Freeman.

Copeland, R., Brown, R., & Hall, R. (1974). The effects of principal-implemented techniques on the behavior of pupils. *Journal of Applied Behavior Analysis, 7*, 77–86.

Cormany, R. (1975). *Guidance and counseling in Pennsylvania: Status and needs*. Lemoyne, Pa.: ESEA title II Project, West Shore School District.

Costello, C. (1964). Ego-involvement, success and failure: A review of the literature. In H. J. Eysenck (Ed.), *Experiments in Motivation*. New York: Macmillan.

Covington, M., & Beery, R. (1976). *Self-worth and school learning*. New York: Holt, Rinehart and Winston.

Craighead, W., Kazdin, A., & Mahoney, M. (1976). *Behavior modification: Principles, issues, and applications*. Boston: Houghton Mifflin.

Cronback, L. (1975). Beyond the two disciplines of scientific psychology. *American Psychologist, 30*, 116–127.

Culross, R. (1982). Developing the whole child: A developmental approach to guidance with the gifted. *Roeper Review, 5*, 24–26.

Cummings, C. (1980). *Teaching makes a difference*. Edmonds, Wash.: Teaching Publishing.

Currence, C. (1984, February 29). School performance tops list of adolescent worries. *Education Week, 3*, 8.

Curwin, R., & Fuhrmann, B. (1975). *Discovering your teaching self: Humanistic approaches to effective teaching*. Englewood Cliffs, N.J.

Darling-Hammond, L., Wise, A., & Pease, S. (1983). Teacher evaluation in the organizational context: A review of the literature. *Review of Educational Research, 53*, 285–328.

Daum, J. (1972). *Proxemics in the classroom: Speaker-subject distance and educational performance*. Paper presented at the annual meeting of the Southeastern Psychological Association.

Davidson, H., & Lang, G. (1960). Children's perceptions of their teachers' feelings toward them. *Journal of Experimental Education, 29*, 109–118.

Davis, J., Laughlin, P., & Komorita, S. (1976). The social psychology of small groups: Cooperative and mixed-motive interaction. In M. Rosenzweig & L. Porter (Eds.), *Annual review of psychology. 27,* Palo Alto, Calif.: Annual Reviews, 501–542.

Davis, R., & Mcknight, C. (1976). Conceptual, heuristic, and S-algorithmic approaches in mathematics teaching. *Journal of Children's Mathematical Behavior, 1* (Supplement 1), 271–286.

DeBevoise, Wynn (1984). Synthesis of research on the principal as instructional leader. *Educational Leadership, 41,* 14–20.

DeCharms, R. (1968). *Personal causation.* New York: Academic Press.

DeCharms, R. (1971). From pawns to origins: Toward self-motivation. In G. S. Lesser (Ed.), *Psychology and educational practice.* Glenview, Ill: Scott Foresman.

DeCharms, R. (1972). Personal causation training in schools. *Journal of Applied Social Psychology, 2,* 95–113.

DeCharms, R. (1976). *Enhancing motivation.* New York: Irvington.

Deci, E. (1971). Effects of externally mediated rewards on intrinsic motivation. *Journal of Personality and Social Psychology, 18,* 105–115.

Deci, E. (1972). The effects of contingent and noncontingent rewards and controls on intrinsic motivation. *Organizational Behavior and Human Performance, 8,* 217–229.

deHirsch, K., Jansky, J., & Langford, W. (1966). *Predicting reading failure.* New York: Harper and Row.

Delefes, P., & Jackson, B. (1972). Teacher-pupil interaction as a function of location in the classroom. *Psychology in the Schools, 9,* 119–123.

Dembo, M. (1977). *Teaching for learning: Applying educational psychology in the classroom.* Santa Monica, Calif: Goodyear.

Denham, C., & Lieberman, A. (Eds.). (1980). *Time to learn.* Washington, D.C.: National Institute of Education.

Dennis, W. (1960). Causes of retardation among institutional children: Iran. *Journal of Genetic Psychology, 96,* 46–60.

DeVries, D. & Edwards, K. (1973). Learning games and student teams: Their effects on classroom process. *American Educational Research Journal, 10,* 307–318.

Dewey, J. (1958). *Experience and nature.* LaSalle, Ill.: Open Court.

Dewey, J. (1963). *Experience and education.* New York: Macmillan.

Diggory, J. (1966). *Self-evaluation: Concepts and studies.* New York: John Wiley.

Dooling, D., & Mullet, R. (1973). Locus of thematic effects in retention of prose. *Journal of Experimental Psychology, 97,* 404–406.

Dorman, G. (1981). *Middle Grades Assessment Program.* Chapel Hill, N.C.: Center for Early Adolescence.

Douvan, E., & Adelson, J. (1966). *The adolescent experience.* New York: Wiley.

Doyle, W. (1979). Classroom tasks and students' abilities. In P. L. Peterson & H. J. Walberg (Eds.), *Research on teaching.* Berkeley, Calif. McCutchan.

Doyle, W. (1983). Academic work. *Review of Educational Research, 53,* 159–199.

Doyle, W. (in press). Classroom organization and management. In M. C. Wittrock (Ed.), *Handbook of research on teaching* (3rd ed.). New York: Macmillan.

Doyle, W., Sanford, J., & Emmer, E. (1982). Managing academic tasks in junior high school: Background, design, and methodology (R & D Rep. 6185). Austin: Research and Development Center for Teacher Education, University of Texas at Austin.

Drabman, R., & Lahey, B. (1974). Feedback in classroom behavior modification: Effects on the target child and her classmates. *Journal of Applied Behavior Analysis, 7,* 591–598.

Drabman, R., Spitalnik, R., & O'Leary, K. (1973). Teaching self-control to disruptive children. *Journal of Abnormal Psychology, 82,* 10–16.

Dreikurs, R. (1968). *Psychology in the classroom: A manual for teachers* (2nd ed.). New York: Harper and Row.

Dreikurs. R., & Cassel, P. (1972). *Discipline without tears: What to do with children who misbehave.* New York: Hawthorn.

Dreikurs, R., Grunwald, B., & Pepper, F. (1971). *Maintaining sanity in the classroom: Illustrated teaching techniques.* New York: Harper and Row.

Dreikurs, R., Grunwald, B., & Pepper, F. (1982). *Maintaining sanity in the classroom: Classroom management techniques* (2nd Ed.). New York: Harper and Row.

Duckworth, E. (1964). Piaget rediscovered. In R. E. Ripple and V. N. Rockcastle (Eds.), *Piaget rediscovered: A report of the conference on cognitive skills and curriculum development.* Ithaca, N.Y.: Cornell University, School of Education.

Duffy, G., & McIntyre, L. (1982). A naturalistic study of instructional assistance in primary-grade reading. *Elementary School Journal, 83,* 15–23.

Duke, D. (1978). How administrators view the crisis in school discipline. *Phi Delta Kappan, 59,* 325–330.

Duke, D. (1980). *Managing student behavior problems.* New York: Teachers College, Columbia University.

Duke, D. (1984). *Teaching—the imperiled profession.* Albany, N.Y.: State University of New York Press.

Duke, D. (1985). School discipline plans and the quest for order in American schools. In D. Tattum (Ed.). *Management of disruptive behaviour in schools.* Chichester, Sussex, England: John Wiley.

Duke, D., & Jones, V. (1984). Two decades of discipline—assessing the development of an educational specialization. *Journal of Research and Development in Education, 17,* 25–35.

Duke, D., & Jones, V. (in press). What can schools do to foster student responsibility? *Theory into practice.*

Dunkin, M., & Biddle, B. (1974). *The study of teaching.* New York: Holt, Rinehart and Winston.

Dunn, R. (1983). Learning style and its relation to exceptionality at both ends of the spectrum. *Exceptional Children, 49,* 496–506.

Dunn, R., Cavanaugh, D., Eberle, B., & Lenhausern, R. (1982). Hemispheric preference: The newest element of learning style. *American Biology Teacher, 44,* 291–294.

Dunn, R., & Dunn, K. (1972). *Practical approaches to individualizing instruction: Contracts and other effective teaching strategies.* West Nyack, N.Y.: Parker.

Dunn, R., & Dunn, K. (1978). *Teaching students through their individual learning styles: A practical approach.* Reston, Va: Reston.

Dunn, R., & Dunn, K. (1979). Learning styles/teaching styles: Should they . . . can they . . . be matched? *Journal of Educational Leadership, 36,* 238–244.

Dunn, R., & Goldman, M. (1966). Competition and noncompetition in relationship to satisfaction and feelings toward own group and nongroup members. *Journal of Social Psychology, 68,* 299–311.

Durkin, D. (1981). Reading comprehension instruction in five basal reader series. *Reading Research Quarterly, 16,* 515–544.

Edmonds, R. (1979). Effective schools for the urban poor. *Educational Leadership, 37,* 15–18.

Edmonds, R. (1981). Making public schools effective. *Social Policy, 12,* 56–60.

Edmonds, R. (1982). Programs of school improvement: An overview. *Educational Leadership, 40,* 4–11.

Eider, E. (1984). Can educational research inform educational practice? *Phi Delta Kappan, 65,* 447–452.

Elardo, P., & Cooper, M. (1977). *Aware.* New York: Addison-Wesley.

Elder, G. (1963). Parental power legitimation and its effect on the adolescent. *Sociometry, 26,* 50–65.

Elkind, D. (1967). Egocentrism in adolescence. *Child Development, 38,* 1025–1034.

Elkind, D. (1979, February). Growing up faster. *Psychology Today, 12,* 38–45.

Elkind, D. (1981a). *The hurried child: Growing up too fast too soon.* Reading, Mass.: Addison-Wesley.

Elkind, D. (1981b). Adolescent thinking and the curriculum. *New York University Education Quarterly, 12,* 18–24.

Ellison, W. (1979). School vandalism: 100-million-dollar challenge. *Community Education Journal, 3,* 27–33.

Emmer, E., Evertson, C., & Anderson, L. (1980). Effective management at the beginning of the school year. *Elementary School Journal, 80,* 219–231.

Emmer, E., Evertson, C., Sanford, J., Clements, B., & Worsham, M. (1982). *Organizing and managing the junior high classroom.* Austin, Tex.: Research and Development Center for Teacher Education.

Emmer, E., Evertson, C., Sanford, J., Clements, B., & Worsham, M. (1984). *Classroom management for secondary teachers.* Englewood Cliffs, N.J.: Prentice-Hall.

Enright, R., Lapsley, D., Drivas, A., & Fehn, L. (1980). Parental influences on the development of adolescent autonomy and identity. *Journal of Youth and Adolescence, 9,* 529–546.

Epanchin, B. C., & Paul, J. (1982). *Casebook for educating the emotionally disturbed.* Columbus, Ohio: Charles E. Merrill.

Epstein, H. (1979). Cognitive growth and development. *Colorado Journal of Educational Research, 19,* 34–35.

Epstein, J. (1981). *The quality of school life.* Lexington, Mass.: Lexington Books.

Epstein, M., Hallahan, D., & Kauffman, J. (1975). Implications of the reflectivity-impulsivity dimension for special education. *Journal of Special Education, 9,* 11–25.

Erikson, E. (1963). *Childhood and society* (2nd ed.). New York: Norton.

Erikson, E. (1968). *Identity, youth, and crisis.* New York: W. W. Norton.

Evertson, C. (1982). *What research tells us about managing classroom instruction effectively.* Palo Alto, Calif.: Teaching and Learning Institute.

Evertson, C., & Emmer, E. (1982a). Effective management at the beginning of the school year in junior high school classes. *Journal of Educational Psychology, 74,* 485–498.

Evertson, C., & Emmer, E. (1982b). Preventive classroom management. In D. Duke (Ed.), *Helping teachers manage classrooms.* Alexandria, Va.: Association for Supervision and Curriculum Development.

Evertson, C., Emmer, E., Clements, B., Sanford, J., & Worsham, M., (1984). *Classroom management for elementary teachers.* Englewood Cliffs, N.J.: Prentice-Hall.

Evertson, C., Emmer, E., Clements, B., Sanford, J., Worsham, M., & Williams, E. (1981). *Organizing and managing the elementary school classroom.* Austin, Tex.: Research and Development Center for Teacher Education.

Evertson, C., Emmer, E., Sanford, J., & Clements, B. (1982). Improving classroom management: An experimental study in elementary classrooms. Austin, Tex.: Research and Development Center for Teacher Education, University of Texas.

Faber, A., & Mazlish, E. (1980). *How to talk so kids will listen and listen so kids will talk.* New York: Rawson, Wade.

Faris, R. (1967). High and low achievement of intellectually average intermediate grade students related to self-concept and social approval. *Dissertation Abstracts, 28,* 1205.

Farquhar, W. (1968). *A comprehensive study of the motivational factors underlying achievement of eleventh-grade high school students.* U.S. Office of Education, Cooperative Research Report No. 846. East Lansing: Office of Research and Publications, Michigan State University.

Federal Bureau of Investigation, U.S. Department of Justice. (1975). *Uniform crime reports.* Washington, D.C.: U.S. Government Printing Office.

Federal Register. (1977, August). *Public Law 94–142.* Washington, D.C.: U.S. Education Department.

Feitler, F., & Tokar, E. (1982). Getting a handle on teacher stress: How bad is the problem? *Educational Leadership, 39,* 456–458.

Fernandez, C., Espinosa, R., & Dornbusch, S. (1977). Discussed in Martin, D. Your praise can smother learning. *Learning, 5,* 43–51.

Fisher, B., & Fisher, L. (1979). Styles in teaching and learning. *Journal of Educational Leadership, 36,* 245–254.

Fisher, C., Berliner, D., Filby, N., Marliave, R., Cahen, L., & Dishaw, M. (1980). Teaching behaviors, academic learning time, and student achievement: An overview. In C. Denham and A. Lieberman (Eds.), *Time to learn.* Washington, D.C.: National Institute of Education.

Fisher, C., Filby, N., Marliave, R., Cahen, L., Dishaw, M., Moore, J., & Berliner, D. (1978). *Teaching behaviors, academic learning time and student achievement.* (Report of Phase III–B, Beginning Teacher Evaluation Study. Tech. Rep. V–1). San Francisco, Calif.: Far West Laboratory for Educational Research and Development.

Fitzpatrick, K. (1982). *The effect of a secondary classroom management training program on teacher and student behavior.* Paper presented at the annual meeting of the American Educational Research Association, New York.

Flanders, N. (1963). Intent, action and feedback: A preparation for teaching. *Journal of Teacher Education, 14,* 251–260.

Flanders, N. (1970). *Analyzing teaching behavior.* Reading, Mass.: Addison-Wesley.

Flanders, N., & Amidon, E. (1967). *The role of the teacher in the classroom.* Minneapolis, Minn.: Minneapolis Association for Productive Teaching.

Flanders, N., Morrison, B., & Brode, E. (1968). Changes in pupil attitudes during the school year. *Journal of Educational Psychology, 59,* 334–338.

Fowler, J., & Peterson, P. (1981). Increasing reading persistence and altering attributional style of learned helpless children. *Journal of Educational Psychology, 73,* 251–260.

Fox, R., Luzski, M., & Schmuck, R. (1966). *Diagnosing classroom learning environments.* Chicago: Science Research Associates.

Fredericks, B. (1975). *Personal communications.* Unpublished Research Project, Teaching Research, Monmouth, Oreg.

Frericks, A. (1974, March). Labeling of students by prospective teachers. Paper presented at the American Educational Research Association Convention, Chicago.

Friedrich, L., & Stein, A. (1973). Aggressive and prosocial TV programs and the natural behavior of preschool children. *Monographs of the Society for Research in Child Development, 38* (4, Serial No. 151).

Fuller, B., & Lee, G. (1981). *Toward more human schools: Exemplary efforts in self-concept, human values, parenting, and school climate.* Sacramento, Calif.: State Department of Education.

Gall, M., Haisley, F., Baker, R., & Perez, T. (1982). *The relationship between inservice education practices and effectiveness of basic skills instruction.* Eugene, Oreg.: Center for Educational Policy and Management.

Gallagher, J. (1965). Expressive thought by gifted children in the classroom. *Elementary English, 42,* 559–568.

Gallup, A. (1984). The Gallup poll of teachers' attitudes toward the public schools. *Phi Delta Kappan, 66,* 97–107.

Gallup, G. (1983). The 15th Annual Gallup Poll of the public's attitudes toward the public schools. *Phi Delta Kappan, 65,* 33–47.

Gallup, G. (1982). Gallup Poll of the public's attitudes toward the public schools. *Phi Delta Kappan, 64,* 37–50.

Gallup, G. (1984). The 16th Annual Gallup Poll of the public's attitudes toward the public schools. *Phi Delta Kappan, 66,* 23–38.

Gambrell, L., Wilson, R., & Gantt, W. (1981). Classroom observations of task-attending behaviors of good and poor readers. *Journal of Educational Research, 74,* 400–405.

Gibb, J. (1964). Climate for trust formation. In L. Bradford, J. Gibb, & K. Beene (Eds.), *T-Group theory and laboratory method.* New York: John Wiley, 279–309.

Ginott, H. (1965). *Between parent and child: New solutions to old problems.* New York: Macmillan.

Glasser, W. (1965). Reality therapy. New York: Harper and Row.

Glasser, W. (1969). *Schools without failure.* New York: Harper and Row.

Glasser, W. (1977). Ten steps to good discipline. *Today's Education, 66,* 61–63.

Glick, P., & Norton, A. (1979). Marrying, divorcing, and living together in the U.S. today. *Population Bulletin, 32,* 1–40.

Goertzel, V., & Goertzel, M. (1962). *Cradles of eminence.* Boston: Little, Brown.

Good, T. (1970). Which pupils do you call on? *Elementary School Journal, 10,* 190–198.

Good, T. (1979). Teacher effectiveness in the elementary school. *Journal of Teacher Education, 30,* 52–64.

Good, T. (1983a). Classroom research: A decade of progress. *Educational Psychologist, 18,* 127–144.

Good, T. (1983b). Recent classroom research: Implications for teacher education. In David Smith (Ed.), *Essential knowledge for beginning educators.* Washington, D.C.: American Association of Colleges for Teacher Education.

Good, T., & Beckerman, T. (1978). Time on task: A naturalistic study in sixth grade classrooms. *Elementary School Journal, 78,* 193–201.

Good, T., & Brophy, J. (1973). *Looking in classrooms.* New York: Harper and Row.

Good, T., & Brophy, J. (1974). Changing teacher and student behavior: An empirical investigation. *Journal of Educational Psychology, 66,* 390–405.

Good, T., & Brophy, J. (1980). *Educational psychology: A realistic approach* (2nd ed.). New York: Holt, Rinehart and Winston.

Good, T., & Brophy, J. (1984). *Looking in classrooms* (3rd ed.). New York: Harper and Row.

Good, T., Ebmeier, H., & Beckerman, T. (1978). Teaching mathematics in high and low SES classrooms: An empirical comparison. *Journal of Teacher Education, 29,* 85–90.

Good, T., & Grouws, D. (1979). The Missouri mathematics effectiveness project. *Journal of Educational Psychology, 71*, 355–362.

Good, T., & Power, C. (1976). Designing successful classroom environments for different types of students. *Journal of Curriculum Studies, 8*, 47–52.

Goodlad, J. (1983a). A study of schooling: Some findings and hypotheses. *Phi Delta Kappan, 64*, 465–470.

Goodlad, J. (1983b). A study of schooling: Some implications for school improvement. *Phi Delta Kappan, 64*, 552–558.

Goodlad, J. (1984). *A place called school.* New York: McGraw-Hill.

Goodwin, S., & Mahoney, M. (1975). Modification of aggression through modeling: An experimental probe. *Journal of Behavior Therapy and Experimental Psychiatry, 6*, 200–202.

Gordon, I. (1966). *Studying the child in school.* New York: Wiley.

Gordon, T. (1970). *Parent effectiveness training: The tested new way to raise responsible children.* New York: Wyden.

Gordon, T. (1974). *Teacher effectiveness training.* New York: Wyden.

Gordon, T., & Breivogel, W. (1976). *Building effective home-school relationships.* Boston: Allyn and Bacon.

Gottfredson, G. (January 23, 1984). School discipline. Testimony before the Subcommittee on Elementary, Secondary, and Vocational Education of the Committee on Education and Labor, U.S. House of Representatives.

Gowan, J. (1960). Factors of achievement in high school and college. *Journal of Counseling Psychology, 7*, 91–95.

Gray, R., Graubard, P., & Rosenberg, H. (1974, November). Little brother is changing you. *Psychology Today, 7*, 42–46.

Greenfield, W. (1982). *Research on public school principals: A review and recommendations.* Paper presented at the NIE Conference on Principals for Educational Excellence in the 1980s, Washington, D.C.

Greenwood, C., & Hops, H. (1976). *Generalization of teacher praising skills over time and setting: What you teach is what you get.* Paper presented at the 54th Annual Convention of the Council for Exceptional Children, Chicago, Ill.

Greenwood, C., Hops, H., Delquadri, J., & Walker, H. (1974). *PASS: Program for academic survival skills.* Eugene: Center at Oregon for Research in the Behavioral Education of the Handicapped.

Gregorc, A. (1982). *An adult's guide to styles.* Maynard, Mass. Gabriel Systems.

Grimes, J., & Allinsmith, W. (1961). Compulsivity, anxiety, and school achievement. *Merrill-Palmer Quarterly, 7*, 247–272.

Groisser, P. (1964). *How to use the fine art of questioning.* New York: Teachers' Practical Press.

Grueling, J., & DeBlassie, R. (1980). Adolescent suicide. *Adolescence, 15*, 589–601.

Gump, P. (1967). *The classroom behavior setting: Its nature and relation to student behavior.* Washington, D.C.: Office of Education, Bureau of Research. (ERIC Document No. EDO15515).

Hagen, J., & Hale, G. (1972). The development of attention in children. In A. D. Pick (Ed.), *Minnesota symposia on child psychology* (Vol. 7). Minneapolis: University of Minnesota Press.

Hall, R., Lund, D., & Jackson, D. (1968). Effects of teacher attention on study behavior. *Journal of Applied Behavior Analysis, 1*, 1–12.

Hargreaves, D. (1967). *Social relations in a secondary school.* New York: Humanities Press.

Haring, N., & Phillips, E. (1972). Analysis and modification of classroom behavior. Englewood Cliffs, N.J.: Prentice-Hall.

Harlow, H. (1958). The nature of love. American Psychologist, 13, 673–684.

Harmin, M., Kirschenbaum, H., & Simon, S. (1973). Clarifying values through subject matter. Minneapolis, Minn.: Winston Press.

Harter, S., & Connell, J. (1981). A model of the relationship among children's academic achievement and their self-perceptions of competence, control and motivational orientation. In J. Nicholls (Ed.), The development of achievement motivation. Greenwich, Conn.: JAI Press.

Hawkes, T., and Furst, N. (1971). Research note: Race, S.E.S., achievement, IQ, and teachers' ratings of behavior as factors relating to anxiety in upper elementary school children. Sociology of Education, 44, 333–350.

Hawkes, T., and Furst, N. (1973). An investigation of the misconceptions of pre- and in-service teachers as to the manifestations of anxiety in upper elementary school children from different racial-socioeconomic backgrounds. Psychology in the Schools, 10, 23–32.

Hawkes, T., and Koff, R. (1970). Differences in anxiety of private school and inner-city public elementary school children. Psychology in the Schools, 7, 250–259.

Hawley, R., & Hawley, I. (1975). Human values in the classroom: A handbook for teachers. New York: Hart.

Hefele, T. (1971). The effects of systematic human relations training upon student achievement. Journal of Research and Development in Education, 4, 52–69.

Henry, J. (1963). Culture against man. New York: Random House.

Heward, W., & Orlansky, M. (1980). Exceptional children. Columbus, Ohio: Charles E. Merrill.

Hewett, F. (1974). Education of exceptional learners. Boston: Allyn and Bacon.

Holinger, P. (1978). Adolescent suicide: An epidemiological study of recent trends. American Journal of Psychiatry, 135, 754–756.

Hollingsworth, E., Lufler, H., & Clune, W. (1984). School discipline: Order and autonomy. New York: Praeger.

Holmes, D., & Barthell, C. (1968). High school yearbooks: A nonreactive measure of social isolation in graduates who later become schizophrenic. Journal of Abnormal Psychology, 73, 313–316.

Holt, J. (1969). The underachieving school. New York: Pitman.

Holt, J. (1972). What do I do Monday? New York: Dell.

Holzman, P., & Grinker, R. (1977). Schizophrenia in adolescence. In S. Feinstein and P. Giovacchini (Eds.), Adolescent psychiatry, Volume V. New York: Jason Aronson.

Hoover, K. (1968). Learning and teaching in the secondary school: Improved instruction practice. Boston: Allyn and Bacon.

Horst, B., & Johnson, R. (1981). Brain growth periodization and its implications for language arts. English Journal, 70, 74–75.

Hosford, P. (1984). Using what we know about teaching. Alexandria, Va.: Association for Supervision and Curriculum Development.

Howard, E. (1981). School climate improvement—rationale and process. Illinois School Research and Development, 18, 8–12.

Hudgins, B., & Ahlbrand, W., Jr. (1969). A study of classroom interaction and thinking. Technical report series No. 8. St. Ann, Mo.: Central Midwestern Regional Educational Laboratory.

Hughes, E., Becker, H., & Greer, B. (1962). Student culture and academic effort. In N. Sanfort (Ed.) The American college. New York: Wiley.

Hundert, J. (1976). The effectiveness of reinforcement, response cost, and mixed programs on classroom behaviors. *Journal of Applied Behavior Analysis, 9,* 107.

Hunter, M. (1976). *Improved instruction.* El Segundo, Calif.: TIP.

Hunter, M. (1981). *Increasing your teaching effectiveness.* Palo Alto, Calif.: Learning Institute.

Hutzell, R., Platzek, D., & Logue, P. (1974). Control of symptoms of Gilles de la Tourette's Syndrome by self-monitoring. *Journal of Behavior Therapy and Experimental Psychiatry, 5,* 71–76.

Hyman, I., & D'Alessandro, J. (1984). Good old-fashioned discipline: The politics of punitiveness. *Phi Delta Kappan, 66,* 39–45.

Ince, L. (1976). The use of relaxation training and a conditioned stimulus in the elimination of epileptic seizures in a child: A case study. *Journal of Behavior Therapy and Experimental Psychiatry, 7,* 39–42.

Irwin, F. (1967). Sentence completion responses and scholastic success or failure. *Journal of Counseling Psychology, 14,* 269–271.

Jackson, N., Jackson, D., & Monroe, C. (1983). *Getting along with others: Teaching social effectiveness to children.* Champaign, Ill.: Research Press.

Jackson, P. (1968). *Life in classrooms.* New York: Holt, Rinehart and Winston.

Jacobs, J. (1971). *Adolescent suicide.* New York: Wiley.

Jacobson, E. (1938). *Progressive relaxation.* Chicago: University of Chicago Press.

Jencke, S., & Peck, D. (1976). Is immediate reinforcement appropriate? *Arithmetic Teacher, 23,* 32–33.

Jessop, D. (1981). Family relationships as viewed by parents and adolescents: A specification. *Journal of Marriage and the Family, 43,* 95–108.

Johnson, D. (1979). *Educational psychology.* Englewood Cliffs, N.J.: Prentice-Hall.

Johnson, D., & Johnson, R. (1975). *Learning together and alone: Cooperation, competition and individualization.* Englewood Cliffs, N.J.: Prentice-Hall.

Johnson, D., & Johnson, R. (Eds.). (1978). Social interdependence in the classroom: Cooperation, competition and individualism; symposium. *Journal of Research and Development in Education, 12,* 1–152.

Johnson, D., & Johnson, R. (1982). *Joining together: Group theory and group skills.* Englewood Cliffs, N.J.: Prentice-Hall.

Johnson, D., & Johnson, R. (1983). The socialization and achievement crisis: Are cooperative learning experiences the solution? In L. Bickman (Ed.), *Applied social psychology annual, 4.* Beverly Hills, Calif.: Sage.

Johnson, D., Johnson, R., Holubec, E., & Roy, P. (1984). *Circles of learning: Cooperation in the classroom.* Alexandria, Va.: Association for Supervision and Curriculum Development.

Johnson, D., Marayama, S., Johnson, R., Nelson, D. & Skon, L. (1981). Effects of cooperative, competitive, and individualistic goal structures on achievement: A meta-analysis. *Psychological Bulletin, 89,* 47–62.

Johnson, R., & Johnson, D. (1983). Effects of cooperative, competitive, and individualistic learning experiences on social development. *Exceptional Children, 49,* 323–329.

Johnson, S. (1970). Self-reinforcement versus external reinforcement in behavior modification with children. *Developmental Psychology, 3,* 147–148.

Johnson, S., & Martin, S. (1973). Developing self-evaluation as a conditioned reinforcer. In B. Ashem and E. Poser (Eds.), *Behavior modification with children.* New York: Pergamon, 69–78.

Jones, C. (1979). Dynamics of transcendence in the middle school setting. *Urban Review, 11,* 37–43.

Jones, R., & McEwin, C. (1980). Creative learning environments for the middle school. *Childhood Education, 56,* 146–150.

Jones, V. (1972). The influence of teacher–student introversion, achievement, and similarity on teacher–student dyadic classroom interactions. *Dissertation Abstracts,* 6205–6206A.

Jones, V. (1972). A junior high school program for emotionally disturbed children. In H. Fredericks, V. Baldwin, W. Moore, J. McDonnel, B. Dalke, & M. Moore (Eds.), *Impact 6 of the Title VI programs in the state of Oregon,* September 1971–August 1972. Monmouth: Teaching Research.

Jones, V. (1973). A junior high school program for emotionally disturbed children. In J. McDonnel, H. Fredericks, V. Baldwin, W. Moore, R. Crowley, R. Anderson, & K. Moore (Eds.), *Impact 7 of the Title VI programs in the state of Oregon,* September 1972–August 1973. Monmouth: Teaching Research.

Jones, V. (1977). Humanistic behaviorism: A tool for creating healthy learning environments. *Journal of School Psycyology, 15,* 320–328.

Jones, V. (1980). *Adolescents with behavior problems: Strategies for teaching, counseling, and parent involvement.* Boston: Allyn and Bacon.

Jones, V. (1981). School discipline: Problems and solutions. *Principal, 61,* 14–17.

Jones, V. (1982). Training teachers to be effective classroom managers. In D. Duke (Ed.), *Helping teachers manage classrooms.* Alexandria, Va.: ASCD.

Jones, V. (1983a). Current trends in classroom management: Implications for gifted students. *Roeper Review, 6,* 26–30.

Jones, V. (1983b). *School-wide discipline: Meeting both students' and teachers' needs. Middle School Journal, 14,* 22–26.

Jones, V. (1984). An administrator's guide to developing and evaluating a building-wide discipline program. *National Association of Secondary School Principals Bulletin 68,* 60–73.

Jones, V. (1985). *The influence of student achievement and family factors on student misbehavior.* Manuscript submitted for publication.

Jones, V., & Jones, L. (1981). *Responsible classroom discipline: Creating positive learning environments and solving problems.* Boston: Allyn and Bacon.

Jorgenson, G. (1977). Relationship of classroom behavior to the accuracy of the match between material difficulty and student ability. *Journal of Educational Research, 69,* 24–32.

Joyce, B., Bush, R., & Mckibbin, M. (1981). *Information and opinion from the California staff development study: The compact report.* Sacramento, Calif.: California State Department of Education.

Joyce, B., & Clift, R. (1984). The Phoenix agenda: Essential reform in teacher education. *Educational Researcher, 13,* 5–18.

Joyce, B., & Weil, M. (1980). *Models of teaching* (2nd ed.). Englewood Cliffs, N.J.: Prentice-Hall.

Kagan, J. (1966). Reflection-impulsivity. *Journal of Abnormal Psychology, 71,* 17–24.

Kagan, J., Moss, H., & Siegel, I. (1963). Psychological significance of styles of conceptualization. In J. C. Wright & J. Kagan (Eds.), *Basic cognitive processes in children. Monographs of the Society for Research in Child Development, 28,* 260.

Kagan, S. (1980). Cooperation-competition, culture, and structural bias in classrooms. In S. Sharan, P. Hare, C. Webb, & R. Hertz-Lazarowitz (Eds.), *Cooperation in education.* Provo, Utah: Brigham Young University Press.

Kamii, C. (1972). *An application of Piaget's theory to the conceptualization of a preschool curriculum.* In R. K. Parker (Ed.), *The preschool in action.* Boston: Allyn and Bacon.

Kandel, D., & Lesser, G. (1969). Paternal and peer influences on educational plans of adolescents. *American Sociological Review, 34,* 213–223.

Kandel, D., & Lesser, G. (1972). *Youth in two worlds.* San Francisco: Jossey-Bass.

Kazdin, A. (1972). Response cost: The removal of conditioned reinforcers for therapeutic change. *Behavior Therapy, 3,* 533–546.

Kazdin, A. (1973). The effect of vicarious reinforcement on attentive behavior in the classroom. *Journal of Applied Behavior Analysis, 6,* 71–78.

Kazdin, A., & Bootzin, R. (1972). The token economy: An evaluative review. *Journal of Applied Behavior Analysis, 5,* 343–372.

Kazdin, A., & Kpock, J. (1973). The effect of nonverbal teacher approval on student attentive behavior. *Journal of Applied Behavior Analysis, 6,* 643–654.

Keirsey, D. (1969). Systematic exclusion: Eliminating chronic classroom disruptions. In J. Krumboltz & C. Thoresen (Eds.), *Behavioral counseling: Case studies and techniques.* New York: Holt, Rinehart and Winston, 89–113.

Kelley, C., & Goodwin, G. (1983). Adolescents' perception of three styles of parental control. *Adolescence, 15,* 567–571.

Kelley, E. (1980). *Improving school climate:* Leadership techniques for principals. Reston, Va.: National Association of Secondary School Principals.

Kelley, E. (1981). Auditing school climate. *Educational Leadership, 39,* 180–183.

Kennedy, B. (1968). Motivational effect of individual conferences and goal setting on performance and attitudes in arithmetic. ERIC: ED 032113.

Kenny, T., Rohn, R., Sarles, R., Reynolds, B., & Heald, F. (1979). Visual-motor problems of adolescents who attempt suicide. *Perceptual and Motor Skills, 48,* 599–602.

Kerman, S. (1979). Teacher expectations and student achievement. *Phi Delta Kappan, 60,* 716–718.

Kerr, M., & Nelson, M. (1983). *Strategies for managing behavior problems in the classroom.* Columbus, Ohio: Charles Merrill.

Klein, R., & Schuler, C. (1974, April). *Increasing academic performance through the contingent use of self-evaluation.* Paper presented at the Annual Meeting of the American Educational Research Association, Chicago.

Kleinfeld, J. (1972). *Instructional style and the intellectual performance of Indian and Eskimo students.* Final Report, Project No. 1-J-027, Office of Education, U.S. Department of Health, Education and Welfare.

Kleinfeld, J. (1975). Effective teachers of Indian and Eskimo students. *School Review, 83,* 301–344.

Knaus, W. (1974). *Rational-emotive education: A manual for elementary school teachers.* New York: Institute for Rational Living.

Kohl, H. (1967). *36 children.* New York: New American Library.

Kohlberg, L. (1964). Development of moral character and moral ideology. In J. L. Hoffman & L. W. Hoffman (Eds.), *Review of child development research.* New York: Russell Sage.

Kohlberg, L. (1970). Stage and sequence: The cognitive-developmental approach to socialization. In D. A. Goslin (Ed.), *Handbook of socialization theory and research.* Chicago: Rand McNally.

Kohlberg, L. (1976). Moral stages and moralization. The cognitive-developmental approach. In T. Lickona (Ed.), *Moral development and behavior.* New York: Holt, Rinehart and Winston.

Kolb, D. (1978). *Learning style inventory technical manual.* Boston: McBer.

Kounin, J. (1970). *Discipline and group management in classrooms.* New York: Holt, Rinehart and Winston.

Krantz, P., and Risley, T. (1977). Behavior ecology in the classroom. In K. D. O'Leary & S. G. O'Leary (Eds.), *Classroom management: The successful use of behavior modification.* (2nd ed.). New York: Pergamon Press.

Kranzler, G. (1974). *You can change the way you feel: A rational-emotive approach.* Eugene: Published by author, Counseling Department, University of Oregon.

Krathwohl, D., Bloom, B., & Masia, B. (1964). *Taxonomy of educational objectives, handbook II: Affective domain.* New York: David McKay.

LaBenne, W., & Green, B. (1969). *Educational implications of self-concept theory.* Pacific Palisades, Calif.: Goodyear.

Landry, R. (1974). *Achievement and self concept: A curvilinear relationship.* Paper presented at American Educational Research Association Convention, Chicago.

Lecroy, C. (Ed.). (1983). *Social skills training for children and youth.* New York: Haworth Press.

Leinhardt, G., & Pallay, R. (1982). Restrictive educational settings: Exile or haven? *Review of Educational Research, 52,* 557–578.

Leonard, G. (1968). *Education and ecstasy.* New York: Dell.

Lepper, M., & Greene, D. (1975). Turning play into work: Effects of adult surveillance and extrinsic rewards on children's intrinsic motivation. *Journal of Personality and Social Psychology, 31,* 479–486.

Levin, G., & Simmons, J. (1962). Response to food and praise by emotionally disturbed boys. *Psychological Reports, 11,* 539–546.

Levin, J. (1980). Lay vs. teacher perceptions of school discipline. *Phi Delta Kappan, 61,* 360.

Levin, T., Libman, Z., & Amiad, R. (1980). Behavioral patterns of students under an individualized learning strategy. *Instructional Science, 9,* 85–100.

Lewin, K., Lippit, R., & White, R. (1939). Patterns of aggressive behavior in experimentally created social climates. *Journal of Social Psychology, 10,* 271–291.

Lewis, R., & St. John, N. (1974). Contribution of cross-racial friendship to minority group achievement in desegregated classrooms. *Sociometry, 37,* 79–91.

Lightfoot, S. L. (1983). *The good high school.* New York: Basic Books.

Lindelow, J., & Mazzarella, J. (1981). *School climate.* (Contract No. 400–78–0007). Washington, D.C.: National Institute of Education. (ERIC Document Reproduction Service No. EA 014 193).

Lipsitz, J. (1984). *Successful schools for young adolescents.* New Brunswick, N.J.: Transaction Books.

Long, N., Morse, W., & Newman, R. (Eds.). (1971). *Conflict in the classroom.* (2nd Ed.). Belmont, Calif.: Wadsworth.

Lorber, M. (1966). Inadequate social acceptance and disruptive classroom behavior. *Journal of Educational Research, 59,* 360–362.

Lovitt, T., & Curtiss, K. (1968). Effects of manipulating an antecedent event on mathematics response rate. *Journal of Applied Behavior Analysis, 1,* 329–333.

Luce, S., & Hoge, R. (1978). Relations among teacher rankings, pupil-teacher interactions, and academic achievement: A test of the expectancy hypothesis. *American Educational Research Journal, 15,* 489–500.

McCarthy, B. (1980). *The 4 MAT system: Teaching to learning styles with right/left mode techniques.* Oak Brook, Ill.: Excel.

McCarthy, B. and Leflar, S. (Eds.). (1983). *4 MAT in action: Creative lesson plans for teaching to learning styles with right/left mode techniques.* Oak Brook, Ill.: Excel.

McClelland, D., & Alschuler, A. (1971). *The achievement motivation development project.* Final report to USOE project No. 7–1231, Bureau of Research.

McClelland, D., Atkinson, J., Clark, R., & Lowell, E. (1953). *The achievement motive.* New York: Appleton-Century-Crofts.

McDaniel, T. (1983, January). On changing teachers' attitudes toward classroom management. *Phi Delta Kappan, 64,* 374–375.

McDill, E., Rigsby, L., & Meyers, E. (1969). Educational climates of high school: Their effect and source. *American Journal of Sociology, 74,* 567–586.

McDonald, F. (1976). *Research on teaching and its implications for policy making: Report on phase II of the beginning teacher evaluation study.* Princeton, N.J.: Educational Testing Service.

McDonald, F., & Elias, P. (1976). *Executive summary report: Beginning teacher evaluation study, phase II.* Princeton, N.J.: Educational Testing Service.

McGinley, P., & McGinley. (1970). Reading groups as psychological groups. *Journal of Experimental Education, 39,* 35–42.

McKenzie, H., Clark, M., Wolf, M., Kothera, R., & Benson, C. (1968). Behavior modification of children with learning disabilities using grades as tokens and allowances as back-up reinforcers. *Exceptional Children, 34,* 745–752.

McKenzie, T., & Rushall, B. (1974). Effects of self-recording on attendance and performance in a competitive swimming training program. *Journal of Applied Behavior Analysis, 7,* 199–206.

McLaughlin, T., & Gnagey, W. (1981, April). Self-management and pupil self-control. Paper presented at the annual meeting of the American Educational Research Association, Los Angeles.

McLaughlin, T., & Malaby, J. (1972). Reducing and measuring inappropriate verbalizations in a token classroom. *Journal of Applied Behavior Analysis, 5,* 329–333.

Madsen, C., Becker, W., & Thomas, D. (1968). Rules, praise, and ignoring: Elements of elementary classroom control. *Journal of Applied Behavior Analysis, 1,* 139–150.

Madsen, C., Madsen, C., Saudargus, R., Hammond, W., & Edgar, D. (1970). *Classroom RAID (Rules, Approval, Ignore, Disapproval): A cooperative approach for professionals and volunteers.* Unpublished manuscript, University of Florida.

Maehr, M. (1974). *Sociocultural origins of achievement.* Monterey, Calif.: Books/Cole.

Maehr, M. (1976). Continuing motivation: An analysis of a seldom considered educational outcome. *Review of Educational Research, 46,* 443–462.

Maehr, M., & Sjogren, D. (1971). Atkinson's theory of achievement motivation: First step toward a theory of academic motivation. *Review of Educational Research, 41,* 143–161.

Maeroff, G. (1982). *Don't blame the kids: The trouble with America's public schools.* New York: McGraw-Hill.

Mahler, M. (1975). *The psychological birth of the human infant.* New York: Basic Books.

Mahoney, M. (1974). *Cognition and behavior modification.* Cambridge, Mass.: Ballinger.

Mannheim, B. (1957). An investigation of the interrelations of reference groups, membership groups and the self-image: A test of the Cooley-Mead Theory of the self. *Dissertation Abstracts, 17,* 1616–1617.

Maple, F. (1977). *Shared decision making.* Beverly Hills, Calif.: Sage.

Martin, B. (1975). Parent-child relations. In F. D. Horowitz (Ed.), *Review of child development research* (Vol. 4, pp. 463–540). Chicago, Ill.: University of Chicago Press.

Martorella, P. (1980). Social studies goals in the middle grades. *Journal of Research and Development in Education, 13*, 47–59.

Maslow, A. (1968). *Toward a psychology of being.* New York: D. Van Nostrand.

Mason, W. (1965). Determinants of social behavior in young chimpanzees. In A. M. Schrier, H. F. Harlow, and F. Stolenits (Eds.), *Behavior of non-human primates* (Vol. 2). New York: Academic Press, 287–334.

Masterson, J. (1980). *From borderline adolescent to functioning adult: The test of time.* New York: Brunner/Mazel.

Mastin, V. (1963). Teacher enthusiasm. *Journal of Educational Research, 56*, 385–386.

Mead, M. (1970). *Culture and commitment: A study of the generation gap.* Garden City, NY: Doubleday.

Medley, D. (1977). *Teacher competence and teacher effectiveness: a review of process-product research.* Washington, D.C.: American Association of Colleges for Teacher Education.

Mehan, H. (1974). Accomplishing classroom lessons. In A. V. Cicourel, K. H. Jennings, S. H. Jennings, K. C. Leiter, R. MacKay, J. Mehan, and D. Roth (Eds.), *Language Use and School Performance.* New York: Academic Press.

Meichenbaum, D., & Cameron, R. (1974). The clinical potential of modifying what clients say to themselves. In C. Mahoney and C. Thoresen (Eds.), *Self-control: Power to the person.* Monterey, Calif.: Brooks/Cole, 263–290.

Mendler, A., and Curwin, R. (1983). *Taking charge in the classroom.* Reston, Va.: Reston.

Mertens, S., & Yarger, S. (1981). *Teacher centers in action: A comprehensive study of federally funded teacher centers.* Syracuse, N.Y.: Syracuse Area Teacher Center.

Messick, S. (1970). The criterion problem in the evaluation of instruction. In M. C. Wittrock and D. E. Wiley (Eds.), *The evaluation of instruction: Issues and problems.* New York: Holt, Rinehart and Winston.

Meunier, C., & Rule, B. (1967). Anxiety, confidence and conformity. *Journal of Personality, 35*, 498–504.

Meyen, E. (Ed.). (1982). *Exceptional children in today's schools: An alternative resource book.* Denver, Colo.: Love.

Middleton, R., & Snell, P. (1963). Political expression of adolescent rebellion. *American Journal of Sociology, 68*, 527–535.

Mohlman, G. (1982, April). *Assessing the impact of three inservice teacher training models.* Paper presented at the annual meeting of the American Educational Research Association, New York.

Moles, O. (1983, April). *Trends in student discipline problems.* Paper presented at the meeting of the American Educational Research Association, Montreal, Canada.

Monohan, J., & O'Leary, K. (1971). Effects of self-instruction on rule-breaking behavior. *Psychological Reports, 29*, 1059–1066.

Moos, R. (1979). *Evaluating educational environments.* San Francisco: Jossey-Bass.

Mordock, J. (1975). *The other child: An introduction to exceptionality.* New York: Harper.

Morris, J. (1978). *Psychology and teaching: A humanistic view.* New York: Random House.

Morrison, A., & McIntyre, D. (1969). *Teachers and teaching.* Baltimore: Penguin.

Morse, W. (1964). Self-concept in the school setting. *Childhood Education, 41*, 195–198.

Moskowitz, G., & Hayman, J. (1976). Success strategies of inner-city teachers: A yearlong study. *Journal of Educational Research, 69*, 283–289.

Mosley, A., & Smith, P. (1982). What works in learning? Students provide the answers. *Phi Delta Kappan, 273.*

Muldoon, J. (1955). The concentration of liked and disliked members in groups and the relationship of the concentration to group comprehensiveness. *Sociometry, 18,* 73–81.

Musser, J., & Fleck, J. (1983). The relationship of parental acceptance and control to college females' personality adjustment. *Adolescence, 15.*

Muuss, R. (1975). *Theories of adolescence* (3rd ed.). New York: Random House.

Nationwide teacher opinion poll. (1983). Washington, D.C.: National Education Association.

Nickerson, C., Lollis, C., & Porter, E. (1980). *Miraculous me.* Seattle, Wash.: Comprehensive Health Education Foundation.

Nielson, G. (1983). *Borderline and acting-out adolescence: A developmental approach.* New York: Human Sciences Press.

Norman, J., & Harris, M. (1981). *The private life of the American teenager.* New York: Rawson, Wade.

O'Leary, D., & Becker, W. (1967). Behavior modification of an adjustment class: A token reinforcement program. *Exceptional Children, 33,* 637–642.

O'Leary, D., Becker, W., Evans, M., & Saudergas, R. (1969). A token reinforcement program in a public school: A replication and systematic analysis. *Journal of Applied Behavior Analysis, 2,* 3–13.

O'Leary, D., & Drabman, R. (1971). Token reinforcement programs in the classroom: A review. *Psychological Bulletin, 75,* 379–398.

O'Leary, D., & O'Leary, S. (1977). *Classroom Management: The Successful Use of Behavior Modification.* (2nd ed.), (Eds.) New York: Pergamon Press.

Osborne, D. (1977). Race, sex, achievement, and suspension. *Urban Education, 12,* 345–347.

Pacard, R. (1970). The control of classroom attention: A group contingency for complex behavior. *Journal of Applied Behavior Analysis, 3,* 13–28.

Page, E. (1958). Teacher comments and student performance. *Journal of Educational Psychology, 49,* 172–181.

Patterson, C. (1973). *Humanistic education.* Englewood Cliffs, N.J.: Prentice-Hall.

Patterson, C. (1982). Self-control and self-regulation in childhood. In T. Field, and A. Huston-Stein (Eds.), *Review of human development.* New York: Wiley.

Patterson, G. (1968). *Living with children: New methods for parents and teachers.* Champaign, Ill.: Research Press.

Patterson, G. (1971a). *Families: Applications of social learning to family life.* Champaign, Ill.: Research Press.

Patterson, G. (1971b). Behavioral intervention procedures in the classroom and in the home. In A. E. Berzin and S. L. Garfield (Eds.), *Handbook of psychotherapy and behavior change: An empirical analysis.* New York: Wiley.

Perline, I., & Levinsky, D. (1968). Controlling behavior in the severely retarded. *American Journal of Mental Deficiency, 73,* 74–78.

Persell, C. H., Cookson, P., & Lyons, H. (1982). *Effective principals: What do we know from various educational literatures?* Paper presented at the NIE Conference on Principals for Educational Excellence in the 1980s, Washington, D.C.

Peterson, P. (1979). Direct instruction reconsidered. In P. L. Peterson & H. J. Walberg (Eds.), *Research on teaching.* Berkeley, Calif.: McCutchan.

Peterson, P., & Swing, S. (1982). Beyond time on task: Students' reports of their thought processes during classroom instruction. *Elementary School Journal, 82,* 481–491.

Piaget, J. (1952). *The origins of intelligence in children* (M. Cook, Trans.). New York: International Universities Press.

Piaget, J. (1970). Piaget's theory. In P. H. Mussen (Ed.), *Carmichael's manual of child psychology* (3rd ed., Vol. 1). New York: Wiley.

Piaget, J. (1977). The role of action in the development of thinking. In W. F. Overton & J. M. Gallagher (Eds.), *Knowledge and development* (Vol. 1). New York: Plenum.

Phillips, E. (1968). Achievement place: Token reinforcement procedures in a home-style rehabilitation setting for "pre-delinquent" boys. *Journal of Applied Behavior Analysis, 1,* 213–224.

Plisko, V. (Ed.). (1983). *The condition of education: 1983 edition.* Washington, D.C.: U.S. Government Printing Office.

Pogrebin, L. (1980). *Growing up free: Raising your child in the 80s.* New York: Bantam Books.

Pollard, A. (1980). Teacher interests and changing situations of survival threat in primary school classrooms. In P. Woods (Ed.), *Teacher strategies: Explorations in the sociology of the school* (pp. 34–60). London: Croom Helm.

Postman, M., & Weingartner, C. (1969). *Teaching as a subversive activity.* New York: Delacorte.

Price, G. (1980). Which learning style elements are stable and which tend to change? *Learning Styles Network Newsletter, 1,* 1.

Purkey, W. (1970). *Self-concept and school achievement.* Englewood Cliffs, N.J.: Prentice-Hall.

Purkey, W. (1978). *Inviting school success: A self-concept approach to teaching and learning.* Belmont, Calif.: Wadsworth.

Purkey, W., & Smith, M. (1983). Effective schools: A review. *Elementary School Journal, 83,* 427–452.

Purkey, W., & Novak, J. (1984). *Inviting school success: A self-concept approach to teaching and learning* (2nd ed.). Belmont, Calif.: Wadsworth.

Putney, S., & Putney, G. (1964). *The adjusted American: Normal neurosis in American society.* New York: Harper and Row.

Ramirez, M., & Castaneda, A. (1974). *Cultural democracy, bicognitive development, and education.* New York: Academic Press.

Reckinger, M. (1979). Choice as a way to quality learning. *Journal of Educational Leadership, 36,* 255–256.

Reese, H. (1961). Relationships between self-acceptance and sociometric choices. *Journal of Abnormal and Social Psychology, 62,* 472–474.

Regan, W. (1966). *Modern elementary curriculum.* New York: Holt, Rinehart and Winston.

Reissman, F. (1964). The strategy of style. *Teachers College Record, 64,* 484–495.

Renzulli, J. (1983, April). *The assessment and application of learning style preferences: A practical approach for classroom teachers.* Paper presented at the annual meeting of the American Education Research Association, Montreal, Canada.

Renzulli, J., & Smith, L. (1978). *The learning styles inventory: A measure of student preference for instructional techniques.* Mansfield Center, CT: Creative Learning Press.

Revans, R. (1964). *Standards for morale: Cause and effect in hospitals.* London: Oxford University Press.

Rim, E., & Coller, R. (1979). In search of nonlinear process-product functions in existing schooling-effects data: A reanalysis of the first grade reading and mathematics data from the Stallings and Kaskowitz follow-through study. *JSAS Catalog of Selected Documents in Psychology, 9,* 92.

Rist, R. (1970). Student social class and teacher expectations: The self-fulfilling prophecy in ghetto education. *Harvard Educational Review, 40,* 411–451.

Robert, M. (1976). *School morale: The human dimension.* Niles, Ill.: Argus Communications.

Robertson, S., Keith, T., & Page, E. (1983). Now who aspires to teach? *Educational Researcher, 12,* 13–21.

Rogers, C. (1958). The characteristics of a helping relationship. *Personnel and Guidance Journal, 37,* 6–16.

Rogers, C. (1969) *Freedom to learn.* Columbus, Ohio: Charles E. Merrill.

Rose, S. (1983). Promoting social competence in children: A classroom approach to social and cognitive skill training. In C. W. LeCroy (Ed.), *Social skills training for children and youth.* New York: Haworth Press.

Rosenkrantz, A. (1978). A note on adolescent suicide: Incidence, dynamics, and some suggestions for treatment. *Adolescence, 13,* 209–214.

Rosenshine, B. (1970). *Enthusiastic teaching: A research review. School Review, 72,* 449–514.

Rosenshine, B. (1976). Classroom instruction. In N. Gage (Ed.), *The psychology of teaching methods.* National Society for the Study of Education, Seventy-Seventh Yearbook.

Rosenshine, B. (1978). Academic engaged time, content covered, and direct instruction. *Journal of Education, 160,* 38–66.

Rosenshine, B. (1980). How time is spent in elementary classrooms. In C. Denham & A. Lieberman (Eds.), *Time to learn.* Washington, D.C.: National Institute of Education.

Rosenshine, B., & Furst, N. (1973). The use of direct observation to study teaching. In R. Travers (Ed.), *Second handbook of research on teaching.* Chicago: Rand McNally.

Rosenthal, R. (1973). The pygmalion effect lives. *Psychology Today, 7,* 56–63.

Rosenthal, R., & Jacobson, L. (1968). *Pygmalion in the classroom: Teacher expectation and pupils' intellectual development.* New York: Holt, Rinehart and Winston.

Rotter, J. (1954). *Social learning and clinical psychology.* Englewood Cliffs, N.J.: Prentice-Hall.

Rotter, J. (1966). Generalized expectancies for internal versus external control of reinforcement. *Psychological Monographs, 80.*

Rounds, T., Ward, B., Mergendoller, J., & Tikunoff, W. (1982). *Junior high school transition study: Volume II—Organization of instruction* (Rep. EPSSP–82–3). San Francisco, Calif.: Far West Laboratory for Educational Research and Development.

Rowe, M. (1974). Wait-time and rewards as instructional variables, their influence on language, logic, and fate control: Part one, wait-time. *Journal of Research in Science Teaching, 11,* 81–94.

Rowe, M. (1978). Wait, wait, wait. *School Science and Math, 78,* 207–216.

Runkel, P., Lawrence, M., Oldfield, S., Rider, M., & Clark, C. (1971). Stages of group development: An empirical test of Tuckman's hypothesis. *Journal of Applied Behavioral Science, 7,* 180–193.

Rutter, M., Maughan, B., Montimore, P., Ouston, J., & Smith, A. (1979). *Fifteen thousand hours.* Cambridge, Mass.: Harvard University Press.

Sadker, D., & Sadker, M. (1985). Is the o.k. classroom o.k.? *Phi Delta Kappan, 66,* 358–361.

Safer, D. (1982). *School programs for disruptive adolescents.* Baltimore, Md.: University Park Press.

Sanford, J., Emmer, E., & Clements, B. (1983). Improving classroom management. *Educational Leadership, 41,* 56–60.

Sanford, J., & Evertson, C. (1981). Classroom management in a low SES junior high: Three case studies. *Journal of Teacher Education, 32,* 34–38.

Schachter, S. (1964). The interaction of cognitive and physiological determinants of emotional state. In L. Berkowitz (Ed.), *Advances in experimental social psychology,* Vol. 1. New York: Academic Press.

Schalock, D. (1979). Research on teacher selection. In D. C. Berliner (Ed.), *Review of research in education* (Vol. 7). Washington, D.C.: American Educational Research Association.

Schlechty, P., & Vance, V. (1981). Do academically able teachers leave education? The North Carolina case. *Phi Delta Kappan, 63,* 106–112.

Schmidt, G., & Ulrich, R. (1969). Effects of group contingent events upon classroom noise. *Journal of Applied Behavior Analysis, 2,* 171–179.

Schmuck, R. (1963). Some relationships of peer liking patterns in the classroom to pupil attitudes and achievement. *School Review, 71,* 337–359.

Schmuck, R. (1966). Some aspects of classroom social climate. *Psychology in the Schools, 3,* 59–65.

Schmuck, R., & Schmuck, P. (1974). *A humanistic psychology of education: Making the school everybody's house.* Palo Alto, Calif.: National Press.

Schmuck, R., & Schmuck, P. (1975). *Group processes in the classroom.* Dubuque, Iowa: Wm. C. Brown.

Schmuck, R., & Schmuck, P. (1983). *Group processes in the classroom.* (4th ed.). Dubuque, Iowa: Wm. C. Brown.

Schutz, W. (1966). *The interpersonal underworld.* Palo Alto, Calif.: Science and Behavior.

Schwebel, A., & Cherlin, D. (1972). Physical and social distancing in teacher-pupil relationships. *Journal of Educational Psychology, 63,* 543–550.

Seagoe, M. (1974). Some learning characteristics of gifted children. In R. Martinson (Ed.), *The identification of the gifted and talented.* Ventura, Calif.: Office of Ventura County Superintendent of Schools.

Sebald, H. (1977). *Adolescence: A social psychological analysis.* Englewood Cliffs, N.J.: Prentice-Hall.

Selman, R. (1980). *The growth of interpersonal understanding: Developmental and clinical analyses.* New York: Academic Press.

Sgan, M. (1967). Social reinforcement, socioeconomic status, and susceptibility to experimenter influence. *Journal of Personality and Social Psychology, 5,* 202–210.

Sharan, S. (1980). Cooperative learning in small groups: Recent methods and effects on achievement, attitudes, and ethnic relations. *Review of Educational Research, 50,* 241–271.

Sharan, S., & Sharan, Y. (1976). *Small group teaching.* Englewood Cliffs, N.J.: Educational Technology.

Sharan, S., Hare, A., Webb, C., & Hertz-Lazarowitz, R. (1981). *Cooperation in education.* Provo, Utah: Brigham Young University Press.

Sharan, S., & Hertz-Lazarowitz, R. (1981). A group-investigation method of cooperative learning in the classroom. In S. Sharan (Ed.), *Cooperation in education.* Provo, Utah: Brigham Young University Press.

Sherif, M. (1958). Superordinate goals in the reduction of intergroup tensions. *American Journal of Sociology, 53,* 349–356.

Sherman, A. (1973). *Behavior modification: Theory and practice.* Belmont, Calif.: Wadsworth.

Shimron, J. (1976). Learning activities in individually prescribed instruction. *Instructional Science, 5,* 391–401.

Shumsky, A. (1968). *In search of teaching style.* New York: Appleton-Century-Crofts.

Siegel, E., & Gold, R. (1982). *Educating the learning disabled.* New York: Macmillan.

Sigel, I., & Coop, R. (1974). Cognitive style and classroom practice. In R. H. Coop and K. White (Eds.), *Psychological concepts in the classroom.* New York: Harper and Row.

Silberman, C. (1970). *Crisis in the classroom.* New York: Random House.

Silverstein, J. (1979). *Individual and environmental correlates of pupil problematic and nonproblematic classroom behavior.* Unpublished doctoral dissertation, New York University, NY.

Simon, S., Howe, L., & Kirschenbaum, H. (1972). *Values clarification.* New York: Hart

Simpson, B. (1973). *Becoming aware of values.* San Diego, Calif.: Pennant Press.

Simpson, R. (1962). Parental influence, anticipatory socialization, and social mobility. *American Sociological Review, 27,* 517–522.

Sirotnik, K. (1982). The contextual correlates of the relative expenditures of classroom time on instruction and behavior: An explanatory study of secondary schools and classes. *American Educational Research Journal, 19,* 275–292.

Sizer, T. (1984). *Horace's compromise: The dilemma of the American high school.* Boston: Houghton Mifflin.

Skinner, B. (1971). *Beyond freedom and dignity.* New York: Alfred A. Knopf.

Slavin, R. (1978). Student teams and achievement divisions. *Journal of Research and Development in Education, 12,* 39–49.

Slavin, R. (1980). Cooperative learning. *Review of Educational Research, 50,* 315–342.

Slavin, R. (1983). *Cooperative learning.* New York: Longman.

Sloane, H., Buckholdt, D., Jenson, W., & Crandall, J. (1979). *Structured teaching: A design for classroom management and instruction.* Champaign, Ill.: Research Press.

Sloggett, B. (1971). Use of group activities and team rewards to increase classroom productivity. *Teaching Exceptional Children, 3,* 54–66.

Smith, C. (1983). *Learning Disabilities—The interaction of learner, task and setting.* Boston: Little, Brown.

Smith, I. (1964). *Spatial ability.* San Diego: Knapp.

Smith, C., Frank, A., Snider, B. (1984). School psychologists' and teachers' perceptions of data used in the identification of behaviorally disordered students. *Behavioral Disorders, 10,* 27–32.

Soar, R. (1977). An integration of findings of four studies of teacher effectiveness. In G. Borich (Ed.), *The appraisal of teaching: Concepts and process.* Reading, Mass.: Addison-Wesley.

Soar, R. (1983, March). *Impact of context variables on teacher and learner behavior.* Paper presented at the annual meeting of the American Association of Colleges for Teacher Education, Detroit.

Soar, R., & Soar, R. (1972). An empirical analysis of selected follow-through programs: An example of a process approach to evaluation. In I. Gordon (Ed.), *Early childhood education.* Chicago: National Society for the Study of Education.

Soar, R., & Soar, R. (1975). Classroom behavior, pupil characteristics and pupil growth for the school year and the summer. *JSAS Catalog of Selected Documents in Psychology, 5*, 873.

Soar, R., & Soar, R. (1979). Emotional climate and management. In P. L. Peterson & H. J. Walberg (Eds.), *Research on teaching* (pp. 97–119). Berkeley, Calif.: McCutchan.

Soar, R., & Soar, R. (1980). Setting variables, classroom interaction and multiple pupil outcomes. *JSAS Catalog of Selected Documents in Psychology, 10*, 2110.

Solomon, D., and Kendall, A. (1976). Individual characteristics and children's performance in varied educational settings: Final report. Rockville, Md.: Montgomery County Public Schools. (ERIC Document Reproduction Service No. ED 125 958).

Spaulding, R. (1963). *Achievement, creativity, and self-concept correlates of teacher-pupil transactions in elementary schools.* Urbana, Ill.: University of Illinois, Cooperative Research Project No. 1352.

Spaulding, R. (1983). A systematic approach to discipline, part 1. *Phi Delta Kappan, 65*, 48–51.

Spaulding, R., & Spaulding, C. (1982). *Research-based classroom management.* San Jose, Calif.: Maple Press.

Spencer Hall, D. (1981). Looking behind the teacher's back. *Elementary School Journal, 81*, 281–289.

Sperry, L. (Ed.). (1972). *Learning performance and individual differences.* Glenview, Ill.: Scott, Foresman.

Stake, R., & Easley, J. (1978). *Case studies in science education* (vols. 1 & 2). Urbana, Ill.: Center for Instructional Research and Curriculum Evaluation and Committee on Culture and Cognition, University of Illinois at Urbana-Champagne.

Squires, D. (1983). *Effective schools and classrooms: A research-based perspective.* Alexandria, Va.: Association for Supervision and Curriculum Development.

Squires, D., Huitt, W., & Segars, J. (1984). *Effective schools and classrooms: A research-based perspective.* Alexandria, Va.: Association for Supervision and Curriculum Development.

Stake, R., & Easley, J. (1978). *Case studies in science education* (Vols. 1 & 2). Urbana, Ill.: Center for Instructional Research and Curriculum Evaluation.

Stallings, J. (1975). Implementation and child effects of teaching in follow-through classrooms. *Monographs of the Society for Research in Child Development, 40*, 7–8.

Stallings, J. (1976). How instructional processes relate to child outcomes in a national study of follow-through. *Journal of Teacher Education, 37*, 43–47.

Stallings, J. (1983). *An accountability model for teacher education.* Paper presented at the annual meeting of the American Association of Colleges for Teacher Education, Detroit.

Stallings, J. (1984). *An accountability model for teacher education.* George Peabody College for Teachers, Vanderbilt University, Stallings Teaching and Learning Institute.

Stallings, J., & Kaskowitz, D. (1974). *Follow-through classroom observation evaluation.* Menlow Park, Calif.: Stanford Research Institute.

Stanford, G., & Stanford, B. (1969). *Learning discussion skills through games.* New York: Citation Press.

Stanish, B. (1981). *Hippogriff feathers: Encounters with creative thinking.* Carthage, Ill.: Good Apple.

Stanton, A., & Schwartz, M. (1954). *The mental hospital.* New York: Basic Books.

Stanwyck, D., & Felker, D. (1974). *Self-concept and anxiety in middle elementary school children: A developmental survey.* Paper presented at American Educational Research Association Convention, Chicago.

Stevens, D. (1971). Reading difficulty and classroom acceptance. *Reading Teacher, 25,* 52–55.

Stinchcombe, A. (1964). *Rebellion in a high school.* Chicago: Quadrangle.

Stipek, D., & Weisz, J. (1981). Perceived personal control and academic achievement. *Review of Educational Research, 51,* 101–137.

Stodolsky, S. (1983). Frameworks for studying the uses of instructional groups in classrooms. In P. Peterson, L. Wilkinson, & M. Hallinan (Eds.), *Organization and processes of classroom groups.* New York: Academic Press.

Stoffer, D. (1970). Investigation of positive behavioral changes as a function of genuineness, non-possessive warmth and empathic understanding. *Journal of Educational Research, 63,* 225–228.

Streit, F. (1980). *Research review 1966–1980: Adolescent problems.* Highland Park, N.J.: Essence.

Sulzbacher, S., & Houser, J. (1968). A tactic to eliminate disruptive behaviors in a classroom: Group contingent consequences. *American Journal of Mental Deficiency, 73,* 88–90.

Swick, K., & Duff, E. (1979). *Parenting.* Washington, D.C.: National Education Association.

Swift, M., & Spivack, G. (1975). *Alternative teaching strategies: Helping behaviorally troubled children achieve.* Champaign, Ill.: Research Press.

Tagiuri, R., Bruner, J., & Blake, R. (1958). On the relation between feelings and perception of feelings among members of small groups. In E. Maccoby, T. Newcomb, & E. Hartley (Eds.), *Readings in school psychology.* New York: Holt, Rinehart and Winston.

Tanner, L. (1978). *Classroom discipline for effective teaching and learning.* New York: Holt, Rinehart and Winston.

Tharp, R. (1982). The effective instruction of comprehension: Results and description of the Kamehameha Early Education Program. *Reading Research Quarterly, 17,* 503–527.

Thomas, D., Becker, W., & Armstrong, M. (1968). Production and elimination of disruptive classroom behavior by systematically varying teacher's behavior. *Journal of Applied Behavior Analysis, 1,* 35–45.

Thomas, J., Presland, I., Grant, M., & Glynn, T. (1978). Natural rates of teacher approval and disapproval in grade 7 classrooms. *Journal of Applied Behavior Analysis, 11,* 91–94.

Thompson, R., White, K., & Morgan, D. (1982). Teacher–student interaction patterns in classrooms with mainstreamed mildly handicapped students. *American Educational Research Journal, 19,* 220–236.

Tjosvold, D. (1977). Alternative organizations for schools and classrooms. In D. Bartel & L. Saxe (Eds.), *Social psychology of education: Research and theory.* New York: Hemisphere Press.

Tjosvold, D., & Santamaria, P. (1977). *The effects of cooperation and teacher support on student attitudes toward classroom decision-making.* Paper presented at the American Educational Research Convention, New York.

Toepfer, C. (1979). Brain growth periodization—a new dogma for education. *Middle School Journal, 10, 3,* 18–20.

Toepfer, C. (1980). Brain growth periodization data: Some suggestions for re-thinking middle school education. *High School Journal, 63,* 222–227.

Torgerson, E. (1977, April 23–29). What teenagers watch and why. *TV Guide,* 4–7.

Torrance, E. (1960). Explorations in creative thinking. *Education, 81,* 216–220.

Travers, R. (1967). *Essentials of learning* (2nd ed.). New York: Macmillan.

Truax, C., & Carkhuff, R. (1967). *Toward effective counseling and psychotherapy: Training and practice.* Chicago: Aldine.

Truax, C., & Tatum, C. (1966). An extension from the effective psychotherapeutic model to constructive personality change in pre-school children. *Childhood Education, 42,* 456–462.

Tuckman, B. (1965). Developmental sequence in small groups. *Psychological Bulletin, 63,* 384–489.

United States Department of Health, Education and Welfare, Public Health Service. (1972). *Behavior patterns of children in school. Vital Health Statistics* (J. Roberts and J. Baird, Jr.).

Usher, R., & Hanke, J. (1971). The "third force" in psychology and college teacher effectiveness research at the University of Northern Colorado. *Colorado Journal of Educational Research, 10,* 3–10.

Vacha, E. (1979). *Improving classroom social climate.* New York: Holt, Rinehart and Winston.

Wagonseller, B., & McDowell, R. (1979). *You and your child: A common sense approach to successful parenting.* Champaign, Ill.: Research Press.

Waksman, S., & Messmer, C. (1979). *Social skills training: A manual for teaching assertive behaviors to children and adolescents.* Portland, Oreg.: Enrichment Press.

Walberg, H., & Anderson, G. (1968). The achievement-creativity dimension and classroom climate. *Journal of Creative Behavior, 2,* 281–292.

Walberg, H., & Waxman, H. (1983). Teaching, learning and management of instruction. In D. Smith (Ed.), *Essential knowledge for beginning educators.* Washington, D.C.: American Association of Colleges for Teacher Education.

Walker, H. (1979). *The acting-out child: Coping with classroom disruption.* Boston: Allyn and Bacon.

Walker, H., & Buckley, N. (1973). Teacher attention to appropriate and inappropriate classroom behavior: An individual case study. *Focus on Exceptional Children, 5,* 5–11.

Walker, H., & Buckley, N. (1974). *Token reinforcement techniques: Classroom applications for the hard-to-teach child.* Eugene, Oreg.: E–P Press.

Walker, H., Hops, H., & Fiegenbaum, E. (1976). Deviant classroom behavior as a function of combinations of social and token reinforcement and cost contingency. *Behavior Therapy, 7,* 76–88.

Walker, H., Hops, H., Greenwood, C., Todd, N., & Garrett, B. (1977). *The comparative effects of teacher praise, token reinforcement, and response cost in reducing negative peer interactions* (CORBEH report #25). Eugene: Center at Oregon for Research in the Behavioral Education of the Handicapped, University of Oregon.

Walker, H., McConnell, S., Holmes, D., Todis, B., Walker, J., & Golden, N. (1983). *The Walker social skills curriculum: The accepts program.* Austin Tex.: Pro–Ed.

Walker, H., Reavis, H., Rhode, G., & Jenson, W. (1985). A conceptual model for delivery of behavioral services to behavior disordered children in a continuum of educational settings. In P. Bornstein and A. Kazdin (eds.), *Handbook of clinical therapy with children.* Homewood, Ill.: Dorsey Press.

Walker, H., Street, A., Garret, B., & Crossen, J. (1977). *Experiments with response cost in playground and classroom settings.* (CORBEH report #35). Eugene: Center at Oregon for Research in the Behavioral Education of the Handicapped, University of Oregon.

Walters, R., Parke, R., & Cane, V. (1965). Timing of punishment and the observation of consequences to others as determinants of response inhibitions. *Journal of Experimental Child Psychology, 2,* 10–30.

Ward, B., & Tikunoff, W. (1976). The effective teacher education program: Application of selected research results and methodology to teaching. *Journal of Teacher Education, 27,* 58–63.

Ware, B. (1978). What rewards do students want? *Phi Delta Kappan, 59,* 355–356.

Warren, R., Deffenbacher, J., & Brading, P. (1976). Rational-emotive therapy and the reduction of test anxiety in elementary school students. *Rational Living, 11,* 26–29.

Watt, N. (1972). Longitudinal changes in the social behavior of children hospitalized for schizophrenia as adults. *Journal of Nervous and Mental Disease, 1, 55,* 42–54.

Watt, N., Stolorowrd-Lubensky, A., & McClelland, D. (1970). Social adjustment and behavior of children hospitalized for schizophrenia as adults. *American Journal of Orthopsychiatry, 40,* 637–657.

Wax, R. (1971). *Doing fieldwork: Warning and advice.* Chicago: University of Chicago Press.

Wayson, W., & Lasley, T. (1984). Climates for excellence: Schools that foster self-discipline. *Phi Delta Kappan, 65,* 419–421.

Wayson, W., & Pinnel, G. (1982). Creating a living curriculum for teaching self-discipline. In D. Duke (Ed.), *Helping teachers manage classrooms.* Alexandria, Va.: ASCD.

Weaver, T. (1979). In search of quality: The need for talent in teaching. *Phi Delta Kappan, 61,* 29–32.

Weber, K. (1982). The teacher is the key: A practical guide for teaching the adolescent with learning difficulties. Denver, Colo.: Love.

Weil, G., & Goldfried, M. (1973). Treatment of insomnia in an eleven-year-old child through self-relaxation. *Behavior Therapy, 4,* 282–294.

Weiner, B. (1979). A theory of motivation for some classroom experiences. *Journal of Educational Psychology, 71,* 3–25.

Weinstein, R. (1976). Reading group membership in first grade: Teacher behaviors and pupil experience over time. *Journal of Educational Psychology, 68,* 103–116.

Wheeler, R., & Ryan, F. (1973). Effects of cooperative and competitive classroom environments on the attitudes and achievement of elementary school students engaged in social studies inquiry activities. *Journal of Educational Psychology, 65,* 402–407.

White, B., & Held, R. (1967). Plasticity of sensorimotor development in the human infant. In B. Staub and J. Hellmuth (Eds.), *Exceptional infant* (Vol. 1). Seattle: Special Child Publications, 425–442.

White, M. (1975). Natural rates of teacher approval and disapproval in the classroom. *Journal of Applied Behavior Analysis, 8,* 367–372.

White, R. (1959). Motivation reconsidered: The concept of competence. *Psychological Review, 66,* 297–333.

Williams, R., & Cole, S. (1968). Self-concept and adjustment. *Personnel and Guidance Journal, 46,* 478–481.

Willis, B. (1970). The influence of teacher expectation on teachers' classroom interaction with selected children. *Dissertation Abstracts, 30,* 5072–A.

Willower, D. (1975). Some comments on inquiries on schools and pupil control. *Teachers College Record, 77*, 219–230.

Wilson, A. (1959). Residential segregation of social classes and aspirations of high school boys. *American Sociological Review, 14*, 836–845.

Witkin, H., & Moore, C. (1974, April). *Cognitive style and the teaching-learning process.* Paper presented at the annual meeting of the American Educational Research Association, Chicago.

Wlodkowski, R. (1978). *Motivation and teaching: A practical guide.* Washington, D.C.: National Education Association.

Wolfgang, C., & Glickman, C. (1980). *Solving discipline problems: Strategies for classroom teachers.* Boston: Allyn and Bacon.

Wood, F., & Johnson, G. (1982). *Staff development and the /I/D/E/A/ school improvement project.* Dayton, Ohio: Institute for Development of Educational Activities.

Wood, M. (1975). *Developmental therapy.* Baltimore: University Park Press.

Woods, P. (1976). Having a laugh: An antidote to schooling. In M. Hammersley & P. Woods (Eds.), *The process of schooling: A sociological reader* (pp. 178–187). London: Routledge & Kegan Paul.

Workman, E. (1982). *Teaching behavioral self–control to students.* Austin, Tex.: Pro–Ed.

Wragg, E. (Ed.). (1984). *Classroom teaching skills.* New York: Nichols.

Wright, W., & Dixon, M. (1977). Community prevention and treatment of juvenile delinquency: A review of evaluation studies. *Journal of Research on Crime and Delinquency, 14*, 35–67.

Wylie, R. (1961). *The self-concept.* Lincoln: University of Nebraska Press.

Yamamoto, K., Thomas, E., & Karnes, E. (1969). School related attitudes in middle-school age students. *American Educational Research Journal, 6*, 191–206.

Yando, R., & Kagan, J. (1968). The effect of teacher tempo on the child. *Child Development, 39*, 27–34.

Yinger, R. (1980). A study of teacher planning. *Elementary School Journal, 80*, 107–127.

Zumwalt, K. (1982). Research on teaching: Policy implications for teacher education. In Ann Lieberman & Milbrey McLaughlin (Eds.), *Policy making in education. Eighty-first Yearbook of the National Society for the Study of Education.* Chicago: National Society for the Study of Education.

Index

AUTHORS

SUBJECTS